Migration, Settlement and Belonging in Europe, 1500–1930s

International Studies in Social History
General Editor: Marcel van der Linden,
International Institute of Social History, Amsterdam

Migration, Settlement and Belonging in Europe, 1500–1930s

Comparative Perspectives

Edited by

Steven King
and
Anne Winter

berghahn
NEW YORK · OXFORD
www.berghahnbooks.com

Published in 2013 by
Berghahn Books
www.berghahnbooks.com

© 2013, 2016 Steven King and Anne Winter
First paperback edition published in 2016

Library of Congress Cataloging-in-Publication Data

Migration, settlement and belonging in Europe, 1500-1930s : comparative
perspectives / edited by Steven King and Anne Winter.
     pages cm. — (International studies in social history ; 23)
   Includes bibliographical references and index.
   ISBN 978-1-78238-145-7 (hardback) — ISBN 978-1-78533-218-0 (paperback)
   ISBN 978-1-78238-146-4 (ebook)
   1. Europe—Emigration and immigration—History. 2. Emigration and
immigration—Social aspects—Europe. 3. Immigrants—Europe—History.
4. Assimilation (Sociology)—Europe. 5. Identity (Psychology)—Europe.
I. King, Steven, 1966– II. Winter, Anne, Ph. D.
   JV7590.M528 2013
   305.9'069120940903—dc23

2013015472

British Library Cataloguing in Publication Data

A catalogue record for this book is available from the British Library

ISBN: 978-1-78238-145-7 hardback
ISBN: 978-1-78533-218-0 paperback
ISBN: 978-1-78238-146-4 ebook

CONTENTS

ILLUSTRATIONS

Figures

Tables

Settlement and Belonging in Europe, 1500–1930s
Structures, Negotiations and Experiences

Joanna Innes, Steven King and Anne Winter

The issues of who 'belonged' to a community, how belonging was claimed and maintained and how it was lost were key concerns of everyday life for Europeans in the period from the 1500s (when life-cycle migration began to intensify) to the 1900s (when national welfare states began to create definitive entitlements usually unrelated to migratory or residence status).[1] On the answer to the question 'who belonged' hinged matters of citizenship, identity, relative and absolute entitlement to welfare benefits and other communal resources, and the nature and locus of power in communities. While some commentators have treated 'belonging' and 'settlement' as co-terminus, in practice settlement – a legal or customary belonging for welfare purposes – played a much larger part in defining the identity, 'place' and 'belonging' of the poor and potentially poor than it did for other groups in local society.[2]

Yet, to many contemporaries – paupers, the labouring poor, officials, lawyers and politicians – the answers to the dual questions 'who belonged' and 'who had settlement' were opaque. Normative definitions of 'settlement' or 'citizenship' enshrined in black letter law across Europe usually proved imperfect for our period, especially in light of increasing inter-state mobility from the nineteenth century. In practice, a combination of local law and bye-law, custom, the judgement of manorial and lordship courts, lineage, and the impact of short-term crises such as war and harvest failure coalesced in often unpredictable ways such that the status of 'belonging' or 'being settled' (and the entitlements that might flow from such status) were given or withheld and claimed and experienced along a complex spectrum within and between European states. In some places, such as England and Wales, national legislation provided a framework within which broad understandings could, theoretically, be formulated.[3] For other states, France for instance, there was an intense resistance to national directive with the result that 'belonging' was tied up with intricate negotiations and multi-level indicators of status at the level of village, hamlet or commune.[4] We return to these issues later in the chapter, but in both sorts of system there were perennial squabbles between places and between officials and migrants about who could claim a 'place', 'settlement' or a 'belonging' and about consequential matters such as the level, duration and scale of entitlements to communal resources. Such disputes were partly a function of the particularities of individual cases. They also reflected what happened when customary understandings of belonging and rights to relief, the finances of individual communities and their ratepayers, the requirements of local employers, the interests of landowners and, crucially, competing notions and levels of citizenship, intersected. A legal or customary 'belonging' to a place was not co-terminus with citizenship. The perennially poor, particularly women, could after all 'belong' but not meet any of the key yardsticks of citizenship such as payment of taxes, philanthropy or contribution to civic society. Such issues became particularly problematic when in the nineteenth and twentieth centuries sustained cross-border migration pitched states as well as communities against each other. Nonetheless, 'belonging' was central to an understanding of the rights and obligations of all ranks in a community. The complex but concretely elaborated tripartite citizenship structure of Switzerland was not common across the Europe of our period.[5] Yet, limits of citizenship were consistently elaborated by law and local practice as communities and individuals across the continent wrestled with the key issues of who had 'a place', how 'settlement' in these terms might translate to different levels and baskets of rights, and who had a liability to pay for the entitlements of others.[6]

The 'problem' of defining belonging was clearly a constant across the period covered by this volume, a reflection of large-scale personal mobility. Indeed, the English and Welsh Old Poor Law and its associated settlement laws, the archetype of a national social welfare system, was probably codified in the seventeenth century precisely because widespread migration for economic betterment meant that 'who belonged' (and therefore who had rights to relief at times of economic stress) became an unanswerable question. Those 'out of their place', largely in urban areas which were in turn forced to provide relief for rural migrants, threatened the very financial and social stability of the early modern English state and others.[7] Yet there is also perhaps a sense in which the problem of defining 'who belonged' intensified significantly over time. While the scale and pace of European agricultural and industrial development varied considerably between and within states, the overlapping imperatives of growing proletarianization, urbanization, more intensive short and long-term migration, and degradation of the ordinary family economy increased the risk and duration of poverty and thus the scale of potential calls on welfare resources. Set against European welfare regimes which remained organized on an essentially local basis until the collectivization movements of the late nineteenth and twentieth centuries,[8] these broad macro-trends created intensive pan-European debate about issues such as: Who belonged? How could belonging be evidenced? What should those who belonged be entitled to? How should the interests of the poor be balanced with those of ratepayers and philanthropists? And what should one do about 'outsiders'? Perhaps inevitably such debates were fiercest in the context of burgeoning urban areas, but even the most rural of Swiss Cantons persistently grappled with such matters, particularly in the context of what to do with returning mercenaries.[9] Growing international labour flows and the proliferation of bilateral treaties on welfare rights in the nineteenth and twentieth centuries significantly escalated these debates and took them to a whole new conceptual plane.[10]

The contributors to our volume deal with different combinations of these intricate questions. The majority of the chapters focus on England and Wales, a corollary of the scale of research on the Old and New Poor Laws,[11] and of the richness and systematic nature of the records that these bodies of welfare legislation generated. Yet the volume also brings together detailed analyses of migration, settlement, entitlement and belonging in Austria, Belgium, France, Prussia, Switzerland and The Netherlands to realize one of our driving concepts: the idea that a systematic incorporation of continental legislation and practice in the settlement law debate would enhance both our understanding of the particularities and generalities of the English/Welsh case, and of the social, economic, cultural and political implications of different definitions of belonging in general. Most of the chapters take a bottom-up perspective, incorporating detailed research on the ways in which belonging/settlement and consequential entitlements for poorer migrants were negotiated *in practice*, rather than according to the normative rules of black letter law. Paul-André Rosental works on a larger canvas, specifically engaging with the question of how the widening of the spatial level of identity from the local to the national or international in the long nineteenth century created new debates about the nature of belonging, new structures of exclusion and new debates about the nature of the social rights conferred by having a 'place'.[12] Collectively, the chapters suggest a highly variegated set of responses to a common problem but also some distinct regularities of approach and intent. By way of context for the chapters, the rest of this Introduction provides a broad overview of the spectrum of European settlement systems, a synthesis of some common principles, and a detailed discussion of the ways in which 'belonging' was negotiated and experienced at the level of the community and individual. In so doing we suggest the central importance of the concepts of belonging, settlement, citizenship and entitlement to the operation of European societies across the period from the 1500s to the 1930s.

Settlement in Perspective

Just as contemporaries struggled perennially with the question of who belonged, so modern historians have wrestled with the task of understanding the meaning, intent and impact of one of the key elements in defining belonging for the poor: 'laws' of settlement. In terms of volume, England and Wales have been the subject of most extensive research and discussion. The codification of the Old Poor Law between the 1590s and 1601 provided the legal and definitional basis for a national system of welfare. Distinguishing between the impotent poor (to whom officials at the level of the Church of England parish were supposed to offer relief), the able-bodied poor (whom parishes were supposed to put to work) and casual paupers such as vagrants (who were to be punished), the Old Poor Law legislation established a local system of funding for poor relief based upon a property tax. Without a system for establishing the relative liabilities of individual places/sets of ratepayers, however, the system was bound to be eroded by large-scale migration to towns and areas of economic development, yielding unsustainable long-term bills for receiving parishes. The initial legislation did not incorporate the sort of rural-urban compensation mechanisms that Marco H. D. van Leeuwen identifies for the Netherlands and Anne Winter for Belgium elsewhere in this volume. Rather, in various local and national legislation between 1601 and 1665 a comprehensive system of 'settlement laws' established how the 'place' of each individual was to be identified. Only in that place would the individual have a right to apply for poor relief – unless in extreme need, when they might be relieved anywhere as 'casual poor'. Settlement was conferred by birthplace of one's father (or place of birth for illegitimate children), marriage, serving a full apprenticeship, paying significant local taxes, renting a house of a certain value, or simply by living in a place for long enough under the eyes of local officials. David Feldman revisits some of these criteria in his chapter below. Those not having a settlement defined in these terms could, under the seventeenth-century legislation, be removed at the will of parish officers (usually in practice if it was feared that they might become dependent upon poor relief), a legislative nod to urban and industrial areas who needed the possibility of a mechanism to remove large numbers back to their parishes of settlement in the event of trade depression.[13]

Between the 1660s and 1790s, the qualifying conditions for a settlement changed subtly – particularly with the restriction of some of the 'softer' options for gaining a new settlement such as residence without disturbance in a place – as did the intent of the system. Nonetheless, from 1795 parishes were allowed to remove someone only once they had actually fallen into dependence. Exceptions were unmarried women with children, people of ill fame and convicts, who were all deemed 'chargeable' and might be removed. In his chapter for this volume Steven King argues that many officials and lawyers simply did not understand the laws of settlement as they developed incrementally over time, but cumulatively there is no doubt that this legislation established the most elaborate normative framework of belonging for the migrant poor in Europe. Only the most recidivist of vagrants, the Irish and Scots or truly itinerant groups such as actors lacked a 'place' under this system. The New Poor Law did not herald immediate change in the settlement laws but by 1846 began to undermine them, initially by treating paupers resident in a place for more than five years as legally settled. The length of residence needed to gain irremovable status fell consistently in the later nineteenth century. This does not mean, as Elizabeth Hurren shows in her chapter, that local officials and elites always followed the law, but in terms of broad intent the cumulative impact of the law in nineteenth-century England was to make settlement by residence easier to obtain – a development that contrasted for instance with the Belgian example explored in the chapter by Anne Winter in this volume. We return to these issues below.

While the earliest historians of the English and Welsh settlement laws saw them as a barrier to labour mobility and a source of hardship and uncertainty for the labouring poor,[14] recent historiography has been more nuanced and provocative. There have been lively debates, for instance, over the basic intent and sentiment of settlement law as practiced at local level – whether it facilitated a comprehensive surveillance mechanism in which those at risk of falling into poverty were regularly and systematically examined as to settlement, and removed where it could not be established; or whether it was a much more pragmatic mechanism related to labour market architecture, character and the attainment of actual poverty.[15] A combination of the Old Poor Law and its settlement laws has been seen as facilitating economic development by providing a community-based safety net for those who failed,[16] and detailed analysis of settlement examinations, migratory systems and family reconstitutions has suggested definitively that the settlement laws were no bar to extensive labour mobility.[17] Indeed, and for women with children in particular, they may have actually have been a protective force.[18] And if a combination of settlement and welfare laws did not establish a definitive legal framework for transfer payments between places so as to allow paupers out of their place to remain in a host community (as in nineteenth-century Belgium) there is now compelling evidence that parishes and communities systematically established such a mechanism themselves once the background conditions (the development of a national market in cheques, better postal systems, and increased supply of small change) allowed such a system to operate reliably.[19] In short, the negative perceptions of settlement law, so ingrained into the analyses of early commentators, have been significantly reversed.

Yet, if this array of research is impressive, it also leaves many avenues inadequately explored. British welfare historians have highlighted great variety in both local relief and settlement practices in the English provinces.[20] The difference between the comprehensive system of settlement examinations discovered for St Martin's in London by Jeremy Boulton in his chapter for this volume and the episodic or non-existent settlement examination and removal activity in some of the parishes highlighted by Steven King is both profound and largely unexplained. Do such differences in activity and intent relate to the nature of local labour markets as Marco H. D. van Leeuwen for Amsterdam and Thijs Lambrecht for Flanders argue in their contributions to this volume? Alternatively, might such differences reflect the fact that a professionalized administration allowed places like St Martin's to operate a system of settlement and removal akin to what was *intended* by the legislation whereas the absence of such an administration elsewhere made enforcement irregular, costly and uncertain? Or perhaps the derogation of settlement and removal decisions from the poor law authorities to large employers and landowners in some places but not others explains such differences? Alternatively, we might be picking up profound urban-rural or industrial-rural divisions. Other questions also remain unanswered, both for England and Wales and the wider European continent. Thus, while there has been a considerable body of work on settlement law, understanding of how such law was used in relation to or in conjunction with other elements in the legal armoury of officials is thin. Faced with a new claim for poor relief, officials might turn directly to a settlement examination, but they could also grant casual relief (under, for instance, legislation for speeding up the transit of soldiers), or implement the various vagrancy and anti-begging laws that stood in distinction to settlement legislation. Or they could turn to extra-legal measures such as writing to the settlement parish of the pauper concerned asking it to pay relief while the pauper was resident elsewhere. More sinisterly they could, as Elizabeth Hurren shows, use a series of underhanded and legally suspect or even illegal measures to undermine the settlement of a pauper and to deny him or her welfare.

How and why officials turned to different aspects of the law or customary practice, and why considerable numbers just seem to have paid relief whether the pauper had a settlement or not, requires more substantial research. Nor have the historians of British welfare done much to step outside the realms of the poor law in analysing how belonging was understood and how the communal benefits associated with such belonging sat within the wider resource context. Endowed charities, voluntary hospitals, dispensaries, almshouses and casual charity operated on a quite different basis to the Old Poor Law and with very different, not to say sometimes diametrically opposed, standards of deservingness. To take a hypothetical example, it is unclear how the average overseer of the poor would have resolved the entitlement of a woman long resident in a community and recognized as 'belonging' through receipt of charitable resources or housing but whose legal settlement was elsewhere because it was derived through marriage. Early poor law historians garnered plenty of examples of removal in such cases, but more expansive later work has suggested that such women were unlikely to have been removed.[21] In urban and industrial areas particularly, the proliferation of voluntary hospital, subscription and *ad hoc* charities, street charity and self-help institutions such as friendly societies meant that those without settlement were not immediately or inevitably thrown onto poor relief. Elizabeth Hurren in her chapter for our volume suggests that it was only at times of fundamental ideological change in welfare terms that issues of settlement came to loom large in the lives of the poor. Steven King likewise points to the comparative absence of settlement activity in most parishes, while even in Jeremy Boulton's St Martins parish there was a surprising disjuncture between being examined under the settlement laws and actually being subject to them.

How far these observations of England and Wales can be applied to other states is still a moot point. Implicit and sometimes explicit in most early accounts of England and Wales is a sense of exceptionality.[22] There are reasons to suspect, however, that while English law and practice may have had some distinctive features, the notion of total English exceptionality is illusory. Rather, it is a product of factors – disjointed continental sources, the masking effect of the way that continental poor relief was organized, the complicating factor of strong intra-continental labour flows, and the way that historians have approached the issue of belonging – that make it difficult to generalize continental experience. Thus, and with the exception of Switzerland for example, long-term, stable codified national systems governing settlement and belonging were a product of the nineteenth century. Against this backdrop, simply establishing the variety of local and regional rules on these issues prior to this period is a major research undertaking in its own right, something that both Anne Winter and Thijs Lambrecht argue forcibly in their chapters. Indeed, one of the contributions of this volume is to bring into sharp relief for the first time the fluid systems of laws, customs and local practices that governed settlement in Prussia, The Netherlands, Belgium, Switzerland and France. Nor does the continental welfare system make it easy to understand settlement and belonging as a discrete topic. While it is now clear that English poor relief arrangements in totem ranged across the same spectrum as in continental Europe, there was a difference in emphasis that carried important consequences for notions of belonging and associated entitlements. In France the intertwining of national and municipal responses to crises such as harvest failures or epidemics, religious charity (partly dispensed via sisterhoods), endowed charities and large-scale day-to-day charitable initiatives on the part of employers, guilds, local elites and aristocrats meant that belonging in a formal sense was not always or mainly connected to community-based welfare entitlements. In this system, membership of a confraternity, employment in a certain trade, catching a particular disease or residence on a certain estate determined eligibility and in many of these areas long residence, rather than formal settlement, may have been by far the most important issue. Thus, although localism was rife in France it was constructed at the level of an intense mistrust of the centre by the localities rather than through a simple dichotomy between migrants and natives.[23] The bilateral agreements between France and other European states on the welfare rights of migrant labour outlined by Paul-André Rosental in the Afterword to this volume were simply superimposed on an already highly complex sense of 'who belonged' to French communities.

Similar observations might be made of other states and against this backdrop the fact that the functioning of relief arrangements, and *a fortiori* of settlement arrangements, in continental regions is underdeveloped vis-à-vis the richness of English research is entirely explicable. Nor should we forget that in many continental traditions, poverty, the poor, poor relief and (by definition) settlement are often packaged up into attempts to understand wider problems, trends and experiences. In Germany, for instance the most exciting recent research on settlement and belonging inscribes these issues into the much wider conceptual and empirical framework of insider/outsider or inclusion/exclusion in which the beggar figures significantly more strongly than in any English historiography.[24] And more generally questions of settlement, belonging and citizenship have, in many historiographical traditions, come to form strands of much wider discussions of philanthropy, urbanization, pan-European migratory flows, labour markets and gender.

Arguably, then, the continental literature provides us with a much more layered picture of the nature of local belonging than that afforded by its English counterpart. In the face of these observations, our contributions on the continental states offer important empirical and theoretical advances as well as the opportunity to properly contextualize and extend the English historiography. Collectively, they suggest that England and Wales were far from unique in the legal structures shaping belonging and settlement, the intent of the settlement and removal systems that were employed, the mechanisms by which legal guidance was transfigured at local levels, and the sorts of outcomes experienced by poor migrants. Moreover, these contributions highlight issues and structures which have thus far garnered little attention in the English literature: the central importance of different concepts of citizenship as a mediating factor between belonging and poor relief systems, most clearly in Prussia and Switzerland; the circumstances under which settlement could be lost rather than simply changed; the capacity for formal and informal agreements between communities, parishes, *Länder*, cantons and even states to shape how paupers of different nationalities, origins, ethnicity or gender experienced settlement systems; the importance of certain cities as 'demographic sinks' which took pressure off settlement systems across whole states; and the central importance of relationships of trust and obligation between parishes when dealing with the poor out of their place. Considered as a whole, then, our contributors suggest that similarity rather than difference is what must drive the future intellectual agenda for research on settlement, belonging and 'place'. It is to some of these issues that the rest of this Introduction turns.

Getting, Maintaining and Losing a Place

As our contributors show, the basic mechanics of European settlement systems were anything but simple, something reflected in emerging evidence that paupers themselves invested a lot of resources into the process of understanding law and practice in this sphere.[25] Europe during our period supported three (discrete or overlapping, depending on period, country or region) settlement systems, each linked to the wider status of 'citizen' in complex ways: work-based, residence-based, or birth-based. Work-based systems ranged from settlement conferred by serving a full apprenticeship,[26] membership of a guild, or a formal or informal work contract of a certain length to the granting of a license to work in a community (the Heimatrecht) that we find in Austrian and German communities. In twentieth-century France, the dual processes of defining who belonged and determining welfare benefits might on occasion pass to employers. Who one worked for could thus also confer de facto, if not legal, settlement since essential workers might be protected from normative rules by influential employers, creating an irremovable but nonetheless non-settled group in some localities.[27]

Residence-based systems, in which migrants acquired settlement after a period of undisturbed residence in a place (sometimes but not always associated with the payment of local taxes or the serving of local offices), tended to be the most complex and hotly contested on the European stage. While Amsterdam acted as a more-or-less willing demographic safety valve for the rest of The Netherlands in the early modern period (see Marco H. D. van Leeuwen's chapter in this volume), for many urban communities residence-based rights of settlement were compromised by the fact that local officials in densely populated areas might be unaware of those arriving. Migrants might thus garner a settlement simply because of their urban invisibility. It is for this reason that the London parish of St Martin's in the Field, the focus of our chapter by Jeremy Boulton, devoted so much administrative effort and expense to the *precautionary examination* of all migrants among the labouring poor. Most parishes and towns could not afford such administrative effort, and during the seventeenth and eighteenth centuries national, regional and local rules governing settlement by residence were constantly amended at the margins to try and restrict migrant rights. In turn, and notwithstanding the Swiss example analysed here by Anne-Lise Head-König, the nineteenth century was to see an increasing importance for residence-based settlement systems as central state administrations asserted more control over local and regional practice. Nowhere was this clearer than in the 1834 English and Welsh New Poor Law under which the centralized authorities gradually sought to both make residence-based settlement the key means of obtaining a place and reduce the amount of time a migrant needed to have been in a host community before claims could be made. Such changes were not well received in most localities, as Elizabeth Hurren demonstrates. Nonetheless, by the turn of the nineteenth century residence-based systems were increasingly dominant in Western Europe as part of a wider collectivization process.[28]

Intuitively the most logical system for assigning settlement, birth-based criteria also posed considerable problems for contemporaries. Birth-based systems would not allow for an understanding of local contribution in weighing up settlement entitlements, and would explicitly negate the potential for formal and informal contracts such as labour and wage agreements to shape belonging. Nor, as both Anne Winter and Thijs Lambrecht show in their contributions to this volume, can birth-based systems cope easily with the implicit resource transfers between rural and urban areas that rural-urban migration would necessarily entail. And birth-based systems also posed serious problems for communities on transit routes or in illegitimacy hotspots, where the chance childbirth of travellers and unmarried women might saddle a community with lifelong bills. In the event that a family was removed from a place, frequent migration might mean that some children would have been born in one place, others in another place, and both parents somewhere entirely different, leading to the break up of the family concerned and potentially to much higher bills for all of the communities involved. Nor was it clear to contemporaries how to deal with orphans. In France, for instance, the Civil Code set out strict guidance on which family members were to adopt such children, but it did not resolve the essential 'belonging' of orphans vis-à-vis their host families.[29] Much national and local law thus developed around the vexed question of whether it was the individual or the family that held a settlement and could exploit associated welfare rights. Moreover, and even more than with other settlement criteria, birth-based belonging exposes the tension between having a settlement, having rights to apply for the suite of social welfare opportunities often associated with settlement, and belonging in the sense of being regarded as a 'citizen'. While many historians have casually and inevitably interconnected the three issues, in fact they were entirely separate.

Unsurprisingly, therefore, questions of settlement and belonging in most European states tended to be mediated through hybrid systems in which there were multiple criteria for settlement and (potentially) multiple levels of welfare rights associated with different types of belonging. The contributors to our volume do much to explore the spatial particularities of these complex systems, while the afterword addresses the vexed issue of what to do with the different generations of international migrants. Yet we can also discern some regularity of experience and intent. Thus, the essential fluidity and adaptability of settlement criteria – malleable by national statute, local law, bilateral international agreements and accumulated practice – is a striking feature of the continental states. Even in England and Wales, as Steven King demonstrates in his chapter, a supposedly national system of criteria might be adapted, ignored or enforced according to the local and regional conditions faced by officials and paupers. Another commonplace is the way that the criteria for gaining a settlement must be read as one of a 'family' of regulations which collectively sought to control migration, access to citizenship and the challenge posed for local social structures by socio-economic change. This 'family' of regulations included vagrancy legislation, restrictions on freedom of labour contract and legal or customary controls on marriage. Finally, all European settlement systems struggled with the issue of exceptional groups. Some were occupationally based, for instance tramping artisans. Serving (but often sick and thus in need of assistance) or demobilized military personnel formed one of the greatest challenges.[30] And of course for many sailors it was often quite impossible to establish a legal settlement. For these groups, special regulations were established or officials adopted pragmatic solutions such as paying small transit allowances.[31] Those with a different nationality or ethnic identity were also problematic for most European settlement systems. As Andreas Gestrich shows in his chapter for this volume, the different Prussian states saw migrants from the others as essentially foreigners.[32] The same is true for Scottish and Irish migrants in England in particular, while black or other ethnic groups posed an insuperable problem in some areas and states.[33] Countries with significant emigration (Switzerland for instance) or immigration (for instance France) sometimes came to bilateral agreements with other states on how migrants were to be treated and who was to pay for them. In this framework it was perfectly possible for an immigrant from one country to be able to claim social rights that were denied a migrant from another where no such agreement existed.[34] And of course some 'exceptional' or problematic groups were created by the operation of settlement criteria themselves. This applies particularly to married women who often lost a settlement of birth to be given a settlement derived from that of their husbands. Where they came from the same place the transition was unproblematic. An increasing number of local studies, however, have pointed convincingly to an established tendency for men to migrate into the communities where they eventually married. In the event of his subsequent death, his widow, who would have lost her own settlement and gained that of her husband, might be removed to a place completely unknown to her.[35] Indeed, most European settlement systems struggled with the issue of derived settlement until residence-based criteria gained widespread traction in the later nineteenth century.

In turn, a consideration of derived settlement brings into sharp focus another feature of the collective contributions to this volume and the wider literature in which they are inscribed. That is, there has been a tendency to focus explicitly on the issue of how settlement was gained, and much less on how it was maintained or lost. Anne-Lise Head-König shows that Swiss people with citizenship and associated settlement and welfare rights had to consciously maintain this status if they lived outside their original canton or even country. Citizenship in one place (and associated rights) could be lost at the same time as citizenship in another place was not gained, leaving the individual effectively rootless. No other European settlement system had such explicit rules. Nonetheless, it is clear from our chapters that policing settlement could be devolved to a variety of officials (welfare officers, policemen, town officers) or bodies (guilds for instance) and that criminality, moral misconduct, fraud and breaking guild or town regulations could all lead to an individual losing his or her settlement. The issue of how to maintain a settlement was thus not always easy for the contemporary poor to understand or predict. In supposedly national systems such as that in England and Wales there was less scope for simply 'losing' a settlement as opposed to being ascribed a different place of belonging. Even in this context, however, it was possible for individual paupers to be placed in legal limbo, effectively losing their settlement, as communities argued for years over their respective settlement liabilities. For officials the question of how settlements and consequent welfare entitlements were maintained was an important ongoing issue – rootless groups in or around a locality presaged criminality, labour market disruption and a challenge to the social order. For paupers, maintaining a settlement presupposes an ongoing and evolving understanding of the law (something explored by Steven King in his chapter), a grasp of one's 'life story' and the construction and accumulation of external reference points (the names of masters or employers, evidence of wage contracts or physical permits) to embellish that story. The energy that even the most humble of paupers invested into this process, evidenced for instance in English pauper letters or German welfare petitions, is itself testimony to the importance of shifting the long-term research agenda away from the issue of gaining settlement to that of maintaining it.[36] Meanwhile, some sense of why European settlement systems were so complex can be gained by looking at both the guiding principles and pragmatic decision-making that they embodied, issues that are the subject of the next two sections.

Shaping Settlement Rules: Guiding Principles

Whether the legislative and operational basis of a settlement system was national (as in England and Wales), cantonal and regional (as in Switzerland) or local (as in Austria), all had to balance six common guiding principles/concerns. Thus, and firstly, at the core of the settlement concept was the implicit trade-off between the economic contribution of migrants and an unwelcome (current or future) drain on local relief resources. It is for this reason that nationally enshrined welfare systems such as that in England and Wales had measures for both labour market intervention *and* relief management inscribed into their very fabric. Indeed, there is evidence that welfare officials sometimes pursued quite sophisticated labour market policies, as for instance when they tried to find work for old and young dependents of adults in local employment but sought to remove unemployed adults or families where the main wage earner looked likely to be unemployed in the medium term. In turn, we have become increasingly aware that this trade-off did not simply pit the interests of employers against those of other ratepayers. Each group was, as Thijs Lambrecht demonstrates in this volume, more variegated than early research allowed.[37] Nonetheless, at least in theory, the implicit trade-off provided an incentive for communities across Europe to pursue selective policies, allowing the immigration of relatively 'productive' migrants but avoiding the settlement of relatively relief-dependent groups. Settlement systems were also of course multi-functional entities and they might be shaped so as to discourage or minimize forms of migration that challenged particular political and economic interests or cultural preferences. This might, as pointed out in the Afterword, apply particularly to international migrants as states decided with whom they would contract bilateral agreements.

If settlement and associated relief systems were partially concerned with control, they also enshrined or generated implicit obligations. Thus, a second guiding principle across much of Europe was that the practice of settlement should not run counter to conceptions of moral economy. Particularly when it came to the treatment of the life-cycle poor such as the aged and disabled, officials had to balance broad conceptions of prior contribution and current deservingness with the law and prior practice of settlement. The acute problems generated by the need to achieve this balance can be seen in the often terse correspondence between officials on the subject of groups such as the aged that is now coming to light in considerable volume across Europe.[38] Sick paupers, and particularly those brought to pauperism because of sickness, represented an even thornier problem for officials. For this group, questions of legal possibility, accumulated past practice, local law, Christian duty and humanity intertwined in many countries to create an implicit obligation not to remove the afflicted, at once excepting a large group of poor migrants from the immediate scope of the settlement system. Moral economy thus trumped both law and the self-interest of welfare funders. As Jane Humphries points out in her chapter for our volume, the treatment of children was also intimately entwined with considerations of moral economy. The very fact that children were often seen as faultless in questions of poverty might explain the marked absence of reference to settlement experiences in the autobiographies of those who had some contact with the English and Welsh poor law during their childhood years.

A third and related principle was that settlement systems should prevent uncontrolled migration and social disorder, particularly at times of socio-economic and political crisis. This partly explains why in countries such as England and Wales settlement and removal policies subtly interlaced with vagrancy policies right from the inception of the national legislative framework. Yet, officials also had to be concerned that their operation of the settlement system did not itself generate unrest. Tempting as it must have been for urban officials in particular to initiate mass removals at times of crisis there would have been a keen appreciation of the discontent amongst employers and neighbourhoods that might be generated by such policies, even where migrants were from other European states. It is no doubt for this reason that pauper letter writers and petitioners across Europe emphasized the support that they had for continued sojourning in their host communities.[39]

A fourth overarching principle was that settlement systems must be malleable according to the underlying structure of communal resources on which they were superimposed, the social and economic status of migrants to which they applied, and the accrued local contribution of these migrants.[40] Schematically, our different contributors suggest that regulation could operate at three main levels: the right to enter a locality and reside there; access to work; and access to certain 'community rights' or 'community resources', which in turn fell into different categories, such as access to commons, political participation, and various public and private relief provisions, and especially the right to beg legitimately. Different criteria could operate in determining rights on these three levels: place of birth, length of residence, marriage, wealth, and work, creating different bundles of rights. On the whole, the more these different rights were bound up together – as when the right of residence also implied access to community rights – the greater the policing effort required (at entry) and the less flexible the response to migration. It amounted to a policy of all or nothing when deciding whether to accept newcomers and their costs and benefits. Migrants either gained a relatively high degree of protection (when accepted) or a high degree of insecurity (when expelled). Conversely, and as David Feldman shows in his chapter, the more these different rights were unbundled, the more flexibly local authorities could try to separate the costs and gains from migration, and to shift the risks of migration onto either migrants themselves, other parties (employers, landlords or the community of origin) or a wider kinship group.[41]

Focussing more narrowly on the access to communal resources implied by belonging to a place, a fifth general principle was that settlement systems should legally enshrine as few absolute rights as possible. Of course, the question of what constituted a right is problematic, and something to which we return below in dealing with spaces of negotiation. For Anne-Lise Head-König the right to relief existed where there was also a right of appeal. Yet there was a difference in essential sentiment between settlement giving a de facto and acknowledged right to relief when certain criteria were met (and an associated right to appeal) and settlement giving an entitlement to apply (which might also be subject to appeal) but without any acknowledged rights of receipt. The difference is a subtle but important one, counterposing as it does the settlement systems of Switzerland (which effectively obliged communities to provide relief when certain conditions were met) on the one hand and England and Wales on the other. For most European states, however, the broad intent of the settlement system was to constrict rights, either at the point of deciding settlement or in the decision of what rights to give to different sorts of paupers. In most places, for instance, there was a difference between the entitlements afforded (and the sense of belonging created by) giving medical relief as opposed to other forms of relief. Rights were, in other words, multi-layered and the relief associated with rights could be bundled in numerous different ways at the individual and community level. In England, and notwithstanding the recent contentions of Lori Charlesworth,[42] gaining a settlement generated no absolute right to relief, merely an ability to apply for it. There is considerable evidence that a substantial proportion of those who applied for relief in the eighteenth and nineteenth centuries were turned away. Even where a pauper was in receipt of relief, there was no inevitable bundling of other welfare provision (such as housing) or of resources outside the welfare system (such as charitable doles). Rights, and the consequences of those rights, were thus minimized in the English and Welsh system. For Belgium, Prussia or The Netherlands rights were seemingly no easier to obtain but officials had more power to bundle and unbundle resource types and sources, including for instance work and begging opportunities (the two often intertwining) according to the nature of belonging. Whatever the consequential relief, however, it is clear that constraining rights and maintaining discretion was a core aim of European settlement systems. It is for this reason that the extension of residence-based settlement criteria and the signing of bilateral entitlement agreements from the later nineteenth century often occasioned fierce debate.[43]

In turn, and finally, settlement systems had to balance the needs and imperatives of centre and locality, a consistent sub-text in most of our contributions. This balance was not always or readily achieved. Central authorities were often more concerned about avoiding disorder, particularly at times of crisis (and therefore strove to curb the incidence of removal),[44] while local authorities were more concerned with relief management. The incidence of removals might therefore be determined mainly by the power relations between the local and the central. David Feldman notes, for instance, that in England and Wales the right to remove was extended in 1662 under pressure from local authorities. Anne-Lise Head-König suggests that restrictive migration policies at the level of Swiss municipalities ran counter to cantonal endeavours to ensure every Swiss had a settlement. Conversely, the decision of Prussian authorities to maintain French settlement rules against the obvious interests of local authorities, especially cities, reflects the strong directive power of the Prussian state. Yet, and perhaps with the singular exception of France, it is clear that in the long-term, centre-local tensions did not prevent the evolution of settlement systems which allowed for migration, immigration and emigration on a grand scale.[45]

How different European settlement systems balanced, embedded and operationalized these general principles is determined by a suite of influences. Foremost amongst them was the nature and scale of in-migration, a common theme across all of our chapters. Nonetheless, there were also other important drivers. These included: the nature of the legislative process, and particularly the scope for local input into national statutes; the effectiveness of information circulation at the national and regional level; the availability of small change on a scale sufficient to allow the transfer of monetary resources between communities as an alternative to formal removal of individuals and families; the nature of intra- and inter-regional relations between the different bodies responsible for welfare; the role of magistrates and other local and regional legal officials; and the presence or absence of a migration safety valve functioning like Amsterdam for The Netherlands and Geneva for Switzerland. The nature of marriage and non-marriage patterns and wider experiences of household size and structure also had profound implications for the operation of rules of settlement within and between European states and over time.[46] Thus, a transition to nuclear family norms in Navarre between the early modern and modern periods changed the way that belonging was conceived.[47] In the Polish territories of the eighteenth century there were radical differences between the nuclear family norms of a broadly conceived 'west' and the more complex families of the 'middle' and particularly 'eastern' Belarusian territories. Such differences imprinted on the nature and scale of migration and consequently on the underlying questions of who belonged and who had access to communal resources.[48] These differences in household structure (and their consequences) might even be played out at the level of contiguous parishes.[49] An ability to finance administrative systems was also a key issue for the practical operation of the settlement system as it evolved at local and regional levels. The question of who officiated over settlement questions might equally shape the character of the system in complex ways. In the Rhine Province, for instance, the task was transferred from the parish to the police, changing the meaning and symbolism of settlement legislation and practice. Landowners might also take on some of the powers of the parish, with equally important symbolic and practical effects. In most of England and Wales, the amateur overseer of the poor was, until 1834, the mainstay of the settlement system. Even thereafter local officials were responsible for the day-to-day operation of the relief and settlement systems. At this level of enforcement, the prescriptions of national and regional laws gave way to a system of practice in which the keyword was negotiation, and it is to this issue that we now turn.

Negotiating Settlement Practice

Whilst migrants' access to bundles of welfare rights and citizenship status was often prescribed broadly by normative provisions, in practice they were shaped by negotiations at different levels: *within* local communities (e.g., between employers and relief payers), between different communities (that of residence and of origin), between local and central authorities (determining local autonomy to diverge from general rules, and feeding back into central legislation), between migrants and the officials who stood between them and local ratepayers or philanthropic donors, and even between European states. At best, therefore, normative prescriptions provided an arena for the ongoing negotiation process. In this arena, the balance of power constantly shifted and the outcomes were often unpredictable.

In the period covered by this volume, negotiating space existed at three core levels across Europe. The first was created by ambiguities, omissions, path-dependency and contradictions in the system itself. These might include: misunderstandings of or confusion over the meaning of the law (something picked up on constantly by our contributors); inconsistencies between local and national law; the lack of a professional bureaucracy which might make selective implementation of the law inevitable; institutional blocks to change, such as heavy prior investment in workhouse-like institutions; the existence of multiple legal entities for dispensation of welfare because new laws failed to repeal the structures put in place by old ones; changes to the socio-economic or financial system that curtailed or increased the capacity of the settlement system to act in some areas; the existence of multiple equivalent ways of dealing with settlement issues (via vagrancy instead of settlement laws for instance); the failure of the law to be sensitive to the nature of the migratory stream faced by communities (as Thijs Lambrecht shows, it mattered very much whether migrants were perceived by host communities to be temporary or permanent); the failure of policymakers to key settlement laws into other aspects of social legislation, particularly that which restricted marriage amongst the poor in several European states;[50] and ambiguities over how communities should respond to the changing composition of the wider economy of makeshifts, particularly the schizophrenic attitudes towards begging often highlighted in our chapters, upon which migrants might draw in addition to or as a substitute for public welfare.

Negotiating space was also created in a second way, by the agency of the paupers, their epistolary advocates or officials who stepped, positively or negatively, beyond the letter and spirit of the law. These individuals drew on an alternative framework of power relations, in which the law had to be understood and interpreted within the boundaries of moral economy, worth, trust, paternalism, custom, duty (to ratepayers, God, the office, or the community), economy, pragmatism and reputation. Not until the late nineteenth century did this alternative reality come under real pressure for much of Europe. At the same time, however, a different and third level of negotiating space opened up. Paul-André Rosental's afterword in this volume suggests that growing international flows of labour forced intra-national settlement and social systems to confront uncomfortable questions about the rights and needs of those who by definition did not belong. The response – bilateral treaties on welfare rights – in turn gave migrants a fixed reference point in their negotiations both with their host and origin communities. As he points out, the granting of rights to one group immediately fed through into demands by workers from other nations for comparable treatment.

Within this multi-layered negotiating space, migrants' belongings and entitlements to relief were sometimes mediated via agreements and practices that were situated *outside* or at least were *complementary to* normative provisions. Even in England and Wales the law was imperfectly, periodically and selectively applied. Before the eighteenth century, London and other urban or industrial areas developed locally orientated conventions about access to 'casual relief' for those out of their place or simply passing through. Migrants who found themselves outside the scope of settlement legislation by virtue of their nationality or ethnicity might also be covered by well-known local conventions which simultaneously kept them outside the reach of vagrancy laws. By the later eighteenth century such local understandings had metamorphosed into a national 'out-parish relief' system which also stood outside the confines of the law.[51] Across Europe the easy assumption of much of the early literature that settlement and removal systems did operate, and did operate according to the law, has given way to an appreciation that communities and officials tailored their policies. It is striking, for instance, that Swiss and Belgian towns were accused of being more 'generous' to rural residents falling into poverty than to their own settled poor because officials could clam back their relief costs. In England exactly the opposite was true. From Prussia to England and Wales, officials rapidly came to an understanding that removal did not work (with people incessantly coming back) and so developed other multi-layered systems of mediation. And Elizabeth Hurren reminds us that as the law on settlement was clarified and liberalized, so localities often turned very deliberately to informal strategies to exclude the non-belonging poor. None of our case studies portray communities consistently and universally turning to expulsion as a remedy to the problem of those who could not labour for their own subsistence. European settlement systems were thus fractured and multi-coloured, such that even contiguous communities could act in very different ways when faced with the same 'sort' of migrant.

In turn, just as officials seem to have had considerable leeway in shaping the settlement system underneath and outside the law, so recent interest in the ego documents of the poor has re-conceptualized paupers as more active in shaping belonging, settlement, entitlement and the form and duration of relief, than has thus far been allowed. Our contributions on England and Wales clearly suggest that paupers had a detailed understanding of settlement law and that they actively shaped what they told local officials so as to generate particular outcomes. Having obtained a right to apply for relief in either settlement or host community, such paupers used notions of custom, Christian duty, precedent, threat and deference to shape the scope of resources that were bundled together (cash relief, medical treatment, clothing, rent payments), the value of what was on offer and the duration of the support offered. By the later nineteenth and into the twentieth century, this sort of claims-making was increasingly layered with issues of national identity, rights afforded by international treaties, and the possibility of using comparability to other groups of migrants as a reference point. The poor had, in other words, a capacity to negotiate and shape their own experience of both poor law and settlement.

Experience

Of course, it follows from these observations that the experiences of paupers in the settlement systems of all of the countries considered in this
volume were more variegated than we recognize if we see migrants as
a lumpen mass. Keith Snell has argued that questions of settlement and
belonging figured strongly in the consciousness of migrants and others in
eighteenth- and nineteenth-century England and Wales.[52] The implication to be drawn from our case studies is that the same contention might
be made across the different European settlement systems, and particularly in states such as Switzerland. Crudely, those 'out of their place'
could never be sure that they would not be removed or denied the bundle
of welfare possibilities that might allow them to stay in a host community,
and hence they invested energy and resources in their stories of belonging. International migrants of a particular nationality also, as Paul-André
Rosental shows, invested energy into constructing comparisons between
themselves and those from other states. Yet, it is a very large step indeed
from this observation to the idea that removal of the non-settled was
either frequent or easy. In practice, and as we have already observed,
officials struggled with the issue of what to do with the aged who were
out of their place, particularly where the person or family concerned had
grown old in their host community rather than simply moving there in
the later stages of life.[53] For this group, positive considerations of contribution, custom, Christian duty and philanthropy had to be balanced
with the threat of long-term bills in the minds of officials. The result,
at least in English and Welsh communities, was the creation of an effectively irremovable group even before the nineteenth-century transition to
residence-based settlement criteria. For other groups, legislation on their
susceptibility to the law and practice of settlement and removal often had
to catch up with the weight of accumulated local decision-making. Adaptive practice melted seamlessly for many countries and communities into
relatively fluid settlement legislation and norms. Groups, such as the sick
or insane, rarely achieved legally enshrined protection from removal, but
across Europe it is possible to find evidence of the fact that poor health
was one of the key arenas for contestation between officials, paupers and
pauper advocates over rights to relief, stable residence and the form and
duration of communal support.[54] Nor should we forget that while the
question of the moral standing of poor migrants took on radically different importance in the decision to relieve or not and remove or not in
different regions and states, there is compelling evidence that even those
regarded as immoral often managed to escape the grasp of the formal
settlement and removal system.[55]

These observations, and the underlying contributions to this volume on which they are based, remind us that the intimate connection between questions of belonging or settlement and of access to welfare and other rights meant that the law, at whatever level it was codified, was always mediated. Even in England and Wales we must regard the Old and New Poor Law and the settlement legislation that stood alongside it as a system of chances. For the officials who enquired into settlement and dispensed benefits, the law was sufficiently vague to mean that right up to the point at which a pauper or family was put onto a cart to be taken 'home' no decision was immutable, no posturing reversible and no document absolute. The analogue for paupers is that while they understood the force of the law of the Old and New Poor Law, most knew they had multiple chances to slip beneath or through it. They faced, in short, a system in which it was possible to manufacture a shared fiction of belonging and deservingness with officials in host and settlement communities. The result was the creation of different (often conditional) levels of protection or security, in which an agreed landscape of claims making – for instance that sickness was a reason not to remove as long as the pauper claimed that his or her ultimate aim was to be well and to return to independence – nullified the force of the law. There is a sense, in other words, in which paupers and officials colluded to create a sliding scale of benefits attached to different types of explanations for poverty and dependence and to the way in which a claim was made. It is for this reason that paupers who wrote to or petitioned local and regional welfare officials always sought to show that relief was requested as a last resort and that it was taken as part (or upon the exhaustion) of much broader support systems which both mitigated the cost for communities and suggested the perennial possibility that the claimant would cease to need formal welfare. Equally, many of these potential claimants would emphasize their contribution to both locality and nation.[56]

We see these basic ideas inscribed most strongly in the literature on England and Wales. Here, pauper letters and other ego documents exist in sufficient numbers for us to be sure that while activity under settlement and removal legislation was sometimes very substantial indeed, and that some communities consistently utilized the legislation, the basic fact is that the level of removal activity in particular was slender compared to the number of people out of their place and becoming poor. English and Welsh communities simply found solutions to such dependence, whether negative or positive. Almost none of those who wrote English pauper letters and who were, by definition, susceptible to removal were actually sent back to their home communities. The lack of reference to settlement issues by those who wrote English autobiographies is, as Jane Humphries shows in her chapter for our volume, even more striking. This is a stark commentary on the reach and significance of the universal settlement legislation that has so often been seen as distinguishing Britain from elsewhere. Work on pauper letters on the continent is less advanced,[57] but as many of our contributors suggest implicitly or explicitly, settlement legislation and accumulated practice was only one consideration in the decision of who and when to remove and what relief package to develop for those who were deemed entitled. While we might argue that Switzerland in particular occupied a distinctive place at one end of the spectrum on attitudes to, and experiences of, belonging, much of the rest of Europe shared with England and Wales a fiction of legal regulation that gave way to pragmatic decision-making over the status and rights of waves of short- and long-term migrants.

Conclusion

Settlement was one of the key cornerstones to identity and the management of communal resources in Europe between the seventeenth and twentieth centuries. It was vital to perceptions of social order, rural-urban relations, the operation of labour markets, and the nature of family life. It is thus unsurprising that the question of how one belonged to a place, at what level and with what benefit, absorbed the energies of migrants rich and poor and of officials and representative groups in the communities to which they travelled. Yet it is clear that even in the most concretely defined system of normative regulations for deciding who belonged – in England and Wales – no universal or consistent answers were to be obtained. While settlement systems provided a mechanism for defining belonging and then removing those who did not fit, in practice relatively few of those potentially subject to removal *were* actually transported back to their places of legal belonging. Between the law and its enforcement stood a landscape in which accumulated institutional infrastructure (such as guilds), long established practice, the evolution of local legal precedent, custom, paternalism, Christian duty, gender relations, the ambiguities of legal statute and a widely understood moral economy facilitated the agency of the poor and the paths for retreat by local officials. In part this reflects path-dependency (the tortuous history of most settlement legislation created an inevitable set of grey areas that undermined black letter or local law), weaknesses at the centre in many European states, and limited administrative budgets. Yet officials also struggled with the very complexity of the migratory systems on which settlement laws and other restrictive initiatives were superimposed. The question of how to respond to long-distance and permanent migration was very different to that posed by short-distance and temporary or seasonal migrants. Old male migrants posed a different challenge to young females, and, as Sandro Guzzi-Heeb points out for the Alpine region, in and out migration might mean something very different if inscribed into a comprehensive spatial kinship system than if migrants were friendless as well as penniless.[58] Settlement law was thus a starting point for making a workable system but not a sufficient framework for its execution. In this sense, the very poorest were afforded multiple opportunities to both shape their own 'belonging' and to escape the formal mechanisms established by states, regions and localities to restrict entitlements to bundles of community resources by using the proxy of settlement legislation.

This did not, of course, mean that the bundle of rights and benefits associated with successful pauper agency could offset the negative life-course impact of falling into poverty as a child. Jane Humphries in her chapter for our volume reminds us forcefully that even an English and Welsh poor law system national in scale and *relatively* uniform in benefits could not prevent a poverty penalty for young children. Yet, she also reminds us that there is a profound danger of overstating the impact of the settlement laws on the mental world of paupers. Few of those who wrote autobiographies seem to have been much animated by such concerns. Whether this reflects biases in the evidence – a sense that those literate enough to write an autobiography were unlikely to reflect on these matters – or a genuine disjuncture between the perspectives of historians and those of contemporaries, is something that requires more extensive testing on the European stage. The particular problems posed by long-distance inter-state migration in nineteenth- and twentieth-century Europe, especially when set against the backdrop of the national collectivization of welfare systems from the 1880s, equally requires a more extensive treatment. As Paul-André Rosental points out in his Afterword, the presence of these migrants might necessitate new forms of law and identification as well as welfare. Superimposed upon often complex regional and national settlement systems, the assumed or bilateral legal rights and aspirations of such groups created new layers of belonging and necessitated new structures by which naturalization to French citizenship could be achieved.[59] States like Britain largely shunned bilateral agreements, but even here questions of naturalization and the willingness or otherwise of communities to support the processes of integration created from the later nineteenth century much more layered senses of who 'belonged'.[60] At the same time, the very act of legislating for one group invents a group of 'others', creating a milieu in which the case for the progressive extension, collectivization and formalization of 'rights' to both belonging and bundles of associated rights takes on a powerful energy. In this space, bundles of rights become intimately inscribed into questions of national identity and international diplomacy. This does not, of course, mean that our period is one in which the locus of discussion about belonging moves inexorably or in linear fashion from the local to the international. As Anne Winter and Thijs Lambrecht show keenly in their chapters, the micro-politics of belonging has enduring power.

Notes

1. In terms of migratory streams these dates also encompass a period which saw a fundamental increase in migration rates, starting with migration rates of 70 per cent in the period 1600–1650 in The Netherlands, and then rippling out across Europe. See J. Lucassen and L. Lucassen. 2009. 'The Mobility Transition Revisited, 1500–1900: What the Case of Europe Can Offer to Global History', *Journal of Global History* 4, 370–373.
2. For the most sophisticated discussion of belonging see K. D. M. Snell. 2006. *Parish and Belonging: Community, Identity and Welfare in England and Wales 1700–1950*, Cambridge. As Jane Humphries points out in her contribution to this volume, however, terms such as 'belonging' in the context of the poor might actually be created by, or have their meaning particularized in the context of, the very administrative systems established to deal with migrants and others who left their place of legal residence.
3. English and Welsh settlement legislation is summarized by Snell, *Parish and Belonging*, 81–161; L. Charlesworth. 2010. *Welfare's Forgotten Past: A Socio-Legal History of the Poor Law*, Abingdon, 74–103.
4. See J.-P. Gutton. 1971. *La sociètè et les pauvres. L'exemple de la Gènèralitè de Lyon 1534–1789*, Paris; K. Norberg. 1985. *Rich and Poor in Grenoble, 1600–1814*, Berkeley; T. Smith. 2003. *Creating the Welfare State in France, 1880–1940*, Montreal.
5. See the chapter of Anne-Lise Head-König in this volume. See also M. Leimgruber. 2008. *Solidarity Without the State? Business and the Shaping of the Swiss Welfare State, 1890–2000*, Cambridge, 1–16.
6. See A. Fahrmeir. 2007. *Citizenship: The Rise and Fall of a Modern Concept*, New Haven.
7. See P. Slack. 1999. *From Reformation to Improvement: Public Welfare in Early Modern England*, Oxford, 26–54; S. Hindle. 2004. *On the Parish? The Micro Politics of Poor Relief in Rural England 1550–1750*, Oxford, 300–360; A. Winter. 2012. 'Regulating Urban Migration and Relief Entitlements in Eighteenth-Century Brabant', in B. De Munck and A. Winter (eds), *Gated Communities? Regulating Migration in Early Modern Cities*, Aldershot, 175–196.
8. S. King. 2011. 'Welfare Regimes and Welfare Regions in Britain and Europe, c. 1750–1860', *Journal of Modern European History* 9, 42–66.
9. See the chapter by Anne-Lise Head-König in this volume. On the propensity of Swiss mercenaries to return 'home' on a much greater scale than those of other states, see F. Redlich. 1964. *The German Military Enterpriser and his Work Force: A Study in European Economic and Social History*, Wiesbaden, 114–117.
10. P.-A. Rosental. 2011. 'Migrations, souveraineté, droits sociaux. Protéger et expulser les étrangers en Europe du XIXe siècle à nous jours', *Annales HSS* 66, 335–373.
11. Summarized well in L. Hollen Lees. 1998. *The Solidarities of Strangers: The English Poor Laws and the People 1700–1948*, Cambridge.

12. For context see G. Noiriel. 1992. *Population, immigration et identité nationale en France: XIXe-XXe siècle*, Paris; A. Fahrmeir. 2000. *Citizens and Aliens: Foreigners and the Law in Britain and the German States, 1789–1870*, Oxford.
13. P. Slack. 1988. *Poverty and Policy in Tudor and Stuart England*, London.
14. S. Webb and B. Webb. 1927. *English Local Government. English Poor Law History, Part 1: The Old Poor Law*, London; G. Oxley. 1974. *Poor Relief in England and Wales 1601–1834*, Newton Abbott.
15. The debate, primarily between Keith Snell and Norma Landau, is excellently summarized in R. Wells. 1993. 'Migration, the Law and Parochial Policy in Eighteenth and Early Nineteenth Century Southern England', *Southern History* 15, 86–139.
16. P. Solar. 1995. 'Poor Relief and English Economic Development before the Industrial Revolution', *Economic History Review* 48, 1–22.
17. For the best summary of British migration patterns see C. Pooley and J. Turnbull. 1998. *Migration and Mobility in Britain since the Eighteenth Century*, London.
18. A. Levene. 2010. 'Poor Families, Removal and 'Nurture' in Late Old Poor Law London', *Continuity and Change* 25, 233–262.
19. S. King. 2005. '"It Is Impossible for Our Vestry to Judge His Case into Perfection from Here": Managing the Distance Dimensions of Poor Relief, 1800–40', *Rural History* 16, 161–189.
20. For a review of this research see Hindle, *On the Parish*, 227–299.
21. J. Taylor. 1991. 'A Different Kind of Speenhamland: Nonresident Relief in the Industrial Revolution', *Journal of British Studies* 30, 183–208.
22. See J. Innes. 1998. 'State, Church and Voluntarism in European Welfare 1690–1850', in H. Cunningham and J. Innes (eds), *Charity, Philanthropy and Reform from the 1690s to 1850*, Basingstoke, 225–280.
23. J. Weiss. 1983. 'Origins of the French Welfare State: Poor Relief in the Third Republic 1871–1914', *French Historical Studies* 13, 47–77; P.-A. Rosental. 1999. *Les sentiers invisibles: Espace, familles et migrations dans la France du 19e siècle*, Paris, 7–23, 63–79; Smith, *Creating the Welfare State*.
24. For the most recent discussion of this framework see contributions to A. Gestrich, L. Raphael and H. Uerlings (eds). 2009. *Strangers and Poor People: Changing Patterns of Inclusion and Exclusion in Europe and the Mediterranean World from Classical Antiquity to the Present Day*, Frankfurt. On the intertwining of issues of settlement with the wider question of begging see contributions to B. Althammer (ed.). 2007. *Bettler in der europäischen Stadt der Moderne: Zwischen Barmherzigkeit, Repression und Sozialreform*. Frankfurt. See also R. Jütte. 2000. *Arme, Bettler, Beutelschneider: Eine Sozialgeschichte der Armut in der Frühen Neuzeit*. Weimar; M. Scheutz. 2003. *Ausgesperrt und gejagt, geduldet und versteckt: Bettlervisitationonen im Niederösterreich des 18. Jahrhunderts*, St Pölten.
25. Snell, *Parish and Belonging*, 1–27.
26. Apprenticeship was a source of rancid dispute between communities across Europe because it both gave long-term security to young migrants and provided an easily manipulable way for officials to offload liabilities onto surrounding communities.
27. See the chapter by Paul-André Rosental in this volume.
28. See P. Baldwin. 1990. *The Politics of Social Solidarity and the Bourgeois Basis of the European Welfare State, 1875–1975*, Cambridge. For a discussion of the relationship between residence-based and other settlement systems, see Winter, 'Regulating Urban Migration', 178–180.
29. G. Brunet. 2011. 'So Many Orphans … How Could One Give Them All a Helping Hand? Family Solidarity in a Context of High Mortality in the First Half of the Nineteenth Century. A Case Study: The Dombes Province (France)', *History of the Family* 16, 1–12. Also M. S. Dupont-Bouchat. 1996. 'Enfants corrigés, enfants protégés: Gènese de la protection de l'enfance en Belgique, en France et aux Pays-Bas 1820–1914', *Droit et Société* 32, 89–104.

30. For the suggestion that 80 million military personnel passed within and between European states between 1500 and 1900 see Lucassen and Lucassen, 'The Mobility Transition', 365–366, 368. Also contributions to M. Asche, M. Herrmann, U. Ludwig and A. Schindling (eds). 2008. *Krieg, Militär und Migration in der Frühen Neuzeit,* Münster.
31. On late nineteenth-century attempts to finally deal with problematic groups see contributions to W. Loth and J.-C. Kaiser (eds). 1997. *Soziale Reform im Kaiserreich: Proteestantismus, Katholizismus und Sozialpolitik.* Stuttgart.
32. See also R. Dorwart. 1971. *The Prussian Welfare State before 1740,* Cambridge; L. Frohman. 2008. *Poor Relief and Welfare in Germany from the Reformation to World War I,* Cambridge.
33. For the suggestion that black people – slaves, ex-slaves and others – formed up to 10 per cent of the population of some towns, see Lucassen and Lucassen, 'The Mobility Transition', 357.
34. Fahrmeir, *Citizens and Aliens,* 68–83.
35. For a particularly good example in the Porto district see C. Viegas de Andrade. 2010. 'Marriage Patterns in Nineteenth-Century Vila de Conde: The Study of an Urban Centre in Northwest Portugal', *History of the Family* 15, 44.
36. L. Gray. 2002. 'The Experience of Old Age in the Narratives of the Rural Poor in Early Modern Germany', in S. Ottaway, L. Botelho and K. Kittredge (eds), *Power and Poverty: Old Age in the Pre-Industrial Past,* Westport, 107–123; S. King, T. Nutt and A. Tomkins (eds). 2006. *Narratives of the Poor in Eighteenth Century Britain,* London; K. Marx. 2008. *Armut und Fürsorge auf dem Land: Vom Ende des 19. Jahrhunderts bis 1933.* Göttingen.
37. Various institutional factors (such as guilds) also complicate any simplistic balancing of interest groups.
38. Steven King and Andreas Gestrich are currently engaged in a project, funded jointly by the DFG and AHRC, to collect and analyse such sources.
39. H. van Wijngaarden. 2000. *Zorg voor de kost. Armenzorg, arbeid en onderlinge hulp in Zwolle 1650–1700,* Amsterdam; Gray, 'The Experience of Old Age'.
40. For a discussion of the importance of this factor see S. Hochstadt. 1999. *Mobility and Modernity: Migration in Germany 1820–1989,* Ann Arbor, 1–16.
41. On kinship obligations and welfare see A. Schmidt. 2007. 'Survival Strategies of Widows and Their Families in Early Modern Holland, c. 1580–1750', *History of the Family* 12, 275; S. King. 2010. 'Forme et fonction de la parenté chez les populations pauvres d'Angleterre, 1880–1840', *Annales* 65, 1147–1174.
42. Charlesworth, *Welfare's Forgotten Past,* 1–7.
43. See W. Mommsen and W. Mock. 1981. *The Emergence of the Welfare State in Britain and Germany 1880–1950,* Newton Abbott; E. P. Hennock. 2007. *The Origins of the Welfare State in England and Germany: 1850–1914: Social Policies Compared,* Cambridge. For local debate see S. Veits-Falk. 2000. *'Zeit der Noth': Armut in Salzburg 1803–70,* Salzburg; Smith, *Creating the Welfare State;* L. Frohman. 2008. 'Break Up of the Poor Laws – German Style: Progressivism and the Origins of the Welfare State 1900–1918', *Comparative Studies in Society and History* 50, 981–1009.
44. Particularly for instance during the nineteenth-century cholera epidemics. See M. Manfredini. 2003. 'Families in Motion: The Role and Characteristics of Household Migration in a 19th-Century Rural Italian Parish', *History of the Family* 8, 326, 335–336; B. Althammer. 2012. 'Poverty and Epidemics: Perceptions of the Poor at Times of Cholera in Germany and Spain, 1830s–1860s', in A. Gestrich, E. Hurren and S. King (eds), *Poverty and Sickness in Modern Europe: Narratives of the Sick Poor, 1780–1938,* London, 93–116.
45. The literature on this area is vast but deftly summarized by Lucassen and Lucassen, 'The Mobility Transition'.
46. See A. Fauve-Chamoux. 2006. 'Family Reproduction and Stem-Family System: From Pyrenean Valleys to Norwegian Farms', *History of the Family* 11, 171–184.

47. J. Sánchez-Barricarte. 2002. 'Developments in Household Patterns in Three Towns in Navarre, Spain, 1786–1986', *History of the Family* 7, 479–499. Also Manfredini, 'Families in Motion'.
48. M. Szołtysek. 2008. 'Three Kinds of Preindustrial Household Formation System in Historical Eastern Europe: A Challenge to Spatial Patterns of the European Family', *History of the Family* 13, 223–257.
49. M. Dribe. 2000. *Leaving Home in a Peasant Society: Economic Fluctuations, Household Dynamics and Youth Migration in Southern Sweden, 1829–1866*, Stockholm; M. Szołtysek. 2007. 'Central European Household and Family Systems, and the 'Hajnal-Mitterauer' line: The Parish of Bujakow (18th–19th Centuries)', *History of the Family* 12, 19–42.
50. See M. Lanzinger. 2003. *Das gesicherte Erbe. Heirat in lokalen und familialen Kontexten. Inichen 1700–1900*, Vienna, 45–86; P. Teibenbacher. 2009. 'Natural Population Movement and Marriage Restrictions and Hindrances in Styria in the 17th to 19th Centuries', *History of the Family* 14, 292–308.
51. King, 'It Is Impossible'.
52. Snell, *Parish and Belonging*, 81–104.
53. For an intriguing study of the scale and impact of Belgian migration in old age, see M. Neven. 2003. 'Terra Incognita: Migration of the Elderly and the Nuclear Hardship Hypothesis', *History of the Family* 8, 273–275.
54. See A. Gestrich, E. Hurren, and S. King. 2012. 'Narratives of Poverty and Sickness in Europe 1780–1938: Sources, Methods and Experiences', in Gestrich, Hurren and King, *Poverty and Sickness*, 1–34.
55. Contrast for instance the central importance of moral standing in the decision of who to relieve and who to remove in some of the Germanic states with the persistent failure to remove even morally suspect pauper beggars from English communities. See Gray, 'The Experience of Old Age'; T. Hitchcock. 2004. *Down and Out in Eighteenth Century London*, London; S. King and A. Stringer. 2012. '"I have once more taken the Leberty to say as you well know": The Development of Rhetoric in the Letters of the English, Welsh and Scottish Sick and Poor 1780s–1830s', in Gestrich, Hurren and King, *Poverty and Sickness*, 69–92.
56. On England see T. Sokoll. 2001. *Essex Pauper Letters, 1731–1837*, Oxford. For Europe, see M. van Ginderachter and M. Beyen (eds). 2011. *Nationhood From Below: Europe in the Long Nineteenth Century*, Basingstoke, 1–17; Gray, 'The Experience of Old Age'.
57. Though see Wijngaarden, *Zorg voor de kost;* Schmidt, 'Survival Strategies', 268.
58. S. Guzzi-Heeb. 2009. 'Kinship, Ritual Kinship and Political Milieus in an Alpine valley in 19th Century', *History of the Family* 14, 107–123. Also Manfredini, 'Families in Motion'.
59. See also Rosental, 'Migrations', 337–338, 334–341.
60. See particularly L. Tabili. 2011. *Global Migrants, Local Culture: Natives and Newcomers in Provincial England, 1841–1939*, Basingstoke, passim.

CHAPTER ONE

SETTLEMENT AND THE LAW
IN THE SEVENTEENTH CENTURY

David Feldman

Introduction

In 1662 Parliament enacted a new law 'for the better relief of the poor of this Kingdom'. This was the first time in six decades that poor law legislation reached the statute book. In 1598 and again in 1601 the structure of the Elizabethan poor law had been codified and consolidated. Parliament had then placed day to day responsibility for raising poor rates, relieving the impotent, and providing work for the able-bodied in the hands of parish officers. Yet neither in 1598 nor in 1601 did Parliament define what class of person each parish was obliged to relieve. The poor were mobile and unlikely to die in the parish of their birth, childhood or even marriage. The question of how to assign to parishes a mobile and chronically vulnerable population was a vital concern for overseers, ratepayers and, of course, the poor themselves. Should the recipients of poor relief be relieved where they were found? Where they were born? Where their parents were born? Where they had lived for three years? One year? A month? Each of these solutions figured in contemporary debate. The 1662 Act addressed, even if it did not fully resolve, the limits of parochial responsibility for welfare.

Above all, the Act encased a limit to parochial responsibility. It empowered Justices of the Peace, acting on complaints from parish officers, to remove migrants within forty days of their arrival if they considered the newcomers 'likely to be chargeable to the parish' at some indefinite point in the future. The only exemption mentioned in the Act was for those incomers who could afford to rent a tenement with a yearly value of £10 per annum. These migrants were not vulnerable to removal. However, those who were vulnerable, the law stated, should be sent to the parish where, in the specifically legal sense, they were last settled.[1] The law of 1662 – as well as a vast body of case law and subsequent legislative additions – set guidelines for parish officers, Justices of the Peace and the higher courts, to determine the parish in which any pauper, or potential pauper, was 'legally settled' and to which they 'belonged'.

The meaning of settlement in the seventeenth century was a narrow one in comparison to later usages. By the early decades of the nineteenth century some poor law commentators claimed that a 'settlement' carried with it an entitlement, in the sense of a right, to poor relief. More recently historians have argued that this understanding of the law shaped the way the poor themselves understood their right to relief in this later period and also contributed to a subjective and inward sense of belonging to a parish on the part of the poor.[2] My concern in this essay is with an earlier period. In the seventeenth century, unambiguously, settlement did not confer a right to poor relief: it merely assigned a person to a parish. Relief lay at the discretion of the overseers and justices.[3] The repeated invocation in the sources of the parish to which this or that person 'belonged' is understood in this essay in the administrative and legal context that generated this formula. These conventional poor law usages do not in themselves provide compelling evidence of a more inward sense of 'belonging'.

In their history of English local government, Sidney and Beatrice Webb made a dramatic and highly negative assessment of the 1662 Act. According to the Webbs, it introduced a set of 'extraordinary provisions' that potentially immobilized 'the entire body of wage-earners of the Kingdom, together with their families' in their parishes of settlement.[4] Just as the Webbs' negative appraisal of the Old Poor Law has come under general revision since the 1960s, so too their particular assessment of the law of settlement has fallen out of favour. In essays published in 1963 and 1976 Philip Styles and James Taylor argued that the 1662 Law of Settlement was neither as significant nor as vicious as the Webbs claimed. They see the Act as a necessary counterpart to the system of parochial poor relief that developed in the late sixteenth century. In his influential and much cited essay, Styles argues that the 1662 Act was not innovative but should be seen as but one symptom of a long standing concern with the mobility of the poor in the sixteenth and seventeenth centuries. The importance of the Act, Taylor tells us, has been 'exaggerated'.[5] And there the matter has stood so far as the 1662 law is concerned. Now historians focus instead on the reform of settlement law at the end of the century. Poor law reforms enacted in 1685, 1691 and 1697 are heralded as significant and progressive, introducing a more flexible regime, promoting labour mobility in an increasingly commercial and dynamic economy.[6]

In what follows, I offer a revision of this account of the law of settlement in the seventeenth century. Although Styles and, more recently, Hindle illumine a century-long history of legal restrictions on the movement of the poor, this chapter will argue that a backward-looking perspective understates the significance of the 1662 Act.[7] I shall also suggest that the character of the legal changes at the end of the century have been misunderstood. In these ways, this chapter aims to contribute to our understanding of the entitlement of migrants within a particular welfare system. Scholars widely make the assumption that 'settlement restrictions are essential to any welfare system based on compulsory provision for the poor by public authority'.[8] Yet historians at least should know better. Settlement restrictions have been neither consistent nor ubiquitous. For example, the eligibility of 'aliens' for poor relief in England was established beyond doubt in 1803 and in the first half of the twentieth century many aspect of the new national welfare system were open to all comers. Moreover, when settlement restrictions have been in force their severity in law and application in practice have also changed over time. Most notably, the law of settlement under the poor law was radically attenuated after 1846. An awareness of the existence of open as well as closed welfare systems should lead us to consider why it was that a particular and increasingly restrictive legal system came into force in the course of the seventeenth century.[9]

Migrants and Governance c. 1580–1640

Movers not stayers were the norm in the sixteenth and seventeenth centuries. Migration reflected myriad individual and familial decisions but this did not make it a random or chance affair. Migration was intrinsic to the central institutions of family and working life – service, apprenticeship, the developing labour market more broadly and marriage. Other sorts of migration were more desperate but equally driven by endemic features of the economy: landlessness, low wages, want of work and a shortage of housing. After mid century this sort of subsistence migration became less common but mobility remained the norm for the labouring poor in and out of work.[10]

In contrast to this precarious and migratory reality for the mass of the population, the Statute of Artificers of 1563 imagined a world from which idleness was banished and in which labour was both adequately re-warded and sedentary. This fantasy of a stable social order whose strength was buttressed by immobility was an abiding theme in social commentary.[11] Accordingly, the mobile poor provoked a torrent of complaint. For example, migrants and vagrants were prominent in the rationale for the 1593 law that aimed to restrict building within three miles of the city gates of London and Westminster. The new law was necessary because of the vast numbers migrating to the capital:

> the great Mischiefes and Inconveniences that daylie growe and increase by rea-son of the pesteringe of Houses with divse Famylies, harboringe of Inmates, and convertinge of great Houses into sevall Tente or Dwellinges, and erectinge of new Buyldinge... whereby great Infection of Sickness & dearthe of Vic-taulles and Fewell hath grown and ensued, and manye idle vagrante and wicked persons have harboured themselves there.[12]

Almost a century after the Statute of Artificers was enacted, the Council of State commissioned a report on towns whose trade had decayed. The same preference for immobility, as well as the association of migrants with disorder, remained in its pithy diagnosis: 'too much beer and too many strangers'.[13]

The laws against vagrancy were used to punish one section of the migrant population. In law, the crime of vagrancy was drawn so broadly that almost any unemployed migrant might have been charged under this heading. A statute of 1597 stated that all 'wandering persons' who were able-bodied but out of work should be apprehended and punished. Yet, in practice, vagrancy was a category that the authorities imposed on only a small minority of the migrant poor. The problem of how to deal with the majority remained.[14]

In the late sixteenth and early seventeenth centuries, parishes and towns were equipped with an arsenal to repel unwanted incomers. Most notably they were armed by the 1589 statute that both forbade building cottages without at least four acres of land and which also insisted only one family or household should live in each cottage. These weapons were used widely by towns against 'inmates' and 'undertenants'.[15] In doing so they were keen to subordinate commerce to low taxes, good order and, in godly places, public edification. To these ends, they not only acted against migrants but also the landlords and tenants who rented space to them. At Finchingfield, in Essex, the town's governing body visited parishio-ners to persuade them to rid themselves of a tenant. If landlords proved recalcitrant, however, they were to be prosecuted for keeping inmates 'contrary to the mind of the town'. In 1626 the vestry of St Bartholomew Exchange, in the City of London, ordered a landlord to eject his lodgers so the parish 'might sustaine no more losse and wronge as they have doone form'ly by some poore allreddie in the same house'.[16] Initiatives such as these sometimes aspired to a close oversight of mobility and commerce. At Braintree in February 1622 the town's governing body (the 'four and twenty') resolved to survey the town and 'bring in account what disordered persons are crept into the parish & what inmates are either intertained already or coming in'. Five years later the same body issued a new regulation:

> Nobody to build any cottage or convert any building in his dwelling house or to receive any strangers without the consent of the churchwarden and six of the Four and Twenty in writing under their hands under pain of fine of £3.[17]

In rural England too, enterprising householders and tenants who found space to rent to migrants aroused the anxiety of local governors charged with the welfare of the wider community. A petition in 1615 from the inhabitants of Leigh (on Mendip) to Ilchester sessions complained that Thomas Bridges, his sons and tenants had 'received divers inmates and undertenants into many houses and small cottages there, contrary to the law; and the said Mr Bridges hath taken away the ground belonging to sundry tenements there, selling them only to poor men, which is likely to be a greater charge to the inhabitants.' In rural areas governors, at times, attempted to uphold the 1589 statute against squatters. In 1599 a group of petitioners persuaded the justices at the Staffordshire Quarter Sessions to issue a warrant of good behaviour against Hughe Bolde from the township of Lyttle Sandon. Bolde had erected buildings for no fewer than 28 people, besides his own family, on his small freehold.[18]

These measures and complaints were aimed at local entrepreneurs as well as at the migrant poor. They expressed a policy which tried to adjudicate between the conflicting demands of the common weal of the town or parish – as local governors saw it – and the commercial energies of individuals. The same priorities meant that landlords, tenants and employers were asked to indemnify towns against any claims for poor relief made by their poor tenants, sub-tenants or labourers. In 1635 one landlord in Gloucester was ordered to make a weekly payment for the relief of the poor to indemnify the parish in case any of his tenants became chargeable. In 1640 Chester Quarter Sessions advised Stockport's Justices to assess fines on those who took in 'poore people' and increase these fines 'weekly or otherwise, as they shall think fitt'.[19]

We only have to remind ourselves of the ubiquity of migrants in early modern England to realize that attempts to impose these laws and by-laws were unsuccessful in both towns and large swathes of rural England. The law against building cottages without four acres of ground was, as

Sharp comments, 'a pious hope unrealizeable in the social and economic reality of Tudor and Stuart England'.[20] We can examine the failure to regulate inmates in an urban context in the case of Southampton. Here, from the last decade of the sixteenth century the Leet Court issued a series of orders that addressed the 'intollerable numbers of inmates and undertennants overmuche increasinge in this Towne to the great annoyaunce of all the honest inhabitants thereof'. As the problem became unmanageable so the town's regulatory energies spiralled. In 1590 the Southampton beadles were instructed to present undertenants to the Leet Court 'from tyme to tyme'. By 1602 this was supposed to occur weekly. The following year the town authorities declared that landlords and tenants should not let or sub-let accommodation to anyone who did not pay tax to parliament on lands and personal property, or who did not 'give good suerties before Mr maior for the time beinge to discharge the Towne & parishes thereof of all charges concerninge themselves or there wives, familie & children'. But in 1604 the order had not come into force and, in so far as it ever did, we know that by 1611 it had fallen into abeyance because in that year there was a call for it to be enforced, a call that was repeated five years later.[21] There was a chronic problem of administrative capacity, in towns and in forest areas especially, as draconian orders were not translated into bureaucratic practice. Though measures against inmates and cottagers were not routinely enforced they nevertheless infused countless lives with uncertainty. The law offered opportunities for vindictive or godly individuals to pursue a quarrel or for busybodies to intervene.[22]

The impact of migrants on the poor rate was a recurrent theme in complaints against inmates and squatters in town and country.[23] Migrants put pressure on the poor rate both directly and indirectly. Indirect pressure arose because they made demands on resources that were intended to supplement or pre-empt poor relief: charity and commons, as Thijs Lambrecht also points out in his chapter for this volume. The authors of the 1601 Poor Law had assumed that local taxation would not be used to support the needy in general but only a particular range of cases – those involving children, the aged and the impotent. The remainder of the poor were meant to improvise with the help of relatives and neighbours, by taking paid work whenever possible, by seeking alms and through access to the commons and wastes.[24] At Chester in 1603 the City Council complained that 'straungers … not only take away or much diminishe the maintenance and relief which belongeth to the poore borne in the said citie but much impoverisheth the state of the commoners of the same Citie.'[25] It is notable that the great codification of the Elizabethan poor law was accompanied by a new law designed to punish 'lewde and idle persons' who 'cut corn or grain, robbed orchards and gardens, dug up fruit trees, broke hedges and fences, and spoiled woods and underwoods'. Explicitly it targeted the despoliation of communal as well as private property. Little wonder that in 1642 Edward Coke complained that squatters' cottages were 'nests to hatch idlenese, the mother of pickings, theeberies, stealing of wood etc, tending also to the prejudice of lawful commoners'.[26]

Migrants created, as I have suggested above, chronic and sometimes acute difficulties for the administrative and material capacities of towns and rural parishes. In this context, the poor law presented both a problem and an opportunity. The problem lay in the comprehensive obligation it placed on parishes to treat the poor. The opportunity lay in the notion – already present in the law on vagrancy – that every poor person had a 'settlement'; a place to which he or she 'belonged'. This concept of a 'settlement' potentially gave parishes the means to redeem their incapacity to control migration. In the face of the failure to regulate mobility by targeting housing and employment, local authorities moved to a second line of defence – entitlement to welfare. Having failed to control mobility it might yet be possible to capture and eject unwanted migrants when they applied for poor relief. At the same time, the poor law itself generated its own regulatory imperative as it forced parishes to assess the limits to their liabilities and to eject paupers or potential paupers for whom they had no legal responsibility or for whom they did not want to take responsibility.

Unfortunately for many parishes the courts quickly declared strict limits to the power of parishes, as they administered the poor law, to remove unwanted migrants. As early as 1598 the Essex Quarter Sessions ruled 'no persons (other as Rouges or Vagabonds) shalbe removed from their present habitation.' This opinion was immediately buttressed in a ruling by the West Yorkshire Justices.[27] The assize judges reinforced this view. At Cambridge in 1629 Sir Francis Harvey held that 'the Justices of the peace (especially out of their Sessions) were not to meddle with the removing, or settling of any poor, but only of Rogues.' In the 1630s the assize judges of the western circuit regularly intervened to prevent parishes from removing immigrants illegally.[28] When John Denham was faced at Devon Assizes with three parishes contending over the settlement of Henry Snooke he dealt with the matter by asserting that the dispute was pointless. Although destitute, Snooke was neither impotent nor vagrant and so the Justices of the Peace had no power to settle him. Denham backed up his judgment with a threat: 'since he [Snooke] is destitute, he is to be put to work at Middlemarsh, where he was last resident, and if the inhabitants allow him to become vagrant he will be settled there.' This policy provided a measure of protection to poor migrants and at the same time placed a requirement on them. It safeguarded them from removal but at the same time it obliged them to labour. In Snooke's case he was put to work by the parish.[29]

Legal obstacles to removing migrants acquired still greater authority in 1633 when Robert Heath, Chief Justice of Common Pleas, issued a series of resolutions that he intended to resolve difficult questions arising from the poor laws and which had been brought to him by Norfolk Justices and by the Privy Council. Heath repeated earlier judgements almost word for word. He too connected a categorical limitation on the legal authority of towns and parishes to expel immigrants to the expectation that the poor 'ought to set them selves to labour, if they be able, and can get work, if they cannot get work the Overseer must set them to labour'.[30] In this way, he made explicit the assumption behind the policy: the unwanted immigrant poor should not be ejected because this would promote vagrancy. At the same time, retaining these paupers would not impose a severe burden on the receiving parish or town because the migrants would work to support themselves, either through the labour market or through the mechanism of the poor law itself.

It is difficult to assess precisely the impact of judgements such as these beyond the individual cases. But it is likely that they did inhibit parishes and municipalities from removing immigrants. The legal force of the decisions is indicated when we find that lawyers adopted these arguments (to good effect) in contesting settlement decisions.[31] Although Judges of Assize had no greater authority than Justices of the Peace in these matters, only a broader area of jurisdiction, in practice Justices relied on the Assizes in matters of interpretation. The Assizes brought together virtually every person of consequence in the county. The decisions made there on poor law matters were certain to be disseminated. Heath's resolutions, moreover, acquired influence because they provided JPs with a ready guide as they enforced the poor law. A further level of authority was added to all these decisions when they were publicized in successive editions of Lambarde's *Eirenarchia* and Dalton's *Country Justice*.[32]

Nevertheless, Dalton observed that poor people 'are much sent and tossed up and down from Town to Town.'[33] The judges' *dicta* were widely ignored. In 1616 the inhabitants of a parish petitioned Taunton sessions to eject a recently married couple. Symon Burrage, a tailor, had married Mary Sealy who is described as the 'daughter-in-law' of Humfry Brownsford with whom the couple then went to live. There was no suggestion here that anyone was either impotent or vagrant. The outcome, nevertheless, was that Burrage and Sealy were removed under the poor law. The Justices ordered the tithingman to take Burrage and Sealy to the parish of Upton 'there to be received and set on work as poor people of the said parish, being the place where Symon had made his last abode for the most part of three years before the making of this order.'[34] At Braintree, in Essex, in October 1619 the town's governing body the 'four and twenty' considered the case of 'one Nicolls' who had left his wife and children in Long Melford, seventeen miles away, and had found work in Braintree as a journeyman. Plainly, he too was neither impotent nor vagrant. Nevertheless, the constables were ordered to send him home 'to his wife and children', lest they too made their way to the town.[35]

We can sum up by saying that in the first decades of the seventeenth century policies towards migration developed as the outcome of two distinct failures. The first failure was the incapacity of towns and rural parishes to arrest the flow of migrants. This was not because they had no weapons but because the weapons they had were ineffective and did not have any discernible impact on the overall movement of people. The disparity between the aspirations expressed in laws and orders, on one side and, on the other, the limited capacities of parochial and town officers did not mean the law went unenforced but it did mean that it was implemented erratically. At the same time as they were faced with an unmanageable volume of migrants, parishes also received responsibility for implementing the Elizabethan poor law which imposed new obligations on local officers to tax inhabitants and administer social welfare. The concept of a 'settlement' gave parishes the means to redeem their incapacity to control migration. Here we find the second failure of policy. For it is clear that the higher courts did not intend the right to remove to be interpreted so broadly. Judicial authorities placed narrow limits on the power to remove but they were incapable of getting magistrates and parish officers to implement the law accordingly. Historians suggest that legal uncertainty between 1601 and 1662 allowed overseers to remove and intimidate new arrivals.[36] There were, indeed, many uncertainties and complexities to the law of settlement as it faced myriad contingencies, as Sir Robert Heath had stated in his 1633 resolutions. But the basic point, that only vagrants should be removed, was not in doubt. The source of uncertainty did not lie in the law itself but in the capacity of the courts and higher judicial authorities to impose their view on parishes, urban corporations and even on Justices of the Peace.

From Workfare to a Law of Settlement

From the 1640s the discrepancy between judicial doctrine and local practice took new directions as the Justices of the Peace sanctioned removal in new terms. It is from this decade that we find phrases such as 'likely to become chargeable' or 'likely to prove a charge to the parish' or 'likely to be very chargeable' thickly distributed through the records. The phrase was always used to the same purpose – namely, to justify the removal of people who though poor were not vagrants. The policy of removal thus attained new legitimacy from the 1640s. The following case is characteristic and was heard at Lewes in Sussex in 1643:

> Upon complaint made to this Court by the parishioners of Hellingly That Harbart Wenham of the said parish hath lately taken one Richard Quithampton the younger a poore man of the parish of Chittingly as an Inmate into his house or Cottage at Hellingly where he is likely to become a parish charge. It is ordered that the said Richard Quithampton shalbe sent back to the said parish of Chittingly there to be setled and provided for according to law.[37]

Legal authorities did not immediately accept this explicit justification for pre-emptive removal. As late as 1649 one magistrate reminded parish officers that people whose leases had expired and servants out of time should not be sent away from town. If able-bodied they should be set to work and if impotent they should be relieved.[38] This reproof, however, also contains a clue to one reason why it fell on deaf ears. The alternative to removal, according to the justices' prescription, was work. We have seen already that this was embodied in Heath's resolutions as well as in particular judgments. Elizabethan legislators intended to set the able-bodied poor to work leaving only the impotent to be provided from the rates. There is plentiful evidence, however, from Emily Leonard's research at the start of the last century to Steve Hindle's at the beginning of the present one, that workfare peaked in the 1630s and fell away thereafter. In towns the chronology of failure was more variable but the overall picture is similar. As Paul Slack notes, 'When workhouses had to be maintained losses were large.' Ambitious schemes to provide work for the able-bodied unemployed were essayed in a number of towns and then abandoned. We will better understand the evolving interpretation of settlement law and the practice of removal if we see both in the context of this broader change in poor law practice.[39]

Here it will be useful if we take up the idea proposed by Peter Solar and Richard Smith that we should regard the Old Poor Law as a form of insurance, rather than as a dole. Their analyses build on the observation that welfare was not restricted to a separate and identifiable class of recipients. In addition to the 5 per cent of the population who received relief at any one time there was a much larger portion who lived in or near poverty and who might at some time claim relief. There was an overlap among the class that funded poor relief and those who received it at some point in the life cycle. In this respect, 'poor relief can be viewed as a form of insurance.' As Solar points out, insurance schemes face two fundamental problems. First, there is the problem of moral hazard, when as a result of being insured against an event an individual acts in ways to make that event more likely: insured against unemployment, for example, he or she may not seek work. Second, there is the problem of adverse selection. This occurs when insurers are unable to distinguish between high and low risk members. Solar suggests that neither of these problems arose under the Old Poor Law. First, in small communities, he claims, it was possible to police the system against moral hazard because applicants were well-known to the authorities. Second, the risk of selecting the wrong people did not apply because everyone was covered.[40] This is too optimistic. The endemic mobility of early-modern England meant that not everyone was well-known to the authorities. Moreover, as we have seen, mobility and the issue of settlement law meant that, at the level of the particular parish not all individuals were covered: some were the responsibility of another parish (another insurer) altogether. Workfare, had it taken root, would have been one way parishes combated these risks. It would have provided a sanction against moral hazard because able-bodied paupers who refused to work could then have been prosecuted under the vagrancy laws. This in turn would have reduced the risks from taking responsibility for all comers and not discriminating among them. However, as workfare dwindled after the 1630s the issue of settlement and eligibility became ever more pressing.

It was against this background, and in the context of the widening implementation of the poor law, that justices in the 1640s and 1650s increasingly allowed overseers to remove incomers not because they were paupers but because they were thought 'likely to be chargeable' at some indefinite point in the future. As the general conditions of poor relief changed, policies towards migrants hardened and overseers and justices developed new strategies for removal. If work was no longer an option, then the objections to removing the able-bodied, articulated by Heath and other judges, lost force. The entitlements to welfare of the migrant poor shrank in the context of other changes in the seventeenth-century welfare regime. In London for as long as 'workfare' lasted the scheme was extended to the 'straggling poor'; that is to say to the migrant poor that filled the capital. With the collapse of the corporations' ambitious plan to set as many as one thousand paupers to work, the only options were either to ignore or remove this large group.[41] When Parliament legislated on settlement in 1662 it thus gave the sanction of law to a practice that had been gaining ground for two decades.

This does leave open the question why it was that Parliament did finally legislate on settlement in 1662. The 1650s had seen Parliament repeatedly incapable of legislating on the poor law. This had not been for want of opportunities to do so. The Interregnum parliaments had been treated to a 'continuous stream of resolutions and committees' on the poor but without any legislative outcome. Bills were sent to committees but they did not return.[42] In 1662 the final Act emerged from four separate bills which had been introduced to Parliament in December 1661 and January 1662. These bills had varied purposes but one was for 'the better relief and employment of the poor, and for the preventing of the poor by the settling of them'. The Commons referred all four bills to a single committee. Here they were consolidated to produce a single measure.[43]

The preamble to the 1662 Act provides reasons why, following six decades of inaction, parliament had now passed this law. The country, it claimed, was menaced by a vast and predatory population of dissolute migrants who lived off of the labours and savings of honest and long-standing parishioners:

> Poor people are not restrained from going from one parish to another and therefore doe endeavour to settle themselves in those parishes where there is the best stock the largest commons or wastes to build cottages and the most woods for them to burn and destroy and when they have consumed it then, to another parish, and at last become rogues and vagabonds, to the great discouragement of parishes to provide stocks where it is liable to be devoured by strangers.

Historians have been unimpressed by these complaints and suggest that the preamble owed more to formulaic stigmatization of the mobile poor than to the behaviour of migrants.[44] Their view receives some support from Clark's finding that long distance subsistence migration became less common after 1640. From the 1620s population growth slowed and around 1650 it stopped altogether. The country entered a new era of falling prices and population stagnation. If this was the new long-term trend, it is also significant that the labouring poor were no longer subject to traumatic crises due to harvest failure. The last such years were in 1630–1631. Migration had been a widespread response to harvest failure as people moved out of marginal uplands to lowland areas, both across the nation as a whole and within individual counties.[45] Thus at mid century there was the onset of a major shift in the pattern of mobility in England.

We should keep in mind, however, that these were long-term and cumulative changes, whereas the social conflicts connected to migration remained a continuing presence. In some areas illegal encroachments reached new peaks in the late 1640s and 1650s. In 1657 a survey of Ashdown Forest carried out for Parliament reported:

> That we find much waste and destruction to have been committed on the said Forest in a total destruction of the Game of Deer in plucking up and carrying

away the pales of the said park now almost wholly dispaled and cutting down the wood which we are informed did in plenty grow there.[46]

Moreover, the onset of the Restoration and the enactment of the Law of Settlement took place in circumstances that further obscured the abatement of population pressure and of crisis-driven migration. First, there was a series of meagre harvests. By 1661 the price of wheat reached 74 shillings per quarter, three times the level in 1654. The widespread distress and the increase in mobility this caused were compounded by the sudden disbandment of the army. This action threw, perhaps, 50,000 men at once on to the labour market. The upshot was an increase in unemployment, underemployment and the presence of wandering beggars on the roads. In 1661 the government issued a proclamation that expressed concern at the rising tide of idleness and vagrancy.[47] Giving his charge to the grand jury at Fakenham in 1664 the Norfolk magistrate Robert Doughty complained that:

the armies lately disbanded have afforded many too old & lazy to learn and labour, and too likely and ready to beg and steal. Yea & a new race of loose or runaway rogues are lately sprung up, who were scarece ever or never well-fixed in any lawful course of life.[48]

In this context, it is perhaps significant that the Law of Settlement emerged from a bill which yoked 'the preventing of the poor by the settling of them' to the 'better relief and employment of the poor'. In others words, in the minds of legislators the origins were connected to the collapse of workfare. In this light the thoughts of Matthew Hale are illuminating. His views are notable because he was close to both judicial and parliamentary discussions on the poor law. He served as a judge under Cromwell, and he was elected MP for the County of Gloucester in 1654, for the University of Oxford in 1658 and again for Gloucester in 1660.[49] In 1659 Hale lamented the way in which the employment provisions of the poor law had fallen into disuse.[50] Like other judges before him he believed that if overseers provided work for the able-bodied poor the issue of settlement would dissolve:

For when every man were once sure that they that would honestly work might have it, and reasonable Wages, every Wanderer and Beggar would be esteemed such a Person as will not work, or will be dishonest in it, and not fit to be relieved.[51]

This was not an isolated opinion. In 1652 a petition from the Council of Officers to Parliament had called for work for the unemployed to put an end to begging and vagabondage.[52] When Hale contemplated the consequences of not providing work his conclusions are especially interesting because they correspond closely to the vision presented in the preamble to the 1662 Act. He believed that the overseers' failure to provide work had given rise to a surfeit of 'idle and unprofitable Persons that consume the Stock of the Kingdom without improving it, and that will daily increase, even to Desolation in time'. This theme of despoliation resulting from idleness recurred in Hale's pamphlet. He enumerated 'thieving and stealing ... cutting and destroying of Woods, pulling of Hedges, and trespasses to Corn and Gras thereby, Alms giving at the door' as among the 'losses' that 'do accrue by the want of a due Provision of Work'.[53] Settling the poor and setting them to work were two answers to a common problem.

Finally, in considering reasons for passing the Law of Settlement soon after the Restoration we should take into account the way migration became invested with negative political meanings in the English revolution. In October 1647 in the course of the Putney debates General Ireton drew a broad distinction between the propertied and propertyless that mapped onto another distinction, one between the mobile and stationary portions of the population:

> I would have an eye to property ... if a man have not a permanent interest he can have no claim ... I mean by permanent local, that is not anywhere else; but he that has no permanent interests, that is here today and gone tomorrow, I do not see he has such a permanent interest.[54]

As he defined the citizenry, Ireton expressed a well established fear of the multitude in motion and the threat they posed to freeholders.

These concerns were dramatically confirmed when on 1 April 1649 Gerald Winstanley and a group of about twenty 'poor men' placed themselves on common land at St George's Hill in Surrey. They began to clear the land, cultivate and also build houses on it. By August, however, having had action taken against them in the courts and some of their goods having been seized, Winstanley and his fellow Diggers moved on to Cobham, two miles away. Here the colony lasted until April 1650 before it was destroyed and dispersed. In these months at least eight other short-lived Digger colonies were established, mostly in counties around London. These experiments bear on the law of settlement: as Keith Thomas suggests, 'The whole Digger movement can be plausibly regarded as the culmination of a century of unauthorized encroachments upon forests and wastes by squatters and local commoners, pushed on by land shortage and pressure of population.'[55]

Local responses to the Diggers highlight some of the social conflicts that migrants provoked and the alliances that formed in response to their presence. At St George's Hill the Diggers were outsiders and opposition to the incomers was led and initiated by local yeomen. In the 1580s and again between 1606 and 1616 the inhabitants of Walton 'had been involved in struggles to prevent incursions on to their commons by outsiders'. For many smallholders access to the commons sustained their capacity to support a livelihood as independent farmers. Winstanley's appeal to the rural poor was overlain by conflict between the local population and incomers.[56]

For Winstanley communal cultivation of the commons and wastes would simply restore to the people what had been taken from them at the Norman Conquest. Not only this, it would also solve the problem of the poor. This much is clear, for instance, in Winstanley's "APPEALE TO ALL ENGLISHMEN" dated 26 March 1650:

> But come, take *Plow & Spade*, build & plant, & make the wast Land fruitfull, that there may be no beggar nor idle person among us; for if the wast land of England were manured by her Children, it would become in a few yeares the richest, the strongest and flourishing Land in the world.[57]

In this way, Winstanley and the Diggers gave a new and dangerous political meaning to conflicts that had been a feature of rural England for more than a century. Under the Commonwealth, Winstanley claimed, the authority of Lords of the Manor was lost since it derived directly from the King. Since the revolution, the Lords' jurisdiction over the commons was at an end and poor men were free to build houses and sow corn on the land.[58]

The Diggers proposed one solution to the urgent social problems of begging and idleness. Their programme would render the poor law obsolete. They conjoined squatters and encroachment with regicide, an attack on local authority and the rights of property owners. They offered a clear challenge to the social order, one that was all the more resonant because of the far wider problems arising from migration and encroachment. For this reason, although they were a short lived phenomenon, the Diggers cast a long shadow which reached the Restoration parliaments.[59] It is, perhaps, no wonder, that parliament in 1662 passed a law whose preamble berated and stigmatized the migrant poor and whose practical consequences made legal the removal of any new arrival, whether a vagrant or not.

1662 and After

In one sense, the 1662 Act continued a history of measures designed to deter and eject strangers and to protect the poor rate and other resources held in common by villagers and townspeople from the depredations of incomers. Nevertheless, this customary emphasis on continuities presents a partial view of the Act's significance. To be sure, the law of 1662 did not give parishes their first weapons with which to resist the streams of migrants that were a ubiquitous feature of English society. Yet it does not follow that because practices for excluding unwanted immigrants were part of the machinery of governance in early-modern England, the Act of 1662 did not produce significant change.

First, from a narrowly legal standpoint the 1662 Act was innovative. As Michael Nolan, an early nineteenth-century authority pointed out, the law now allowed placed vagrant beggars and the impotent poor 'on the same footing' in one important respect:

> Prior to this statute, no persons could be removed unless they were in a state of vagrancy, or had actually become chargeable to some other place than that of their settlement. But this act regards all people of an inferior condition who change their habitation as vagrants and vagabonds, unless they come to reside upon a tenement of £10 in value.[60]

Whereas in law, if not in administrative practice, before 1662 no one who was not a vagrant could be removed, now it only required a complaint 'made by the Churchwardens or Overseers of the Poore of any Parish to any Justice of Peace' that an incomer was 'likely to be chargeable' to have him or her sent away. Of course, in many cases the formal protection of the law had been no help to migrants ejected from parishes and towns. But we have also seen that local governors were aware of legal constraint and that this inhibited them from taking still more swingeing action against the migrant poor. The law's prophylactic formula adopted a form of words that had been used by Justices of the Peace since the 1640s. But even here, to say that the new law simply codified existing practice is too bland. In part, this is because the formula did not date back to the enactment of the Poor Law itself but was a relatively recent invention. In part, too, we need to recognize that from 1598 to 1662 there was a steady erosion of the legal protection offered to able-bodied migrants; this had been attenuated from the broad immunity that judges regularly asserted in the period up to the 1640s, to the extra-legal formulas adopted by magistrates from the 1640s, to the legal transformation effected by the 1662 Act.

A still more significant shift followed from the impact of the 1662 Act on the techniques of exclusion. The law against inmates was still used by some parishes and corporations in the 1670s and even the 1680s.[61] By the late seventeenth century, however, these measures of control had largely faded away. Functionally, the law of settlement took their place.

This became the principle mechanism through which local authorities strived to control both migrants and their rights. As this change occurred it brought about a shift in how local governors allocated the risks and costs that migration generated for local communities. At the beginning of the century the regulatory regime had placed risks and costs on landlords and employers who were required to offer bonds or sureties for the strangers they accommodated as tenants or set to work. They were inhibited by coalitions of fellow-inhabitants who protested that their profit-seeking activities were 'contrary to the mind of the town'. After 1662, however, commerce was set free from these obligations. Once parishes and corporations were certain of their powers to remove poor migrants there was far less need than before for them to demand securities and bonds from their landlords and employers. In this way, the 1662 law diffused and hence, to a degree, defused a host of local conflicts that arose between landlords and large famers and manufacturers, on one side, and the larger body of ratepayers, on the other, over the burden placed by the migrant poor on the poor law and other collective resources. The risks of migration to the wider community were now borne by the poor migrants themselves and by their parishes of settlement.

Finally, the suggestion that the law of settlement merely codified preceding practice glosses over the capitulation it registered on the part of the centre in the face of local intransigence. Thanks to the work of historians such as Michael Braddick and Steve Hindle, we now have a keen sense of how the growth of the state in sixteenth- and seventeenth-century England took place and was carried out with the co-operation of the parochial and county elites.[62] There was conflict as well as cooperation here and the centre's dependence on local agents placed limits on its capacity to enforce the law. For enforcement depended on local initiative and this allowed the law to be implemented according to local needs. In the case of the poor law this meant that the policy on removal was set by Justices of the Peace, vestries, corporations and overseers and not by national officials and that, in this case, local desires contradicted national prescriptions. Rather than clarify and codify the law, what the reform of 1662 did, therefore, was to legitimize ways in which the law had been evaded.[63]

The 'laws for the settlement of the poor' were revised again when Parliament reconvened in 1685 following the accession of James II. Further legislation was passed in 1691 and 1697. The first of these changes, in 1685, addressed the disadvantage at which the law had placed overseers of the poor. 'Forasmuch as such poore persons at their first coming to a Parish doe commonly conceale themselves', the new statute now required migrants to give written notice of their arrival in a parish either to a churchwarden or an overseer. This announcement had to include both the location of the migrant's house and the number in his family. The qualifying period of 40 days would begin only after the incomer passed written notice of his arrival to the overseer of the poor. In 1691 the mechanism for registering and overseeing migration was strengthened still further: now the notice of arrival had to be read out in church and registered in the parish poor book. However, the 1691 Act also set out a number of ways through which migrants could gain a settlement: by serving an annual public office in the parish, by being charged with rates and paying them, by being bound as an indentured apprentice and (if they were unmarried and childless) by being hired into service for a year. In 1697 the law was amended again to permit parishes to certificate labour migrants. Overseers and churchwardens could provide an emigrant from their parish with a document declaring that the parish of origin would be responsible for the emigrant whenever he or his family became chargeable.

Historians have suggested that, in contrast to the backward-looking Act of 1662, these reforms set a new and flexible framework for the next century and a half. These later measures, they say, reflected new attitudes to labour and 'facilitated labour mobility in pre-industrial England'. The reforms also introduced a series of pathways based on 'merit' though which migrants could be accepted as members of the parish community.[64] It is not difficult to see why historians have reached this conclusion: certification promoted labour mobility, and entitlements based on service or a level of income that led to paying local taxes generated an apparent affinity with the idea of individual merit. Nevertheless, once we explore the legal context for the reforms we shall see that this interpretation is at best partial and in important respects misleading.

First, the emphasis on the how the acts opened up labour markets and parochial membership gives too little weight to the central and restrictive features of the 1685 and 1691 reforms. The requirement to give written notice took away from overseers the burden of seeking out incomers. Instead, migrants were now obliged to declare themselves if they wanted to become eligible for poor relief. Richard Burn observed, 'the giving of notice is only putting a force upon the parish to remove.'[65] By requiring migrants to give notice in writing the law now made it impossible for a migrant to gain a settlement merely by moving to a parish and keeping a low profile for forty days.

What of the reforms that did allow migrants to gain a settlement? The idea of 'merit' is an anachronism in this context. The issue of eligibility was discussed irrespective of the personal qualities of the individuals concerned. It is easy to see that ideas of 'merit' and 'membership' might be imputed to the entitlement gained by men who served an annual public office in the parish and by those who were charged with rates and who paid them. In reality the logic of these exemptions was located elsewhere – in the requirement on migrants to give notice – and in the developing idea of what constituted notice. This was made clear in a settlement dispute that reached the court of King's Bench in 1689. The Paine family had migrated from Hebridge in Essex to the parish of St Peter in Malden where they paid rent at £3 per annum. This was too low a level of rent to gain a settlement. However, at the same time, the household was assessed by parish officers for both poor and church rates which Paine duly paid. A year and half later Paine died, leaving his family 'poor and indigent'. The Justices at Quarter Sessions ruled that Paine had not given notice to the Parish Officers and, illogically, that the family should *not* be removed to another parish. This contradictory judgement may have been delivered precisely because the justices wanted guidance from a higher court. This, at any rate, is what the King's Bench provided. The judges there ruled as follows:

> the parish officers had Notice sufficient within the Intent of the Statute, though not within the letter, because the Assessing this Man to the parish rates and receiving the Money assessed is a sufficient evidence, that they knew he was an inhabitant there.[66]

Their view turned not on merit but on what constituted notice. Serving in a public annual office on one's own account generated a settlement in the same way as paying rates. Here too, performance of office was equivalent to notice in writing because of, as Burn put it, 'the notoreity of the thing'.[67]

What of the other avenues to acquire a settlement? Do these indicate a shift from settlement by residence to settlement by merit? If we look at the way the law was formulated we shall be able to see that settlement by residence – the forty-day rule – remained fundamental. What was new was that the law clarified those cases in which the authorities could not object to newcomers during their initial forty days in the parish. This indulgence did not arise on account of these migrants' personal worth, however, but because they arrived bound to contracts that were so weighty that these bonds trumped even the interests of ratepayers. Apprentices and servants gained a settlement by forty days' residence. But theirs was a special sort of residence because it arose from a contract that the overseers were not allowed to break. This was not a matter of merit but of the special status of the agreements contracted by apprentices and servants. The contract did not confer a settlement but it did stand in the way of removal. Then once forty days had passed a settlement had been acquired.[68] In the case of servants, a covenant for a year's service had been regarded as good grounds for a settlement since at least the early seventeenth century. This had been confirmed in the 1662 Act which stated that forty days' residence should give a settlement to an 'apprentice' and a 'servant' as well as to a householder and sojourner. The 1691 law did not, therefore, provide a settlement to apprentices and servants for the first time. Rather, the law in 1691 merely exempted apprentices and servants from the recent requirement to give notice in writing.[69]

The law of settlement as it applied to servants was further amended in 1697. In that year legislators required them to remain in their places for an entire year before they gained a settlement. It is important to see, however, that even here the forty-day rule remained intact. Having served for a year, it was the servant's last forty days' residence that determined his or her settlement. The stipulation of a year's service, Burn suggested half a century later, arose not from considerations of merit but the reverse. The ease of gaining a settlement had made servants 'insolent', he claimed. On this interpretation the qualifying period was a form of labour discipline. The law gave rise to notorious practices on the part of employers who dismissed servants just short of their full year of service. This suggests a different interpretation of the origins of the requirement on servants to remain in place for a whole year. Namely, that this was a device to reconcile ratepayers to the needs of employers at the expense of the servants' entitlements.

In the case of certificates it is true that the 1697 reforms legislated to promote labour mobility but the law of that year itself was less innovative than has been supposed. The certificate system was an important development in the period from the mid seventeenth century and not from the 1690s. The reform to the poor law of 1662 had recognized certificates as one way to secure labour mobility. In 1697 Parliament did not intervene to initiate but to resolve a problem that had arisen in the system of granting certificates. As the 1697 Act itself explained, 'the Certificates that have been given in some cases have been oftentimes construed into a notice in Handwriting.'[70] Parishes receiving migrants who carried a certificate found themselves with an apparent obligation to support the incomers from the poor rate. In other words, the practice of giving and accepting a certificate had become so subverted that it now had the opposite outcome from the one intended.

The assessment of changes in the law of settlement presented here, though revisionist in its legal history, fits well with those trends in the broader historiography of settlement which emphasize the significance of the local context in shaping the welfare entitlements of migrants. The law did not predict poor law practice in any particular locality. Rather, it created a framework of constraints and opportunities within which local practices developed. There remained more than one interest at stake when it came to the local impact of migration: farmers and other entrepreneurs welcomed migrants in ways that other ratepayers did not.[71] Moreover, administrative incapacity, particularly in urban England, remained a continuing problem. These are two reasons why examination and removal under the law of settlement continued to encompass just a minority of those who were vulnerable to action under the law. If, indeed, labour markets did become more fluid in the first half of the eighteenth century and the protection offered to migrants by the poor law became one source of the industrial revolution, then this was not due to the far-sighted legislation of the Stuart parliaments but a combination of the initiative and the incapability of local officials.

Conclusion

The reforms of the late seventeenth century amounted to an elaboration of the system put in place in 1662. They did not significantly change it or the principles on which it operated. This should not be surprising. Mobility across parish and corporation boundaries remained a persistent feature of English society. Although the number of people in danger of starvation markedly declined in the seventeenth century, the number who were simply poor and lacked fuel or clothes, for example, increased to the same degree.[72] In a society in which poverty was endemic and in which additional population would not only exert downward pressure on wage rates but also, because of the problem of diminishing marginal returns, would eventually operate as a drag on per capita output, we can readily understand why migration was widely regarded as a problem and why poor law overseers and vestries frequently chose to target migrants.[73] The ways in which this happened emerged as the problem of migration interacted with the broader institutional and social context. First, as we have seen, the law of settlement developed both from the logic of a parochial based welfare system and also from the need to address problems arising from the widespread failure to set the poor to work. Second, although migrants created difficulties for local economies taken as a whole and for ratepayers, they were also a source of profit for individual petty landlords and entrepreneurs. The law of settlement instigated and elaborated a system that shifted the social costs of migration away from these rent and profit seekers and on to both the migrants themselves and the more distant parishes to which they belonged. In this way, whatever its impact on the poor, the law of settlement contributed to social peace among the middling sort.

Notes

The author would like to thank the British Academy and the Arts and Humanities Research Council for supporting the research and research leave which allowed him to produce this essay.

1. 14 Car.II. c.12.
2. K. D. M. Snell. 2006. *Parish and Belonging. Community, Identity and Welfare in England and Wales 1700–1950*, Cambridge, 81–161. For recent historians, see P. Sharpe. 1997. '"The Bowels of Compation": A Labouring Family and the Law, c. 1790–1834,' in T. Hitchcock, P. King and P. Sharpe (eds), *Chronicling Poverty. The Voices and Strategies of the English Poor, 1640–1840*, London, 87. For a dissenting view from the mid nineteenth century, see House of Commons Papers. 1851. *Report of George Coode, Esq to the Poor Law Board on the Law of Settlement and Removal of the Poor*, 113–125.
3. On relief and discretion in the seventeenth century, see S. Hindle. 2004. *On the Parish? The Micro-Politics of Poor Relief in Rural England c. 1550–1750*, Oxford, 404, 445–446.
4. S. Webb and B. Webb. 1927. *English Local Government: English Poor Law History: Part 1. The Old Poor Law*, London, 314.
5. P. Styles. 1963. 'The Evolution of the Law of Settlement', *Birmingham Historical Journal* 9, 33–63; J. S. Taylor. 1976. 'The Impact of Pauper Settlement 1691–1834, *Past and Present* 73, 44, 49.
6. Taylor, 'The Impact', 50–53; A. Fletcher. 1986. *Reform in the Provinces. The Government of Stuart England*, New Haven, 205–6; P. Slack, *Poverty and Policy in Tudor and Stuart England*, London, 1988, 194–195; N. Landau. 1988. 'The Laws of Settlement and the Surveillance of Immigration in Eighteenth-Century Kent', *Continuity and Change* 3(3), 391–420; P. Solar and R. Smith. 2003. 'An Old Poor Law for the New Europe. Reconciling Local Solidarity with Labour Mobility in Early-Modern England', in P. David and M. Thomas (eds), *The Economic Future in Historical Perspective*, Oxford, 472–473.
7. Styles, 'The Evolution'; Hindle, *On the Parish*, ch. 5.
8. Taylor, 'The Impact', 45. For the same assumption made in a contemporary context, see G. Dench, K. Gavron and M. Young. 2006. *The New East End. Kinship, Race and Conflict*, London.
9. On the history of closed and open systems see D. Feldman. 2003. 'Migrants, Immigrants and Welfare from the Old Poor Law to the Welfare State', *Transactions of the Royal Historical Society, Sixth Series* 13, 79–104.
10. A. Kussmaul. 1981. *Servants in Husbandry in Early Modern England*, Cambridge; P. Clark and D. Souden (eds). 1987. *Migration and Society in Early Modern England*, London; D. Levine and K. Wrightson. 1991. *The Making of an Industrial Society: Whickham 1560–1765*, Oxford, 180; M. Kitch. 1992. 'Population Movement and Migration in Pre-Industrial Rural England', in B. Short (ed.), *The English Rural Community*, Cambridge, 62–84; B. Stapleton. 1992. 'Marriage, Migration and Mendicancy', in B. Stapleton (ed.), *Conflict and Community in Southern England*, New York, 59; K. Wrightson and D. Levine. 1995. *Poverty and Piety in an English Village: Terling 1525–1700*, Oxford, 79, 81.
11. D. Woodward. 1980. 'The Background to the Statute of Artificers: The Genesis of Labour Policy 1558–63', *Economic History Review* 33(1), 35–37, 40; M. Braddick, *State Formation in Early Modern England c. 1500–1700*, Cambridge, 2000, 108–110.
12. 35 Eliz. c.6.
13. F. A. Inderwick. 1891. *The Interregnum. Studies of the Commonwealth Legislative, Social and Legal*, London, 93–94.
14. P. Slack. 1974. 'Vagrants and Vagrancy in England, 1598–1664', *Economic History Review* 27, 360–379; A. L. Beier. 1981. 'Social Problems of an Elizabethan Country Town: Warwick 1580–1590', in P. Clark (ed.), *Country Towns in Pre-Industrial England*, Leicester, 62; J. R. Kent. 1981. 'Population Mobility and Alms: Poor Migrants in the Midlands During the Early Seventeenth Century', *Local Population Studies*, 27, 35–51; P. Clark. 1983.

The English Alehouse: A Social History 1200–1830, London, 129; Braddick, *State Formation*, 150–155.

15. Styles, 'The Evolution'; Hindle, *On the Parish*, 302.
16. E. Freshfield (ed.). 1890. *The Vestry Minute Book of St Bartholemew Exchange, 1567–1764*, London, 88; F. G. Emmison (ed.). 1970. *Early Essex Town Meetings*, Chichester, 107, 112–114.
17. Emmison, *Early Essex Town Meetings*, ix, 14.
18. E. H. Bates (ed.). 1907. *Quarter Sessions Records for the County of Somerset*, vol. 1 (1607–1625), Somerset Record Society, 135; S. A. H. Burne (ed.). 1936. *The Staffordshire Quarter Sessions Rolls, vol. 4 (1598–1602)*, Stafford, 95–96.
19. Bates, *Quarter Sessions*, 206; J. H. E. Bennett and J. C. Dewhurst (eds). 1940. *Quarter Sessions Records with Other Records of the Justices of the Peace for the County Palatine of Chester, 1559–1760*, vol. 1, 100–101; W. B. Willcox. 1940. *Gloucestershire. A Study in Local Government*, New Haven CT, 256; J. S. Cockburn (ed.). 1976. *Western Circuit Assize Orders 1629–1648: A Calendar*, London, 120.
20. B. Sharp. 1980. *In Contempt of All Authority: Rural Artisans and Riot in the West of England, 1586–1660*, Berkeley CA, 158.
21. F. J. C. Hearnshaw and D. M. Hearnshaw (eds). 1905. *Court Leet Records, vol. 1*, Southampton, part 1, 284, 369; part 3, 386, 402, 439.
22. Cockburn, *Western Circuit Assize Orders*, 79; P. Slack (ed.). 1975. *Poverty in Early Stuart Salisbury*, Devizes, 131.
23. P. Clark. 1977. *English Provincial Society from the Reformation to the Revolution*, Hassocks, 302.
24. S. Birtles. 1999. 'Common Land, Poor Relief and Enclosure. The Use of Manorial Resources in Fulfilling Parish Obligations 1601–1834', *Past and Present*, 165, 91, 105–106; Hindle, *On the Parish*, 147–148.
25. M. J. Groombridge. 1956. *Calendar of Chester City Council Minutes 1603–42*, Blackpool, 9.
26. 43 Eliz c.7; E. Coke. 1642. *The Second Part of the Institutes of the Laws of England*, London, 740.
27. Hindle, *On the Parish*, 307–308.
28. M. Dalton. 1666. *The Countrey Justice*, London, 116; Cockburn, *Western Circuit Assize Orders*, 28, 55, 67.
29. Cockburn, *Western Circuit Assize Orders*, 51.
30. Dalton, *The Countrey Justice*, 115, 123.
31. Cockburn, *Western Circuit Assize Orders*, 31–32.
32. T. G. Barnes. 1961. *Somerset 1625–40. A County's Government during the Personal Rule*, Cambridge MA, 187; T. G. Barnes (ed.), 1959, *Somerset Assize Orders 1629–40*, Frome: xxvi; Slack, *Poverty in Early-Stuart Salisbury*, 2.
33. Dalton, *The Countrey Justice*, 115–116.
34. Baker, *Quarter Sessions*, 183–184.
35. Emmison, *Essex Town Meetings*, 3.
36. Fletcher, *Reform*, 204; Hindle, *On the Parish?*, 306–310. Contrary to Fletcher, W. Sheppard. 1652. *The Whole Office of the Country Justice of Peace*, 2nd ed. London, part 1, 97–98 does not dissent from the interpretation elucidated in this chapter.
37. B. C. Redwood (ed.). 1954. *Sussex Quarter Sessions Order Book, 1642–49*, Lewes, 47. Of course, the timing of change was not uniform and in some places it can be found a little earlier: Emmison, *Essex Town Meetings*, 94.
38. M. Nolan. 1825. *A Treatise of the Laws for the Relief and Settlement of the Poor*, 4th ed. London, vol. 1, 271; Inderwick, *The Interregnum*, 91.
39. E. Leonard. 1900. *The Early History of English Poor Relief*, Cambridge; W. MacCaffrey. 1958. *Exeter 1540–1640*, Cambridge MA, 115; Slack, *Poverty in Salisbury*, 153–155; D.

Underdown. 1992. *Fire From Heaven: The Life of an English Town in the Seventeenth Century*, London, 222; Hindle, *On the Parish*, 185.

40. P. Solar. 1995. 'Poor Relief and English Economic Development Before the Industrial Revolution', *Economic History Review* 48(1), 1–22; see also R. Smith. 1996. 'Charity, Self-Interest and Welfare: Reflections from Demographic and Family History', in M. Daunton (ed.), *Charity, Self-Interest and Welfare in Britain, 1500 to the Present*, London, 23–50; Solar and Smith, 'An Old Poor Law'.

41. V. Pearl. 1978. 'Puritans and Poor Relief. The London Workhouse, 1649–60' in D. Pennington and K. Thomas (eds), *Puritans and Revolutionaries. Essays in Seventeenth-Century History Presented to Christopher Hill*, Oxford, 225; Styles, 'The Evolution', 177.

42. M. James. 1930. *Social Problems and Policy During the Puritan Revolution 1640–60*, London, 283–286.

43. Webb and Webb, *English Local Government (...) Part 1*, 325–326.

44. Webb and Webb, *English Local Government (...) Part 1*, 324; Taylor, 'The Impact', 50.

45. J. Walter and K. Wrightson. 1976. 'Dearth and the Social Order in Early Modern England', *Past and Present* 71, 22–44; P. Clark. 1979. 'Migration in England during the Late Seventeenth and Early Eighteenth Centuries', *Past and Present* 83, 57–90; J. Walter. 1989. 'The Social Economy of Dearth in Early Modern England', in J. Walter and R. Schofield (eds), *Famine, Disease and the Social Order in Early Modern Society*, Cambridge, 123–125.

46. L. Merrick. 1994. '"Without Violence and by Controlling the Poorer Sort": The Enclosure of Ashdown Forest 1640–93', *Sussex Archaeological Collections* 132, 118. See also J. Thirsk. 1978. *Economic Policy and Projects. The Development of a Consumer Society in Early Modern England*, Oxford, which connects the 1662 Act to a long history of squatting and despoliation.

47. Webb and Webb, *English Local Government (...) Part 1*, 323; Fletcher, *Reform*, 211.

48. J. M. Rosenheim (ed.). 1989. *The Notebook of Robert Doughty 1662–1665*, Norfolk, 118.

49. J.B. Williams. 1835. *Memoirs of the Life, Character and Writings of Sir Matthew Hale*, London, 34, 40–48, 83.

50. Cited in Webb and Webb, *English Local Government (...) Part 1*, 323–324.

51. M. Hale. 1683. *A Discourse Touching Provision for the Poor*, London, 24–25. The pamphlet written in 1659 was not published until 1683.

52. A. Woolrych. 1982. *Commonwealth to Protectorate*, Oxford, 41.

53. Hale, *A Discourse*, 19–20, 26.

54. Cited in D. Rollison. 2010. *A Commonwealth of the People. Popular Politics and England's Long Social Revolution*, Cambridge, 455–456.

55. K. Thomas. 1969. 'Another Digger Broadside', *Past and Present* 42, 58. See also A. Howkins. 2002. 'From Diggers to Dongas: The Land in English Radicalism 1649–2000', *History Workshop Journal* 54, 5–6.

56. D. Gurney. 2007. *Brave Community. The Digger Movement in the English Revolution*, Manchester, 1–20.

57. G. H. Sabine (ed.). 1941. *The Works of Gerard Winstanley*. Ithaca, NY, 408.

58. Ibid., 410–412.

59. D. L. Smith. 1999. *The Stuart Parliaments 1603–1689*, London, 147.

60. Nolan, *A Treatise*, vol. 1, 275. As Nolan points out the law was innovative in other ways too: it placed beyond doubt that a settlement continued until a new one was acquired, it gave power to JPs to rule in cases of removal and settlement, it prevented settlement from being acquired by the mere act of residence for forty days without being chargeable, and it gave a right of appeal to the next quarter sessions. Ibid., 280–282.

61. F. R. Sharpe. 1965. 'The Order Book of Ormskirk 1613–1721' in F. R. Sharpe (ed.), *A Lancashire Miscellany*, [s.l.], 32–33. At Coventry the constables stopped presenting inmates between 1662 and 1673 but did so regularly between 1673–82. L. Fox (ed.). 1986. *Coventry Constables Presentments, 1629–1742*, Oxford.

62. M. Braddick, *State Formation;* S. Hindle. 2000. *The State and Social Change in Early Modern England, c. 1550–1640,* London.
63. In this respect, the Law of Settlement was a characteristic piece of Restoration legislation that derogated the authority of the centre and devolved power to local elites. See G. C. F. Forster. 1983. 'Government in Provincial England under the Later Stuarts', *Transactions of the Royal Historical Society, Sixth Series* 33(1), 29–48.
64. For the notion of merit, see especially Taylor, 'The Impact'.
65. R. Burn. 1780. *The Justice of the Peace and the Parish Officer,* 14th ed. London, vol. III, 444.
66. Carthew. 1728. *Reports of Cases Adjudged in the Court of the King's Bench from the Third Year of King James the Second to the Twelfth Year of King William the Third,* London, 28.
67. Burn, *The Justice of the Peace,* vol. III, 451.
68. Ibid., 367–368, 392–393.
69. 3 Gul&Mar c11 ~ vi, vii.
70. On the problems that arose, see Carthew, *Reports,* 346.
71. On these conflict of interest in the next century, see R. Wells. 1993. 'Migration, the Law and Parochial Policy in Eighteenth and Early Nineteenth Century England', *Southern History* 15, 86–139.
72. P. Slack, *Poverty and Policy,* 188–189.
73. E. A. Wrigley. 2004. *Poverty, Progress and Population,* Cambridge, chs. 7–8.

CHAPTER TWO

DOUBLE DETERRENCE
Settlement and Practice in London's West End, 1725–1824

Jeremy Boulton

In the Parish of St Martin in the Fields, it has, for a very long period, been the custom to admit into the Workhouse all Persons that were destitute, without, in the first instance, enquiring to what Parish they belonged; to relieve their actual and immediate wants, and afterwards, if necessary, to pass them to their legal places of settlement. (*St Martin in the Fields. Report on the subject of Casual Poor admitted by relief tickets into the Workhouse of the Parish of St Martin in the Fields*, London, 1839, 3)

Introduction

This chapter represents the first full length study of how the laws of settlement were applied in Georgian London. Such a study is now seriously overdue. Although historians are increasingly using London's voluminous settlement material (mostly examinations and removal orders) to study such topics as the treatment of lunatics, vagrancy, bastardy, childcare, domestic service and family breakdown, it is rare for such studies to contextualize their source material within the wider welfare system(s) of eighteenth-century London.[1] More importantly, however, the effects of the Landau-Snell debate over the nature and reach of the eighteenth-century settlement laws continues to cast a pall of uncertainty over both the motives for examination and who exactly was subject to that process.

This despite the fact that Landau's argument – that settlement laws were used to regulate and monitor migration rather than responding only to destitution – related only to males in rural areas and that she took pains to make it clear that her original 'article most certainly does not deny that a very large number of those examined as to their settlement were in need of poor relief'.[2]

Since this chapter concerns settlement practice in the metropolis it has little relevance to that often highly technical debate and does not seek to re-open it. Apart from the legal framework of the settlement laws, virtually every other historical variable in London – population size, structure, density and mobility, economic specialization, bureaucratic sophistication, documentary survival, levels of wealth, poverty and literacy – were radically different to that found in rural areas. As the quotation at the start of this chapter indicates, too, parishes might, in practice, run their local welfare systems directly against the strict letter of settlement law. Moreover, for much of the eighteenth century most of those seeking poor relief in the metropolis faced what can be termed 'double deterrence'. An application for poor relief, in theory, would trigger an enquiry into one's settlement. For those applicants who were, or who suspected that they might be, legally settled elsewhere this might be a significant deterrent to applying at all since it could mean physical removal. After 1723, however, all large London parishes erected substantial workhouses under the Workhouse Test Act. These institutions, like those erected under the New Poor Law, were designed partly to deter the poor from applying for relief. Those refusing to enter could be denied aid by officials. For most of the eighteenth century therefore, applicants for poor relief in London faced the double deterrent of the settlement laws *and* the possibility of entering a parish workhouse.[3] Since only a (substantial) minority of parishes in provincial England used or operated workhouses in the eighteenth century, their ubiquity in the capital represents another significant difference between the metropolitan and rural experience.[4]

This chapter will exploit the rich documentation surviving for the Westminster parish of St Martin in the Fields to answer key questions about settlement and belonging in the capital which stem from the historiography outlined above: How did the settlement laws actually operate in the nation's capital? Who was actually examined under the law of settlement? All migrants or just the destitute? What impact did these laws have on the lives of the poor? How did settlement law mesh with local welfare structures and practices? And, bearing in mind that both Landau and Snell uncovered significant changes over time in the ways in which the law of settlement was applied in provincial England, can a chronology for the working of settlement law be uncovered? The answer will need to start with a description of the parish and its administration. Settlement documentation, local changes in policy and practice will then be discussed and the essay will finish by taking a bottom up rather than a top down view of settlement law via a case study of two paupers.

The Parish of St Martin in the Fields

The parish itself contained within its 286 acres between 25–35,000 inhabitants for most of the period. It seems to have experienced no particular surges of population growth and was already built up in 1725.[5] It contained large numbers of both rich and poor people within its boundaries and encompassed various government offices and buildings as well as part of St James's Palace. Throughout the period the parish hosted members of the titular aristocracy, including the Dukes of Northumberland whose seat at Charing Cross was a prominent landmark. Naturally its occupational structure included large numbers of tradesmen and artisans serving the rich and powerful, as well as an army of domestic servants.[6] The parish's social structure can be best summed up as heterogeneous.

A census of Westminster's population in 1821 (Table 2.1) reveals a fairly typical metropolitan age structure, with a notable bulge in the 20–29 age group, produced by the immigration of large numbers of servants and apprentices. That many of these were female domestics explains the low sex ratio in the latter age group.[7] The 1821 census can provide only the roughest of guides to the likely demographic structure of Westminster's population in the eighteenth century. Preliminary work on sex ratios at burial suggests that St Martin's had an unusually large surplus of females in its population compared to that of the metropolis as a whole, although this difference may have been diminishing towards the end of the eighteenth century.[8]

Migration is key to contextualizing how the settlement laws operated and London, of course, was a city of migrants. One quarter of Dr Bland's 1618 married couples using the Westminster General Dispensary between 1774 and 1781 were native Londoners and 58 per cent came from other counties in England and Wales. Women were more likely to be native Londoners than men. Things were little different in 1840 when only 29 per cent of working-class Westminster inhabitants gave their 'country' as 'London'. The majority, 55 per cent, came from 'other parts of England' and Wales, with 16 per cent coming from Ireland and Scotland. Over time Westminster seems to have experienced a fall in Scots and foreigners, and a rise in the number of those born in Ireland.[9]

Table 2.1. Westminster Age and Sex Structure in 1821

Age	Males	Females	Total	%	Sex Ratio
0–4	5,801	5,948	11,749	*11.0*	98
5–9	4,435	4,734	9,169	*8.6*	94
10–14	4,289	3,984	8,273	*7.8*	108
15–19	4,880	5,498	10,378	*9.8*	89
20–29	10,201	13,083	23,284	*21.9*	78
30–39	8,402	9,476	17,878	*16.8*	89
40–49	6,364	6,457	12,821	*12.0*	99
50–59	3,688	3,889	7,577	*7.1*	95
60–69	1,677	1,974	3,651	*3.4*	85
70–79	555	769	1,324	*1.2*	72
80–89	91	187	278	*0.3*	49
90–99	1	17	18	*0.0*	6
100+	1	1	2	*0.0*	100
Total	50,385	56,017	106,402	*99.9*	90

Source: Census of Great Britain, 1821, Abstract of the answers and returns made pursuant to an Act, passed in the first year of the reign of His Majesty King George IV, entitled, "An Act for taking an account of the population of Great Britain, and of the increase or diminution thereof." Preliminary observations. Enumeration abstract. Parish register abstract, 1821, BPP, 1822 XV (502), 197.

Such migrants faced a formidable welfare system. St Martin's, like most other parishes in suburban London, operated a large workhouse. This opened in 1725 and was rebuilt and greatly expanded in 1772. Notwithstanding its workhouse, however, St Martin's operated a poor law system which balanced both outdoor and indoor relief throughout the eighteenth and early nineteenth centuries. The local poor law rested on a very substantial tax base. In 1726, 2,569 ratepayers raised £4,102. After the inflation of the later eighteenth century, in 1799, 3,099 tax payers produced £10,200 and further inflation meant that by 1829 the parish's then 2,912 rate payers were contributing no less than £21,839. Between 1725 and 1750 the overseers' accounts reveal total expenditure hovering around £4,000 per year, rising to between £10,000 and £12,000 from the mid 1770s to the 1790s. Even allowing for inflation, this represented a substantial increase in real terms. As far as one can judge, income from the poor rate and other sources more than kept pace with expenditure throughout the eighteenth century.[10] Given its huge population, per capita spending on the poor, although reasonably generous, was far from exceptional when compared to some of its West End neighbours and many of the wealthy parishes in the City of London.[11]

Substantial funding of this sort paid for an extensive parish bureaucracy, rarely found elsewhere. For poor law purposes the parish was
sub-divided into individual wards. In 1766 five overseers managed nine
wards of the parish. By 1794 nine overseers were responsible for nine
wards, with one exceptionally large ward (Charing Cross) sub-divided
into two parts.[12] The parish's streets, courts, lanes, yards and alleys were
patrolled by an army of beadles, watchmen and constables. Beadles, in
particular, played an important role in the daily operation of the settlement laws. Constables dealt with bastardy cases and were also responsible for conveying vagrants to Bridewell. Watchmen occasionally brought
paupers to the workhouse or the local lock-up and sometimes arrested
vagrants.[13] Incoming overseers were inducted by the ward beadle.[14] Yet,
although Overseers and Churchwardens continued to be recruited from
the higher social ranks of ordinary parishioners, this does not mean that
the poor law was actually run and maintained solely by self-serving ama-
teurs. In fact, there was a professional parish bureaucracy which did most
of the routine clerical work. Two paid clerks and their deputies churned
out poor law documentation. The vestry clerk looked after legal business
on behalf of the parish, which included handling criminal prosecutions,
keeping the Register of the Infant Poor, managing settlement appeals
and prosecuting the fathers of bastard children for maintenance. The
post required formal legal training. Until 1772 vestry clerks seem to
have served as clerks to the overseers of the poor. The vestry clerk had
less to do with poor law matters after that date since a vestry minute
records the granting of extra salary to compensate for the loss of business caused by the overseers appointing their own clerk 'of late'. The
rebuilding and expansion of the parish workhouse in 1772 was thus part
of a local reorganization of poor law administration. At that time the
workhouse clerkship seems to have been merged with that of the Clerk
to the Overseers of the Poor, whose office was located on the workhouse
site.[15] This official played a central role in local settlement business thereafter, particularly in the case of one T. Samuel Lemage (1784–1785,
retired 1808) who was succeeded by his son and former deputy William
Samuel Lemage (1808–1817). The clerk following the Lemage dynasty
in 1817, William Toone, was a professional poor law administrator who
published a number of guides to poor law procedure and practice.[16] This
clerkship paid well.[17] On 9 April 1794 Lemage was given a gratuity of
£20 in consideration of the 'many litigations of settlements which have
occurred during the last year, & in which this parish has succeeded'.[18] In
the following year he was to act as agent for a number of parishes to op-
pose 'the objectionable Clauses in the Bill now depending in Parliament,
relating [to] the removal of the poor'.[19]

Settlement and Poor Law Documentation

The parish bureaucracy was far from idle. Documentation exists for this single parish in quantities that would be more appropriate for an entire county. The most important sources are settlement examinations. Between 1725 and 1794 some 25,881 individuals were examined, and their testimonies written down in an unbroken series of numbered 'examination books'. Earlier books date back to 1708 and are equally voluminous. The post-1725 books included bastardy examinations and examinations of individuals passed under vagrancy and settlement laws. It is clear from their format, and later additions, that the entries were referred to on a regular basis and would presumably have formed the basis of fair copies to accompany removal orders and any other legal process. They formed a permanent archive of settlement examination which might be consulted long after the event by interested parish administrators. Despite (or perhaps because of) the extensive nature of this material these examination books have not been exploited by previous historians as much as one might have thought although J. S. Taylor makes reference to the St Martin's examinations in his classic article on the subject.[20]

These books essentially contain drafts. Those which were the basis of subsequent removal orders and which thus required a copy were signed by at least one local justice, and details therein sometimes updated if necessary. Some of the examinations thus include marginal notes to the effect that there was an 'Original in the Bundle of Ex[aminations]'.[21] Many of the pre-1725 entries contain a note to the effect that there was an 'original on the file'.[22] Whether these examinations were taken at a formal petty session or not is currently unclear, although given the number that were unsigned it seems very unlikely.[23] Most of the examinations took place before only one JP, but many were undated and some have no reference to any JP being present at all, or a blank where the name of the JP should be. Clerks, notably T. Samuel Lemage, could be assiduous in checking testimonies, searching out information, correcting and amplifying testimonies and detecting outright fraud. Such investigations are only recorded, however, in a small minority of cases. Officials like Lemage could and did call on a network of family members, neighbours, landlords and former employers to establish the veracity of a claim for settlement, or record an examinees' later life history. Occasionally such people were given cash rewards, or reimbursed for the expense involved. Thus, for example, John Pegg, overseer, gave 5s 3d to 'Catherine Lloyd for her Trouble in swearing to the Settlement of a Child left in this Parish' in 1772. Particularly effective parish officers, as well as clerks, might also be rewarded: 'Paradise for diligence in finding out Settlements' was given 2s 6d by an overseer in 1785.[24] However, it would be pushing things too far to use cases of fraud or evasion to argue that manipulation of the law of settlement by the examined was widespread. One could argue that the care taken by parish officials actually made such tactics less likely to succeed.

These 'examination books' are probably the closest thing we have in Britain to an entire extant record of an urban early modern parish seeking to operate the law of settlement in the eighteenth century. They represent the first contact that parish officers had with the parish poor and newcomers of all sorts: vagrants, unmarried mothers, migrant workers, displaced families, the homeless and recent arrivals. There is a gap in the record between 1795 and 1816, but from the latter date until 1827 a large number of what are termed 'rough examinations' exist and have been used here to carry the analysis into the nineteenth century. The huge number of draft examinations, and the creation of a permanent parish archive from them, represented an element of regulation and surveillance, perhaps to act as an *aide memoire* to inform future poor relief decisions.

This chapter also deploys, in addition to the examination books, and for the years 1710–1742 only, books called 'register of removals' (containing records of removals from the parish, certificates issued for parishes elsewhere and vagrancy passes) and 'books of complaints' (removal orders from other parishes back to St Martin's). Between the years 1719 to 1734 inclusive these, together with the examination books, provide what seems to be a complete record of settlement-related business in the parish.[25] In addition to the settlement material, the Pauper Biographies Project from which it is drawn has digitized a complete series of workhouse admission and discharge registers between 1725 and 1824. This enables us to match settlement activity to fluctuations in workhouse admissions, and also to build individual pauper biographies. This is important since it is thereby possible to measure the extent to which 'chargeability' was linked to examination. Lastly, a complete set of payments made to the 'extraordinary' poor in 1726–1727 are also available. This means that it is possible to see who exactly was receiving both indoor and outdoor relief in that one accounting year.[26]

Settlement Practice and the Workhouse

Figure 2.1 is based on a count of all the examination books.[27] There is a clear chronology. Examination seems to have been at its most intensive between 1725 and 1740 and declined to about 400 per year thereafter. The number recorded in the books slumps dramatically after 1785 for reasons which are not clear, but might relate to changes in local poor law

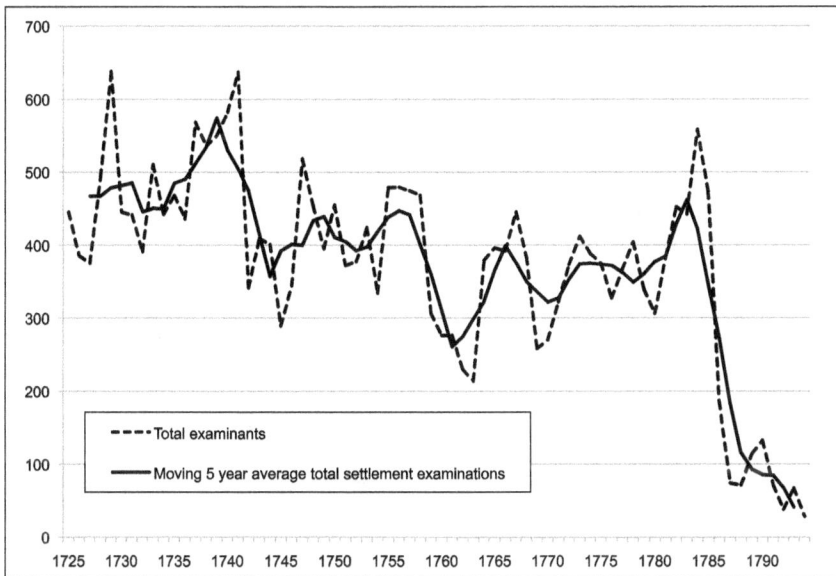

Figure 2.1. Total Number of Settlement Examinations in St Martin in the Fields, 1725–1794

policy. Until 1785 there is a reasonably close relationship between the annual number of examinations and the numbers of paupers admitted into the parish workhouse. There is also a very similar seasonality in the two series, with a winter peak and a spring trough.[28] This is hardly surprising, since, rather in the manner of the quotation at the head of this chapter, it quickly became standard practice to examine paupers only *after* their admission into the workhouse. Figure 2.2, which shows the percentage of examinations said to have taken place in (or occasionally at) the workhouse, probably underestimates the practice, since it is demonstrable that workhouse residence was not always mentioned in examinations. For most of the period, then, at least one third, and sometimes as many as 40 per cent of all those examined were already resident in the parish workhouse. Many more of those examined were sent to the workhouse shortly afterwards. Here, therefore, is strong evidence that a large number of examinations under the settlement law were tied to destitution, rather than being 'likely to become chargeable' even before legal changes in 1795 made actual chargeability the trigger for settlement considerations. It was presumably easier to examine paupers on site and at leisure. That said, however, the proportion examined in the workhouse declined, and the absolute number of examinations remained stable, after it was *enlarged* in 1772. This suggests a new stringency regarding examination, perhaps

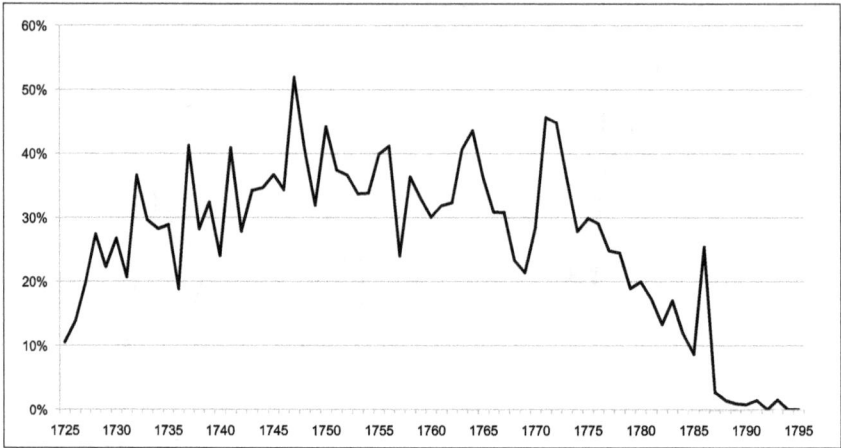

Figure 2.2. Percentage of Examinations Taken in the St Martin's Workhouse, 1725–1794

associated with the local poor law reorganization that accompanied the rebuilding.

What is equally clear, however, is that settlement activity continued into the nineteenth century, such that the period of the most intensive scrutiny occurred in the 1810s. It would be quite wrong, therefore, to think that the 1795 legislative change necessarily led to a *reduction* in regulative activity via the settlement laws in London. 'Rough' settlement examinations were taken in huge numbers in 1817 (1,856) and 1818 (1,280).[29] Thereafter they returned to levels comparable with the first three-quarters of the eighteenth century. When set against the likely age distribution of the parish population as suggested by the 1821 census (see Table 2.1), it can be estimated that around 10 per cent of all those aged thirty or older would have been examined by the parish in 1817. It would require an intensive study to uncover the motives behind this extraordinary regulative effort. [30]

Why were individuals examined in the first place? To answer this question it is helpful to look at the basic characteristics of those examined. Table 2.2 presents the age and gender of all examinants between 1725 and 1794. It excludes 812 people whose age was not given. The figures relate only to the person who was the chief subject of the examination rather than dependents or spouses. Clearly, in the eighteenth-century metropolis, the examined, like those admitted to the parish workhouse, were disproportionately female, with a particular bulge in the 20–29 age group reflecting the effects of gender-specific migration revealed in Table 2.1. The clear and unremarkable message of the table is that females were

Table 2.2. Age and Gender of Those Examined under the Settlement Laws in
St Martin in the Fields, 1725–1794

Age	Males	Females	Total	%	Sex Ratio
0–19	570	1,871	2,441	*10*	30
20–29	998	6,023	7,021	*28*	17
30–39	1,204	4,088	5,292	*21*	29
40–49	1,082	2,596	3,678	*15*	42
50–59	1,000	1,946	2,946	*12*	51
60+	1,363	2,328	3,691	*15*	59
Total	6,217	18,852	25,069	*101*	33

at far greater risk of falling into need and destitution than were men at
virtually all ages. Bastardy, death of spouse, desertion and insecure female
employment explain the gender bias.[31]

Both the gender bias of those examined, and the extent to which examination took place after workhouse admittance, confirm that actual destitution explains a great deal of the examination taking place in St Martin's
under the settlement laws. To investigate this topic further a sample of 415
examinations was taken for the accounting year 1726–1727 and the individuals therein sought in the overseers' accounts of 'extraordinary' payments and the workhouse admissions register. This is a tricky exercise, as
one needs to identify not only examinants but also their dependents. Since
poor law accounts only usually supply forenames and surnames of those
relieved the resultant linkage exercise contains a degree of error caused by
individuals of the same name, common surnames, non-standardized spell-
ings, as well as the difficulty of identifying dependents. Thus, Table 2.3
may underestimate the extent to which the 415 examinations are related
to the receipt of indoor or outdoor relief in 1726–1727 but it is probably
broadly accurate.[32] Overall 70 per cent of the examinations (289/415) can
be linked to either indoor or outdoor relief of some sort. Obviously individuals are found in more than one category. Detail in the poor accounts
suggests that many of those examined only appear in the poor accounts
because the payment involved their removal out of the parish. That is,
examination and subsequent removal involved a cost. At the very least,
however, 30 per cent (126/415) of those examined do not seem to have
been given immediate relief by the parish. Of these, just fourteen appeared
in order to get a settlement certificate from the parish allowing them to
reside elsewhere. A further twenty of those 126 were linked to a removal
order, which might have explained their examination. All told 93 examinations could not be linked to either a removal order, a certificate or any
form of poor relief payment within the accounting year in question.[33]

The sex ratio of those examined in the 1726–1727 sample was typically low, with 36 males per 100 females, similar to the overall examined population (Table 2.2). Only those few examinants granted settlement certificates were overwhelmingly male – just as Landau has argued those certificated were far less likely to be in need of poor relief at the time of examination.[34] There is nothing especially striking about the 30 per cent of the sample who were not given poor relief of some sort, although there were a few more males than in the sample population. It seems a reasonable conclusion, especially given the female bias, that most were examined because they were thought 'likely to become chargeable' in some way, i.e., they were sick, deserted, unemployed, pregnant, bereaved, recent arrivals or homeless. Whatever the case, it seems undeniable that some of those examined did not immediately fall on the parish.[35]

Settlement Laws, Removal and Migration

Table 2.3 suggested that only about one-third of the draft examinations in 1726–1727 were associated with either an incoming or outgoing removal order. Landau also found that the majority of examinations at her Kentish Petty Sessions did not produce either a certificate or a removal.[36] Since these examinations are the much more numerous 'draft' documents, one would expect the rate of removal to be lower. As noted in the Introduction, surviving books of complaints and removals, together with existing settlement examinations, can be used to uncover the exact relationship between the settlement laws and enforced migration in this parish. As far as can be judged these books, albeit for a relatively short period, record all incoming and outgoing removals. Moreover, they seem to contain a complete record of certificates granted out of the parish and of orders of sessions determining the results of appeals against removals. They also contain some bastardy orders and over one hundred removals under the vagrancy laws. Table 2.4 compares the number of paupers subject to removal orders issued by St Martin's against the total number of examinations between 1719 and 1734 inclusive. It also compares the number of certificates issued during the same period. Most of those examined were not subsequently removed from the parish. One in seven of those examined in this period were the subject of outgoing removal orders, most of which were certainly carried out, paupers and dependents being carried or accompanied out of the parish and delivered to their opposite numbers by parish officers.[37] As far as can be judged from the parish documentation, very few removal orders (69 for this period) were appealed. Some involved overturning removal orders out of the parish,

Table 2.3. Links between Poor Relief, Removals and Settlement Examinations, 1726–1727

Examinations	Number of Examinations	%	Sex Ratio of Examinants
Linked to an overseer's payment	220	53	27
Linked to a workhouse admission	149	36	31
Linked to a hospital payment	30	7	36
Linked to an incoming or outgoing removal order	144	35	32
Linked to the granting of a certificate	16	4	433
Not linked to either an overseer's payment, a hospital payment or a workhouse admission	126	30	52
Not linked to any poor law payment or to any incoming or outgoing removal order, or to a certificate	93	22	39
Total Sample of Examinations	415		

Source: Linkage of overseers' accounts for 1726–1727, workhouse admission registers, settlement examinations and removal orders and certificates. COWAC F462; F4002; F4073; F4074; F5019-F5021; F2217-F2218. Categories overlap.

while others related to the overturning of 1,224 incoming 'complaints'. Such figures suggest that only about 3 per cent of all removal orders resulted in an appeal at sessions, a rate comparable to that found from the mid eighteenth century in some parts of Kent.[38] If the rate was so low, it may be that this is partly due to the professionalism of London bureaucrats, who weeded out unreliable and unconvincing testimonies before issuing removal orders.

A significant difference between St Martin's and Landau's Kentish parishes appears to be the relatively small number of certificates issued by the metropolitan parish.[39] Of 287 certificates known to have been granted by the parish between 1710 and 1742, 90 were granted to women, 196 to men, and 1 to a person of indeterminate sex. Most were granted to married men with wives. Many certificates, moreover, were granted for parishes *outside* the London area. This suggests two things. Firstly, that few London parishes expected or demanded settlement certificates from newcomers and, secondly, that relatively few of those leaving the capital sought certificates. In St Martin's many of those granted certificates appear to have *already* been living outside the parish, and travelled in specially to apply, presumably after pressure from their parish of residence.

Table 2.4. Settlement Examinations, Removals and Certificates in St Martin's, 1719–1734

Year	Number of Examinations	Removal Orders	Certificates Issued	Percentage of Examinations that Led to a Removal
1719	414	56	10	*14%*
1720	396	60	24	*15%*
1721	415	55	25	*13%*
1722	541	39	35	*7%*
1723	472	49	21	*10%*
1724	507	60	28	*12%*
1725	445	67	27	*15%*
1726	385	80	19	*21%*
1727	375	88	17	*23%*
1728	493	79	18	*16%*
1729	638	80	19	*13%*
1730	445	78	16	*18%*
1731	441	66	5	*15%*
1732	391	60	7	*15%*
1733	510	57	7	*11%*
1734	442	45	3	*10%*
Total	7,310	1,019	281	*14%*

Source: Removals and certificates taken from COWAC F2217-F2222; F5013-F5027.

Drafting certificates seems to have been a part of the routine business of the parish bureaucracy and is rarely itemized in accounts, nor is there any record of fees paid by recipients. In 1776, 'filling up, Swearing to & executing two certificates for persons residing in the Country' cost an overseer 10s in total, 5s each.[40] The cost of issuing such certificates was itself a disincentive for the parish but it is also clear that parish policy was to 'grant' certificates (use of the word grant is revealing) only to those perceived to be 'low risk'. This prudent policy was articulated explicitly in 1718, when one Abram Johnson, on examination, desired 'a Certificate from our Parish to Tunbridge'. The local Justice noted 'I think there is a Necessity to grant this Certificate and no Charges is likely to ensue And I order a Certificate to be made'.[41]

There were, of course, methods other than the settlement laws to address the problem of the destitute or unwanted, an observation common to other chapters in this volume. Use of the vagrancy laws to remove those apprehended as rogues and vagabonds was one.[42] This does not seem to have occurred on a large scale compared to the numbers removed under the law of settlement. The books of complaints and removals show that between 1720 and 1742 only 85 individuals were sent to St Martin's as vagrants, and the parish sent only 14 to other places between 1729 and 1733. A different and less troublesome method of getting rid of the unwanted was simply to bribe them to go away. Difficult to quantify it is clear that such informal action was reasonably common both here and elsewhere in Europe. The twenty-seven-year-old William Ware, examined in 1723, had a claim to settlement in the parish and was seeking a certificate to the hospital, but instead a parish officer 'Gave him 25s to go into the Country he being never to Trouble the Parish any more'.[43] In the 1726–1727 overseers' accounts more than 50 paupers were paid small sums of money 'not to trouble the parish' again. In many (although not all) of these cases there was a clear expectation that paupers would physically leave. All in all some 147 individuals and their families were paid sums of money to leave the parish or not to trouble it any more, *without* a corresponding removal order. Such paupers were said to have been passed away, their passage paid, that they had gone into the country, or were to go out of the parish. Sometimes these payments could be very small, like the 6d paid to an anonymous 'poor person to go out of the parish'. Such payments were essentially bribes like the 2s 6d paid to 'A man in princess Court ill of a Fever to go out of the parish' and might extend to travel subsidies. John Green 'and Wife going to Windsor not being to trouble the parish any more' also received 2s 6d. Costs rose if a chair or coach was required, and the parish lashed out relatively large sums to send paupers out of London, such as the guinea paid to Catherine Poll and her 'four children going to feversham [Faversham, Kent] and not to trouble the parish any more' or the same sum paid to Margaret Benskin and child 'to go to Bishops' Castle in Montgomeryshire [now in Shropshire]'. The heaviest payments were made following justices' orders that forced the parish to pay for the passage of paupers to Ireland.[44]

Individuals sent out of the parish without formal removal orders included 31 adults (plus dependent wives and children) who seem to have been travelling through, or removed from, the parish 'with a pass' or 'with a permissive pass'. Such passes (presumably those described by Dorothy George as 'walking' or 'begging' passes) were used to send paupers back to their place of alleged settlement – without recourse to settlement or vagrancy procedures and costs:

It is a common practice to send paupers who have committed no act of vagrancy by passes, instead of orders, to save expense to the parish removing ...
Some get travelling passes signed by a magistrate generally of some corporate town, under which they beg or rather extort money from parish officers, who

are induced to give it them for fear of worse consequences, upon their promise to quit that place immediately. Others procure themselves to be sent by passes to places where they have no settlement, for reasons best known to themselves, and the money given for apprehending them too often facilitates this means of imposition upon the public, by rewarding some accomplice in the fraud'.[45]

Parishes subject to Gilbert's Act (1782) were forbidden to remove paupers without a legal order of removal. That Act noted:

whereas it frequently happens that poor Children, pregnant Women, or poor Persons afflicted with Sickness, or some bodily Infirmity, are enticed, taken, or conveyed by Parish Officers, or other Persons, from one Parish or Place to another, without any legal Order of Removal, in order to ease the one Parish or Place, and to burthen the other with such poor Persons.[46]

Such individuals were usually given small sums of money – sixpence or a shilling was typical – to send them on their way. Sometimes they were military-related, such as the 'poor woman with a pass from the Warr Office' or the 'Six Seamen with a permissive pass being disabled'. Many were anonymous. Payments on account of such permissive passes occur regularly in the overseers' accounts throughout the eighteenth century.[47] Those sent out of the parish with 'permissive passes', like those removed under the vagrancy laws, travelled relatively long distances to counties outside London, including Ireland and Scotland. Those removed under the settlement laws tended to travel relatively short distances, due to the expense involved.[48]

Permissive passes are worth more attention, because they were a significant method by which individuals were removed from the parish, albeit many must have been only temporary residents and travellers. Those removed from the workhouse with permissive passes were probably only a small fraction of the total number issued, and are only identified from 1785, perhaps reflecting a change in local policy.[49] Overseers' accounts can be used to make an estimate of the extent to which such passes were issued by the parish (Figure 2.3).[50] Although the sums involved are trivial in comparison to the huge expenditure on annual poor relief, the graph is striking. This preliminary analysis suggests that there were sharp peaks in the use of permissive passes in the years 1780–1784, 1810–1811 and 1815–1817. The first peak may well represent a surge in regulative activity following the shock of the Gordon Riots in London in 1780.[51] The last probably relates to the rise in unemployment and applications for poor relief following the demobilizations of 1815 already referred to. This latter was a metropolitan-wide phenomenon. The number of vagrants passed from Middlesex increased six-fold between 1811 and 1820.[52] Although the sums of money spent on these permissive passes were usually very

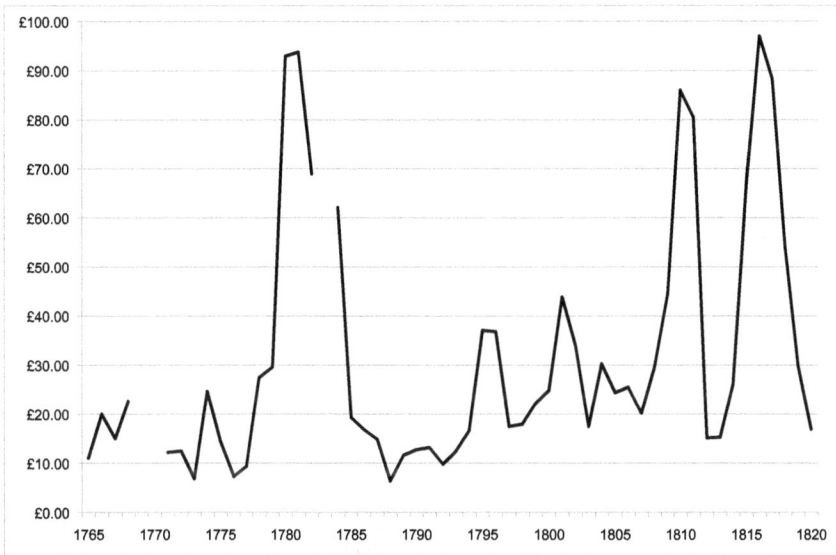

Figure 2.3. Spending on 'Permissive Passes' in St Martin in the Fields, 1765–1821

small, they could still translate into large numbers of people. If between 1765 and 1818 dealing with each poor person with a pass cost the parish on average two shillings (double the modal sum in 1726) this would imply that during peak periods at least 800 to 900 people were being removed from the parish *each year* using this method. The actual numbers of individuals passed this way must have greatly exceeded the number removed formally under the settlement laws, and resonates with other chapters in this volume which draw attention to the suite of legal and extra-legal measures which could be combined to curtail belonging and restrict the entitlements associated with such a status.

The Pauper Experience of Settlement Laws:
Two Case Studies

Two reconstructed life histories help to illustrate and amplify this parish-based study. The first concerns a plain maker called William Franklin, who visited St Martin's in 1727 and was examined by the parish before a local justice:

William Franklin aged about 29 years living in Oxford saith he was married to Catherine his Wife at St. Abbs in the City of Oxford about five Weeks agoe.

Saith he was bound an apprentice by Indenture, Eight years ever since May last, for seven years, to one Richard Mealing a Plain maker who then lived in Great Queen Street by Lincolns Inn Fields where he served him about two years and then his Master removed to Cross Lane in Long Acre and he this Deponent with him where he served him the Remainder of his time. Saith he never lived a year in Service since, never kept house, hath no Children.

Although his examination did not mention it, William was seeking a settlement certificate from the parish authorities. The fact that he asked for a certificate five weeks after his marriage suggests that the parish of St Abbs, Oxford, was behind his request. The St Martin's authorities duly granted a certificate to the Oxford parish on the same day of his examination. Nothing was heard from William again, but *thirty years later,* in 1758, his wife Catherine was admitted to the St Martin's workhouse. The day after her admittance she, too, was examined by the parish:

Catherine Franklin aged 67 years and upwards in the Workhouse of and in the parish of St Martin in the Fields Upon her Oath saith she is Widow of William Franklin (who died about Twelve Years ago) to whom she was Married at St Abb's Church in the City of Oxford about 31 years ago. That he was a Plain maker by Trade and so this Examinant hath been informed was bound an Apprentice by an Indenture to Richard Mealing a Plainmaker in Great Queen Street by Lincoln Inn Fields and there served him about two years and then his Master removed to Cross Lane in the Parish of St Martin in the Fields aforesaid and this Examinant with him and there served the Remainder of his time. That she this Examinant saith That she this Examinant now (when at Oxford) lives in and Rents an House and hath lived in and Rented an House in the Parish of St Abb's in the City of Oxford for several Years at the Yearly Rent of Three Pounds and paid the Poors Rate. Taken in the Workhouse the 25th October 1758.

After a week in the workhouse Catherine 'Left the House November the 1st. following & return'd to Oxford'. She seems to have remained in Oxford for a further eighteen years until an entry in the St Martin's overseers' accounts reported in 1776, that £3 11s was 'paid the Guardians of the Poor of the Parish of St Abbs in the City of Oxford for Maintenance of Catherine Franklin a Certificated person (now dead)'. This is a classic example of how a certificate was supposed to work: an elderly pauper was cared for in her final illness by the parish in which she had lived for some fifty years, which then received reimbursement from her parish of legal settlement. The rarity of entries reimbursing host parishes caring for certificated poor in the overseers' accounts again, however, suggests that relatively few certificates can have been issued by the parish.[53]

Another compelling story is the case of Robert Metcalf.[54] We initially meet him at his first settlement examination, when he entered the parish workhouse for the first time at the age of twenty-two. Robert 'Medcalf' and Mary his wife had been passed from the parish of St Giles in the Fields back to St Martin's, his parish of legal settlement, on a removal order dated 16 November 1738.[55] His then wife Mary, who the workhouse registers show was heavily pregnant, was admitted with him on the same day:

> Robert Metcalfe aged 22 years in the workhouse saith that he was bound an apprentice by indenture for 7 years to one Edward Ward a Last Maker in Cross Lane in the parish of St. Martin in the Fields whom he there served the whole which expired about 2 years ago, since which time he never kept any house rented £10 by the year, paid any parish taxes or was a yearly hired servant, that he was married to Mary his wife at the Barbers Pole in the Fleet 11 months ago.[56]

Admitted to the parish workhouse on 17 November 1738, Robert and Mary (then aged just under twenty-one) were discharged on the 2 January following. During this short incarceration, a daughter Elizabeth was born and baptized, but, as was all too common for workhouse progeny, she lived less than a month, dying on 15 December 1738.[57] The settlement examination, taken shortly after his entry into the workhouse, was silent about the fact that Robert's pregnant wife Mary was also present in the workhouse with him (the couple were gender-segregated on entry, as was routine). There is no unambiguous record of Robert's marriage to Mary in the voluminous registers in the Fleet.[58]

Robert was, however, examined three times under the settlement law. His second examination took place in July 1748:

> Robert Metcalf aged 37 years lodging at Mr Potts a Chandler's shop the lower end of St Martin's Lane in the Parish of St Martin in the Fields upon his oath saith that he is a Last Maker by trade and was bound apprentice by indenture to Mr Edward Ward a Last Maker in Cross Lane in Long Acre in the Parish of St Martin in the Fields for seven years and there served six years and then parted by consent which is about 16 years ago and never kept house rented a tenement of 10 pounds by the year paid any parish taxes or was a yearly hired servant in any one place for 12 months together since, that he was married to his present wife Mary at the Fleet about 14 years ago, that he has one [child] living by his said wife to wit Mary aged seven years and upwards now with this Examinant. Sworn this first Day of July 1748 before James Fraser.[59]

This second examination is interesting on a number of levels. Robert's age was now given as thirty-seven, when it should have been about thirty-three. He had followed the trade of last making, but was clearly still eking out a living in lodgings. His settlement was based on his apprenticeship with his master Ward. However, this second examination reveals that Robert had not in fact served out his time since he and his master had 'parted by consent' before the term of his apprenticeship had been completed, supposedly sixteen years previously. There is no evidence that Robert himself entered the parish workhouse at this time. The examination reveals that a seven-year old daughter, Mary, was with Metcalf and that his wife Mary was still alive.

At this point we should turn our attention to Metcalf's wife Mary. If Robert does not appear to have entered the workhouse in 1748, there is quite a bit of evidence that his wife became a regular burden on the parish. In March 1749 a Mary 'Midcalf', aged thirty-one, spent a few days in the workhouse, entering with two young children, an infant, Robert, and Mary (aged eight). Mary left with Robert after a three-day stay. She was 'Dischargd 21st following with her young Child had 2s 6d given her'. Mary the daughter was 'took out by her Mother' after a six month stay on the 29 September 1749. Mary might have been readmitted again in April 1750 and it is likely that the daughter Mary, and a young brother John, were readmitted into the workhouse in September of the same year. Mary was then nine and John was a year and a quarter. Both were taken out by their mother after four or five months in the institution.[60] The two Metcalf children appear, therefore, to have been dumped at the workhouse.

This was not the elder Mary Metcalf's last contact with the parish. In fact the workhouse admission and discharge registers suggest that Robert's wife made seven or eight separate trips into the workhouse between her first admission with Robert and what may have been her last in 1760. Thus, in 1757 Mary was admitted twice into the parish workhouse, both times with some of her children. In June of that year, Mary (now forty) was admitted with two children: John (aged eight) and a new daughter Frances (aged three). All were discharged after a two-week stay. Within a month they were back: all three were admitted again on 15 July 1757. This time their fortunes were very different. Mary, the mother, left both her children in the workhouse and was discharged after only a week. John Metcalf stayed for three years in the workhouse, before being 'Bound Apprentice to William Cannell, of the Broad Place New-InnYard in the Parish of St. Leonard Shoreditch Weaver' in October 1760. Frances, after five months, died in the workhouse on 28 December 1757.[61] Mary the mother returned three times to the workhouse thereafter, her last visit being in 1760, after which she was discharged and does not appear to have been admitted again, although it is actually possible that she was resident until 1763. All this is less conjectural than it might have been, because Mary herself was examined under the settlement laws in 1757:

> Mary Metcalf aged about 40 years Destitute of Lodging upon her Oath saith she is the Wife of Robert Metcalf (gone from her) to whom she was Married

at the Fleet 20 years ago. That her said Husband is a Last maker by trade and was bound an Apprentice by an Indenture for seven years to Mr Edward Ward Last maker in Cross Lane in the Parish of Saint Martin in the Fields and there served about six years and then parted by consent which is about Twenty Five Years ago. That he never kept house rented a Tenement of Ten pounds by the year paid any Parish Taxes nor hath been a yearly hired servant since to this Examinants Knowledge. That she has two Children living by her said Husband to wit John aged 8 years and Frances aged 3 years both now with this Examinant. The Mark of Mary Metcalf
Sworn the 6th day of May 1757 Before Benjamin Cox
[Annotated] L A Wd [Long Acre Ward][62]

Mary thus had a settlement in the Long Acre Ward of the parish. The examination confirms the identity of Frances and John and reveals that her husband Robert had 'gone from her' at some unspecified time, but clearly within the previous three years. Mary can be found inhabiting the workhouse, and receiving small handouts of clothing and shoes from the parish, up until at least 1763.[63] So, by 1760, Robert Metcalfe's career as a last maker and erstwhile workhouse inmate had spawned three settlement examinations and a number of admissions to the workhouse by himself and members of his family. The parish had apprenticed one of his children, buried two of them, and taken care of the wife and children he had clearly deserted. His wife and children may also have received ad hoc out relief, but such payments are not visible in the accounts after the middle of the century.

However, this was far from the end of Robert's contact with the parish. In 1780 he reappears, in the overseers' accounts, now an old man, when the parish paid the staggering sum of £47 5s 10½d for 'expences on an appeal concerning the settlement of Robert Metcalfe, wife and four Children against the Parish of St Martin in the Town of Birmingham'.[64] Said to be seventy-four but apparently no less active then before, he had been readmitted to the parish workhouse on 16 February 1781 together with four members of what was a *completely new family:* his new wife Catherine (forty-seven) and three children Thomas (fourteen), George (four) and Elizabeth (six months). He was also examined for the third and last time:

Robert Metcalfe aged 74 years removed by an order of removal from the Parish of Birmingham in the County of Warwick to the Parish of St Martin in the Fields upon his oath saith that he was bound an apprentice by an indenture for 8 years to Edward Ward a Last maker in Cross Lane in the said Parish of St Martin in the Fields, and there served his said master for the space of five years and one month, and then his said Master assigned him over to John Worder a Last maker in the city of Dublin in the Kingdom of Ireland and with the said Mr

Worder served the remainder of the said term out in the city of Dublin which expired about 53 years ago, that he never kept house rented a tenement of 10 pounds by the year paid any parish taxes nor been a yearly hired servant in any one place for 12 months together since, that he was married to his present wife Catherine in the Parish Church of St Martin in Birmingham about 22 years ago by whom he hath four children to wit Catherine aged about 17 years, Thomas aged about 10 years, John aged four years and upwards, and Elizabeth aged about six months all now removed with this Examinant, that the said Catherine his daughter and Thomas his son were never apprentices nor a yearly hired servant in any one place for 12 months together, nor was his said daughter ever married. Sworn the 17th Day of February 1781 before William Hyde.[65]

Clearly this last examination is more revealing than the previous two (neither of which seem to have been remembered or consulted in this particular case). The marriage of Robert to a Catherine Adey can in fact be independently documented. It took place on 25 May 1756 at St Martin's, Birmingham.[66] It was therefore, bigamous, since his first wife Mary we know was then still alive and was in the workhouse shortly after this second marriage. Informal separations and remarriages of this sort were a relatively common means of popular divorce in the eighteenth century amongst the poor, although their incidence is impossible to measure.[67] The examination had taken place in the workhouse (although this was not recorded), to which Robert and Catherine, and his youngest children had been admitted the day before. After what was probably a short stay, all five members of the family were 'Discharged and sent by Appeal of Quarter Sessions to Birmingham' again, sometime in 1781. If most of his second family disappeared, the same cannot be said for Robert, who returned *again* the following March when he was readmitted to the workhouse at the age of seventy-five, finally dying of 'old age' there two years later in June 1784.[68]

Conclusion

It is now possible to answer some of the questions posed at the beginning of this chapter. Despite the huge numbers of people milling about within its boundaries, the 'city-sized' parish of St Martin's was able to impose a formidable level of regulation under the settlement laws. It is likely that the ability to run and finance a professional bureaucracy was particularly important here, and in this sense the parish stands in contradistinction to others in England and Wales. The examination books formed a dynamic archive; some pauper records were consulted and updated sometimes years after they were taken. Most paupers had their 'entitlement' or otherwise memorialized by parish bureaucrats. In turn, levels of examination in the parish fluctuated over time. Activity was most intensive following the Napoleonic Wars, and other chapters in this volume have noted an equally irregular pattern of activity. Those who study the settlement laws, too, clearly need to contextualize them within the larger welfare system. In St Martin's settlement quickly became integrally bound up with admission to the workhouse. For much of the period, indeed, short-term relief in the workhouse was often given before a legal settlement was established although there are signs that this practice declined rapidly from the 1770s for reasons which need to be explored. As elsewhere, the issue of who belonged and what to do with those who did not must be understood holistically.

The law of settlement could clearly be an intrusive presence in the lives of the poor, although (outside years such as 1817) its proportional impact in any one year would have been relatively small. For those remaining within the parish for a reasonable period of time, however, the chances of being subject to examination, and placed on permanent record, increased significantly. Of course it goes without saying that the number of *people* affected by the law was always much greater than the number examined, due to the number of dependents (sometimes but not always) mentioned in the examination. What is also particularly striking is that many individuals were being removed by the parish *without* formal resort to the law of settlement at all. We clearly need to know more about the informal or semi-legal means by which parishes erected and maintained barriers to settlement and belonging, something to which Elizabeth Hurren's chapter also draws attention for the late-Victorian period.

Lastly, the two case studies provide further perspectives on how pauper lives interacted with settlement practice. The case of the Franklins shows how a family's parish of legal settlement might play only a peripheral part in its life-history. Robert Metcalf's story reveals messy realities and individual strategies that are usually hidden from view. His time in Ireland (which had no settlement law) only emerged in his last examination. He was exceptionally mobile: moving to Ireland to finish his training and raising a second family in (presumably) Birmingham. However, the settlement law clearly affected his residence. His 1781 examination prompted forcible removal to Birmingham and that same law was used to remove him from Birmingham when aged. The law worked, after a fashion, since both parishes used it to remove a potentially expensive burden, but for neither parish did it produce a lasting result. Birmingham saw Metcalfe's entire family return; St Martin's still ended up maintaining Metcalf in their workhouse in his last years. Metcalf's movements do not seem to have been *inhibited* by the law of settlement.[69] His removal from

Birmingham where he may have lived for over twenty years (since his second marriage) actually recalls Keith Snell's observation that the aged poor might be returned by parishes to their place of settlement when they fell into poverty.[70] In the end, Metcalf's case serves to underline the gap that often existed between pauper strategies and the existing legal frameworks that shaped and constrained them. His convoluted family and settlement history remind us that perspectives on settlement centred on administrative units – be they parish, town, county or even nation – do not necessarily uncover or represent the reality of pauper lives.

Notes

I would like to thank those who have worked on the Pauper Biographies Project, from which this chapter is drawn. Leonard Schwarz has been co-director since its inception. John Black, Rhiannon Thompson and Peter Jones collected much of the raw material for this project, as did latterly, Tim Wales. The research was funded by the ESRC Research Grant, RES-000-23-0250, the support of which is gratefully acknowledged.

   1. The best and most recent overview of poverty in later-eighteenth- and nineteenth-century London is D. R. Green. 2010. *Pauper Capital. London and the Poor Law, 1790–1870*, Farnham. For studies using London settlement material, some of it from St Martin's, see A. Suzuki. 1988. 'The Household and the Care of Lunatics in Eighteenth-Century London', in P. Horden and R. M. Smith (eds), *The Locus of Care: Families, Communities, Institutions, and the Provision of Welfare since Antiquity*, London, 153–175; D. A. Kent. 1989. 'Ubiquitous but invisible: female domestic servants in mid-eighteenth-century London', *History Workshop* 28, 111–128; N. Rogers. 1989–90. 'Carnal Knowledge: Illegitimacy in Eighteenth-Century Westminster', *Journal of Social History* 23, 355–375; D. A. Kent. 1990. '"Gone for a Soldier": Family Breakdown and the Demography of Desertion in a London Parish, 1750–91', *Local Population Studies* 45, 27–42; N. Rogers. 1991. 'Policing the Poor in Eighteenth-Century London: The Vagrancy Laws and Their Administration' *Histoire Sociale / Social History* 24, 127–147; J. Boulton. 2000. '"It is extreme necessity that makes me do this": Some Survival Strategies of Pauper Households in London's West End during the Early Eighteenth Century', *International Review of Social History*, Supplement 8, 47–70; A. Levene. 2010. 'Poor Families, Removals and 'Nurture' in Late Old Poor Law London', *Continuity and Change* 25(2), 1–30.
   2. N. Landau. 1991. 'The Eighteenth-Century Context of the Laws of Settlement', *Continuity and Change* 6(3), n. 1, 431–432. For the debate, see also N. Landau. 1988. 'The Laws of Settlement and the Surveillance of Immigration in Eighteenth-Century Kent', *Continuity and Change* 3, 391–420; N. Landau. 1990. 'The Regulation of Immigration, Economic Structures and Definitions of the Poor in Eighteenth-Century England', *Historical Journal* 33, 541–572; K. D. M. Snell. 1991. 'Pauper Settlement and the Right to Poor Relief in England and Wales', *Continuity and Change* 6, 375–415; K. D. M. Snell. 1992. 'Settlement, Poor Law and the Rural Historian: New Approaches and Opportunities' *Rural History* 3(2), 145–172; N. Landau. 1995. 'Who Was Subjected to the Laws of Settlement? Procedure Under the Settlement Laws in Eighteenth-Century England', *The Agricultural History Review* 43(2), 139–159. For some London settlement evidence, see also Lynn Hollen Lees. 1998. *The Solidarities of Strangers. The English Poor Laws and the People, 1700–1948*, Cambridge, 1–111.

3. For workhouses in eighteenth-century London, see D. R. Green. 2009. 'Icons of the New System: Workhouse Construction and Relief Practices in London under the Old and New Poor Law', *London Journal* 34(3), 264–284; Green, *Pauper Capital*, 57–69. For their origins and deterrent effect, see T. Hitchcock. 1992. 'Paupers and Preachers: The SPCK and the Parochial Workhouse Movement', in L. Davison, T. Hitchcock, T. Keirn and R.B. Shoemaker, *Stilling the Grumbling Hive. The Response to Social and Economic Problems in England, 1689–1750*, Stroud, 145–166. For workhouses in provincial England, see J. Kent and S. King. 2003. 'Changing Patterns of Poor Relief in some English Rural Parishes circa 1650–1750', *Rural History* 14(2), 119–156; S. Hindle. 2004. *On the Parish? The Micro-Politics of Poor Relief in Rural England, c. 1550–1750*, Oxford, 186–191. The Webbs are still worth reading on this: S. Webb and B. Webb. 1927. *English Local Government: English Poor Law History: Part 1. The Old Poor Law*, London, 243–245.

4. S. King. 2000. *Poverty and Welfare in England 1700–1850. A Regional Perspective*, Manchester, 38–39.

5. Readers should note that the parish of St George Hanover Square was carved out of St Martin's in 1725. Before 1725 therefore the parish was both bigger and had significantly more wealthy inhabitants.

6. C. E. Harvey, E. M. Green and P. J. Corfield. 1999. 'Continuity, Change, and Specialization within Metropolitan London: The Economy of Westminster, 1750–1820', *Economic History Review* 52, 469–493; C. Spence. 2000. *London in the 1690s. A Social Atlas*, London, 63–171.

7. The 1821 census has been analysed by L. Schwarz. 2001. 'Hanoverian London: The Making of a Service Town', in P. Clark and R. Gillespie (eds), *Two Capitals: London and Dublin, 1500–1840*, London, 93–110.

8. J. Boulton and L. Schwarz. 2011. 'Domestic Service and the Law of Settlement in the West End, 1725–1824', paper presented to LPSS Conference on Domestic Service in England, 1600–2000, 16 April 2011, available at http://research.ncl.ac.uk/pauperlives/esrcpresentations.htm.

9. 'Report of a Committee of the Statistical Society of London, on the State of the Working Classes in the Parishes of St. Margaret and St. John Westminster', *Journal of the Statistical Society of London* 3(1), 1840, 24; M. D. George. 1976. *London Life in the Eighteenth Century*, Harmondsworth, 118.

10. This bald summary of parochial finances is drawn from the overseers accounts kept at the City of Westminster Archive Centre (COWAC): F459A, F462, F465, F468, F472, F476, F478, F482, F485, F488, F492, F495, F498, F501, F504, F515, F519/348, F529, F547, F549, F551, F553, F559, F561, F563, F565, F567, F569, F571, F573, F575, F577, F579, F581, F585, F587, F589, F591, F593, F595, F597, F599, F601, F603, F605, F607, F609, F611, F613, F615, F617, F619, F621, F623, F625, F627, F629, F631, F633, F635.

11. Compare the numbers of houses and total expenditure on the poor in the mid 1720s listed for each parish in W. Maitland. 1739. *The History of London, from its Foundation by the Romans, to the Present Time*, vol. II, 353–520; vol. VII, 715–743; vol. VIII, 744–783; vol. IX, 784–800. Only St James Westminster raised more money than St Martin's in the mid 1720s. Maitland's count of houses showed that St Martin's was the fourth biggest parish in London at this time, exceeded only by St Dunstan Stepney and St James and St Margaret, Westminster.

12. COWAC F549; F605.

13. On these, see J. M. Beattie. 2001. *Policing and Punishment in London. 1660–1750*, Oxford; P. Griffiths. 2008. *Lost Londons. Change, Crime and Control in the Capital City, 1550–1660*, Cambridge, 361–399.

14. The Long Acre overseer in 1726 recorded payments 'To the Beadle showing me and my partner around the ward when we first collected the same', F462/276–7.

15. The workhouse quickly became the centre of poor law administration in Chelsea: Tim Hitchcock and John Black (eds). 1999. *Chelsea Settlement and Bastardy Examinations, 1733–1766*, London, vii–xii.

16. Toone was appointed at the end of 1817 at a huge salary of £300 pa plus £50 for a clerk and allowances for prosecutions, see COWAC F2077. He was a former magistrate's clerk and the author of *The magistrate's manual: or, a summary of the duties and powers of a Justice of the Peace*, London, 1813; and *A practical guide to the duty and authority of overseers of the poor*, London, 1815.

17. The clerk's salary was raised following a petition by Lemage to £150 per year in 1792 'exclusive of any privileges he now enjoys', COWAC F2075/10. The clerk's salary was raised to £180 in 1803, and £200 by 1805, ibid., F2075/353, F2076/31. Lemage's son was 'appointed assistant clerk to this Board under the superintendence of his father at the salary of £31 10s pa' in 1805, F2076/26. Lemage senior retired on health grounds in 1808, after serving the parish for twenty six years, and was succeeded by his son, F2076/104–5.

18. COWAC F2075/74.

19. COWAC F2075/102.

20. Taylor's article sets out a research agenda which has still not been addressed. For London, he singled out the parishes of St Martin in the Fields and St Botolph Aldgate to be of 'special note' for their extensive collections of surviving examinations. J. S. Taylor. 1976. 'The Impact of Pauper Settlement 1691–1834', *Past and Present* 73, 72. See note 2 for previous work on these books.

21. COWAC F5020/252.

22. F5018/144–45. There over 180 occurrences of this phrase between 1718 and the end of 1724. In that same period 28 per cent (802/2866) of draft examinations were sworn by a named local Justice.

23. I am currently working on a more detailed examination of the workings of the law of settlement in the parish. Some Petty Sessions are listed separately in the examination books before 1725, but not thereafter. They dealt with settlement and especially poor law business, often confirming or ordering pension payments to some of those examined. A valuable account of the creation of a far smaller and fuller set of examinations created at monthly petty sessions, which has some parallels but some differences to that found in St Martin's, is in Hitchcock and Black, *Chelsea Settlement and Bastardy Examinations,* vii–xvii.

24. COWAC F561, F587.

25. COWAC F2217, F2218, F2219, F2220, F2221, F2222, F4001. There are also other bundles of removal orders, for single years and other settlement material, for later periods.

26. Unfortunately records detailing individual poor relief payments made to the 'casual poor' do not exist after 1750, and regular payments to the 'settled' or pensioner poor disappear from overseers accounts in 1782.

27. Since the workshop in 2010 the sample has been expanded to include date, gender, age and workhouse residence data for the entire collection, over twenty-five thousand examinations. Thanks are due to Tim Wales who gathered the information.

28. For this in Chelsea, see Hitchcock and Black, *Chelsea Settlement and Bastardy Examinations,* xii.

29. Green, *Pauper Capital,* 28–35. There was a surge in workhouse admissions between 1817 and 1820. See COWAC F6015/pt2, F6104, F6105/pt1.

30. For an authoritative survey of settlement and removal in London in the early nineteenth century, see, Green, *Pauper Capital,* 213–224. For two insightful treatments of the immediate post-war surge in St Martin's, see L. MacKay. 1995. 'A Culture of Poverty? The St Martin in the Fields Workhouse, 1817', *Journal of Interdisciplinary History* 26, 212–214; L. MacKay. 2001. 'Moral Paupers: The Poor Men of St. Martin's, 1815–1819', *Histoire sociale / Social History* 67, 115–131.

31. As the Webbs concluded, 'at all times, it was the unattached woman, whether single or widowed, who suffered most from the Law of Settlement': Webb and Webb, *English Local Government (...) Part 1*, 342, n. 2.
32. The accounting year ran from mid April to mid April.
33. Obviously those examined at the end of the accounting year might appear in the next year's overseers' accounts. To check for this effect the linkage exercise was restricted to the 204 examinations taking place on or before 31 October 1726. Of these, 106 (52 per cent) were linked to a poor relief payment, 71 (35 per cent) to a workhouse admission and 13 (6 per cent) to a hospital payment. All told 33 per cent could not be linked to any indoor or outdoor payment, mirroring the results for the whole sample in Table 2.3.
34. Landau, 'The Eighteenth-Century Context', 424, 436, n. 36.
35. Hitchcock and Black, *Chelsea Settlement and Bastardy Examinations*, xii–xiii, commenting on the seasonality of examination, argue in similar vein that 'the balance between these two factors, unemployment and surveillance, is almost impossible to determine with any certainty'.
36. Landau, 'The Laws', 402.
37. Almost all removals had a matching examination, but since a few did not the percentages must be regarded as maximum figures.
38. Landau, 'The Laws', 395. Further investigation of this issue could be done by matching removal orders to the justices' papers available at the *London Lives* website, http://www .londonlives.org/.
39. Landau, 'The Regulation', 545. This difference might have been typical of large urban settlements if the experience of Birmingham at this time is any guide. St Martin's was actually more generous than Birmingham. A. Parton. 1987. 'Poor Law Settlement Certificates and Migration to and from Birmingham 1726–57', *Local Population Studies* 38, found only 225 certificates issued by that town (population in 1731 of 23,000) between 1720 and 1757, six per year.
40. COWAC F569.
41. There is no evidence, unusually, that this particular certificate was ever granted, COWAC F5013/45.
42. The best article on London vagrancy in this period, by far, is still Rogers, 'Policing'. Passing vagrants was finally abolished in 1824 in favour of one month hard labour in a House of Correction. Ibid., 146. See also T. Hitchcock. 2004. *Down and Out in Eighteenth-Century London*, London.
43. COWAC F5016/117.
44. COWAC F462/324, 219, 175, 200, 166.
45. Thomas Gilbert, 1775, quoted in George, *London Life*, n. 124, 359.
46. XLI. For Remedy whereof, be it further enacted, That when any Guardian, or other Person or Persons, shall so entice, take, convey, or remove, or cause or procure to be so enticed, taken, conveyed, or removed, any such poor Person or Persons from one Parish or Place to another, which shall adopt the Provisions of this Act, without an Order of Removal from two Justices of the Peace for that Purpose, every Person or Persons so offending shall, for every such Offence, forfeit a Sum not exceeding twenty Pounds, nor less than five Pounds. *An Act for the better Relief and Employment of the Poor.*
47. After the middle of the century these passes are not itemized but lumped together as a single item of expenditure by the overseers of each ward. Overseers were buying quires of vagrant (and once 'permissive') passes at 1s 6d a time in 1784/5, F585, F587. The passes were sometimes described as payments to 'Sundry Poor Persons with Passes to different Counties', again suggesting that they were employed to send paupers out of London. Rogers, 'Policing', 138, argues that the main difference between those subject to settlement examination, and those caught by vagrancy laws was 'that the majority of vagrants were drawn from outside the metropolitan area'.

48. This is apparent from an analysis (not presented here for reasons of space) of those removed from the workhouse under settlement law, those passed from other parishes, the 249 workhouse inmates discharged by 'permissive passes' and 92 sent as vagrants to other parts of the country. An Act of 1792 prohibited the promiscuous granting of permissive passes, but it proved inoperable, George, *London Life*, 359. For a good account of free passes, see Webb and Webb, *English Local Government (...) Part 1*, 387–391. The restricted distances travelled by those removed under the settlement laws was reported by contemporaries: Green, *Pauper Capital*, 218.
49. The vestry attempted to limit spending on casual relief and the payment of permissive passes in 1785, COWAC F2008, 28th March 1785. Those not seeking to 'inhabit' in a parish, that is vagrants and travellers, were technically not subject to removal under the Law of Settlement: Webb and Webb, *English Local Government (...) Part 1*, 334–335.
50. Note that this method relies on the separation of the casual and 'passed' poor in the accounts. Payments for permissive passes were included in 'casual poor books' (no longer extant) but were usually set down separately in the overseers' accounts. In 1773, Suffolk Ward made no such distinction, so the payment for that ward's passes is hidden. Charing Cross ward made no such payment in 1777. Some payments under this head were quite small, and it is just possible that none were made in these wards in such years.
51. Rogers, 'Policing', 144.
52. Ibid., 138, 146. The passing of vagrants was farmed out to contractors in the eighteenth century. For the statistics generated see, ibid., 138 and n. 36.
53. COWAC F569; F5049/545; F5021/4; F2221/143; F4075.
54. Medcalf or Metcalf(e).
55. F2222/263.
56. COWAC F5030/252.
57. COWAC F4073.
58. A database of all those marrying in the Fleet from 'St Martin's' does include the marriage of one Robert Medcaff, 'Lashmaker', a bachelor, who married the spinster Anne Tate, on 11/08/1737, TNA RG 7/159 but there is no sign of a Mary.
59. COWAC F5039/98.
60. COWAC F4007/169, 173, 174.
61. COWAC F4075, F2469.
62. COWAC F5048/397.
63. The Churchwardens and Overseers' minutes detail more time Mary spent in the workhouse, and her gifts of clothing and shoes, COWAC F2225/99, 157, 251, 263, 264; F2070/33, 57, 99.
64. COWAC F577/47r.
65. COWAC F5067/72.
66. Information from IGI.
67. S. Colwell. 1980. 'The Incidence of Bigamy in Eighteenth- and Nineteenth-Century England', *Family History* 11, 91–102; D. M. Turner. 2005. 'Popular Marriage and the Law: Tales of Bigamy at the Eighteenth-Century Old Bailey', *London Journal* 30(1), 6–21.
68. COWAC F4078/431, F4079/231, 419/238.
69. P. Clark. 1979. 'Migration in England during the Late Seventeenth and Early Eighteenth Centuries', *Past and Present* 83, 80, 83.
70. K. D. M. Snell. 1984. 'Parish Registration and the Study of Labour Mobility', *Local Population Studies* 33, 35–37.

CHAPTER THREE

POOR RELIEF, SETTLEMENT AND BELONGING IN ENGLAND, 1780s TO 1840s

Steven King

Introduction

On 4 June 1818, the overseer of the poor for Thrapston in the English county of Northamptonshire received a letter from the pauper Jacob Curchin. He had written because although he was resident in the parish of Wisbech (Cambridgeshire, some 100 km away) his legal settlement was in Thrapston.[1] The letter ended with the observation:

> For Sur we Must have Relief and I appeals to the Gentlemen to consider my Case Trade is slow here and I cannot get Half of what we need and if the Gentlm will not Pay then I must send her [his wife] and the childer *Home to you where I have a Place* and you Know Sir that will not be so Cheap. Please to send Immediately.[2]

This letter is a classic of its type.[3] Curchin was keenly aware of his 'place' of settlement where he had a right to apply for poor relief (though not a right to receive it). He pointed to factors beyond his control (slow trade – he was a Cooper – and sickness) and tried to use the 'out-parish relief system' to get Thrapston to pay an allowance while he remained in Wisbech.[4] In turn, the overseer of Thrapston was anything but convinced. He wrote to his counterpart in Wisbech (Mr Walters) asking for more information on Curchin and his condition and warned, 'I urge you

to beware of this man. He is crafty and not to be trusted and we are convinced that he does not manage well'.[5]

On 5 June the overseer of Thrapston received a second letter, this time
from William Thorne. He too was resident in a hamlet just outside Wisbech
but had a legal settlement in Thrapston. Thorne's letter outlined a tale of
sickness (himself, wife and a daughter), pointed out that one daughter still
in work had been supporting them but it was 'now outside her power',
and made a plea for the rent and some 'trifling expenses'. He asked:

> Please Gentlemen to consider my case for trade is short [like Curchin, he was
> a Cooper] and we have been much in need and would not have come to you
> if we could but make do without *help from Home*. If you do not support my
> request, then *we must come home directly* for I cannot watch my wife and chil-
> dren starve.[6]

These are in and of themselves interesting cases of paupers actively
engaging with the relief process. Both appear confident and well-rooted
in their host communities and neither seems to particularly fear removal
from Wisbech. Yet at this point the fates of the two men diverge. The
overseer of Thrapston wrote saying that he would not pay relief for either
the shady and disreputable Curchin or the morally upstanding Thorne.
The response of Mr Walters when faced by two men with the same trade,
roughly the same family circumstances and the same needs, was to give
some relief to Curchin but remove Thorne to Thrapston.

Moving from the particular to the general this chapter will explore the
differential application of the settlement laws highlighted by these individual narratives, drawing on the most substantial collection of pauper
letters and overseer correspondence ever assembled. Numbering some
5,500 individual items and covering most counties in England and either
side of the Welsh borders[7], the underlying data set allows us to ask five
fundamental questions about the operation and impact of the settlement
laws: How common was recourse to the laws of settlement and removal?
Why did parishes use the law against some paupers and not others? How
did parish officials understand both the law of the law of settlement and
its intersection with the wider concept of belonging to a community?
How did paupers understand the law of settlement and elaborate that understanding in their engagement with officials and third parties? And how
did the poor, officials and the epistolary advocates of the poor construct
a multi-layered sense of belonging to a place? One of the core arguments
of the chapter will be that between the 1780s and 1840s, the poor and
their advocates defined, in their engagement with officials, an accepted
ground of contestability over belonging which bore little relationship to
settlement law.

How Common Was Recourse
to the Laws of Settlement and Removal?

The intersection between an obligation on English and Welsh parishes to consider relief for the deserving poor, but only to do so for those who had a legal settlement, has been well explored in the secondary literature.[8] We know that settlement and removal disputes at parish level were sometimes numerous and that parish officials occasionally contested their liability under the law well beyond the limits of economic rationality. In this sense, all poor law historians have a suite of fabulous settlement and removal stories in which paupers were unceremoniously moved about the country in disputes which cost many times the amount of relief that would have had to have been given to the pauper over many decades. Certainly it is clear that in some places the prospect of removal loomed alarmingly frequently for paupers, with James Taylor and Keith Snell drawing attention to compelling caches of settlement examinations and removal orders.[9] Unsurprisingly, parish officials writing between each other often sought to emphasise the economy of prompt action to pay for relief in a host parish rather than incurring the cost of a settlement examination, removal order and the removal process. This said, for most parishes and towns it is often striking how little settlement and removal documentation exists for the later eighteenth century and, where it does, its periodicity. Such a situation might reflect the fact that sources have not been preserved, but a consideration of the overseers' accounts (in which the costs of conducting settlement examinations and attending meetings of magistrates etc., were recorded) also suggests that for many places there genuinely was little formal settlement and removal activity.

This observation (itself not new; Oxley remarked on the same issue in the 1970s[10]) might be explained by some of the generalizations about settlement which dominate the welfare historiography: The system of out-parish relief, developing most rapidly from the 1780s, may have obviated the need for formal settlement and removal activity. In other places, and as David Green has recently shown for London, the scale of population growth may simply have made it impossible to consistently monitor the poor and enforce settlement legislation even if the will was there.[11] Or limited settlement and removal activity may have represented the needs of the labour market trumping the idea of economy for ratepayers. Certainly there is evidence for this. The Lancashire industrialist David Whitehead established his spinning mills in one of the most inhospitable and bleak areas of England (Rawtenstall, Lancashire) and was obliged to run both his own shop and a housing association for his workers. When power or demand fell short, losing this workforce would have been fatal, as Whitehead acknowledged frequently in his autobiography. He thus encouraged workers to save for the bad times via a savings bank, subscriptions to clubs etc., but ultimately bad times meant the appearance of numerous spinners and machine minders of both sexes on the relief lists and irrespective of their settlement credentials. In the same fashion, when rioters came to Rawtenstall in 1826 the Whitehead workers defended the factory and machines from burning but had to agree to suspend work, the result of which was a surge of relief payments to underemployed Whitehead workers.[12]

These are convenient explanations, but as the examples of Thorne and Curchin hint they are by no means adequate. Rather, the relative dearth of settlement and removal documentation for the late eighteenth and early nineteenth centuries can be explained by the fact that the law was differentially applied to some migrants and not others. This contention comes into sharp focus if we shift our attention to the vexed question of the number of people *liable* to settlement examination and removal at any point in time. At the broadest level, most of those undertaking family reconstitutions have been able to create full life histories for only small minorities of residents in any place. While the nature of truncation bias varies according to place and time, much of it is lower level truncation (i.e., an inability to trace baptisms for individuals who subsequently appear in other records or to find baptisms for marriage partners), de facto evidence of inward migration and a strong likelihood that the people concerned did not have a legal settlement. The analogue of this experience – high level truncation in the sense of being unable to link a life history to death – is what we partly see in pauper letters as people leave a place of settlement to live and die elsewhere.[13] Any historian familiar with settlement examinations or other legal testimonies can also see the tendency to move from place-to-place, clouding settlement entitlement, writ large.

Unsurprisingly, then, when historians have tried to link those receiving poor relief to prior demographic histories played out in a single place, the figures have been uninspiring. Richard Smith and myself found linkage levels of around 40 to 50 per cent for Whitchurch (Oxfordshire) and Calverley (West Yorkshire) respectively, but in other places linkage rates have been lower. Samantha Williams managed to link only 26 per cent of paupers in this way for two Bedfordshire parishes, while for Birstall (West Yorkshire) and Shepshed (Leicestershire) the figures are under 20 per cent.[14] Of course the number of reliable family reconstitutions in England and Wales is slim, but even without them, analyses of surname turnover tend in the same direction. Buckatzsch observed in the 1960s that surnames rarely lasted in English parishes for more than three generations.[15] There is, in other words, evidence that the migrant, probably with no or contestable settlement credentials, was the majority resident of some English parishes. We see the same thing evidenced where parishes maintained separate accounts for out-parish relief payments rather than mixing them in, without denotation, with the rest of the overseers' accounts. In Kirkham (Lancashire) more than 40 per cent of relief payments apparently made to the poor were either financed by other parishes or sent from Kirkham to other places. The list of 'Kirkham poor' was much slimmer than we would have expected in a parish of the same size and location, suggesting just how inaccurate a superficial reading of overseers' accounts can be.[16] Similarly, in Hulme, a small town in the shadow of Manchester, at least two-thirds of the population by the early nineteenth century were in-migrants without a settlement and the majority of poor relief payments for the 'Hulme poor' were actually made to other parishes.[17]

In short, the level of actual settlement and removal activity after 1780 was muted both in an absolute sense *and* in relation to the number of those in any community who *could* have been caught up in it. This remains true even after the 1790s and the instigation of the legal requirement that someone be actually dependent rather than 'potentially dependent' for proceedings to begin. The generality of overseers could, in other words, have followed the example of some of their individual peers and systematically and comprehensively enforced settlement legislation, but they did not. This issue has prompted a vigorous debate about how much of a disciplinary effect settlement law and the surveillance that went with it had.[18] Yet, stepping aside from this debate it is clear that in most places, where an individual or family was removed (especially if we ignore vagrants) there was something that differentiated them in the minds/reasoning of officials vis-à-vis others in the community who could also have been removed. This is what we see with the pauper letter writers Curchin and Thorne.

Differential Use of the Laws of Settlement

Analysing *how* the laws of settlement came to be differentially applied is beset with both methodological and source problems. Some 13 per cent of all the pauper letter writers appealing for relief to their settlement parishes in the underlying sample eventually 'came home', voluntarily and with the financial assistance of the settlement parish. Only around (a further) 5 per cent were forcibly removed under settlement legislation.[19] These figures are interesting, but they tell us about the reasons for differential application of settlement legislation only if individual cases left a paper trail and/or we come across groups of directly comparable paupers, as in the case of Thorne and Curchin. The situation is no less problematic in places where we have systematic settlement/removal data, a family reconstitution, and overseers' accounts. In Calverley, for instance, there are 43 removal orders and 52 settlement examinations between 1780 and 1834, amounting to less than one removal case per year and less than 4 per cent of all people who would have been liable for removal on the basis that they were both dependent and did not obviously have a settlement. Not all of those who 'failed' a settlement examination were removed and at least three people who clearly had a settlement in Calverley were nonetheless removed. The occupational profile of removals stretched across the range from small clothiers through to labourers and the majority were women. Here then is differential use of the settlement laws writ large, but the reasons for it are opaque. Why should Thomas Hargreaves (weaver aged 43, his wife and three resident children) be removed while the person who literally lived next door, Jonathan Spacey (labourer, 47, wife, four children) who had moved into the parish and did not have a settlement, be given poor relief when they both applied in February 1794?[20] Such questions are difficult to answer but are the focus of the rest of this section of the chapter.

It is important initially to discount some of the stock explanations from the secondary literature already encountered briefly above. Thus, there is little convincing evidence in the primary sources that in most places judgements on the moral worth of the pauper informed differential application of the settlement laws. The shunting of unmarried pregnant women (who might generate a potentially lifelong settlement liability for the parish of birth) across parish boundaries has become a stock-in-trade image of the settlement laws. Yet, a study of the illegitimacy examinations, filiation orders, bond payments and removal orders for parishes in Lancashire, Somerset and Wiltshire suggests no evidence of sustained attempts to remove pregnant women whether they had a settlement or not.[21] Similarly, when cross-linking the Constable and Churchwarden accounts (in which those responsible for petty offences from urinating in the churchyard to minor assaults were recorded) to the overseers' accounts, settlement examinations and removal orders for the parish of Calverley, there is almost no evidence that those who were morally suspect were targeted for removal. Indeed, looking at pauper letters one is struck by how infrequently the very worst characters (often acknowledged as such by host and settlement parishes) were the subject of removal orders. Jacob Curchin is one of more than two dozen reprobates who wrote multiple times in the letter sample underpinning this chapter and who could have been subject to removal orders but never were. The existence of an out-parish relief system, a second potential explanation for the differential application of settlement laws, does *not* explain this. Settlement parishes usually refused to pay or at least pay regularly for their reprobates and yet not a single removal order was ever issued.

A third variable lacking explanatory power is occupation or the periodicity of the labour market, in the sense of skilled men being less likely to be removed than unskilled labourers and all workers less likely to be removed in good times than in bad. The detailed examples already drawn here have dwelt on people with the same sort of occupational label and of similar ages but with different outcomes. Curchin and Thorne were both coopers but one was removed and the other not. In Garstang (Lancashire) the closure of the calico printing works resulted in some calico printers being removed but others, equally subject to the basic laws of settlement, not. Even in decidedly rural areas such as Welton (Northamptonshire) some labourers were removed after the harvest and others not.[22] If removal was connected to the nature of work, skill or the labour market, then the relationship was probably, at least after the 1780s, mediated by a number of intervening variables such as who one worked for rather than what one did.

Other variables have more explanatory purchase. Four in particular loom large. Thus, there is no doubt that in a framework where removal and payment of relief were discretionary issues, personal relationships with officials mattered. It is clear from the more than 2,300 pieces of correspondence between overseers collected for this chapter that officials could generate a definite respect for some paupers, both those who were morally unstained and those not. Two examples locate the different ends of the spectrum. On 26 January 1829, the overseer of Billington (Lancashire) received the eighth letter in a series from his counterpart, Richard Palmer in Howick (Westmorland) on the subject of the Ormerod family. It said:

Sir

James Ormerod's wife is very poorly indeed and the relief which they have had is thought by all who are acquainted with her situation to be quite insufficient: I have consulted Mr Hesmondhalgh [a magistrate] on the subject and we have come to the following conclusion:

"That the overseer give a ticket to Richard Hesmondhalgh for 11s per week to furnish the old people with milk until such a time as they can provide for themselves."

James Seed had, therefore, better send a ticket to that effect with J. Ormerod to R. Hesmondhalgh.[23]

James Seed (the overseer of Billington and one of the most parsimonious officials in Britain) did not send a ticket and did not pay extra relief, but Palmer did not remove the old couple as he was entitled to do. We might infer from the tone of his letter that he (and others in the town) actually respected the Ormerods, who were thus not removed. At the other end of the spectrum we see the grudging respect for the pauper Elizabeth Watson, resident in Wing (Rutland) but settled in Oundle (Northamptonshire) and the subject of a series of letters between officials in the two places. One of 1 June 1832, a letter asking whether Watson should get further relief while living in Wing, occasioned a reply from Oundle township that:

> Sir
>
> Eliz Watson was in our workhouse some short time ago & derived great benefit from the treatment. Indeed got as she herself said quite well & left it. She has been for some years constantly on our Parish Books & we were much astonished at her very [double underlined] quick recovery [double underlined] from her treatment at the workhouse and my orders were not to allow her any more money or relief out of the house but from your own signatures which tell me that it is right. I am willing to allow what you ask.
>
> PS We considered that she came the old soldier over us to use a Common phrase for the last year or more.[24]

Despite the fact that she had come over the old soldier (that is, deceived the parish) the overseer was willing to sanction further relief. In simple legal terms he had no reason to do this. He would certainly have won any appeal to the magistrates. She could have been removed at minimal expense but the Oundle overseer did not push for it and the Wing overseer did not instigate removal even when, on several future occasions, he had to find relief from the pockets of his own ratepayers, suggesting a grudging respect.

A second potential explanation of the differential application of settlement legislation, for some places at least, was ethnicity. British welfare historians are familiar with concerted attempts by parish authorities to keep the Irish on the move using combinations of vagrancy and transit legislation, legal provisions for the relief of demobilized soldiers, and settlement legislation. Less familiar is a tendency for settlement legislation to be applied by English parishes to Welsh migrants. In the parish of Hulme, for instance, whereas those with broadly Welsh surnames made up 12 per cent of household heads in 1811, the Welsh were involved in 94 per cent of all removals between 1800 and 1834. While it would be appealing to see this as an example of English xenophobia, it was also partly tied up with the fact that many Welsh parishes either would not work within the confines of the out-parish relief system or could not afford to. Thus, William Lloyd wrote from Rhayadda parish to the overseer of Hulme on 18

January 1828 to say that he could not consider paying an allowance for Thomas Thomas while he lived in Hulme because 'we are a small parish and out [rate]payers are little more than paupers themselves. Please to return him and his family home by the cheapest method.'[25]

Two other explanatory variables have an even stronger evidential base. It is clear from the underpinning letter sample, for instance, that the density of family connections in the settlement or host parish strongly influenced the likelihood of removal. In our opening example, William Thorne was removed, while Jacob Curchin was not. One of the key things that distinguished the two men was that Curchin had other family in Wisbech whereas Thorne's mother and brother were still resident in the parish of Thrapston, something that he had reminded the overseer of in an earlier exchange of letters.[26] Thorne was thus removed to the place where he had the strongest family connections.

We can extend this observation by moving north to the parish of Calverley and the township of Sowerby (near Halifax), both of which have detailed reconstitutions available. Between them they boast 293 removal order and settlement examinations for the period 1780–1834, and we can identify a further 23 removals from overseers' accounts and other sources.[27] Eleven of the removal orders were bilateral. Linking these to the reconstitutions for both places reveals that 8 of the 11 had no other kin in the community *from which* they were removed while all but one (a widow removed from her place of marriage, Calverley, to the settlement of her husband, Sowerby) had significant kin in the community *to which* they were removed. In 1798 when Thomas Hoyland and James Spacey were removed to Sowerby, there were at least five other Sowerby families who were dependent upon some aspect of poor relief and had not met the criteria for a Calverley settlement and yet who were not removed. All had family in the parish whereas Hoyland and Spacey did not. A related explanatory variable is religion. In Calverley it is striking that not a single Methodist, Baptist, Unitarian or Moravian was the subject of a settlement examination or removal proceedings. This may have reflected anticipatory action by members of the different circuits, providing financial support to those tipping into dependence or moving people on through the nonconformist 'circuit' before parishes had a chance to remove them. Yet, there is also something more going on. Work on the epistolary advocates of the poor reveals nonconformist ministers to have been very active indeed in petitioning parish authorities on behalf of their flocks and writing to officials to prevent removal, serving as a *de facto* family in the host parish.[28]

There are, of course, other potential explanations for differential application of the laws of settlement. One might simply be bad luck – the

need for a host parish to choose someone who could be used as a deterrent example for the rest of the population. Levene has also recently
argued, in an elegant article, that the law offered protection to women
with young children making it much more difficult to remove this group
than those at other stages of the life and family-cycle.[29] The rest of this
chapter, though, will suggest that the key variable shaping who could
legitimately be removed was the intersection of the understandings of
the law of settlement and the custom of belonging held by both officials
and paupers, something which created a mutually understood territory of
contestability when it came to removals.

Official Understanding of the Law of Settlement

On 18 June 1831, John Ormerod, the overseer of Ramsbottom (Lancashire), received a letter from Mr James Braidwood, a solicitor. It related
to an opinion sought by Ormerod in the case of the settlement examination of Henry Ramsbottom and Elizabeth Pilling. An enclosure opened
with the sentence 'I thought proper to give you account of the statutes
ordering the settlement of the poor as followeth'. Starting with an act of
1662 the list of acts and Braidwood's assessment of the degree to which
they had subsequently been amended ran through 1685 and 1691 right
up to an element of case law in 1808. Thereafter we find a long and involved discussion of the Ramsbottom and Pilling case, centring initially
on whether apprenticeship indentures had been formally signed and
sealed, then moving on to the issue of whether Ramsbottom or/and his
father had paid taxes and whether the officials of the town had accurately
recorded their payment. Braidwood suggested that the township 'had the
advantage' in the sense that the Justices had already in effect dismissed
the charge of inadequate accounting because they had allowed an initial
removal order. Nonetheless, Braidwood warned Ormerod that he must
attend Haslingden sessions with past overseers and to take 'all your kinsmen with you' because it was likely that Ramsbottom would attend with
his father and their local kinsmen to further testify that they had a belonging in the parish.[30] We return to this issue below.

   Henry Ramsbottom may have had a point in his claim of shoddy accounting practices.[31] The key thing in this case, however, is both the
longevity and complexity of settlement law, and the plethora of considerations that could impact on its enforcement. While he did not say it
explicitly, Braidwood 'sat on the fence' because he was just not sure what
the outcome would be. Ormerod himself was clearly uncertain as to the
right path because he took the advice to the ratepayers a week later. The

vestry was also somewhat confused and 'Resolved not to pursue the case further it not being worth the candle', a reflection of the fact that they did not understand, and could not afford, action under settlement legislation.[32] This is the analogue to the protracted and expensive settlement cases that were the stock-in-trade of early settlement historians and it is reflected in hundreds of other cases in the data underpinning this chapter. Thus, John Nourse, the overseer of Box (Wiltshire) reported to his vestry that he had received legal opinion on the case of the removal of John Armitage to Salisbury but that it was 'not all to our side'. With much regret, because Armitage was a 'saucy fellow', he concluded that the law of settlement 'might fail us in this case and occasion the need for a special rate in consequence'. The Box officials were afraid that the law itself left so many loopholes that it would be difficult for them to win.[33] One such loophole was ambiguity over how long a putative parish of settlement had to appeal against a removal order. When William Clarke, Master of the Oxford House of Industry wrote to Samuel Lucas, overseer of Tilehurst (Berkshire) on 5 November 1832 to follow up non-payment of relief for John Meller he noted:

> it must be recollected that an Order *unappealed against is conclusive to all the World** & their order was not disputed … [written sideways in margin:] *Rex v Kenelworth 4v. Burn or 2VNP 14th where an order, though in error, unappealed against was conclusive – I hope you will look to this case.[34]

This was both a demonstration of detailed legal knowledge, but also a reminder that case law could be unpredictable in refining black letter law. Another loophole was the facility afforded to overseers by settlement law to obtain a removal order but suspend it where there were compelling reasons (for instance ill-health) which would dictate a parish offering relief and removing later. Examples of this practice quite literally litter overseers' correspondence and an interesting case is the letter from Thomas Heath, overseer of Preston, to Billington, on 29 November 1835, which said:

> The wife of William Shuttleworth, belonging your township, has applied here in consequence of her husband having enlisted and the lying in, in a most deplorable state without any means of support for herself and 3 children; she says you sent her 3/ and 23d just and promises to call on her on Saturday last I trust that you will take her situation into your serious consideration, and give her such further Relief – as may be necessary for a person so situated – which will save us trouble and expense of Removal under suspended.[35]

While Heath took it that he had an absolute right to obtain and then suspend a removal order, the legal basis for the threat and assertion is by no means as secure as his letter implies. Suspended removal orders were always supposed to be the exception rather than the rule, and contrary assumptions on the reach of this aspect of law opened up considerable scope for the contestability of removal. More widely, there are some 150 examples in the underlying dataset where officials corresponding with each other pointed specifically to the contestability of the law. By way of example, the overseer of Christchurch (Surrey) wrote to his counterpart in Pangbourne on 3 October 1829 to acknowledge a letter withdrawing the regular weekly allowance previously paid for Widow King. He said:

> I cannot help, for the sake of the poor woman, expressing my regret that you should have sent me such an order … nothing was wanting to complete her miserable situation that the withdrawal of this pittance. However I have communicated to her, your determination, & advised her to apply to the magistrate, at Union Hall for advice under her very distressing circumstances.[36]

Reflecting on examples such as this it is hard to escape the sense that late-eighteenth- and early-nineteenth-century officials did not invoke settlement law consistently, did not act on legal opinion that they had sought, and did not often pursue the law, where they did start to act, to its fullest extent because they felt that they could not trust the actuality of settlement law rather than just the threat or language of it. In turn, we see latent concerns over the complexity of the law reflected in the increasing number and length of 'how to be an overseer' guides from the later eighteenth century onwards.

These ideas, entwined with the human dimension of the decision to remove or not, made life difficult for some overseers. The problem is beautifully hinted at in a letter from Thomas Lyon of Bolton to James Seed, overseer of Billington on 13 May 1824:

> Mr James Seed
>
> Sir I take this opportunity of informing you that I have seen the overseer of Great Bolton to day and he tells me that he will put Richard Eastwood under a suspended order on Monday next if no relief comes betwixt and then for he is starving for want and we cannot do for him any longer as he has cost us six or seven shillings a week ever since he began to be poorly.[37]

Bolton, then, had been paying regular relief to Richard Eastwood even though they knew him to have a settlement elsewhere. They must equally have known that they could have had a removal order at any time but also that suspending it (Eastwood was 'starving', not sick or in some other condition that would have held legal water as a ground for suspension) would have been a contestable decision. In the sense that James Seed was well known in Lancashire for his determination to contest liability, Bolton must also have been aware of the likelihood of significant legal bills in the event that they did seek a removal order. In this case Billington did not pay and Bolton did not remove, carrying on a payment to Eastwood for some four months. Officials in both Bolton and Billington clearly had an understanding not only of the law but also of the very large grey areas of contestation explicit and implicit in a law of settlement that had built up incrementally layer by contradictory layer.

This still does not, however, fully explain why Bolton failed to remove and, more widely, why parishes removed some people and not others. Some signpost to a more nuanced explanation is to be had by returning to the case of Ramsbottom and Pilling. The vestry of the parish of Ramsbottom were, to be sure, defeated in part by the vagaries of the law, but there was also another issue played out in this instance: the pair could muster an extensive set of local people (kinsmen might mean relatives but in Lancashire often meant friends and work colleagues too) to testify that they 'belonged' to the parish and one reading of the case is that at its core is a contested understanding of different, extra-legal, versions of belonging. Building on such a reading, the last sections of this chapter will contend that there is explanatory value in the idea that paupers and their advocates also understood and could rhetoricize the law of settlement law and that this, allied with the deployment of a suite of yardsticks of belonging, explains why some people were removed and others not.

Pauper Understandings of Settlement Law and Belonging

That by the later eighteenth and early nineteenth centuries paupers had an understanding of the law of settlement is not to be doubted. As Geoffrey Oxley and James Taylor both pointed out in early work, paupers targeted for examination were either deliberately vague or unerringly precise in what they said and the life-cycle they recounted, actively seeking to shape how the law would be applied.[38] Moreover, Peter King has argued persuasively that paupers actively turned to the law via magistrates to shape the way they were treated by officials.[39] Certainly the pauper letters and overseer correspondence that underpin this chapter provide a vivid exemplification of some of the ways that paupers were able to frustrate the operation of settlement law. James Tomblin wrote from Thrapston (Northamptonshire) to Henry James, a Peterborough magistrate on 25 October 1833 to say:

> As you are a magistrate of the city of Peterborough *of which place I am a native and to which place I belong* I take the liberty of troubling you which I hope

you will excuse. *My circumstances are well known* to many of the inhabitants of
Peterborough, having had for a long time a series of domestic affliction the lat-
est and most considerable of which is that my wife has been very ill for nearly
twelve months ... I am totally unable to meet these expenses [rent], and must if
not assisted in some degree *come home* to Peterboro. If assisted to pay the rent I
will endeavour to discharge the other accounts as far as I can which I hope will
not be refused. I applied to the overseers personally a few weeks ago *and went
away under the hope that something would be done for me as I was not positively
refused* but promised that my case should be considered and an answer sent. I
have received no answer.[40]

The letter has something of a legalistic feel. His appeal in person was
'not positively refused' and he had come away with an expectation that
his case would be successful, such that the act of not refusing became a
de facto guarantee. Equally, his circumstances were well known to the
inhabitants of the town, suggesting that there can have been no reasonable excuse for failing to consider his request favourably. Having got no
decision Tomblin showed a keen appreciation of his legal right to apply
directly to a local magistrate.

Another example is William Cooke, writing to Mr Wetherhead, justice
and vicar of Peterborough in an undated letter to say, 'This is to aquaint
you that I am left a widower with 5 small childer and 2 of them very ill
and has nothing to support with but what I have hard to endeavour for
which is not sufficient ... if not answered [helped] I must be obliged to
apply to the overseer of Bradford for relief to the present support of my
childer or otherwise me and my family to be brought to Peterborough.'[41]
Cooke displayed none of the legalistic poise of Tomblin, but he had a
clear sense that his position (a widower with 5 children and 2 of them
very ill) generated an entitlement and that it allowed him to write directly
to a magistrate to prevent removal. John Lovegrove elaborated a more
robust and direct interpretation of the law when writing from London to
Pangbourne (Berkshire) on 1 November 1816 to ask where his money
was for looking after his mother. Dealing with a new overseer, he suggested that 'the other overser aloud her 3 shillins per week I know a
magistrate would alow it her and she stay in her place if you do not send
the mony soon you may expect to hear from me a gain'.[42] Lovegrove
deployed a sophisticated argument in which past practice and belonging
to a place allied with a right of appeal to the magistrate intertwined to
generate a compelling case for the new overseer to act. Frances Soundy,
writing from Battersea to Pangbourne on the subject of her sick husband
and unemployed son on 12 October 1826 offered that 'Gentillman if you
have any doubts of the truth if you sand any person I will take them to
him of gentillmen If you will sand word wot you wish him to do or he will

gentillmen if it will give satisfackion he will go to a magistrate and make oth of his statement of his disstres'.[43] Many other paupers availed themselves of this facility, with 260 letters written to magistrates by paupers in the underlying letter sample.

There is also much more direct evidence of pauper engagement with and understanding of the laws of settlement. William Ellis, living in Brighton but settled in Rothersthorpe asserted in 1811 that the 'Act of His Majesties Parlement of 1795 means that you must take into consideration my case and remit me some relief and not to Remove me'. While his understanding of the timing of the Act and the nature of its provisions was imperfect, Ellis, and hundreds of others like him, nonetheless felt confident in quoting the law.[44] Another example is that of Martha Fellowes, writing from Bath to Rothersthorpe, who suggested:

> If you cannot see youre way to sending me a trifle Gentlmen then I will apply to Bath and they will not hesertate so I am Told to Put me under a Removal and Serspended for I am to Sick to travel back Home and then the Cost to you Gentlmen will be much the greater for You must pay the price of the Order and the trifle that We will gette.[45]

Many letters in the same vein could be analysed, but what seems clear is that a substantial proportion of paupers had knowledge of the law, running along a spectrum from the hazy and the speculative/hearsay through the rudimentary, and to the relatively sophisticated. And there is evidence that having such knowledge and being able to elaborate or rhetoricize it made paupers less vulnerable to removal. A comment in the Vestry book of Welton (Northamptonshire) that the parish would 'not fight Jonathan Samuels *again*' over his settlement typifies such evidence.[46]

This familiarity with and use of the law on the part of paupers is mirrored in the way that the epistolary advocates for the poor (doctors, overseers, ministers, landlords, etc., in more than 400 letters) often framed their interaction with officials. An unnamed correspondent writing from St Werburgh parish (Derby), to the vestry at Earl's Barton (Northamptonshire) on 1 December 1829 is typical. The writer lamented the fact that the overseer of Earl's Barton had neglected to send an allowance of 2s. per week for the pauper Sarah Robins, who

> would beg if you have any mercy in you that you would send the money immediately and not suffer a poor old woman of 74 years of age to die of starvation she has no means of support but the small pittance you have allowed her and if the statement of Mr Moody's [the St Werburgh overseer] is correct I think you are very much to blame in not remitting the money when due ... if you do not think well to send the money the magistrates here shall be applied to and they

will compell mr moody to do something for her for it is impossible for her to be
removed and I trust the magistrates will give the poor woman that full support
that her case requires.[47]

This sophisticated letter combines an implication that the law is being
broken with a sense that the morals of the Earl's Barton overseer are
suspect, and a specific threat to go to a magistrate to compel favourable
treatment of the pauper *in situ* rather than removal. In short, the law
suffuses this letter. In similar fashion, the Rev. John Mitchell wrote from
Isleworth (Hertfordshire) to the Vestry Clerk of Rothersthorpe in June
1824 to remind him that 'It will be no good having recourse to the Law
to bring about a removal. I am quite determined that this old couple
[John and Sarah Harris] will lose all if they are taken from Isleworth
and will go to the law myself.'[48] There are many more examples of this
sort, but the core point is that the epistolary advocates of the poor seemingly had a good grasp of the complexities of the legal system and especially its uncertainties. At a human level, would the overseer of Isleworth
have removed the Harris family given the Rev. Mitchell's letter? Would
the overseers of either place have been willing to test the Rev. Mitchell's
determination that the settlement laws would not be instituted in this
case? Having an advocate may thus have been an important predictor of
whether the law would be applied to any individual, and there is plenty
of evidence that advocacy of this sort was common both for those inside
their settlement parishes and for those further away.

In turn, the Mitchell letter confirms one already highlighted discriminating factor which may have shaped the operation of the law of settlement – a sense of belonging. The tension between belonging to a 'home'
(that is, settlement) parish and living in and belonging to a host parish is
apparent in many pauper letters and much overseer and other correspondence. It leads to paupers who did not want to move and overseers who
might not want to remove them, elaborating multi-layered structures of
belonging to a host parish as a justification for relief. Elizabeth Maunders,
writing from Old Brentford (Berkshire) to her settlement parish of Woo-
ton (Oxfordshire) on 6 January 1827 is typical. Responding to the suggestion that she come 'home' Maunders noted that once she had left Old
Brentford she would have left for good, saying, 'I should lose the little
employ I have & I trust at my time of Life <u>65</u> the Gent^{n} will not wish me
to leave here as I am content with what they allow me.'[49] The underlining
here, firmly in the original and underscored several times, clearly implies
that Maunders felt that old age conferred both a legal and moral right
to receive relief and *also* to receive it in her host community, where she
clearly (in her view) belonged.

Other paupers trod a delicate balancing act between rhetoric of belonging to the settlement parish *and* to their current place of residence in order to prove both a general entitlement and the absolute need for them not to be removed from a host parish. The former might involve subtle references to 'my parish', 'being the place I belong to', 'I must come Home to you', or being 'removed home', as well as direct questions such as 'whether I may expect relief from my own parish'. Sometimes a sense of belonging could be conveyed in a veiled threat, as in the case of Joseph Richards writing from Warwick to Thrapston, who suggested that 'you *must* take me and keep me as I cannot do any longer'.[50] Paupers might also claim personal connection to officials and other prominent people in the settlement parish, as did Anthony South writing from Brighton to Peterborough and claiming first that 'Mr White knew my father well' and then that 'I did not however know when I wrote that you are at present acting as head overseer of that Parish, otherwise would have addressed the letter to you as being well acquainted with my father and which you told me when I was last at Peterboro'.[51] The analogue to these claims, often in the same letter, was to emphasize either the economy of leaving a pauper in their host community or the moral imperative for leaving them be. Such a case might involve phrases such as: 'Hope you will be so obliging to pay it as I may keep where I am I can't get my bread if I come to Peterboro' (Joseph Yates, 12 September 1799) or 'I am in other Cases much embarrassed' (Mary Gunnell, writing from Manchester to Oxendon (Northamptonshire) on 22 January 1834 to emphasize that her credit networks were under threat).

Many paupers also sought to show that they were rooted in local kinship and friendship networks, which would keep down the long-term cost of relief for the settlement parish, as for instance with Joseph Richards whose letter of 6 August 1826 noted 'was it not for some of our children that have been kind to us we must have come wolly [wholly] to you before now', or Margaret Walcott, whose letter of 23 January 1819 noted 'our friends can do no more having kept us for these years' and 'our son and Dr has been of so much help to us otherwise we must have come home before this'.[52] The epistolary advocates of the poor were even more forthright about the belonging of paupers to their residence parishes. Thomas Adams's letter of 30 January 1826 'On behalf of Thomas Drage, a man living here and belongs to your parish' is typical of hundreds of others. It went on: 'he is a most deserving character and *much respected here* but from age and bad health (a paraletik stroke) he is unable to support himself without a trifle assistance *I believe he would do any thing rather than come to Thrapston*.'[53] To be able to strongly evidence belonging to a host parish, especially if other kin were present, could thus make the difference between being removed and not. In this sense we come full circle to Jacob Curchin and William Thorne.

Conclusion

At the core of this chapter is the basic question: why were the settlement laws differentially applied in most communities so that one pauper with a given set of circumstances would be removed and another with a roughly identical set would not? Understanding this issue is more than a mere technicality in poor law history. It gets to the heart of much wider debates about the experience of being poor, the mobility of the poor, understandings of the law, the operation of the poor law as an administrative entity, the nature and structure of power relations and the mental world of communities in the period between the late eighteenth century and the advent of the New Poor Law. The substantial sample of pauper letters, official correspondence and the letters of epistolary advocates assembled for this chapter in turn does more than simply provide an entertaining way into the operation of the poor law. The individual examples can be useful, but at least for this chapter they simply exemplify striking regularities in the way that paupers and officials understood, rhetoricized, addressed and avoided the settlement laws across a very large and (spatially and chronologically) wide data set.

These data suggests that some of the stock explanatory variables for the differential application of settlement legislation – the moral standing of paupers or the nature of labour demand, for instance – are blunt instruments. A range of other potential explanations – including unfashionable ones such as religion and personal chemistry – appear to have been more important. Above all, however, the settlement laws were differentially applied because of the complex intertwining of three broad explanatory variables: the lack of confidence that overseers had in the law itself, with competing readings of the law of settlement introducing an element of contestability to removal decisions; understanding and elaboration of the law by paupers threatened with removal; and the ability of paupers to construct multi-layered arguments of belonging (often bolstered by epistolary advocates) that made the decision to remove or not by either settlement or host parish anything but straightforward. These observations do *not* mean that: the settlement and removal system had no force – all communities were episodic in their application of settlement examination and removal – or results of such activity were benign. Clearly the threat of removal could hang over paupers and drive them to duplicitous lengths to avoid it. Yet it is hard to escape the sense in looking at pauper letters that many writers felt they had little chance of *actually* being re-moved. Statistically this is quite true. What is surprising about removal orders, even if we allow that a good proportion of them may have been lost, is how few there are rather than how many. It is even more surprising how infrequently removal orders were issued compared to the number that *could* have been issued had the law been completely enforced. At least for the later eighteenth and early nineteenth centuries, then, we see the evolution of a framework of contestability for removal. This resulted in the differential application of the law but it also suggests that we ought to fundamentally rethink the nature of power in the welfare system and locate paupers within a mental world of officials and ratepayers which was rather less monolithic and negative than has often been asserted for the closing decades of the Old Poor Law.

Notes

1. For the two best reviews of how settlement was generated, see K. D. M. Snell. 2006. *Parish and Belonging: Community, Identity and Welfare in England and Wales, 1700–1950*, Cambridge; and L. Charlesworth. 2010. *Welfare's Forgotten Past: A Socio-Legal History of the Poor Law*, Abingdon.
2. Northamptonshire Record Office (hereafter NRO) 325P/193, 'Letter book'. My italics.
3. For the definitive overview of pauper letters and a discussion of their reliability, see T. Sokoll. 2001. *Essex Pauper Letters, 1731–1837*, Oxford.
4. On the out-parish system, see S. King. 2005. '"It is impossible for our vestry to judge his case into perfection from here": Managing the distance dimensions of poor relief, 1800–40', *Rural History* 16, 161–189.
5. NRO 325P/193, 'Letter book'.
6. NRO 325P/194, 'Letter book'. My italics.
7. Pauper letters are much rarer for Scotland given the fact that it employed a very different welfare system to England and Wales. See A. Gestrich and J. Stewart. 2007. 'Unemployment and Poor Relief in the West of Scotland, 1870–1900,' in S. King and J. Stewart (eds), *Welfare Peripheries: The Development of Welfare States in Nineteenth and Twentieth Century Europe*, Bern, 125–148.
8. See, for instance, L. H. Lees. 1998. *The Solidarities of Strangers: The English Poor Laws and the People 1700–1948*, Cambridge; S. King. 2000. *Poverty and Welfare in England 1700–1850: A Regional Perspective*, Manchester; S. Hindle. 2004. *On the Parish? The Micro-Politics of Poor Relief in Rural England c. 1550–1750*, Oxford.
9. J. S. Taylor. 1991. 'A Different Kind of Speenhamland: Nonresident Relief in the Industrial Revolution', *Journal of British Studies* 30, 183–208; Snell, *Parish and Belonging*.
10. G. Oxley. 1974. *Poor Relief in England and Wales 1601–1834*, Newton Abbott.
11. D. Green. 2010. *Pauper Capital: London and the Poor Law 1790–1870*, Aldershot.
12. These episodes are documented in Whitehead's autobiography. See S. Chapman (ed.). 2001. *The Autobiography of David Whitehead of Rawtenstall (1790–1865): Cotton Spinner and Merchant*, Helmshore.
13. For a description of the process of family reconstitution and of truncation bias, see S. Ruggles. 1992. 'Marriage, Migration and Mortality: Correcting Sources of Bias in English Family Reconstitutions', *Population Studies* 46, 507–522.

14. D. Levine. 1977. *Family Formation in an Age of Nascent Capitalism,* New York; S. King. 1997. 'Reconstructing Lives: The Poor, the Poor Law and Welfare in Rural Industrial Communities', *Social History* 22, 318–338; R. Smith. 1998. 'Ageing and Well-Being in Early Modern England: Pension Trends and Gender Preferences under the English Old Poor Law c. 1650–1800', in P. Johnson and P. Thane (eds), *Old Age from Antiquity to Post-Modernity,* London, 64–95; S. Williams. 2004. 'Caring for the Sick Poor: Poor Law Nurses in Bedfordshire, 1770–1834,' in P. Lane, N. Raven and K. Snell (eds), *Women, Work and Wages in England, 1600–1850,* Woodbridge, 102–118.

15. E. Buckatzsch. 1961. 'The Constancy of Local Populations and Migration in England before 1800,' *Population Studies* 5, 23–42.

16. Lancashire Record Office (hereafter LRO) PR811, 'Out parish accounts'; PR812, 'Settlement and removals'; PR834, 'Bills and receipts'.

17. Manchester Local Studies Library (hereafter MLS) M10/808-817. These large ledgers contain bills, orders, examinations and correspondence for the parish. They were consulted before the recent preservation process and the large amount of loose material defied any systematic ordering.

18. Reported most keenly in Snell, *Parish and Belonging.*

19. These sorts of low numbers are repeated in Essex. See Sokoll, *Essex Pauper Letters.*

20. King, 'Reconstructing Lives'.

21. S. King. 2005. 'The Bastardy Prone Sub-Society Again: Bastards and their Fathers and Mothers in Lancashire, Wiltshire and Somerset, 1800–1840,' in A. Levene, T. Nutt and S. Williams (eds), *Illegitimacy in Britain, 1700–1820,* Basingstoke, 66–85. Also for Essex, see T. Nutt. 2010. 'Illegitimacy, Paternal Financial Responsibility, and the 1834 Poor Law Commission Report: The Myth of the Old Poor Law and the Making of the New', *Economic History Review* 63, 335–361.

22. LRO DDX 386/3, 'Minutes of the Select Vestry of Garstang'; Northamptonshire Record Office (hereafter NRO) 356p/18, 'Welton Vestry minutes'.

23. LRO PR2391/2–47, 'Billington overseer correspondence'.

24. NRO 249p/216, 'Oundle letter book', underlining in the original.

25. MLS, M10/812, 'Letters and accounts'.

26. Hence paupers had to be careful what they told overseers about their family circumstances, something very evident in the chapter by Boulton elsewhere in this volume.

27. Material for this section is drawn from P. Hudson and S. King. 2014 forthcoming. *Industrialisation, Material Culture and Everyday Life,* Cambridge.

28. See S. King. 2011. 'The Residential and Familial Arrangements of English Pauper Letter Writers, 1800–40s,' in J. McEwan and P. Sharpe (eds), *Accommodating Poverty: The Housing and Living Arrangements of the English Poor, c. 1600–1850,* Basingstoke, 145–168.

29. A. Levene. 2010. 'Poor Families, Removals and 'Nurture' in Late Old Poor Law London', *Continuity and Change,* 25, 233–262.

30. This letter was examined in 1995 at Rawtenstall Library Local Studies Collection. It has subsequently been deposited at the LRO.

31. On the evolution of poor law accounting practice, see S. King. 2011. '"In These You May Trust". Numerical Information, Accounting Practices and the Poor Law, c. 1790 to 1840', in T. Crook and G. O'Hara (eds), *Statistics and the Public Sphere: Numbers and the People in Modern Britain, c. 1750–2000,* London, 51–66.

32. These vestry minutes were examined in 1995 at Rawtenstall Library Local Studies Collection. They have subsequently been deposited at the LRO.

33. Wiltshire Record Office 1719/4–8, 'Box vestry minutes 1793–1824'.

34. Berkshire Record Office (hereafter BRO) D/P 132/18/25, 'Letter', underlining in original.

35. LRO PR2391/21, 'Letter'.

36. BRO D/P 91/18, 'Letters'.

37. LRO PR2391/2–47, 'Billington overseer correspondence'.
38. Oxley, *Poor Relief;* J. S. Taylor, *Poverty, Migration and Settlement in the Industrial Revolution: Sojourners' Narratives,* Palo Alto, 1989.
39. P. King. 2004. 'Social Inequality, Identity and the Labouring Poor in Eighteenth Century England,' in H. French and J. Barry (eds), *Identity and Agency in England, 1500–1800,* Basingstoke, 60–87.
40. Tomblin was settled in Peterborough St John parish. See NRO 261P Vii/Bundle 244/3, 'Letter'. My italics.
41. NRO 261P Vii/Bundle 244/11, 'Letter'.
42. BRO D/P 132/18/44, 'Letter'.
43. For the full Soundy correspondence, see S. King, T. Nutt and A. Tomkins, *Narratives of the Poor in Eighteenth Century Britain,* London, 2006, 9–38.
44. Rothersthorpe correspondence was consulted in the parish chest in October 1994. On amendments to settlement law, see Charlesworth, *Welfare's Forgotten Past.*
45. Rothersthorpe correspondence was consulted in the parish chest in October 1994.
46. NRO 356p/18, 'Welton Vestry minutes'. Underlining in the original.
47. NRO 110p/138, 'Letters'.
48. Rothersthorpe correspondence was consulted in the parish chest in October 1994.
49. Oxfordshire Record Office Woot. P.C. IX/iv/9.
50. NRO 325P/194, 'Thrapston letter book'.
51. NRO 261P Vii/Bundle 244/26, 'Letter'.
52. NRO 261P Vii/Bundle 240/11, 'Letter'; NRO 251p/98, 'Letters'; Rothersthorpe correspondence was consulted in the parish chest in October 1994.
53. NRO 325P/194, 'Thrapston letter book', my italics.

CHAPTER FOUR

MEMORIES OF PAUPERISM

Jane Humphries

Introduction

The English and Welsh poor law has had a mixed reception among historians.[1] Traditional perspectives emphasized its Tudor origins in social control and pro-agrarian state policy and its reformulation in 1834 to fit an emergent industrial economy with its need for labour mobility and work incentives.[2] Such straightforwaradly functionalist interpretations with their emphasis on a structural break in 1834 have fallen out of fashion. Rather, recent historians have demonstrated the long roots of the ideas and policies broached in the Poor Law Report and the many ways in which local authorities, overwhelmed by rising expenditures, had hardened their position on relief long before the Poor Law Amendment Act of 1834 introduced the New Poor Law. Others have emphasized the persistence of traditional behaviour into the New Poor Law era and the difficulties that the Poor Law Board faced in ensuring that local administrators fell into step with the new regime.[3] Commentators have also noted regional variation in the policies and practices of overseers under the Old Poor Law and Guardians under the New.[4] Empirical investigations have persistently pointed to a complex relationship between theory and practice under the New Poor Law at the same time as they have not always exculpated the Old Poor Law from the charge that it was inefficient and counterproductive.[5]

These same empirical investigations also suggest the need for further revisionist work. The classical political economists considered the Old Poor Law an obstacle to economic development and structural change: settlement laws inhibited migration from areas of underemployment to expanding new centres where labour was needed; allowances in aid of wages prevented labour markets from equilibrating and undermined self-reliance; outdoor relief blunted incentives and prudence; and, family allowances encouraged early unconsidered marriages. These and other criticisms influenced the investigative framework of the Royal Commission (the 'Rural Queries') and the subsequent famous (infamous?) 1834 Report. Many developments that contemporaries thought products of the Old Poor Law, however, have been reinterpreted by historians as independent changes within the socio-economic system that then in fact elicited an increase in parish expenditures.[6] In this context, an interesting strand in the recent literature has been to turn the standard account on its head and argue that the Old Poor Law encouraged rather than inhibited growth and structural change,[7] and that it operated to shore up human capital formation and provide lifelines back to independence for the economically and socially disadvantaged.[8]

The ways in which children fared under the Old Poor Law and, in particular, how the system of pauper apprenticeships operated, has provided an important yardstick to assess the social impact of the poor law in recent research.[9] While providing a rosier view of the Old Poor Law, such work raises interesting questions about the transition to the New Poor Law and its implications for the social and economic treatment of poor children. Did 1834 actually lead to deterioration in the treatment of pauper and impoverished children and fewer and less robust lifelines back to stable employment and respectable society? Scholars have speculated that shifts in the way the poor laws operated contributed to the deregulation of the child labour market in the early nineteenth century, a deregulation which promoted an increase in child labour and a deterioration in the terms and conditions of children's employment.[10]

The limitations of the sources available hamper investigation of the outcomes for children under different poor law regimes. Most quantitative poor law history relies on aggregated administrative records. While these are useful for many purposes, they cannot support an enquiry into the nature and consequences of children's encounters with the poor law authorities. Local studies of particular towns or parishes can uncover how children were treated and how such treatment changed, but again the consequences of different interventions remain speculative. Honeyman's important study of parish apprenticeships assembled voluminous evidence on how overseers selected likely children, and then distributed them to a variety of traditional workplaces and new factories. Nor did her investigation stop as the young apprentices arrived at their destination. The 1802 legal requirement that parishes monitor the well-being of children placed at distance from their homes appears to have been taken more seriously than hitherto expected. Correspondence between poor law officials and factory owners and records of follow-up visits by overseers to factories taking parish children provide insight into their treatment once in place.[11] However while this material supports Honeyman's rejection of any blanket condemnation of Old Poor Law functionaries, many of whom strove to do their duty by the children in their care, it provides only limited insight into the subsequent history of such children, though she promised further work on what happened to parish apprentices when they gained their indentures.

These lacunae in relation to children are part of a wider problem with the literature, with historians struggling to provide an account of the poor law 'from below'. Characterizations of the poor and paupers almost invariably come from above, representing the views of officials, social commentators and middle-class observers.[12] The historical record provides little evidence on the lived experience of pauperism outside of the pauper letters explored by Steven King elsewhere in this volume. How did the poor, and here poor children, access and respond to poor relief? Most importantly, how did they survive assistance that was usually conditional and often harsh? Did poor relief constitute a permanent stigma or could pauper children in particular recover economic independence and social standing? Pauper letters, a chief source for historians struggling to excavate the clients' perspective, rarely describe the treatment of children and even less commonly provide evidence on subsequent histories, but educational and occupational outcomes are essential evidence if the system is on trial.[13] Our understanding of how episodes of poverty, receipt of poor relief and the operation of the settlement system intertwined to affect the life chances of children is equally fragile, tied up as it is with a focus on families rather than individual members.

This chapter addresses such questions using a source that is remarkable for its ability to capture the ways in which children's encounters with the poor laws moulded their lives in both the short and long run: surviving memoirs by working people born in the crisis years of the Old Poor Law from the 1780s and into the New Poor Law. Working-class autobiographies are not unproblematic as sources, raising questions of selectivity, memory, authorial intention and representativeness akin to those that must be asked of pauper letters. Nonetheless, and as European historians in general are increasingly coming to realize, they are unique in providing evidence about family circumstances and poor law involvement; they furnish accounts of what the recipients thought about poor relief in its various forms and how they understood welfare dependency. Moreover, they allow historians to track what happened next, to see how a child who had received poor relief fared in later life. In my recent book, *Childhood and Child Labour in the British Industrial Revolution,* I digitized relevant information from the life stories of 617 working men born between 1627 and 1878 to develop quantitative measures of age at starting work, occupational inheritance, probability of apprenticeship, duration of schooling and factors conditioning human capital formation. In this chapter, I focus on the effect of involvement with the poor law in its broadest sense on subsequent occupational and educational outcomes. Thus, it is possible to measure the effect of poverty on children's life chances and even to do so controlling for other relevant factors such as family structure, numbers of siblings, date of birth, etc. Digging deeper it might also be possible to identify whether the transition from the Old to the New Poor Law involved a change in the treatment of impoverished children. The New Poor Law might have continued to impose precocious labour on impoverished boys as part of 'less eligibility'. On the other hand, the Guardians might have tried to substitute education for early labour in the hope of breaking the cycle of pauperism and instilling the desire and ability to be independent.

An encounter with the poor law was not a trivial event in the lives of the autobiographers, many of whom provided a detailed account of the circumstances and nature of relief. Some assistance might have gone unreported given the associated stigma, but it is more likely that such embarrassment would operate to obscure pauperism in adulthood than in childhood. A child's inability to be independent did not signal personal failure in the same way as did adult indigence, something well understood in contemporary debates. Working men did not hide childhood encounters with the parish. Indeed they are often presented as formative influences. Even so, the quantitative analysis has obvious limitations. For example, it was not possible to categorize the nature and duration of poor law involvement in a child's upbringing to distinguish the effects of different kinds of intervention and differentiate intrusion and control from support. Too few autobiographers provided the detail necessary. The best achievable is to conflate all forms of contact to form a categorical variable. Sixty-two autobiographers either received outdoor relief within some kind of family structure or were relieved within the workhouse during their childhood; these represent my pauper sub-sample and provide the basis for controlled statistical comparison with a peer group of the independent poor.[14]

However, the autobiographical evidence does not just underpin this unique quantitative investigation. Myriad individual stories illustrate the nature, causes and consequences of working people's contact with the poor law, putting flesh on the statistical bones of the correlations, enhancing the macro account and identifying themes for further research.

Their silences, particularly on issues such as settlement and removal, are equally telling when set against the backdrop of the aims of the volume as a whole. In this way, working-class memoir facilitates the weaving together of quantitative and qualitative research to edge forward beyond what is realisable by a one-dimensional investigative strategy. The next section develops the quantitative analysis discussed above and the third follows up with the micro-history and a more explicit discussion of issues of settlement and belonging.

Measuring the Effects of Pauperism

At the centre of my analysis of child labour in the industrial revolution was an attempt to chart trends in, and explain age at starting work, which I took as an important indicator of life chances.[15] Children who started work at young ages were disadvantaged: work crowded out schooling, while hard, hazardous jobs impaired children's health and inhibited their growth. Very young working represents an insult to a child's development and to his or her subsequent well-being. On the other hand, work in any form influenced the sense in which the child 'belonged' as an individual, as opposed to being part of a family and, in both theory and practice, complicated his or her status under the settlement laws. This was especially the case after legislation in 1795 made actual destitution the trigger for invoking settlement activity and simultaneously made removing women and young children considerably more difficult. In the rest of this section, then, the focus is on the effect of the English Poor Laws on age at starting work.

The first question is whether men who recorded receiving poor relief as children worked at younger ages than did their peers. Fifty-six autobiographers who received poor relief also reported their age at starting work. The mean age for these poor-law boys can be computed and compared with the mean for the 460 boys whose age at starting work is known and whose families appeared independent throughout their childhoods. Thus, the boys in the pauper sub-sample started work on average aged 9.51. The 460 boys who grew up in working-class but independent families started work aged 10.89, a difference that is unlikely to have occurred by chance.[16] The sample can be sub-divided to reflect the different welfare regimes associated with the Old and New Poor Laws in (say) 1830.[17] Of those boys born before 1830, 27 reported contact with the overseers and on average they started work aged 9.37 years, while their (239) peers who did not report any such contact started work aged 10.62, again a difference unlikely to have occurred by chance.[18] Of those boys born in

1830 or later, 28 reported contact with New Poor Law guardians, and on average they started work aged 9.55 years, while their (217) peers who did not report any such contact started work aged 11.14, again a difference unlikely to have occurred by chance.[19] Both pauper and non-pauper boys started work older in the later era but not much older in the case of the poor-law boys.[20] As a result, the gap in age at starting work between the subsamples widened from 1.3 years under the Old Poor Law to 1.6 years under the New Poor Law: a first sign of the less than beneficent effects of the New Poor Law.

Childhood and Child Labour included an analysis of the relationship between receipt of poor relief and age at starting work using multivariate regression, a technique which controls for other potential influences affecting working age.[21] The results of the regression analysis, discussed at length in *Childhood and Child Labour*, were consistent with expectations. The relevant finding here is the negative and significant effect of the receipt of poor relief. Boys in families that suffered an episode of welfare dependency started work about nine months younger than did their independent peers. Such a negative relationship is to be expected. Poor relief was associated with poverty and poverty with youthful working. Any test of the pure effect of parish relief on age at starting work would have to identify and compare the ages at starting work of boys who received relief with those of boys in identical circumstances in a regime without relief. It would also have to compare the working ages of those boys who were legally settled and not subject to removal with those of boys who were removed because the simple act of removal might make work more or less likely. Such counterfactuals are impossible to construct; the autobiographical detail is simply not available for a large enough sample. However, it is important to note that several explanatory variables included in the model attempt to control for family poverty, (some of fathers' occupational groups, for example casual and soldiering, mothers' labour force participation, dead and absent fathers), all of which have the right signs. Even in the presence of such controls, contact with parish officials reduced age at starting work. At the very least then, the involvement of the poor law did not protect impoverished children from early working.

In *Childhood and Child Labour*, I also explored the longer-term effects of childhood experience on life chances by correlating autobiographers' final CAMSIS rankings, measures of their occupational and economic status, with a number of explanatory variables linked to opportunities for health and human capital formation.[22] A cross-tabulation of CAMSIS scores with the poor law dummy highlights the enduring deleterious effect of a childhood encounter with early industrial welfare agencies. For the sample as a whole, 60 boys reported receiving poor relief during childhood and simultaneously provided enough evidence to impute a CAMSIS rating to their final occupation. Their average CAMSIS rating was 38.97 points. Contextualizing, shoemakers enjoyed a rating of 39, shipwrights and sawyers of 38, and personal service workers and seamen of 37. In comparison, boys who grew up in independent working-class households achieved on average a CAMSIS score of 49.57. Again, to put this in context, engineers, coopers and painters had a ranking of 50 points and small and medium farmers, plumbers, leather workers and mechanics a ranking of 49. The mean differences in scores represents a historically as well as statistically significant difference in occupational and economic status.[23] It would be intriguing to undertake a similar analysis comparing the life chances of children whose families received relief in their parish of settlement with those where an application for poor relief occasioned removal. However, the rarity of references to settlement in general and removal in particular in these sources makes such analysis impossible while simultaneously supporting the suggestion by Steven King elsewhere in this volume that settlement legislation was relatively unimportant.

Cutting the sample at a date of birth of 1830 provides a rough test of whether the disadvantage was sensitive to the particular poor law regime. Thirty boys born before 1830 reported a poor law encounter and a final occupation. Their experience can be compared with the average of the 295 boys who apparently remained independent in childhood and can be assigned a CAMSIS score. The poor-law boys' final CAMSIS rating was on average 33.30 while their independent peers also born before 1830 achieved a rating of 49.97. Thus, while the control group fared about the same as did the independent working-class throughout the whole period, the poor-law boys did badly. To put their relatively low CAMSIS rating in context, fishermen scored 34, building trades workers 33 and bricklayers 31. The gap between the poor-law boys and their independent peers was larger than for the overall sample and unlikely to have occurred by chance.[24] Turning to those autobiographers born during or after 1830, twenty-eight reported an episode of assistance and provided sufficient information to be assigned a final CAMSIS score, in this case 45.43, roughly the status of cutlers and metal fabricators. The control group of 239 boys attained a final CAMSIS score of 49.03, roughly the same as in the earlier period. This gap is both historically and statistically insignificant.[25]

In short, bruising as it might have been, an encounter with the New Poor Law appears not to have had the same enduring adverse effects as a similar encounter with the Old Poor Law, and this despite the evidence that the post-1834 utilitarian regime was associated with a widening gap between poor-law boys and other lads in age at starting work. However, it might not be that the New Poor Law was less damaging to its youthful charges than the earlier regime, but simply that the later period afforded more second chances, opportunities for training and education that even ex-poor law boys could seize. The New Poor Law itself may also have offered more second chances. Certainly the focus of overall expenditure under the New Poor Law moved decisively away from the cash payments of the Old Poor Law and rather more towards 'rehabilitative' spending such as that on education, clothing and food which while unexciting probably combated malnourishment better than similar spending under the Old Poor Law. Moreover if, as seems likely and particularly after 1846, fewer people were subject to settlement and removal, the mere fact of leaving children cemented into their communities for longer may have afforded them more chances to make a success of their lives. The qualitative material might help uncover the extent and nature of such second chances, but before turning to the micro-histories, a final piece of quantitative evidence merits attention.

Thus *Childhood and Child Labour* included a regression analysis of the determinants of autobiographers' final CAMSIS scores.[26] While the aim in the book was to identify the effects of schooling on CAMSIS outcomes within a model that corrected for both ability bias and measurement error, the poor law variable was included in the regression analysis. Space constraints militate against reproducing the complete results here but I note that in the simple OLS regression, a childhood encounter with the poor law was shown to influence an adult's CAMSIS rating negatively and significantly, but in the preferred 2SLS model, the effect was muted. One inference might be that the adverse effect of childhood pauperism operated primarily through schooling, particularly through the displacement of schooling and especially where poor relief was associated with removal. The extent to which the different poor law regimes embodied different educational stances might then explain the less enduring effects of early pauperism in the later nineteenth century. If the New Poor Law was less likely to crowd out schooling (especially if an analogous decline in removal activity left children in a single place for longer), or indeed even actively provided schooling, it may have compensated for its apparent insistence on relatively early working. Again, this intriguing suggestion can be followed up in the individual accounts below.

Experiencing Pauperism

The quantitative material cited above, while suggestive, remains subject to interpretation. In this section, individual life stories are used to cast light on the links implied by the statistical correlations. I draw both on the extensive autobiographical evidence used in *Childhood and Child Labour* and work in progress on contemporaneous memoirs by working women. The material supports three main conclusions: first, outdoor relief in regular or occasional instalments, combined with the absence of removal, was vital in maintaining family integrity and enabling children to grow up in something approaching a secure and caring environment; second, the workhouses of both the Old and the New Poor Law operated hugely varied welfare regimes and a (perhaps surprising) number of people recalled their sojourn therein with affection; and third, the poor laws (whatever the regime) encouraged child labour and promoted early working, which under the New Poor Law was freed from the restraints of pauper apprenticeship indentures.

The first finding concerns the way in which outdoor relief and the apparent absence of removal enabled families to remain intact and raise their children who could then climb back to self-sufficiency and even respectability. If the reason for their indigence was permanent, assistance could be prolonged as was often the case for female-headed households, the widespread product of the "breadwinner frailty" that afflicted families in this era.[27] John Castle's mother, on the death of her husband and after various trials and tribulations, obtained seven shillings a week from the parish to raise her three boys.[28] Access to relief, as in this case, might require widows to move their bereaved families to where they had a legal settlement, at least prior to 1795. This exacerbated disruption and strained potentially supportive ties to friends and family. Even when secured, the subsidies were not munificent. They did not imply a life of leisure, or even of survival, without contributions from mothers and growing children, but in comparison with agricultural wages or the potential earnings of unskilled workers, these doles represented a level of support in touch with common standards. Indeed, commentators have suggested that outdoor relief was in relative terms more generous than current levels of support to female-headed households.[29]

Recipients were not oblivious to the relative generosity however much they might still feel the pinch of poverty. The author of the Ashby family history in recalling the weekly dole of six or seven shillings on which Elizabeth Ashby-Townsend struggled to raise her two legitimate children and older illegitimate child noted the poverty it implied but observed too that the family's income was not much below the village average. Some men earned only seven or eight shillings as agricultural labourers and had many more children than Elizabeth's three. Low earnings and large families operated to put other local families in the same straitened circumstances as the Ashby-Townsends. As a result of the family's poverty, Elizabeth sought employment herself in the houses and fields of her community and was pressurized to withdraw her cherished and clever elder son, aged eleven (in 1870), from school to send him to work as an agricultural labourer.[30] Similarly, when Will Thorne's father died in the early 1860s, his widowed mother made little delay in applying for poor relief. Perhaps she was in too great distress to care about any shreds of respectability, or perhaps the poor's revulsion from formal assistance has been exaggerated, but at any rate, she succeeded in obtaining outdoor relief of four loaves of (bad) bread and four shillings per week. Again this was not enough for family subsistence, but, supplemented by her sweated labour in sewing hooks and eyes on cards and Will's work as a rope spinner, the family survived.[31] In these cases as in many others spanning both Old and New Poor Laws, families were preserved and did not always have to resort to the workhouse. Nor were they removed. However, the strategy relied upon the mother's ability to contribute, and children's early work. More widely, it is striking how often pauper letters make the case for relief outside of settlement communities based upon the fact that local opportunities for child labour could keep down the claims for assistance and so the overall cost of relief for the parishes of actual settlement.

 Other families for which prolonged poor relief appeared vital were those headed by men caught up in the wars of the eighteenth century. Army and navy pay rarely arrived, so they relied on the earnings of other family members and the munificence of the parish, both for subsistence and for avoiding removal. Thomas Sanderson, a soldier's son, grew up in a household dependent on the washtub earnings of his mother and aunt supplemented by poor relief. Not surprisingly under these circumstances he was only eight when 'taken away from school to assist in making a fend for myself'.[32] Thomas recounted too the problems created by the settlement laws for the families of soldiers and sailors. His family had followed Sanderson senior to London, but on his discharge, 'although steeped to the lips in poverty, [my father] would not allow my poor mother to go and receive any more parish money, which at that time was six shillings per week ... consequently off we all went to Sheffield', his parish, walking all the way, he and mother carrying John by turns.[33] As in this case, when men returned from fighting, they were often neither willing nor able to resume the role of breadwinning. Thus, the perpetual warfare of the eighteenth century and its aftermath effects on working-class households was probably an important and under-appreciated contributor to the pressures on the Old Poor Law. The story also begins to suggest, of course, why parishes often did not have to resort to settlement examinations and removal orders.

 Inadequate though it was alone, poor relief gave bereaved or deserted women a breathing space within which to devise a survival strategy geared to their reduced circumstances, and by subsidizing if not replacing potential earnings allowed them room to care for their children.[34] On the other hand, society expected men to provide for their dependents, so if widowed or deserted they found it hard to obtain relief, and impossible to secure the ongoing assistance that combined with occasional or part-time work would have enabled them to raise their children. They were also more likely to be removed. Lone fathers sometimes clung onto their children but survival strategies usually involved remarriage or the deposit of children with other kin, which often turned into permanent adoption.[35]

Of course, for each family that relied long-term upon relief there were several who thanked the parish for help in overcoming sporadic crises. Permanent doles characterized specific types of (frail breadwinner) families, but occasional relief had many triggers: unemployment, sickness, childbirth, accident and migration. The life stories contain illustrations of many such emergencies and the responses of the parish officials. Some calamities illustrate astonishing generosity, going well beyond legal requirements and subverting the law and intent of settlement. Mary Saxby was no meek deserving supplicant. She was a traveller and her autobiography – subtitled *Memoirs of a Female Vagrant Written by Herself* – suggests that by the standards of the time she was of uncertain morality. Yet when a terrible tragedy befell her, she experienced real kindness. In the summer of 1774, several travelling families including Mary's had pitched camp in the fields near Northampton, from which base they proposed to visit the neighbouring villages and ply their wares. While the older children accompanied the grown-ups, Mary had two infants. She carried the baby in her arms but left the toddler, the survivor of twins, in the care of an elderly man who remained at the base making baskets and guarding the travellers' property. While the guard went out to tend to the baggage, the huts caught fire. When he returned they were in flames and there was no sign of the child. In desperation, he threw himself into the inferno and pulled her out, still alive. She implored him to carry her to her mother. Leaving the huts to burn to the ground, and with the child on his back, the man ran as fast as he could to Wellingborough, where he knew he could overtake his comrades. In Wellingborough, the people were amazed and horrified at the sight of this man with his clothes hanging in charred rags and his pitiful bundle, and he was so incoherent with shock that he could barely make himself understood. Eventually he managed to locate Mary. She, poor woman, recognized neither the man nor her child so disfigured were they by the fire. As the child clung to life, Mary recalled the people of Wellingborough found the family lodgings and provided medical and other sorts of assistance – aid extended to a family that was neither settled nor 'deserving'. Notions of settlement and belonging were, as others have shown in this volume, elastic. Mercifully, the child eventually died but Mary did not forget the kindness shown during this heartbreak. On another occasion, when she was left a widow with four young children, an application to the parish resulted in a weekly dole of 3s. Mary continued to receive poor relief and charitable support for much of the rest of her long (and increasingly pious!) life.[36]

These forms of outdoor relief were supplemented by various incarnations of Old Poor Law workhouse. For children *in extremis* such asylum was vital. The alternative was exploitation, hunger, neglect and criminality. On the death of both his father and mother, John Shipp and his brother were in 'utter destitution'. For these lads, as he emphasized, 'there was one place of refuge, and one place only, in which two hapless orphans could obtain, at once, food, clothes, and shelter; and that one asylum was the village poor-house'.[37] Some workhouses offered more than sanctuary. Jonathan Saville grew up in Horton Workhouse and after being brutalized as a pauper apprentice, he was returned there helpless and deformed.[38] In his disabled state, he saw the workhouse as a haven: 'and never did a prince long for his crown so much as I did to get there'.[39] Successive workhouse masters then provided some homely physiotherapy, having him bathed several times a week and encouraging him to swim in a damned-up section of the local river. He was fitted with crutches, and fed well. Through these efforts, he had sufficient mobility restored to become economically self-supporting. Moreover, Jonathan learned to read:

> There was an old pensioner in the house, who had lost the use of one side. The master said to him, 'John, I'll give thee a pint of beer to thy drinking, if thou wilt teach these lads to read'. And I well remember my creeping between the old man's shaking knees to say my lesson to him. Within a year, I became a tolerable reader in the Bible.[40]

Both his restored mobility and his literacy were of use to Jonathan later as an agent collecting and distributing materials to textile outworkers. More treasured by him perhaps was the way in which literacy enabled his Methodist Sunday school teaching and missionary work. In turn, Henry Price's memoir provides another picture of a humane if ramshackle Old Poor Law workhouse:

> We were all happy there, well fed, nurs'd and doctor'd went in and out just as we pleas'd dress'd like others. Fields and gardens all around us we fattend our own Pigs made our own bread, Brew'd our own Beer. The Old men had their bit of Baccy. The Old women their bit of snuff. We gather'd round the fire at night. The old soldiers sang their songs, the old salts their ditties… I must say that Poor Houses at that time for the infirm, and the Fatherless and Motherless children was a real refuge from the stormy blast and a thoroughly good Home.[41]

Pleasant workhouse memories are almost exclusively of Old Poor Law institutions, however. The essential aspect of reform in 1834 was to test the neediness of applicants for relief before providing help. Need could not be assessed by appearances or histories; it could only be gauged by the willingness to submit to an existence which was palpably less enviable than that of the independent poor. Outdoor doles, however miserly, could not ensure less eligibility. With contributions from other family members, as we have seen, recipient families could meld in with their peers and avoid settlement legislation. Moreover, if reform required restriction of outdoor relief, it also required that life within the workhouse take on unattractive and uncomfortable features. Living there had to be sufficiently unpleasant to deter frivolous appeals for help and had too to reform the lazy and imprudent through discipline and work. How pauper children were to be accommodated in these reformed institutions was problematic. While it was recognized that they were not responsible for the destitution or death of their parents, they could not be exempted from less eligibility without impairing incentives. Contemporary social theory implied too that whatever the source of child poverty, pauper children were in danger of inheriting or imbibing vicious and degenerate traits. The same less eligible regime that tested grown-ups, in child-sized form, might break the cycle of dependency and rehabilitate the young.[42]

Increasingly for frail breadwinner families, then, the workhouse was the only option. Thus, when Lucy Luck's father deserted her mother and his children, the family faced the New Poor Law in an area of high pauperism. Application to the parish produced an invitation to enter the workhouse, though not a removal. The family resided therein for several years during which Mrs Luck's health deteriorated and an invalid sister died. Lucy and her brother escaped only when dispatched, before their ninth birthdays, to work in the local silk mill.[43] In contrast to families in similar predicaments in an earlier period (though note the segregation practiced in St Martin's workhouse and reported in this volume by Jeremy Boulton), the Luck family was broken up, with the children separated from their mother and passing their formative years in a gloomy and repressive institution where they were taught like John Reilly that they lived 'under law and not under Grace'.[44] Similar fates befell other poor children post-1834. George Barber and his little brother found life after the death of their mother 'a hard experience' being placed in lodgings with uncaring even cruel minders while their father sought work. The New Poor Law showed even less compassion when their father fell ill and they had to enter the workhouse. Here the brothers fell foul of regulations that broke up families. Writing many years later and in the third person perhaps to try and distance himself from painful memories,

George remembered the harsh separation[45]: 'At that time George was seven years of age and Edward two … circumstances were such that they were compelled to go into separate wards … for three months, remaining there until their father had recovered'.[46] Similarly, Charles Shaw remembered experiencing violence, terror and anguish at being separated from his mother, during his sojourn in a New Poor Law Bastille.[47] This said, and as historians have often observed, even after 1834 the pragmatism of local guardians could soften the operation of the law, under which 'relief must be made painful and even disgraceful'. Generosity was particularly likely towards the settled poor of the community especially if they had once numbered among the respectable. The Ashby-Townsends enjoyed outdoor relief long after 1834, their treatment probably premised on the knowledge that the family's forbears had long resided in the parish and indeed themselves once been overseers, distributing not receiving relief. Moreover, as the family historian recalled, in Tysoe it took some time before the widowed and the fatherless came to regard poor relief with shame and Elizabeth and her family maintained their self-respect.[48]

Nonetheless, it is clear that the New Poor Law strongly affected workhouse children. Separation from mothers and siblings was remembered, as we have seen, with horror, and, more generally, less eligibility bore down on child inmates. Henry Morton Stanley, illegitimate and fatherless, was passed from relative to relative eventually washing up aged six, and clearly against the strict letter of settlement law, in St Asaph Union Workhouse,

> an institution to which the aged poor and superfluous children of the parish are taken, to relieve the respectabilities of the obnoxious sight of extreme poverty, and because civilisation knows no better method of disposing of the infirm and helpless than by imprisoning them within its walls.[49]

Stanley left a moving account of the conditions in this institution, the regimentation and stigmatization, the unappetising and monotonous diet, and above all the bewilderment of a child denied all affection and care. Henry Price's memoir is particularly relevant here since he was resident in the Warminster Workhouse in the transition from the Old to the New Poor Law and compared the two systems from his client's perspective. He ends his eulogy to the Old Poor Law poorhouse with an ominous warning that a change was underway. Although not blind to the drawbacks of the easy-going regime he first encountered, and certainly a stern critic of allowances in aid of wages, Price had no doubt that the new law was detrimental and led to harsher conditions. The autobiographical accounts provide several blood-chilling examples of physical abuse of children, all located in New Poor Law workhouses. This is not surprising. Physical

force was an entrenched part of eighteenth- and nineteenth-century social control and was institutionalized in workhouse punishment books.
Adolescent working-class boys, especially workhouse boys, especially after
1834, were located at the sharp end of its delivery. Even New Poor Law
workhouses were not uniform however and at least one autobiographer
remembered his with affection. George Elson spent some years of his
childhood in a New Poor Law workhouse and reported 'grateful recollec-
tions of the kind treatment I experienced. Workhouse reminiscences are
seldom cherished by former inmates; perhaps mine are exceptional'.[50]

One final aspect of the New Poor Law deserves particular attention
in the context of the rehabilitation and training of child inmates: its progressive educational provisions. Some education and training had always
been provided as reflected in the case of Jonathan Saville cited above.
The New Poor Law replaced sometimes effective but haphazard provision with a requirement to educate. Improvement did not always follow.
Henry Price, who remember was in a position to compare both regimes,
favoured Old Poor Law provisions. Under the old regime, as we have
seen, a fellow inmate, who was crippled with rheumatism but nonetheless
'a scholar for those times', taught the boys and girls to read, write and
cipher. Their lessons involved hymns, verses of the New Testament and
sums. The curriculum was unimaginative and the learning was by rote
but lessons went well beyond the basics taught in working-class schools
of the era. Under the New Poor Law, the boys were sent outside to a local school but the townspeople objected. A schoolmaster was hired but,
as Henry Price observed, 'with no more knowledge than myself'.[51] The
educational provision deteriorated alongside the food and treatment.

Indeed, overworked and untrained teachers who resorted to rigid discipline and ritualized violence proliferated in the working-class schools of
the era. Not surprisingly, workhouse schoolmasters exhibited these tendencies in spades. The master in charge in Henry Morton Stanley's workhouse school was a sadist 'soured by misfortune, brutal of temper and
callous of heart'.[52] Presided over by this dictator, the workhouse school
appeared a world within a world. Five of the thirty boys it contained
were, according to Stanley, just as clever as the brightest in the best public schools, and this elite attracted praise from Inspectors of Schools and
the Board of Guardians. Despite the miseries of the environment and
the terrors of the schooling, Stanley reported two reasons for gratitude:
first that he discovered 'God by faith as the father of the fatherless' and
second that he learned to read.[53] In an era when perhaps a third of all
boys remained illiterate, this was not less eligibility. Indeed Stanley remained in the school until at least 1856, not entering the labour force
until much older than the majority of his peers. Moreover, the curriculum

went beyond mere literacy though Stanley provided little detail. When the boys in his group began to leave the workhouse aged about fourteen, they were able to obtain employment for which education was a requirement. Stanley himself was earmarked to become second in command in the detested workhouse school! Although he baulked at this posting, the education he had received allowed him to mount the economic and social ladder when he subsequently emigrated. Lucy Luck, George Elson and Joseph Bell, educated in similar workhouse schools, learned to read, write and compose.[54] Sojourns in New Poor Law workhouses may have been psychologically damaging but they often offered an education that was not less good than the schooling available to the sons of poor but independent workers. In their own way, then, such workhouses fostered layers of belonging and participation amongst those who might otherwise have been left to the mercies of the external labour market or even removed to communities where they were unknown and about which they in turn knew little.

So far, the autobiographical evidence has supported the idea that 1834 did see significant discontinuity in welfare provision and that this discontinuity affected children. However, my third finding is one of continuity. My argument is that both Old and New Poor Laws encouraged early working, but they did so in different ways and with different implications. *Childhood and Child Labour* contains overwhelming evidence suggesting that children valued family life, loved parents (especially mothers), cared for siblings and benefitted from the stability and affection provided. Families also provided education, training and many of the basic lessons of life. The doles provided by the Old Poor Law to families in distress allowed them to survive temporary crises and even to persist longer term. Their children were not scattered among distant kin or placed in the poorhouse, and at least some of them were enabled to stay in host communities when they might otherwise, and according to the strict letter of the law, be removed. In short, the support to fragile families enabled them to raise their children, who therefore enjoyed similar care and protection as the children of the independent poor. Bill H ____ grew up in a large family headed by an agricultural labourer whose chronic under- and unemployment stranded the family on the margins of survival and periodically prompted Bill's mother to ask for assistance, with all the consequent risks associated with settlement laws. Bill's later life was chequered; he found it hard to settle down, frequently fell out with employers and even spent time in jail (where he learned to read and write). His mother, whose other children became responsible members of the community, held him responsible for her grey hairs. However, through his many trials and tribulations, Bill remained in contact with his mother and siblings and eventually, with family support turned over 'a new leaf'.[55] The Ashby-Townsends, permanently dependent on parish relief, also sustained a meaningful family life. Elizabeth worked in the fields and houses of her community to support herself and her children, but she still found time to read to them and even to model and play with little clay figures. Her son grew up to become a respected public servant and local historian and his son to be an authority on that same Oxfordshire poor law that had come to his grandmother's rescue.

However, assistance came at a cost. As emphasized above the doles were insufficient alone to support families, which, under both Old and New Poor Law, were expected to help themselves. A key component of this self-help involved the contributions of children. Parents, children and poor law officials shared the expectation that it was children's duty to contribute and the level at which assistance was offered was usually enough to prompt early work. Bill H____ started work aged seven and Joe Ashby at eleven, both young for their time.[56] Problems might arise when no traditional work was available locally. Then parents and poor law officials might come into conflict about the propriety of certain jobs. This was especially likely if the parish proposed sending children some distance to work in factories or signing them up to the merchant service or royal navy. Sometimes parish officials had to get tough and make a family's relief conditional on the employment of its older children, but usually poverty, leavened but not relieved by the finely calibrated subsidies, was sufficient. On the other hand, employment gave a sense that children belonged to their host communities and may have made removal less likely. Certainly, as we have seen, the lack of reference to settlement laws and removal in these autobiographies is compelling.

Parish apprenticeship provided the traditional channel through which poor children came to work. Modelled on its private counterpart, it resembled the familiar and trusted institution whereby children received board, lodging and training, which they paid for by current and future labour services. Traditional parish apprenticeships extended beyond pauper to merely poor children and involved a wide range of village trades. It must have looked like a sensible way to enable the poor to become semi-independent as children and productive adults who might then support families. Its popularity and persistence suggest some success. Settlement examinations show that parish apprenticeships did provide training and most ex-apprentices worked at their trades. The autobiographical evidence supports this finding since it contains examples of boys and youths actively seeking to enlist parish help with a placement. Such lads clearly valued apprenticeships, even those arranged by the poor law. Moreover, Honeyman's recent work suggests that the incorporation of the new demand from textile factories into the traditional traffic did not always lead to degeneration and exploitation.[57] Parish apprentices even in factories were fed and clothed, learned discipline and skills, and often continued in employment as adults. Parish officials were not always uncaring brutes who sent local children to dead-end jobs far away so as to evade possible future liabilities.

The autobiographical evidence is replete with material with which to explore such structures. Orphan John Shipp was boarded with a local farmer. Although the farmer's wife was kind and motherly, the farmer himself could not brook Shipp's natural boisterousness and so resorted to violence. Shipp acknowledged his own shortcomings but his account emphasizes the way in which unwanted children often imposed on unwilling and resentful guardians were likely victims.[58] Not surprisingly, such children collaborated with poor law officials in agreeing to apprenticeships as a way out of such unhappiness. Shipp himself volunteered for the army, and served in a poor-law regiment, a forgotten but effective way of disposing of dependent children. Brutal though this story sounds, in fact Shipp subsequently did well for himself. In the army, Shipp picked up some education and twice won commissions from the ranks. He ended on an army pension as master of Liverpool workhouse. Children incarcerated in workhouses were also likely to agree to an apprenticeship, especially if it was given the right gloss. Robert Blincoe was famously promised a diet of roast beef and plum pudding and a training that would enable social mobility, but a desire to get away could ensure compliance even if the advertising was less romantic. Robert Collyer's father and mother, both the orphans of sailors lost at sea, met after being sent to the same West Riding textile factory. Collyer senior was sent from London:

> He told me they gave him the free choice to go or stay and wanted him to stay; but he said 'I will go'. And so it was he went out, not knowing whither he went, was bound apprentice, and served his time.[59]

Nonetheless, the burgeoning market for child labour may have crowded out traditional pauper apprenticeships as illustrated by the history of the Marcroft children, orphaned around 1820 in Middleton Lancashire.[60] Destitute children in this flourishing area of family farms and handloom weaving were hired out to farmers and weavers. The Marcroft children were placed in four different families: Betty to weaving; Frank to be a boatman; Sally to be a farmer's girl; and, Joseph to be a collier. None appear to have been formally apprenticed. The family book notes that 'The career of each child was much varied. Like pieces of timber from a wreck on a troubled sea, no person can tell when and where they would come to rest'. Betty, a 'strong active girl', and by dint of hard work and a sensible marriage, made her way back into the respectable working-class from which she had fallen. Frank was employed in the rough and dangerous work of stone carrying and was crushed to death in a loading accident a few years later. Joseph worked at a coal pit for a year or two, became very fond of horses and 'having no one to lead him to a well-paid class of work', became a carter. He spent his life in this poorly paid, unhealthy and dangerous job. Sally, despite being a clever textile worker, without parental protection and guidance foundered in a sexually predatory environment.[61]

Although pauper apprenticeships were discouraged for the first decade of the New Poor Law, children continued to be placed with families seeking cheap labour. The demand for boy labour from the rapidly expanding coal industry provided one important outlet. Thomas Ince was sent out of Wigan Workhouse and George Lloyd was handed over by the Cardiff authorities both to colliers looking for boys to assist in underground work. George, it transpired, was too young to work underground. He was passed on carelessly to become 'apprentice' to a shoemaker even though this contravened his original master's agreement to return the boy if the placement was unsuccessful. While George enjoyed shoemaking, his master soon acquired a potato ground and pigs, which became George's responsibility: 'What with the allotment the pigs and shoemaking I was between the devil and the deep sea. Jack of all trades and master of none'. Eventually George ran away and after several adventures found a better situation again as a collier's boy but with a decent family, a placement that resembled the boarding out of earlier times.[62] Similarly J. H. Howard, whose earliest memories were of 'hunger, loneliness, and the exasperation of [being] a not-wanted child in the various houses of my mother's poor relatives', ended up in an orphanage near Swansea, where

> [u]pon reaching the age of thirteen, children of the Homes were given out to families who applied for boys or girls, – not of necessity, with the object of adoption, but usually, for the purpose of apprenticeship, or cheap labour.[63]

By this time there was little to distinguish pauper apprenticeship from cheap labour; they had elided.[64] Certainly John Edward Reilly reported from Sheffield Workhouse:

> In those years, when tradesmen or miners wanted a strong lad who could do the work of a man, act as a messenger boy and do most of the domestic service in the kitchen, they applied to the Guardians. These were never loath to part with their charges to make room for the stream of new-comers.

John was placed with a brutal drunkard, who beat both his wife and new 'apprentice' but when he absconded back to the workhouse, he was birched and returned 'on the understanding that I now belonged to this man'.[65] Other examples abound. Lucy Luck and her brother were both sent from the workhouse to a local silk factory when they were not yet nine years old without the protection and support that an apprenticeship (even a pauper apprenticeship) provided. Lucy's complaint was not about the work she was required to do but the disreputable lodging found for her by the relieving officer.[66] If children of an earlier era were vulnerable to abuse by being bound to a particular employer, children of a later one were threatened by being cast adrift without structure or support in a frightening and dangerous world. It remains striking against this back-drop that the autobiographical evidence contains almost nothing by way of a discussion of the ways in which such pauper children belonged to their communities or of the issue of settlement. Indeed, one of the few explicit references to settlement in these sources suggests the laxity of the machinery of scrutiny and removal with respect to children. Attracted by a little red-headed dog, Snowden Dunhill followed a cart from Bever-ley to Spaldington and so somehow became separated from his parents. Dunhill was not the type of child to blend into the background but his stay in Spaldington became extended; indeed, he said, '[b]eing consid-ered in the light of an orphan, having no father or mother to look after me, I was much noticed by the farmers in the place, so much so as to be finally considered by them as having gained a settlement'.[67]

Meanwhile, Henry Price's reminiscences of the relationship between the workhouse and the labour market hint at the possibilities for cor-ruption embedded in this interface. Boys from Warminster Poorhouse, where Price was resident from 1832, were employed at an old factory where they manufactured chair seating. Aged about eight, Henry was put to work making horsehair seating. The work was dull and monotonous and the boys received no wages, but the employment was irregular, and at least in Henry's case, left time for schooling. Later a carpenter 'in want of an apprentice' came to the House and selected Henry. Terms were agreed. There was to be a two-month trial during which time Henry was to live with the family, subsidized by the parish to the tune of eighteen pence per week. Henry fared well under these arrangements, though not learning much carpentry. Alas eventually the subsidy stopped and Henry was returned to the workhouse.[68] Whether this was a New Poor Law economy measure or marked a pre-arranged milestone by which Henry was supposed to have become so productive that the subsidy was no lon-ger needed remains unknown.

While the Old Poor Law's apprenticeships were undoubtedly always less eligible tickets into less desirable trades and potentially disastrous if children fell into the hands of cruel masters, in many instances they provided lifelines. Spiralling costs of relief, increasing numbers of abandoned and orphaned children, and perhaps even an increasing reluctance to use the settlement and removal system to its full extent put pressure on traditional arrangements. Batch apprenticing to textile factories was just one of the ways in which standards declined. The rejection of pauper apprenticeship by the New Poor Law, allied with reforms to the settlement system which progressively made residence-based criteria the key to belonging, meant that some children who previously would have been trained in the community were instead retained in the workhouse where they received some schooling. This enabled them to seize opportunities that came along in later life. However, as is evident from the autobiographies, the old impulses to farm children out soon reasserted themselves supported by a burgeoning market for child labour. Children perhaps even younger than the pauper apprentices of the previous regime were abandoned to fend for themselves in an unregulated labour market unprotected by the formalities of indenture and with the authorities disclaiming further responsibility. Left in an entirely unsuitable and indeed perilous situation, with no skills and no friends, thirteen year old Lucy Luck exemplified the New Poor Law's fit with the capitalist labour market: 'The parish people sent me a parcel of clothes: no box to put them in. They had quite done with me now'.[69] While historians have engaged in increasingly complex ways with the means by which belonging could be claimed, evidenced and maintained, for pauper children it remained a fragile notion indeed.

Conclusion

Quantitative analysis of a large sample of working-class autobiographies suggests that neither Old nor New Poor Laws were able to compensate for the adverse effects of poverty on pauper children. A childhood encounter with the parish authorities meant children started work at younger ages and achieved lower occupational outcomes than did peers growing up in poor but independent families. Perhaps it was impossible for parish officials to extend the same opportunities to child paupers as those enjoyed by the independent poor. Indeed, the principle of less eligibility required pauper children to experience disadvantage. What we do not know is what would have happened to these children in the absence of the poor law.

To what extent did help from the authorities improve their life chances even though it did not place them on a par with the children of the independent poor? In their life stories, many autobiographers, while complaining of the miserliness of the Old Poor Law or the bleakness of the New, nonetheless acknowledged that without help things could have been much worse. Outdoor relief held families together when children were small, even defying the letter and logic of settlement law. Poorhouses saved orphans and abandoned children from beggary, crime and 'utter destitution', and perhaps from removal where the settlement status of their fathers was unclear. Assistance took many forms. It could be small: a suit of clothes enabling a child to take a job in service or a pair of shoes to prevent chilblains from becoming a disability. It could be large: an apprenticeship premium or passage to join emigrant kin in the United States. It could be pleasant – more or nicer food, for example – or it could be less digestible such as workhouse schooling. As the Introduction to this volume suggests, rights and benefits could be bundled and unbundled at the will of officials. But within the packages of assistance, perhaps wrapped in unpalatable or painful conditions, pauper children often found lifelines back from indigence and deprivation to self-respect and independence. The poor law really was a system of chances as well as constraints and controls.

As far as the change to the New Poor Law is concerned, a new institutional coldness replaced the benign neglect and haphazardness of the Old Poor Law. Over time, all children started work later, but under the New Poor Law the gap between pauper children and the independent working-class actually widened. The New Poor Law effectively dismantled the regulation of child labour through parish apprenticeships and the related statutes while continuing to place workhouse children in employment. At the same time, families lucky enough to get outdoor relief were probably prepared to send children to work younger to avoid the workhouse. However, if the gap in age at starting work widened, the longer-term effects of poverty on occupational outcomes appear to have faded. Perhaps the New Poor Law's educational provisions enabled graduates of workhouses to seize subsequent opportunities and to make their way in the world. It would be interesting in this sense to know the difference between the life chances of those who managed to avoid the settlement and removal system and those who did not. The fact that so little material is available on this issue suggests that the intent of the 1795 legislation restricting the ability of officials to remove women and children, allied with changes to settlement criteria occasioned by the formation of unions of parishes under the New Poor Law, had indeed been played out. Children, in other words, may have been progressively excluded from the settlement system.

Children who grow up in care in modern Britain do poorly in educational and occupational terms. They are more likely to become addicted to drugs or alcohol, to become pregnant as teenagers and to be homeless on our cities' streets. Since we in our rich society lack the political will to remedy this injustice, we should look with less condescension on institutions which cared for handicapped children like Jonathan Saville, educated unwanted bastards like Henry Morton Stanley, and which raised drunkard's daughters like Lucy Luck, and even attempted to rehabilitate vagabonds like Snowden Dunhill, while enabling all four to write vivid and moving accounts of their encounters with the English poor laws.

Notes

Humphries's recent book, *Childhood and Child Labour in the British Industrial Revolution* (Cambridge, 2010), used a large number of published and unpublished autobiographies by working-class men to document children's experiences of this momentous economic transition. The book presented estimates of age at starting work, occupational inheritance, probability of apprenticeship, duration of schooling and factors conditioning human capital formation, each richly contextualized by qualitative material drawn from the life stories. In this chapter, she uses the same sources to focus in detail on the effect of involvement with the poor law on subsequent occupational and educational outcomes and to gauge the effects of poverty and different welfare regimes on children's life chances. She is currently extending her study of these sources to include women's memoirs, which reveal hitherto hidden gendered aspects of working people's experiences of industrialization. The author is grateful for support provided through an ESRC Professorial Fellowship (RES-051-27-0273).

1. There is a considerable literature on the history of the poor laws. No attempt is made here to provide a comprehensive survey, though the Introduction to the volume does offer a synthesis.

2. The classic account remains S. Webb and B. Webb. 1927. *English Poor Law History Part 1: The Old Poor Law*, London; S. Webb and B. Webb. 1929. *English Poor Law History Part 2: The Last Hundred Years*, London. For a recent survey, see D. Englander. 1998. *Poverty and Poor Law Reform in Nineteenth Century Britain, 1834–1914*, London. For the aims and objectives of the 1834 reformers and an annotated guide to the Poor Law Report, see S. G. Checkland and E. O. Checkland (eds). 1974. *The Poor Law Report of 1834*, London.

3. A. Digby. 1976. 'The Rural Poor Law,' in D. Fraser (ed.), *The New Poor Law in the Nineteenth Century*, Basingstoke, 149–170; A. Kidd. 1999. *State, Society and the Poor in Nineteenth Century England*, Basingstoke.

4. S. King. 2000. *Poverty and Welfare in England 1700–1850: A Regional Perspective*, Manchester.

5. The classic positions are scrutinized econometrically in G. R. Boyer. 1990. *An Economic History of the English Poor Law 1750–1850*, Cambridge. See also G. R. Boyer. 1989. 'Malthus was Right After All: Poor Relief and the Birth Rate in South-Eastern England', *Journal of Political Economy* 97(1), 93–114.

6. See M. Blaug. 1963. 'The Myth of the Old Poor Law and the Making of the New', *Journal of Economic History* 23(1), 151–184.

7. P. Solar. 1995. 'Poor Relief and English Economic Development before the Industrial Revolution', *Economic History Review* 48(1), 1–22.

8. S. Horrell, J. Humphries and H.-J. Voth. 1998. 'Stature and Relative Deprivation: Female-headed Households in the Industrial Revolution', *Continuity and Change* 13(1), 73–115; S. Horrell, J. Humphries and H.-J. Voth. 2001. 'Destined for Deprivation; Human Capital Formation and Intergenerational Poverty in Nineteenth-Century England', *Explorations in Economic History* 38(3), 339–365.

9. See K. Honeyman. 2007. *Child Workers in England, 1780–1820: Parish Apprentices and the Making of the Early Industrial Labour Force*, Aldershot; J. Humphries, *Childhood*; A. Levene. 2010. 'Parish Apprenticeship and the Old Poor Law in London', *Economic History Review* 63(4), 915–941.

10. P. Kirby. 2003. *Child Labour in Britain, 1750–1870*, London, 29–30; Humphries, *Childhood*.

11. Honeyman, *Child Workers*.

12. Exceptions include: K. D. M. Snell. 1985. *Annals of the Labouring Poor: Social Change and Agrarian England, 1660–1900*, Cambridge; J. S. Taylor. 1989. *Poverty, Migration and Settlement in the Industrial Revolution: Sojourners' Narratives*, Palo Alto.

13. T. Hitchcock, P. King and P. Sharpe (eds). 1997. *Chronicling Poverty: The Voices and Strategies of the English Poor 1640–1840*, Basingstoke; T. Sokoll. 2001. *Essex Pauper Letters 1731–1837*, Oxford.

14. Details concerning the definition and measurement of the various variables used in the study are provided in Humphries, *Childhood*.

15. Humphries, *Childhood*, 172–209.

16. The difference between means is 1.33 years (t-stat = 3.675; sig. = .000).

17. Unfortunately this involves the loss of five cases where date of birth is unknown.

18. The difference between means is 1.25 years (t-stat = 2.227; sig. = .027).

19. The difference between means is 1.59 years (t-stat = 3.392; sig. = .001).

20. Any subdivision of the sample around 1834 produces the same result which is not sensitive to the particular cut-point adopted here.

21. For more methodological details, see Humphries, *Childhood*, 203–207.

22. CAMSIS rankings are explained in Humphries, *Childhood*, 89.

23. The difference between means is 10.60 points (t-stat = 3.635; sig. = .001).

24. The difference between means is 16.67 points (t-stat = 4.78; sig. = .000).

25. The difference between means is 3.61 points (t-stat = .825; sig. = .410).

26. See Humphries, *Childhood*, 246–253.

27. For more on 'breadwinner frailty', see Humphries, *Childhood*, 172, 367–368.

28. See Humphries, *Childhood*, 69, 193. Other autobiographers who grew up in fatherless families partially supported by poor relief include George Meek, Will Thorne, Joseph Ashby and John James Bezer, and their circumstances are discussed in *Childhood*. Unless otherwise stated further details of and supporting documentation for the cases discussed below can be found in *Childhood*.

29. K. D. M. Snell and J. Millar. 1987. 'Lone Parent Families and the Welfare State: Past and Present', *Continuity and Change* 2(3), 387–422.

30. Cited in Humphries, *Childhood*, 193.

31. See Humphries, *Childhood*, 120–121, 244–245.

32. See ibid., 75, 99, 186, 302.

33. T. Sanderson. 1873. *The Life and Adventures of Thomas Sanderson*, Darlington, 10.

34. Snell and Millar, 'Lone Parent Families'; J. Humphries. 1998. 'Female-Headed Households in Early Industrial Britain: The Vanguard of the Proletariat', *Labour History Review* 63(1), 31–65; S. Williams. 2005. 'Poor Relief, Labourers' Households and Living Standards in Rural England c. 1770–1834: A Bedfordshire Case Study', *Economic History Review* 58(3), 485–519.

35. For further discussion of lone fathers' experiences, see Humphries, *Childhood*, 70–72.

36. M. Saxby. 1806. *Memoirs of a Female Vagrant Written by Herself*, London, 24–27. The 1806 version is held in the British Library and a transcription has been made by Stuart Hogarth of King's College, London. A later edition is held in the Angus Collection at Regent's Park Library, Oxford.

37. See Humphries, *Childhood*, 297–298.

38. See ibid., 248, 299, 301.

39. J. Saville. 1848. 'Autobiography', in F. A. West, *Memoirs of Jonathan Saville of Halifax; Including his Autobiography,* London.
40. Saville, 'Autobiography', 8.
41. Cited in Humphries, *Childhood,* 327.
42. For further discussion of the problematic position of children in New Poor Law workhouses, see J. Humphries. Forthcoming. 'Care and Cruelty in the Workhouse: Children's Experiences of Residential Poor Relief in Eighteenth and Nineteenth-Century England,' in N. Goose and K. Honeyman (eds), *Children and Childhood in Industrial England: Diversity and Agency, 1650–1900,* Aldershot.
43. See Humphries, *Childhood,* 70, 199.
44. See ibid., 136, 199.
45. For other cases of separation in the workhouse, see Humphries, 'Care and Cruelty'.
46. See Humphries, *Childhood,* 70.
47. See ibid., 363.
48. See ibid., 69, 144, 174, 193.
49. Cited in Humphries, *Childhood,* 324–325
50. Ibid., 325–326.
51. Ibid., 328.
52. Ibid., 324.
53. Ibid.
54. For further detail on these cases and relevant references, see Humphries, *Childhood.*
55. B. H____. 1861–62. 'Autobiography of a Navvy', *Macmillan's Magazine* 5, 146–148, 151.
56. Note that other contributors to this volume, Anne-Lise Head-König and Andreas Gestrich, think that these ages at starting work are high in comparison with continental Europe.
57. Honeyman, *Child Workers.*
58. For this and similar cases, see Humphries, *Childhood,* 248, 297–298, 136, 199, 303.
59. Cited in Humphries, *Childhood,* 301–302.
60. For the history of the Marcroft family, see W. Marcroft, *The Marcroft Family,* Manchester, 1886.
61. Marcroft, *Marcroft Family,* 17.
62. See Humphries, *Childhood,* 199, 303, 71, 174, 199, 303.
63. Cited in Humphries, *Childhood,* 78–79, 162–163.
64. Howard's own placement was partially motivated by a need for a collier boy. Fortunately, his adoptive mother was a generous and loving woman.
65. Cited in Humphries, *Childhood,* 303.
66. Humphries, *Childhood,* 304.
67. S. Dunhill. 1831. *The Life of Snowden Dunhill, Written While a Convict at Hobart Town,* Beverley.
68. Cited in Humphries, *Childhood,* 304.
69. Ibid., 305.

CHAPTER FIVE

BELONGING, SETTLEMENT AND THE NEW POOR LAW IN ENGLAND AND WALES 1870s–1900s

Elizabeth Hurren

Introduction

In the 1830s, a London barrister, George Benson Coode, was appointed assistant poor law commissioner. He was asked by Edwin Chadwick to write the legal framework of the Poor Law Amendment Act (1834).[1] Coode had a reputation for drafting legislation in plain language, something that was considered vital if the New Poor Law was to be administered more uniformly in England and Wales. Coode later published a new legal handbook,[2] which subsequently became a core text for poor law officials.[3] He took a great deal of interest in settlement laws, which seemed to him archaic, a block on mobility of labour and simply far too complex.[4] Coode acknowledged that for practical reasons overseers of the poor often paid welfare claims for their non-resident poor living elsewhere, but this was a convenient custom without legal status.[5] This, and the multiple layers of case law that attached to the settlement system in 1834, made poor relief a game of chances. For him a lyrical poem from 1805 still best summarized the situation in respect of settlement laws:

A woman having a settlement
Married a man with none;
The question was, he being dead,
If what she had, was gone?

Quoth *Sir John Pratt* – Her settlement
Suspended did remain,
Living the husband: But, him dead,
It doth revive again
Chorus of Puisne Justices
Living the husband: But, him dead,
It doth revive again.[6]

This type of legal farce came about because of what historians like David Green describe as 'half remembered facts stretching back over many years'.[7] Nobody really understood the precise meaning of settlement clauses and there was a great deal of difference between settlement rights in law, practice and custom. Custom, Coode suggested, created a powerful sense of moral entitlement which would not be eradicated under the New Poor Law. He thus informed Edwin Chadwick that unless the laws of settlement were fundamentally altered the New Poor Law would be compromised.

Of course, and as is well-known, settlement law was not fundamentally altered in 1834.[8] By the 1840s, however, and especially in the light of increasing evidence of entrenched regional differences in the scope, locus and scale of relief, the appetite for reform was rekindled. George Benson Coode was once again commissioned, this time to review the settlement system and a Royal Commission on the Settlement Laws was established. Coode was asked to investigate the Midlands heartland as a test case and he concluded in an article for the *Justice of the Peace* journal of May 1848 that Leicester, Cambridge and Huntingdon constituted a 'locality fit for enquiry'.[9] He did not take long to reach the conclusion that his instincts of 1834 had been correct, writing in his final report that: 'I have been unable to find a single … man who could give me any evidence how the law of settlement works'. Coode suggested that settlement law was 'a law of repression' limiting employment mobility and opportunities to practice self-help, increasing both indoor and outdoor relief claims. Moreover, the existing laws created 'universal discontent' amongst guardians, relieving officers, overseers of the poor, and employers. From the perspective of the 'respectable poor' such laws were much resented, especially by those living on the threshold of relative to absolute poverty who sometimes paid rates and at other times came into the ambit of the New Poor Law at vulnerable lifecycle moments.[10]

The *Report of George Coode, Esq. to the Poor Law Board on the Law of Settlement and Removal of the Poor* is regarded by welfare historians as a formative document. Coode proposed that the old settlement terms (by birth, marriage, apprenticeship and so on) should be replaced by a simpler residency-based system. He appreciated that guardians of the poor might be concerned about a highly mobile workforce moving from one poor law union to next and overwhelming ratepayers with new claims. Coode thus proposed that each person had to reside for a minimum of five years in a new location before he or she gained the right not to be removed back to the notional parish of settlement. While these proposals were in fact enacted, they caused as many problems as they solved. Most guardians conceded that they could no longer after five years of permanent residency insist that a poor relief claimant be sent back to their home parish. Nor, as had previously happened in many cases, could officials write back to a place of birth or marriage to insist that each community pay for its non-resident parishioners, a mechanism common in Belgium and The Netherlands as others in this volume suggest. This did not mean, however, that after five years residency each person automatically gained the right to claim poor relief in his or her new location. Many people rented property and they often moved around an area to work, shifting premises to do so. If they crossed a poor law union boundary – and this was easy to do at the edge of cities or county towns that bordered suburban and rural areas – then technically they had to accumulate a new five-year residency qualification. Landlords soon got wise to the new system and many insisted that at annual rate assessment time on Lady Day (25 March) their rental occupants had to leave the premises overnight and move out of the immediate area.[11] This then meant that the families in question were not legally resident for five continuous years. Given that the same property owners elected guardians it soon became apparent that those who paid the bills for the poor law were essentially seeking to cancel the new settlement rights and thus reduce local welfare bills.

The poorest were, unsurprisingly, attuned to these legal shenanigans. They responded by being evasive about their whereabouts when the rating officer or the relieving officer came to call. Men who worked out of the area often returned on Sunday to maintain visibility in the local community, thereby ensuring they technically did not lose their five-year residency-based settlement rights. In crowded cities it soon proved to be impossible to monitor the movement of residents into, and out of, busy lodging-houses, and that confusion gave rise to opportunities to evade the law.[12] Nonetheless it was also the case that some guardians took evasive action by interpreting the 'irremovability' clause in an underhand way. Some said that whilst the law prevented a claimant from being removed after five years, technically it did not state explicitly that this meant they were in turn entitled to make a poor relief claim where they now resided. In other words, they could stay put but they had to be self-reliant, too.

For individual paupers, these complexities of the 1830s and 1840s could have devastating results. By way of example, in 1823 Mary Wil-

liams, a pauper from the parish of Cwmyoy in Bwlch near Powys made
a request for poor relief. She was described by the overseer of the poor
as being a woman of 'weak intellect' who lived with her 'Uncle David
Norman ... assisting him on his farm'. The economy in this area of south
Wales was not, however, robust and she soon became a drain on the
household finances. Mary's brother therefore agreed 'to take and maintain his sister' with one proviso: James and Ann Williams (his wife) asked
the vestry of Cwmyoy in Bwlch to supplement Mary's subsistence with
an allowance to be paid to the overseer in Longtown over the border in
the Wye Valley where they lived. Once the New Poor Law came into force
in 1834, however, this arrangement was disputed on the grounds that it
was contrary to settlement law. A settlement examination was taken as
follows:

> Examination of Ann Williams of the Township of Longtown ... touching the
> place of the legal settlement of Mary Willliams ... who upon her oath saith, The
> said Mary Williams the pauper has been of weak intellect for many years past
> and is unfit now from derangement of her intellect to be examined upon oath
> as to her settlement. In or about the year [1823] my late husband who was her
> brother agreed with the Overseers of the Poor of the Hamlet of Bwlch ... to
> take care of and maintain her at his house in the said Township of Longtown.
> She came to live there with us, the sum agreed for was seven shillings a week.
> I received money from Daniel Morgan then one of the Overseers of the poor
> of the said Hamlet of Bwlch several times during the first year after she came
> to live with us for and towards her maintenance. The Overseers of the Poor of
> the said Hamlet of Bwlch lowered the weekly payment for the pauper time after
> time till it was reduced to about half a crown a week and I received the money
> for her from several Overseers of the Poor of the said Hamlet until after the
> New Poor Law Act was passed in the year 1834. I am certain that the said Mary
> Williams was never married and that she hath done no act whereby to gain
> any parochial settlement since the year [1823]. The said Mary Williams is now
> chargeable to the said Township of Longtown and I receive weekly the sum of
> Two shillings from the overseers of the poor of the Township for maintainance
> [*sic*] and taking care of her. [Signed] Ann Williams.
>
> [Note on reverse:]
>
> I took the said Pauper to Giles Dukes on Saturday 15th day of August 1846 in
> the Hamlet of Bwlch. [Signed] James Parry.[13]

Notwithstanding a long history of reciprocal payments, Mary Williams
had no legal settlement in the New Poor Law union that contained Longtown over the English border. The settlement examination thus resulted
in her being physically removed back to the hamlet of Cwmyoy in Bwlch.
Ironically, within weeks of Mary Williams' removal to Wales, she obtained
the legal right to go back and live with her nuclear family again under the

Poor Law Removal Act of 1846 (10 and 11 Victoria c. 110), which for the first time introduced formalized residence-based settlement rights. This was little use to Mary who would then have had to wait a further five years to build up her 'irremovability' settlement rights despite having lived with her brother and sister-in-law from 1823 until 1846.

The situation was only marginally less unsatisfactory for ratepayers and employers. The New Poor Law had singularly failed to deal with the question of what should be done about workers or their families in need of temporary relief, during trade downturns or at slack times of the agricultural year. In such cases, and whatever the letter of settlement law, it was cheaper to pay a little from the rates to retain a workforce so that when local economic conditions improved businesses could expand production. Likewise many women worked when they could to supplement their family incomes, but in childbirth for instance they needed temporary respite from the workplace. A small outdoor relief allowance helped them get back on their feet to start earning again. It did not make economic sense to reject the 'respectable' poor who wanted to work but often needed a little bit of community support from time to time, whether or not they met residence-based or other settlement criteria.

Faced with such realities, central government issued three new sets of guidance to clarify legal entitlements for the able-bodied and their kin: The Outdoor Labour Test (1842), Outdoor Relief Prohibitory Order (1844), and the Outdoor Relief Regulation Order (1852).[14] The Labour Test conceded that work patterns were often seasonal. It was therefore permissible to give temporary outdoor relief allowances. Ideally guardians had to employ those fit for work inside workhouses during the day but they could then return home to their families at night. In urban areas unions still constructing workhouses welcomed this new rule because they could now employ local labour on welfare-to-work schemes. The second regulation order meanwhile applied to rural areas where outdoor relief seemed more lax. In winter when work was scarce and during autumn once harvest was finished, relief levels kept rising outside the workhouse. Many farmers persuaded relieving officers to use outdoor medical orders to fund the local workforce. The aim therefore was to restate that outdoor relief was illegal except under exceptional circumstances, in the hope that this legal clarity would stop abuses in the agricultural heartland. Nevertheless guardians retained the right to fund cases of 'sudden and urgent necessity', and this continued to be interpreted liberally. The third regulation order gave guardians the option of funding women who needed short-term relief without subjecting them to the same labour test as men. It also served to complicate issues of entitlement and settlement. All claimants, whether able-bodied or not, could now make a claim for up to 50 per cent 'in kind' assistance. Some guardians started to pay for a wide range of measures that had previously fallen under medical outdoor relief orders. This included: buying work tools, supplementing rents, purchasing food, paying doctors' bills and funding pauper funerals. The key point to appreciate about this 'in kind' system was that central government never said what its upper limit should be, only that it must not exceed 50 per cent of a total outdoor relief payment. There was thus no financial check on the goods, rent and general provisions that the poor law could be expected to provide, and for many guardians faced by a growing sense of entitlement in these matters (particularly in urban areas), the five-year residency-based settlement qualification introduced in 1846 (which would become effective in 1851–1852) threatened an unprecedented rating crisis.

The Late-Victorian Poor Law: Retrenchment Rules and Settlement Law

Certainly by the late 1850s, the New Poor Law appeared to have reached a crisis point, a sense encapsulated in this well-known pauper poem:

> What's the use of savin', when they help yer if ye're ill?
> Four bob every week Jemmy, and pay your Doctor's bill!
> What's the use of savin', wi' the Parson close at the door,
> And allays in his kitchen, and he so good to the poor?
>
> What's the use of savin', or putting away your cash,
> And just when you want your money, your club is sure to smash?
> What's the use of savin', and they bury yer too when dead;
> Coffin o'elm, that's all, but who wants a coffin of lead?
>
> There's some abuse them Guardi'ns and say they're hard as stone;
> But folk come to like 'em better the more they're known.[15]

The national welfare bill had risen by 16 per cent annually despite a falling cost of living index.[16] Central government was convinced of the laxity of local administration. Guardians strongly disputed any accusations of mismanagement, pointing to the impact of agricultural recession, an ageing demography, and workhouses ill-equipped for the types of poverty that were most common. Critics also pointed to the settlement laws, blaming them for a lack of labour mobility. A five-year residency qualification seemed excessive at a time when Britain's competitive edge in domestic and world markets was being challenged for the first time.

It was, a general consensus emerged, time to review poor law rules and regulations once more, and especially to revisit settlement law.

Against this backdrop, a trio of legislative changes sought both to control poor relief and to place the issue of settlement at centre stage. The first was the Irremovability Act of 1861 (28 and 29 Victoria c. 79), which reduced the residency period for settlement from five years to three.[17] Its aim was to make the labour force more mobile and thus ameliorate a rising unemployment trend. The problem with the new legislation is that it still did not clarify many of the questions that had remained intractable since 1846.[18] For instance in the intervening years, case law had established that widows could not be removed from their place of residency during the first year after their husband's death. It was unclear, however, whether they were then entitled to make a poor relief claim too. Likewise it was very difficult to refuse emergency medical aid to the sick and dying because case law had established that this group could claim medical relief for a period of up to twelve months even if they technically did not satisfy the three-year residency qualification. The 1862 Parochial Assessment Act was also directly related to questions of settlement.[19] It prevented landlords from interfering with rating procedures and decreed that if a property was empty but was known to have had tenants living in it even for a short time during the previous twelve months, then it would warrant no reduction in poor rates. Central government hoped that this would prevent unscrupulous ratepayers from evicting tenants temporarily and mean that the new three-year settlement residency-qualification would benefit local employers.

The Union Chargeability Act of 1865 further buttressed these changes and fundamentally altered the financial basis of poor law accounting for the next thirty years. A complicated act, its essence was that rather than making each parish in a New Poor Law union pay for its poor, the union collectively became responsible for the poor of all parishes. In other words, 'property rather than poverty' was now 'the basis of parish contributions to the common expenses of the union'.[20] Civil servants hoped that this would stop small parishes acting like 'quarrelling member states' within each poor law union area, and persuade them not to interfere with the residency-based settlement system because it would no longer be financially worthwhile pushing the poor away to the next village, town or parish.[21] To further bolster these changes a decision was taken to reduce once more the period of residency-settlement qualification from three years to one year by the end of 1865.

In theory, then, gaining and keeping a settlement should have become much easier in the 1860s, a precursor to more secure relief entitlements.

Yet, and as we have seen above, important flaws in the legal provisions existed for both paupers and ratepayers. For the latter group, especially in urban and industrial areas, an accelerated rate of spending coincident with easier settlement terms loomed from the late 1860s. In turn, it was this threat, combined with central perceptions of the stubborn failure of relief costs to fall, that led directly to the crusade against outdoor relief in the 1870s and 1880s, a movement which was to have a profound effect on pauper experiences of both poor relief and the settlement system.

The crusade began with a decision by civil servants at the Poor Law Board (PLB) in the late 1860s that they needed to work more closely with large charitable bodies – especially the Charitable Organisation Society (COS) – to better co-ordinate welfare and philanthropic spending and to establish local level welfare partnerships which could work both to eradicate outdoor relief claims and reduce random acts of charity.[22] This objective was outlined in a new central government circular known as the Goschen Minute (1869) that became the first stage in the 'crusade against outdoor relief'. Boards of Guardians were now encouraged to co-opt COS members. Each poor law union would then function as a pauper 'clearing house'. Relieving officers were to report all claims to guardians, but not before claimants had a home visit from a COS visitor. If after scrupulous enquiry the claim was judged to be 'deserving' then the pauper would get a temporary outdoor relief payment for a maximum of four weeks. Those whose circumstances did not improve were referred back to their poor law union and offered only indoor relief. This new claims system tried to ensure that only genuine claimants obtained help and the work-shy would be disciplined in workhouses.

In 1871 the PLB merged with the newly created Local Government Board (LGB) to form a ministry of state controlling most aspects of local government administration.[23] The LGB was more powerful than its predecessor because it ranked amongst the most senior government departments and its president had a seat in Cabinet. From its inception LGB staff had to find new ways to reduce outdoor relief nationally. The Poor Law division had the biggest budget deficit and therefore dominated the LGB policy-making agenda. Alarm was expressed when senior civil servants calculated that only about 16 per cent of paupers were being relieved within workhouses, despite extensions to workhouses being built everywhere after the Union Chargeability Act.[24]

The LGB secretary, Henry Fleming, took personal responsibility for re-examining outdoor relief procedures. He concluded that a new set of guidelines should be issued to every poor law union. The Fleming Circular of December 1871 was underpinned by a sense that Guardians had failed in their duty to protect ratepayers by refusing outdoor relief claims.[25]

Fleming stressed the need for cost-saving initiatives. Guardians must only grant outdoor relief in very exceptional circumstances, and for a maximum period of three months.[26] This policy change had an immediate impact on the 'makeshift' economies of the poorest. Women who had been able to claim relief under the 1844 and 1852 Orders now had their funding cancelled. Single mothers deserted by their spouses had to enter the workhouse with their offspring (legitimate and illegitimate). If a young mother could go back to work she was encouraged to hand over the care of the children to workhouse staff. Older men had to enter the workhouse or be self-sufficient. All outdoor claims were to be inspected on a regular basis, by means of a home visit from either relieving officers or a District Medical Officer for the Poor (DMOP). No poor law doctor, however, was allowed to override the relieving officer, even on medical grounds. All able-bodied cases were reviewed weekly and medical cases once a quarter. The Fleming Directive thus initiated the second stage of the crusade against outdoor relief. Although, at first, guardians supported the new central government orders, many soon changed their minds because they were angry about residency-based settlement qualifications being reduced to just one year and the consequent increases in potential rate liabilities.

In 1873 meanwhile the LGB commissioned a third report on outdoor relief. It investigated if the Fleming's Directive had been a uniform success. This review was undertaken by Henry Longley, one of the LGB's most senior inspectors.[27] He found that there was still a high degree of local variability. What became known as the Longley Report (1873–1874) was thus the third and final stage in the crusade against outdoor relief. It reiterated the themes of the Goschen Minute of 1869 and the Fleming Circular of 1871, but also proposed more radical measures. Longley made a firm statement that all outdoor relief was now to be abolished. Once offending poor law unions had been identified, they would be pressurized into conforming. Officially, then, a full-scale crusade against outdoor relief had begun by 1873–1874, and it was unquestionably linked to fears about the financial implications of 'irremovability' amongst ratepayers. It is to the question of pauper experiences of the poor law and settlement system during this key period of poor law history that the rest of this chapter turns.

The Crusade against Outdoor Relief

For two decades, from 1873 to 1893, a sustained campaign to eradicate outdoor relief thus dominated central and local government thinking.[28] Guardians could avail themselves of a matrix of explicitly allowed or implicitly tolerated cost-cutting measures such that we cannot trace a single uniform 'crusade against outdoor relief' and there is often considerable discrepancy between 'what the state *thought* should happen ... [and] what actually *did* happen'.[29] Centrally collected statistics on the adoption of 'crusading' measures – which would seem to show that only around 7 per cent of all poor law unions, containing 16 per cent of the entire English population, followed a harsh 'crusade' policy – are misleading in this context.[30] In this very British set of cost-saving initiatives guardians might champion some crusading policies and at the same time ignore orders they disliked. Similarly, they might support a respectable aged pauper and try to reject the sick pauper who cost a lot more. Or they might start out as ardent crusaders and later turn into moderates once they had made enough savings to satisfy their ratepayers. They could consistently ignore central government, or react when pushed to do so, usually at inspection or audit times. Ad hoc and regionality were the two major watchwords of this period.[31] This said, the reduction in residency-based settlement qualifications to just one year after 1865 was both an important catalyst for the retrenchment experiment and a constant thread in the measures deployed to realize it. Overall it is possible to identify six 'crusading' features that were tried at a regional, intra-regional and local levels. All aimed to both reduce relief levels per se and manipulate the various legal complications of the one-year residency-based settlement qualification to avoid paying outdoor relief claims.

Measure 1: Reducing Medical Bills

Medical outdoor relief was expensive and tended to be a long-term drain on welfare resources.[32] Under the Old Poor Law around 25 per cent of the local community had some form of medical care paid from the poor rates by the early nineteenth century. Cancelling it was therefore emotive. An added complication for both the Old and New Poor Law was that the definition of 'medical relief' differed both regionally and often between neighbouring places.[33] What was custom in one area was not necessarily practised in another. Where custom did exist, it tended to be valued highly and to apply to all poor irrespective of settlement. It was necessary therefore for guardians to use some very creative techniques when attacking medical aid. In practice, the best way to be underhanded was to delegate the unenviable task of cutting relief lists to the DMOP. It might seem surprising that they were prepared to co-operate. Yet, it is easy to overlook the subtle strategy 'crusaders' used to appeal to the local medical profession. They argued that poor law doctors (usually on the lowest career-rung) were enhancing their professional appeal in a district by both being guardians' allies and defending the genuine sick poor. This would enhance their medical reputation in the vicinity and give them a better foothold in an overcrowded medical marketplace.[34] 'Crusading' was thus a logical business move.

In one key example Mr Williams, DMOP from Guilsborough parish in the Brixworth Union (located in mid-Northamptonshire) explained in a letter to the *Lancet* how the crusade seemed to promise to promote his professional services in the 1870s.[35] Later, by September 1890, Williams realized his folly. He complained that 'crusaders' tricked him into instigating medical changes that demeaned the sick poor:

> Some 20 years ago I worked hard and ... with the Board to try to reduce the Outdoor relief (which was then very great) by not allowing Medical extras, except in cases of almost Life and Death, depending on them; ever since the numbers have been steadily decreasing and now the number of orders given by the Board are very few. But I constantly give advice to paupers who are not in any club and cannot afford to pay a doctor ... these cases of course are not returned in the weekly reports but my work must be judged from the number of [official] *list* returns.[36]

Williams noted that the number of poor law doctors had been cut from four to one in the 1880s because fewer medical outdoor relief claimants called for less medical men, saving rates. This meant that he had to travel extensively across the union to attend urgent cases. His contract had also been amended. In an emergency he had to contact the relieving officer to authorize all medical expenditures. Non-urgent cases had to be transferred to the Northampton Infirmary, where guardians contracted-out medical care because it was cheaper. Requests for medical relief relating to 'sudden-accidents' were no longer accepted. Medicines were only issued at the Brixworth Union workhouse dispensary. Extras, like alcohol, bread, meat, and tobacco, were cancelled too. For the first time in poor law history medical aid to the poor was under radical attack. The wider context of these practices can be traced in the LGB annual report of 1881–1882.[37] It announced that although there were 4,042 poor law doctors in 647 poor law unions, distribution was uneven. In moderate areas there were on average six doctors per poor law union; in regions where crusading was popular there were just four. The LGB welcomed this trend pointing to the increasing numbers of Inspectors of Nuisance (ION) who assisted poor law doctors and could eventually replace them altogether. But, of course, they omitted to say that most IONs were not medically qualified and were much cheaper replacements on average salaries of just £10 a year compared to a poor law doctor's pay structure of £50 to £75 per annum.[38]

Other attacks on medical relief were more specifically framed around issues of settlement. In 1877, the LGB decided to tighten medical aid particularly in East Anglia because Norfolk poor law unions were very resistant to change being of a radical political tenor. A new retrenchment offensive was co-ordinated by Courtenany Boyle, poor law inspector for the area.[39] He was instructed to specifically find out the best way to cancel all medical outdoor relief services for the elderly. Boyle surveyed the aged poor on outdoor medical orders. He reported that in Swaffham union there were 372 medical paupers aged between sixty and ninety-five; in Hoxne union there were 432 medical cases aged between sixty-six and seventy; in Kings Lynn union there were 361 cases aged between sixty-five and seventy-nine. The problem had been exacerbated by changes in settlement law. The one-year residency-qualification gave rise to a greater demand for medical services and more claims for assistance at home by rural labourers who did heavy fieldwork and were physically worn out by fifty years of age and who under older legislation could have been removed. He concluded that the best way to tackle this problem was to compel medical outdoor paupers to go 'into almshouses' and then in-sist they support themselves after a month. When that policy failed, they could be moved to workhouses. This was the only way to keep shuffling people around the system to avoid paying for their long-term care on outdoor relief.

Poor law unions elsewhere adopted equally effective underhand mea-sures. Sheffield Guardians, for example, dealt with their outdoor medical relief applications by categorising claimants on a 'deserving-scale' – Class A merited 5s, whereas the less deserving got only 4s, 3s, down to 2s 6d per week, respectively.[40] Only 'respectable' paupers received a Class A allowance. At the same time a general policy statement was made that if terminal illness merited the expense, then claimants were directed to the expanded workhouse facilities in many areas. Manchester Union 'claimed that 51.24%' of its pauperism was the result of 'causes directly arising from drinking habits' and so it vigorously attacked medical outdoor relief extras like alcohol for pain relief.[41] In Liverpool outdoor numbers fell from 11,601 in 1871 to 3,233 by 1877, primarily through an attack on medical relief for the newly settled poor.[42]

Measure 2: Making Children Pay for their Parent's Upkeep

Generally when 'crusading' got underway it was led by a number of com-mitted zealots. Typically they would be COS members such as the Rev. Phelps at Oxford or Mr W. Griffin at Southampton poor law unions. Men like this were also sometimes national figures with a political standing who believed they could lead a 'crusade', like the leading Whig peer 5th Earl Spencer or Mr Albert Pell Conservative MP for South Leicestershire. Often, as at Birmingham (Joseph Chamberlain MP) and Manchester (Mr Alexander McDougall Jr), prominent businessmen dominated poor law administration. These people insisted that their business expertise and ideological drive would deliver savings.[43]

In this context the elderly in particular were judged expensive long-term claimants to be discouraged. It was hard to ignore them and impossible to get rid of them. One aspect of the crusade was thus a new emphasis on family duty and kinship responsibility, particularly for those newly settled under reduced residency clauses. Such responsibilities were forcefully highlighted in anti-welfare circulars posted in the waiting room of each workhouse and at church doors in provincial districts.[44] At the same time, adult children of ageing parents who claimed poor relief were prosecuted for their maintenance in local petty session courts.[45]

Court records, as David Thomson explains, are 'filled with reports of … prosecutions of sons, and a few daughters as well' after 1870.[46] Returning to the Brixworth union in mid-Northamptonshire, twenty-six prosecutions were made between April 1872 and April 1877.[47] Magistrates adjudicated that adult children should be responsible for their parent's upkeep. Court orders for maintenance allowances were fixed at 2s 6d per week. If the sum was paid to the court, then the relieving officer paid a matching outdoor relief dole. If the maintenance order was not paid to the court officer, the allowance was halted. Though, in this example, the numbers might seem small, the impact of the prosecutions was to make more children come forward to maintain their relatives. Since Brixworth eventually cut its outdoor relief bill from around £6,000 to just £350 per annum, most accepted they had to make a permanent contribution. Cambridge union had a similar practice but it hoped to avoid expensive court costs through a pledge system, known as an 'Agreement to Contribute'.[48] Guardians persuaded all the friends, relatives, and kin of elderly paupers to sign pledges. All were reminded that non-payment would result in formal prosecution. At Banbury union Rev. C. D. Francis suggested that outdoor relief tended to 'undermine that sense of duty we owe to parents, which nature and religion has planted within us' and so court orders were justified.[49]

Ordinary people were not of course impassive in the face of such attacks. The National Agricultural Labourers Union (NALU) defended its members charged with this type of poor law maintenance order. For example, at Fakenham in Norfolk in 1875 the Swaffham NALU branch employed a solicitor, T. M. Wilkin from Kings Lynn, to defend Robert Towers, 'a labourer summoned by Richard Horsley Relieving Officer of

the Walsingham union to contribute towards the maintenance of his father John Towers.' He was prosecuted under '43 Eliz., c2, sec. 7. Act' and
ordered to 'relieve and maintain' his elderly parents 'being of sufficient
ability to do so'. Wilkin defended that due to weather 'vicissitudes' Towers 'did not have sufficient ability' to maintain his parents throughout the
year. The solicitor asserted that this 'was an application to relieve the Poor
Law Union and not to maintain the parent'.[50] As in most instances, the
case was lost. Clearly, it did not matter if an elderly person had a one-year
residency-based settlement qualification when his or her access to regular
poor relief was being undermined in a concerted way.

Measure 3: Enhancing Charitable Contributions

Central government statistics traced cost savings of some 35 per cent
nationally once crusading was underway. Civil servants produced a series of league tables and praised zealous 'crusaders' while condemning
the recalcitrant. Historians often dismiss the psychological importance of
this annual reporting scheme. Eager 'crusaders' took the statistics very
seriously, competing against each other to achieve record annual savings.
Privately however they were also aware that after the initial savings had
been achieved, it would get harder to reject the most needy-cases. The 5th
Earl Spencer (Chairman of Brixworth Union) admitted for instance that
'reform *must* be slow when dealing with old people'.[51] The challenge was
to institute year-on-year savings. One way to overcome this problem was
to persuade local charities to bear a heavier burden. In Brighton, Leicester, London, Oxford, Reading and so on, this was co-ordinated by the
local branch of the COS.[52] In those crusading unions where the COS had
a minor presence, the situation was more complex.

Thus, in major cities like Manchester and Liverpool, and large rural
unions, such as Atcham (Salop), Bradfield (Berkshire) and Brixworth
(Northamptonshire), Guardians established Charity Visiting Committees.[53] They reviewed all sick clubs, burial societies, clothing clubs, coal
charities, as well as bread and meat gifts, managed by leading philanthropists. Those findings were used to calculate what financial benefit
charitable provision was on average to the labouring poor in their area.
Using this information the mixed-economy of welfare was tabulated into
a matrix against which outdoor relief allowances were reassessed. The
best documented examples of how this operated are contained in the land
agents records and private papers of leading 'crusaders' in the Brixworth
union.[54] The case of the Griffen family of Haselbech parish is illustrative
of many.

Table 5.1. The Griffen Family – Income and Outdoor Relief Assessment

Actual Family Income Per Week		
Value of Charity, Gleaning and Casual Wages	13s	2d
Value of Weekly Medical Outdoor Relief Allowance	8s	4 ½ d
Money 4s		
Five Loaves 4s 4½d		
Estimated Income per week – charity and poor relief	21s	6½d
Total Family Outgoings Per Week before Poor Relief	13s	2d
Rent, Food, Clothing, Linen and Club Subscriptions		

Note: The surplus = The value of the medical outdoor relief allowance

Mrs Griffen's outdoor relief allowance was reassessed as part of a general charity review in 1873–1874. A guardian produced a household budget from his enquiries showing that the family makeshift economy relied on four income streams – medical outdoor relief; charitable donations (milk, firewood and clothing); customary right to glean; and casual wages – and his summation of the situation is reproduced in Table 5.1.[55] Yet these figures should not be taken at face value because the way that guardians calculated the family income was unfair. The weekly benefit of customary rights and casual wages were estimated and no allowance was made for their unpredictability. With a sick husband and five children under fifteen years old, the Griffens needed a combination of reliable welfare and charity income streams to stay outside the workhouse. In fact, Mrs Griffen estimated that the right to glean garnered seventeen stone of flour, an annual value of '50s' enabling her to pay her rent over the winter; milk, firewood and clothing charitable payments were worth '25s' per year. Any extra financial pressures would force the whole family into the workhouse. This family was living on the economic margins of their community and this third 'crusading' measure threatened their independence. They were instructed to fall back on more charity provision. But this was impossible.

Charities in the area protested that their endowments were intended to supplement poor relief, not replace it. The Chairman of Harlestone Charity summarized the feelings of many when he wrote to guardians in May 1878 explaining why a blind widower named John Howard's request for a pension of 2s 6d to replace outdoor relief was rejected:

> The Great Question to be decided between the Brixworth Guardians and the Parish of Harlestone is this:- Is such a man as Howard which is nearer 80 years of Age ... and now blind ... without any means of his own, after having worked

all his days whilst he was able, on the Land at Harlestone to be supported by the occupiers of the Land or merely sympathised with and sent for help to the Trustees of a Fund the Donors of which never imagined that their gifts would be used to lessen the burden imposed on ratepayers.[56]

Two issues worried local charity administrators: that this third crusading measure was destroying customary notions of reciprocity; and that withdrawing relief might trigger deep social unrest. But those leading the crusade were undeterred, even though both the Griffen family and John Howard would cost more to admit to the workhouse. Guardians hoped that creating a climate of fear would persuade potential claimants, many of them newly settled after the change in the length of residence criteria, to migrate. The Griffen family did and Northampton union soon inherited their poor relief problem.[57]

Measure 4: Pushing the Settled Poor Out

A fourth crusading measure was thus simply to increase out-migration amongst the poorest, such that moderate poor law unions in the vicinity of a crusading union often inherited their neighbours' socio-economic problems. Indeed, sampling poor law returns to central government clearly reveals that savings in one area tended to mean the opposite nearby. The process was of course made possible by changes to settlement law and the advent of the one-year residency qualification. Guardians could ignore the fact that they had shifted their social problems and rate costs onto their poor law union neighbours because within a year they would have a permanent solution to the problem of poor individuals and families. Inter-union disputes could drag on for months or years, giving the migrant poor rights of settlement before contentious cases were anywhere near resolved.

Examples of these practices abound, even if they rarely appear in the secondary literature. Manchester Poor Law Union issued crusading rules in 1875. They were very influential, copied throughout Lancashire and further afield such as Brighton, Carmathen and Ruthin.[58] Yet, whereas Manchester outdoor relief numbers fell to around 16 per cent of the total population by 1890, those nearby at Chorlton and Salford had '62.5 per cent and 49.5 per cent rises', respectively. A similar pattern emerged at Birmingham so that even the LGB inspector, Mr F. D. Longe, admitted that success had impacted on suburban ratepayers at the union's fringes. At Brighton outdoor relief numbers fell from a peak of 4,503 in 1871 to just 2,000 by 1880, but paupers simply moved to the surrounding rural districts of West Sussex.[59] Likewise, Northampton union guardians complained that inward migration was happening on a regular basis. They stated clearly that the reduction in settlement law to a one-year residency qualification made this feasible. For example, in July 1882 they reported to the LGB that 56 unemployed vagrants from the Brixworth union had to be taken into the workhouse.[60] There were also 158 children under sixteen years of age admitted. Rural neighbours may have been a crusading success but this was only because Northampton ratepayers now footed the bill for their rejected poor. To these paupers, the law of settlement and residence-based criteria had little functional meaning.

Measure 5: Moving the Insane

There is an extensive historiography detailing care in the community versus the expansion of county asylums in the Victorian era.[61] The Poor Law Amendment Act decreed that

> nothing in this Act contained shall authorize the detention in any workhouse of any dangerous lunatic, insane person, or idiot, for any longer period than fourteen days; and every person wilfully detaining in any workhouse any such lunatic, insane person, or idiot, for more than fourteen days, shall be deemed guilty of a misdemeanour: Provided always, that nothing herein contained shall extend to any place duly licensed for the reception of lunatics and other insane persons, or to any workhouse being also a County Lunatic Asylum.[62]

For the purposes of this chapter it is essential to concentrate on how funding changes for mental-health provision (broadly defined) impacted on some of the most vulnerable members of the pauper community by the later Victorian period.[63] In theory, they had residency-settlement rights after one year by the 1870s, but in reality they were often shuffled around the poor law system to save costs, making a mockery of the law.

Traditional accounts of the expansion of workhouse care, the building of infirmaries and the construction of county asylums emphasize that the insane poor were examined more and concentrated together with the expansion of the mental health system.[64] Yet, the majority were in fact still cared for within their family and kinship circles.[65] For others, specialist institutions concentrated resources where they were needed most by caring for those that were sometimes violent and needed to be removed from the community; those that had a sexually transmitted disease like tertiary syphilis or epilepsy; or those that were socially ostracized because of a medical history connected to a severe physical disability. During the crusade these categories of pauper were targeted.

Historians agree that the Lunacy Amendment Act (25 + 26 Victoria c. 111 1862) started a process of shifting insane paupers around the welfare and healthcare system. Ruth Hodgkinson explains that it primarily 'aimed at the movement of chronic patients out of crowded asylums into workhouses to make room for others'.[66] It is important to keep in mind that this trend happened during a decade when the Treasury was very alarmed by the spiralling costs of poor relief bills. The Lunacy Commission had new powers to 'order the transfer of lunatics from workhouses to asylums at the same time as giving local asylum visitors and poor law guardians the power to provide for a limited number of chronic lunatics in workhouses'.[67] So the vulnerable in mental ill-health were moved more frequently around the system, to and fro, depending on how much they cost local ratepayers to keep. If it was cost-effective to care for them in a workhouse then that is where they resided; but as soon as it was made more financial sense to go to a county asylum, they were removed. Then if the position was reversed, they were sent back again. By the time therefore that the Metropolitan Poor Act (1876, 30 and 31, Victoria C.6) came into force there was a lot of debate inside the system about who should pay and for how long. If there was now to be a common fund for London and it would pay for the cost of lunatics then unsurprisingly guardians decided to transfer patients to the capital's asylums. They quickly filled up and poor law unions now decided to transfer their cases to any town or city with an asylum that would take them in. After all, the Common Fund would pay for the overflow. A lot of poor law unions that had made provision for the insane now found that lunatics were being removed to their infirmaries wherever there was any capacity.[68] Against this backdrop, and to encourage the building of more county asylums the Treasury agreed with the LGB that once it was established in 1871 a new grant-in-aid payment of '4 shillings per week' would be paid for each outdoor relief pauper labelled 'insane', 'idiot', 'imbecile' or incapable of leading an independent life, to relieve ratepayers.[69] They would be compensated for expensive poor relief bills and the extra payment would act as an incentive to transfer insane paupers from a workhouse infirmary to a county asylum. Officially the insane poor were treated like children when it came to settlement law (having rights with their birth parish and then on the basis of residency with kin), but in reality the system was set up to facilitate their regular removal on cost grounds.

Recent historical work on this grant-in-aid system has concluded that the financial incentive was not enough to convince guardians to forcibly remove paupers from a locality. Robert Ellis takes the view that historians have exaggerated the human 'effect of a grant that transferred a proportion of the cost of asylum care from local to central funds'.[70] His study of admissions to two county asylums in Yorkshire concluded that there is 'little evidence to suggest that the grant was responsible for a change in either the size or composition of the asylum population'. He reached this conclusion by doing record linkage work between asylum admission books and their annual reports to the Lunacy Commission. It is important to appreciate, however, that linking asylum records and central government reports on insanity has important limitations. Both sources provide only a snapshot of admission flows to and from the asylums and this means it is very difficult to get a sense of how pauper lunatics were being moved around the entire welfare system. What is missing from this historical landscape are the poor law records of those guardians most committed to keep insane paupers on the move for financial incentives.[71] Without this sort of record, those paupers who were moved far away, sent back, redistributed locally, stayed just six months, returned home for a short time, then had to claim relief again and re-enter the asylum system are usually undercounted. In practice, the 'crusaders' were very creative in the ways that they kept moving people on. Indeed, it is worth remembering that the grant-in-aid could be claimed more than once, so if someone was sent to an asylum, then recovered, and was released but soon found they needed help at a later date, guardians could claim for them twice because they had re-entered the system as a new lunatic patient each time. In effect some of the most vulnerable became balance-sheet entries, removed from their localities.

Nationally an estimated 40,345 outdoor paupers were categorized lunatic between 1853 and 1893 and removed under this creative accounting system.[72] Initial research has begun to throw up some intriguing evidence of its practical implications in Bolton Union, which had a growing lunatic expenditure problem that it was desperate to resolve.[73] In the period April to September 1882 the union spent a total of £6,284 on 435 lunatics.[74] To add perspective, this bill was more than the entire annual indoor poor relief costs of nearby unions. As Table 5.2 shows, Bolton guardians attacked medical outdoor relief for those with mental ill-health, losing 100 claims between 1882 and 1885. This however meant that the insane became an indoor relief burden and so the logical way to off-set that bill was to move them onto local asylums. Any that were released back and then needed care later had to endure the process all over again. This ebb and flow is very difficult to envisage from central government insanity and pauperism returns but was clearly something which stood outside the 'rights' seemingly engendered in settlement law.

Table 5.2. Bolton Lunatic Admissions, 1882–1885

Year	1882	1883	1884	1885
Outdoor	364	293	299	268
Indoor	89	142	127	174

Sources: Compiled from BRO, GBO, 23/2, 'Summaries of Bolton indoor relief, 1851–97'; GBO/9/58–62, 'Bolton workhouse admissions and discharge registers'.

Measure 6: Cutting Support Staff

Historians agree that the 'crusading experiment' sometimes contradicted its own political economy.[75] It promoted cost-savings but the methods used to achieve cost-effectiveness sometimes increased overall poor law expenditure. Outdoor relief was attacked, but then indoor relief costs rose at a faster rate because of the number of vulnerable people who needed to come into the system. This meant that capital costs had to grow to fund more building programmes, with higher loan charges ironically increasing rates by some 62 per cent nationally from 1871 to 1893.[76] Part of the response to this problem was salary savings. Although there were more building schemes, and fixture and fittings expenditure rose as extensions were built to workhouse infirmaries, this did not mean that care inside the new premises improved. Staff salary reductions got lost in the statistics, merged into financial accounts that disguised an overall reduction in personnel. In fact, reducing staff both inside and outside the workhouse was cost effective. Forcing the needy into the workhouse meant that salary bills were spread over more paupers and so unit wage costs fell. Buildings may have been built around an ageing pauper population *but* the key point is that in general there were fewer staff in them. One example in this short review is illustrative of many in the Midlands.

Staffing in the Brixworth union was contentious.[77] In 1873–1874, two relieving officers, four local doctors, and six midwives administered poor relief outside the workhouse. Workhouse personnel included a master, matron, chaplain, schoolmistress, porter, children's nurse and adult nurse. Once the crusade was underway the staffing profile was reviewed. Guardians reduced the number of relieving officers from four to one, increasing the post's salary to £150 per annum. This made the relieving officer one of the highest paid poor law officials in England and Wales. They judged that since he was at the forefront of major cost-savings initiatives, taking tough decisions, a higher salary was justified as a form of performance-related pay, motivating him to achieve targets. But how was this salary paid without ratepayers objecting to the expense? To compensate, around 1880 the number of poor law doctors was also reduced from six to just one, and no further payments were made to midwives. The remaining doctor's salary was reduced from '£78 to £50 per annum' to reflect the fact that he now attended fewer outdoor medical cases, encouraging him to seek more private work. Whereas in the past a poor law doctor might have lobbied hard on behalf of the poor, now the sick were encouraged to enter the workhouse quickly. As a result, an annual saving of £282 to the salary bill for those staff that had previously dealt with outdoor relief cases was achieved.

Coinciding with these salary changes for outdoor personnel, two decisions were taken to reduce staff costs for those working inside the workhouse too. First, Guardians broke the rule that the number of family members inside a workhouse should be limited. Instead they employed the Giles family as master (father), matron (mother), schoolmaster (son) and schoolmistress (daughter), assisted by the Levin family who were porter (husband) and nurse (wife). Keeping indoor relief management *in the family* meant that retrenchment guidelines were followed closely. Second, they needed to make further savings to pay for the relieving officer's high salary. Indoor relief salaries were thus frozen and this even included the master, paid at '£50 per annum'. Unsurprisingly, by the 1880s, there was a high turnover of staff. But, by then, this suited guardians. It created the impression that the workhouse was poorly staffed and therefore to be avoided. For the same reason, many larger provincial poor law unions did not pay their masters well. Liverpool paid £350, Birmingham £250 and Manchester £240 per annum respectively.[78] Medical historians are right to point to well funded sick wards and infirmaries but they do not take account of salary changes, personnel reductions, and what this might be telling us about falling standards of medical care where 'crusading' was popular in the late Victorian era. The rights afforded to the settled and newly settled poor as the law changed meant little if the poor were frightened into not exercising them.

Conclusion

Settlement law in England was complicated and yet it shaped the experience of being poor until the turn of the twentieth century. In theory a revised residency-based system under the New Poor Law (moving from a five- to one-year qualification by the 1880s) should have benefitted the poor. The problem was that like so much nineteenth-century legislation, key terms, such as 'irremovability', were never defined. Expensive and time-consuming case law had to be used to settle disputes. It was therefore how settlement law was *interpreted and acted upon* that really mattered. This chapter thus ends with a human story that epitomizes just how much a poor relief claimant could get shuffled around the system of chances that was the New Poor Law of the late-Victorian decades.

On 9 July 1890 a Church of England chaplain from Spratton village in mid-Northamptonshire wrote a lengthy letter to the LGB about the Brixworth Union Board of Guardians. He set out the sad case of a labourer who had recently died after being shuffled around the poor law system.[79] John Llewellyn Roberts explained that John Wykes (aged twenty-seven) was the main breadwinner for his wife (aged twenty-five) and two small children (aged six and two). After harvest in 1889, John contracted 'quinsy' and then by Christmas he caught 'influenza ... for five weeks in all'. During his illness he relied on the goodwill of neighbours and his savings rather than make a claim for medical relief because he was a proud man and hard worker. In early April 1890, 'he returned to work in the Iron pits' but then developed 'pleurisy and inflammation of the lungs of an exceedingly severe character'. The chaplain claimed that 'during this time he [John] was destitute and dependent upon private Charity'. At the end of six weeks of severe illness, John had no choice but to make a claim for medical outdoor relief.

Dr Harpur, the local medical officer, made a house visit and found that John Wykes 'was still dangerously sick and not in a fit state to be removed'. But the relieving officer refused to accept a prognosis that removal was life-threatening and the Board of Guardians backed his decision. John was told that there was no medical outdoor relief and he had to come into the workhouse. The chaplain then explained that whilst this long bureaucratic process was going on, 'in the meantime the pulmonary inflammation had resulted in an ulceration of the lung with constant discharge of a most malignant and offensive character'. Harriet Wykes knew her husband was dying and she asked the chaplain to visit their sick room to give John spiritual comfort and the last rites.

On entering the sick room, the chaplain told central government that the smell of decay and death was so foul that 'it was difficult for either Mr Harpur or myself to remain even for a few minutes in the room'. He admired the fact that John Wykes was 'nursed day and night by his wife and mother ... I may add to my belief that no other persons in the village would have been induced to nurse him'. The chaplain tried to persuade John to go into the workhouse so a paid doctor could attend him but he replied that he knew he was dying, and 'he wished to die at home'. The chaplain then spoke to the guardians on the family's behalf, quoting John's words:

> First, the feeling that if he was to die, he wished to die at home; Secondly, that he knew that there was no-one to nurse him in the [work]house – that no paid person would endure the horrible offensive stench and that he should be left to the attendance of the aged male paupers, who would desert him in his hour of need; Thirdly, that there was no trained nurse in the [work]house whose duty it was to sit up with him all night.[80]

Again the guardians refused him any medical care at home. Dr Harpur was so concerned about the man's deteriorating physical condition that he supported the chaplain's plea for outdoor medical relief, but to no avail. John Wykes started to fade away while everyone argued about the cost of his basic welfare needs. Meanwhile, the guardians insisted to central government that:

> John Wykes ... would receive the necessary support and attendance [in the workhouse] arrangements for nursing such cases are amply sufficient. Had John Wykes accepted the offer of the [work]House he would have been placed in the upper sick ward which is at present empty and would have had very necessary attention under the direction of the Medical Officer. His wife would have been permitted to remain with him and assist in the nursing.[81]

When this information was conveyed to the chaplain and Dr Harpur they both questioned why central government did not think that there was something suspect about an empty sick ward and low staffing levels. After all, poor people were living longer and so more, not less, should have been inside the workhouse of an agricultural district. The local poor feared the Briwxorth workhouse and the parsimonious nature of healthcare indoors. They avoided seeking help at all costs and often until it was too late. This was why the infirmary rooms were empty. Harriet Wykes was permitted to nurse her husband but this was because there was only one daytime staff member and no night-duty nurses to care for the poor anymore. Despite the fact that they told central government that John Wykes was 'dangerously ill and not in a fit state to be *removed*' the system wanted to keep moving him on, or shuffling his case around, but certainly it did not want to accede to a dying wish to take his last mortal breath at home. Eventually, John Wykes was in so much pain that Harriet and her mother-in-law had to put him on a cart and convey him to the workhouse. There he died soon after, removed from his place of belonging.

John Wykes had options whilst he was able-bodied. He could have moved to Northampton town and benefitted from the new settlement laws. It would only have taken twelve months for him to gain residency-rights by the 1890s. Yet he had kin and family locally, worked hard, and was a respected member of his community. For these reasons he chose to live and work in the Brixworth Union. That however was a critical mistake once he became seriously ill. There were no palatable choices or good outcomes for someone like John Wykes who had paid rates when in work but was judged an economic failure when seriously ill. Settlement laws that ought to have empowered John Wykes were to no avail when guardians systematically sought to undermine the law.

Notes

1. For central government reports by B. G. Coode on his New Poor Law legal work in 1833–1834, see http://www.nottingham.ac.uk/mss/online/online-msscatalogues/cats/newc_5thduke12cat.html.

2. B. G. Coode. 1845. *On Legislative Expression: Or, the Language of the Written Law*, London.
3. On this transition, see S. A. King. 2000. *Poverty and Welfare in England, 1700–1850, A Regional Perspective*, Manchester, 18.
4. On Coode's attitude, see D. Feldman. 2003. 'Migrants, Immigrants, and Welfare from the Old Poor Law to the Welfare State', *Transactions of the Royal Historical Society, Sixth Series* 13, 92.
5. D. R. Green. 2010. *Pauper Capital: London and the Poor Law, 1790–1870*, London, 55.
6. R. Burn. 1805. *The Justice of the Peace and Parish Officer*, 20th ed. London, vol. 1, 766.
7. Green, *Pauper Capital*, 55.
8. K. D. M. Snell. 2006. *Parish and Belonging: Community, Identity and Welfare in England and Wales, 1700–1950*, Cambridge, 81–161, on settlement law and disputes.
9. B. G. Coode. 1848. 'Law of Settlement', *Justice of the Peace*, 6 May 1848, 299.
10. The National Archives [TNA], British Parliamentary Papers [BPP], 1851. *Report of George Coode, Esq. to the Poor Law Board on the law of settlement and removal of the poor, being a further report to those printed in 1850–1851*, London, 1–352.
11. E. T. Hurren. 2007. *Protesting about Pauperism: Poverty, Politics and Poor Relief in late-Victorian England*, Woodbridge, 72.
12. T. Crook. 2008. 'Accommodating the Outcast: Common Lodging Houses and the Limits of Urban Governance in Victorian and Edwardian London', *Urban History* 35, 414–436.
13. Herefordshire Record Office [HRO], G71/53/11, 'Resettlement order for a Longtown pauper, Mary Williams from Cwmyoy, Bwlch', dated 1846.
14. Hurren, *Protesting*, 19–20.
15. Quoted in A. Pell. 1900. 'Outrelief: A paper read at a poor law conference as chairman of the central committee held at the Crewe Arms hotel on Tuesday October 14th 1890', *Tracts, 1843–1893*, London, 1–16.
16. Hurren, *Protesting*, 45–52.
17. L. H. Lees, *The Solidarities of Strangers: The English Poor Laws and the People, 1700–1948*, Cambridge, 1998, 219.
18. K. D. M. Snell. 1985. *Annals of the Labouring Poor: Social Change and Agrarian England, 1660–1900*, Cambridge, 80.
19. D. Englander. 1998. *Poverty and Poor Law Reform in Nineteenth-Century Britain, 1834–1914: From Chadwick to Booth*, New York, 20–21.
20. Englander, *Poverty*, 21.
21. M. E. Rose. 1981. 'The Crisis of Poor Relief in England, 1860–1900', in W. Mommsen and W. Mock (eds), *The Emergence of the Welfare State in Britain, 1850–1950*, London, 59.
22. A. Kidd. 1999. *State, Society and the Poor in Nineteenth-Century England*, Basingstoke, 45–48.
23. C. Bellamy. 1988. *Administering Central–Local Relations: the Local Government Board in its Fiscal and Cultural Context*, Manchester, for the LGB's record of administration.
24. R. Humphreys. 1985. *Sin, Organized Charity and the Poor Law in Victorian England*, Basingstoke, 21–28.
25. Humphreys, *Sin*, 24.
26. Humphreys, *Sin*, 24–25, analyses the Fleming Report.
27. K. Williams. 1981. *From Pauperism to Poverty*, Manchester, 96–107, on the Longley Strategy.
28. Hurren, *Protesting*, 2–3.
29. King, *Poverty*, 18.
30. Williams, *From Pauperism*, 98–104.
31. Though from 1871 to 1876, *all* poor law unions in England and Wales tried with some success to stop outdoor relief. The consolidated bill for poor relief (indoors and outdoors)

fell by some £551, 000 (7 per cent), with indoor relief bills rising slightly and outdoor relief falling by £903,000 (25 per cent).

32. See R. Hodgkinson. 1967. *The Origins of the National Health Service; the Medical Services of the New Poor Law, 1834–1871*, London.

33. M. Flinn. 1976. 'Medical Services under the New Poor Law', in D. Fraser (ed.), *The New Poor Law in the Nineteenth Century*, London, 45–66. See also E. C. Midwinter. 1969. *Social Administration in Lancashire, 1830–1860: Poor Law, Public Health and Police*, Manchester.

34. For context, see C. Hamlin. 1988. *Public Health and Social Justice in the Age of Chadwick, Britain 1800–1854*, Cambridge; V. Berridge. 1990. 'Health and Medicine', in F. M. L. Thompson (ed.), *Cambridge Social History of Britain, 1750–1950*, vol. 6, Cambridge, 171–242.

35. *The Lancet*, 23 February 1887, 5.

36. TNA, MH12/8705, letter dated 19 September 1890.

37. TNA, BPP 1881–2. *The 11th Annual Report of the Local Government Board*, London: HM Stationary Office, 51.

38. Hodgkinson, *The Origins*, 1–66.

39. TNA, MH32/8, Courtenay Boyle's report on East Anglia Poor Law unions, medical relief survey dated 1877.

40. Lees, *The Solidarities*, 267.

41. Kidd, *State*, 41.

42. Humphreys, *Sin*, 42.

43. Ibid., 29–50.

44. Williams, *From Pauperism*, 98–99.

45. M. A. Crowther. 1981. 'Care of the Elderly in England: Family or State Responsibility', *Historical Journal* 25(1), 131–145.

46. D. Thomson. 1991. 'Welfare of the Elderly in the Past, a Family or Community Responsibility?', in M. Pelling and R. Smith, *Life, Death and the Elderly: Historical Perspectives*, Oxford, 217.

47. E. T. Hurren. 2000. '"Labourers are Revolting": Penalising the Poor and a Political Reaction in the Brixworth union, Northamptonshire, 1875–1885', *Rural History* 11(1), 37–55.

48. D. Thomson. 1984. '"I Am Not My Father's Keeper": Families and the Elderly in Nineteenth-Century England', *Law and History Review* II, 282.

49. Ibid., 283.

50. TNA, MH12/8700, 'Agricultural labourers, petty sessions, Fakenham Norfolk', 1874–6 files.

51. British Library, Manuscript Department (BL), Althorp Papers, K159, Spencer to Pell, 28 January 1877.

52. Humphreys, *Sin*, 29–49.

53. Hurren, *Protesting*, chapters 1–4 recount this in detail.

54. See Northamptonshire Record Office (NRO), Spencer Papers, Sox 551–71, land agent records; BL, Althorp Papers, K26, K428, K431, misc. volumes 5th Earl Spencer, 1860–1910.

55. NRO, Spencer Papers, Sox 551. Note that an earlier version confirms this budget's accuracy as it appeared in TNA, BPP, *Royal Commission on the Employment of Children, Young Persons and Women in Agriculture*, 1867, evidence of A, Pell, q. 12–13b, 20–22, 426–427, 431–434. These sources have been cross-checked against NRO, RO, 7f5, Misc. Vol., 'The number of poor and working class people in Brington parish, 1871–3', which provides evidence of a local 'mixed-economy of welfare'.

56. NRO, Brixworth Union Guardian Minute Book, PL2/19, David Morton, Rector of Harlestone to the guardians, 9 May 1878.

57. NRO, Misc. Vols., Northampton Union Guardian Minute Books, 1870–1900. These are un-catalogued, having been rediscovered by this author.
58. Humphrey, *Sin,* 35, details Manchester and its influence.
59. Ibid., 41.
60. TNA, BPP, *The 11th Annual Report of the Local Government Board,* London: HM Station-ary Office, report dated 1 July 1882, Northampton Poor Law Union, 264.
61. See, notably, D. Wright, and P. Bartlett (eds). 1999. *Outside the Walls of the Asylum: the History of Care in the Community, 1750–2000,* London.
62. Poor Law Amendment Act (c. 1834, Section 45).
63. J. Oppenheim. 1991. *Shattered Nerves: Doctors, Patients and Depression in Victorian England,* Oxford.
64. See for example A. Scull. 1979. *Museums of Madness: The Social Organisation of Insanity in Nineteenth-Century England,* London and New York; W. F. Bynum, R. Porter and M. Shepherd (eds). 1985–1988. *The Anatomy of Madness, Essays in the History of Psychiatry,* 3 vols., London.
65. An overview of regional studies can be found in J. Melling and W. Forsythe (eds). 1999. *Insanity, Institutions and Society 1800–1914: A Social History of Madness in Comparative Perspective,* London.
66. Hodgkinson, *Origins,* 586.
67. Ibid., 586.
68. Ibid., 151–152.
69. Anon., *Plain Words on Outrelief,* London, 1894, focuses on this financial context for the welfare of the insane poor.
70. R. Ellis. 2006. 'The Asylum, the Poor Law and a Reassessment of the Four-Shilling Grant: Admissions to the County Asylums of Yorkshire in the Nineteenth Century', *Social History of Medicine* 19(1), 55, 71; R. Ellis. 2008. 'The Asylum, the Poor Law and the Growth of County Asylums in Nineteenth-Century Yorkshire', *Northern History* 45(2), 279–329.
71. Dr Cathy Smith, Northampton University, is working on a project that reconstructs Northampton Infirmary, Berrywood Asylum and Northamptonshire poor law unions re-cords in this way. She is spotting the type of trends referred to here. I am grateful to her for sharing her formative research.
72. TNA, BPP, 1882. *Appendix C to the Twenty-Second Annual Report of the Local Government Board,* 268.
73. Bolton Record Office (BRO), GBO, 12/10–13 – 'Bolton board of guardians, newspaper cutting books, 1887–1907 – How to reduce pauper lunatic bills – the single most impor-tant expenditure.'
74. BRO, GBO, 14/2 – 'Half yearly financial statements by the Bolton board of guardians, 1867–1887.'
75. Hurren, *Protesting,* 259.
76. Williams, *Pauperism,* 88–104.
77. Compiled from TNA MH 9/3 – Brixworth union staff returns; NRO, Microfilm M368.
78. M. A. Crowther. 1981. *The Workhouse System: The History of an English Social Institution,* London, 130.
79. TNA, MH12/8705, Letter 9 July 1890, Rev. John Llewellyn Roberts about John Wykes sad case to the Local Government Board, and reply, 2 August 1890.
80. TNA, MH12/8705, Letter 9 July 1890.
81. TNA, MH12/8705, Official Reply, 2 August 1890.

CHAPTER SIX

CITIZENS BUT NOT BELONGING
Migrants' Difficulties in Obtaining Entitlement to Relief in Switzerland from the 1550s to the Early Twentieth Century

Anne-Lise Head-König

Introduction

The question of migrants' entitlement to poor relief has been a much-disputed topic in Swiss history up to the early twentieth century, a reflection of the fact that a high degree of communal autonomy prevented agreement on this matter at cantonal and national levels. From about 1550 to the early twentieth century, to be entitled to poor relief it was necessary to possess 'full' citizenship, which in turn combined three levels of belonging: national, cantonal and local. Local citizenship – the *droit de bourgeoisie/Bürgerrecht* – was the most important: only a commune where one held local citizenship could issue a 'certificate of origin' (*acte d'origine/Heimatschein*). Its possession implied the right to settle freely where one wanted and to be allowed to return to one's commune of origin, and an entitlement to the poor relief given by the *commune of origine/Bürgerort* in case of need, wherever one lived. Migrants' municipalities of residence, for their part, stressed their right to control mobility and to eject newcomers in need of relief who did not possess local citizenship.

So, for a commune, welfare rights were restricted to an identifiable category of recipients: those who possessed local citizenship. Such a status was, from the mid sixteenth century, passed on from father to son and daughter (*ius sanguinis*). An alternative means to acquire it was by

purchase, a costly undertaking since it implied the possession of sufficient financial means never to become a burden on the commune. Many
of the criteria employed elsewhere in Europe and explored by different
contributors in this volume – length of residence, type of work, apprenticeship, payment of taxes – had no purchase in Switzerland. Indeed, over
time localized rules dealing with the acquisition and loss of citizenship
became more and more constraining, such that in the course of the eighteenth and the first half of the nineteenth centuries the acquisition of
local citizenship in one's place of residence became nearly impossible.
Consequently, those whose ancestors had failed to acquire *droit de bour-
geoisie/Bürgerrecht* at the time when it was created remained excluded
from welfare benefits and had little chance to settle elsewhere, a point to
which we return below.

The longevity of these rules is remarkable. For four hundred years the
principle that it was the perennial responsibility of the commune of origin
to assist its own needy citizens according to its own rules survived intact
in most cantons.[1] This reflected the fact that until 1848 Switzerland was
a federation of states in which each canton – and in some cantons each
commune – had its own codes and statutes. These defined the rules of belonging or for being stripped of one's citizenship and right of residence,
for acquiring citizenship where it had not been inherited, for being deprived of civic rights when dependent upon poor relief, and for defining
who could migrate from one canton to another or even sometimes from
one municipality to another within the same canton. Moreover, even after 1848, when Switzerland had become a federal state, the question of
citizenship and the entitlement to relief remained within the competence
of the local authorities and of the cantons. The Federal constitution did
not allow unlimited mobility within Switzerland for those who risked becoming dependent on assistance or were already being assisted. Indeed,
poor relief for those domiciled outside their commune became a matter
for federal legislation only in the 1970s. It was then decided to set a limit
to the responsibility of municipalities and cantons for poor citizens living outside their boundaries so that the financial commitments did not
continue forever after people had left. It is this trajectory from the 1550s
to the twentieth century that forms the basis for the discussion in the rest
of the chapter.

From the Indiscriminate Distribution of Alms to Local Citizenship

In common with many of the European countries analysed in this volume,
the foundation stones for the system of assistance, which in Switzerland

lasted until the twentieth century, were laid in the middle of the sixteenth century.[2] Population growth in a time of economic difficulties produced an ever-increasing number of vagrants and beggars but no opportunities for work. The usual measures of distributing alms indiscriminately proved to be quite inadequate to address the resulting poverty. At their 1551 annual meeting, the cantonal governments decided on a *Bettel Ordnung* which introduced the notion of belonging to a commune or parish, and thus took the first steps to making the specific territorial entity to which they legally belonged – the *commune d'origine/Bürgerort* – responsible for the relief of its poor wherever they might live, inside or outside of Switzerland. The measure had several purposes: to reduce the mobility of the numerous vagrants who needed relief; to expel the 'foreign vagrants and welsch beggars'; and to oblige each community and each parish in the Swiss Confederation to look after its own poor according to its means and resources and thus prevent them from begging elsewhere than in their place of origin.

The concomitant question of how to define belonging and thus who should be entitled to relief confronted contemporaries (as well as subsequent historians) with thorny problems. The issue must be firmly set in the demographic context of the time. Thus, decisions taken in 1551 to address the increasing number of people with no fixed abode was also a reaction against the policy, often practised at the beginning of the sixteenth century, of encouraging an influx of newcomers – from Swabia, Piedmont, Lombardy, etc. (the last two groups being often qualified as 'welsch') – because of local labour shortfalls (*Mangel an Arbeitskräften*). Increasing the workforce had then been necessary as a result of epidemics but also because of a proliferation (*überwunchernden*) of the mercenary service, with its high death rate.[3]

The 1551 decisions were also, however, an indicator of the numerous frictions between the city-states and the more rural cantons, the upland regions and the lowland ones. In times of crisis, the towns of the city-states and the smaller urban centres were often overwhelmed by masses of poor people looking for work, who resorted to begging when there was none to be found. But the poor in need of help were then not only foreign (*fremde*) beggars. They were also indigenous (*heimisch*) people from other Swiss regions. Thus, the new policy, which aimed at lessening the social burden on the towns and the lowlands, was also at least partly an indicator of the huge contrast in communal organization as it existed in the sixteenth century. In most towns, with their often quite elaborate communal institutions and administrative authorities necessary for organizing assistance, it was relatively easy to establish the necessary criteria for defining those who belonged and needed to be helped. In rural areas nothing similar existed, either because such communities had few resources to create a relief fund or their inhabitants had not yet even organized themselves as an independent community. Moreover, in some regions – as was the case in the Jura Vaudois in the seventeenth century – where demographic pressure was not particularly strong and the commune had adequate resources, questions of belonging were hardly pressing.[4]

Perhaps unsurprisingly when set against this context, initial adoption of the 1551 decisions was patchy, and the question of who belonged and what they were entitled to in different places remained uncertain. Nonetheless, by the second half of the seventeenth century, and particularly due to increasing population pressure, the relevant directives had been implemented in nearly all the cantons, albeit with some reluctance.[5] This brought about a number of significant changes, since the decision taken by the cantonal governments to devolve to the municipalities or the parishes the responsibility for looking after their own people had unexpected and highly undesirable consequences: municipalities started restricting access to local citizenship and toughening the rules towards migrants whose work did not generate enough income to survive. In the course of the eighteenth and early nineteenth centuries nearly all cantonal or regional legislations were amended to reinforce defence mechanisms against the settlement of strangers from near or far.

This does not mean that policies were uniform. In most city-states – with their extensive landed possessions – the elites sought to foster mobility within the borders of the state rather than allow in-migration. This was to favour the relocation of labour to less populated rural or upland regions where entrepreneurs needed a cheap and abundant labour force to drive the expansion of cottage industry. For the rural municipalities, though, the influx of large numbers of unqualified immigrants looking for work was of no economic interest. With very few exceptions in underpopulated and peripheral regions, they always favoured restrictive migration policies since they had no direct share in whatever economic benefit – for instance extra-local tax revenues – these migrants produced. And in times of labour crisis they were confronted with the risk that a migrant's commune of origin would not assist them. So, for the municipalities, the objective was to define the concept of belonging as restrictively as possible in order to avoid being overburdened with too many citizens and to insist on the proof that the commune of origin would provide poor migrants with poor relief. The views of municipalities and parishes concerning their responsibility towards the poor were often quite the opposite of those of cantonal governments. The latter maintained that all Swiss should be able to obtain local citizenship, providing them with access to communal resources and a commune to which they could turn in times of need.

The Regulation of Entitlement and Different Layers of Belonging

The cumulative consequence of the policies and normative frameworks outlined above was that different categories of inhabitants existed in local Swiss communities. Their entitlement to poor relief varied from eligibility to total exclusion, which in turn had an impact on their migratory behaviour. Broadly speaking, there were four categories of inhabitants up to 1848, their number varying during the period under observation depending on the individual cantons and on the legislation and practice of the local communities.

To the first group belonged those who benefited from the advantages conferred by full local citizenship and whose economic and 'moral' behaviour entitled them to receive an *acte d'origine/Heimatschein*, similar to the English settlement certificate. Its possession certified that in case of need its owner could return to his or her place of origin, and thus would not become a burden to the commune of residence. In as much as the *acte* guaranteed he or she would not need relief, it allowed its owner to move and settle freely within Switzerland – and abroad – depending on the exact rules on migration employed by receiving municipalities. Without such a *Heimatschein* it was difficult to settle anywhere in Switzerland. Communal authorities delivered a *Heimatschein* only to citizens whose actions were in no way prejudicial to their economic interests or to those who were not at risk of being removed from their place of residence at the cost of the commune. In turn, there were many reasons for refusing to deliver a *Heimatschein:* to avoid long-term obligations towards outmigrants; to prevent movement of people who had accumulated welfare debts to their municipalities, a frequent case at the beginning of the nineteenth century; to control those who were morally suspect or economically useful; to restrict the movement of those who had come into conflict with the law; and to control and punish those who had fathered or given birth to illegitimate children.

The second group comprised the *Hintersassen*.[6] These were people who did not possess local citizenship, but did hold a right to settle in the canton where they lived (*Landrecht*). They often had been unable to acquire full citizenship for financial, political or religious reasons.[7] But their status gave them no rights in the commune, which meant no entitlement to the poor fund, and no share in communal resources, such as forests, pastures and plots of land. Even their social rights – such as the right to marry – were severely curtailed. The precarious status of the *Hintersassen* can be observed in the canton of Glarus in the seventeenth and eighteenth centuries, where this group often had no choice but to stay put in the canton for risk of losing their right to return to their original place of residence if they moved out even for a short period.[8] Their treatment with regard to poor relief was never the object of negotiation; rather right up to the beginning of the nineteenth century they were threatened with expulsion whenever they dared demand better treatment. These citizens – in 1920 called *personnes à demi-droits* – were hardly ever mentioned in the lists of persons to be assisted by the commune. In periods of economic difficulties they received only casual help and had either to survive on alms given them by private persons or by ecclesiastical institutions or alternatively, in some cantons such as Bern, they would be assisted by the canton.

The third group, made up of those who were tolerated in different degrees. *Tolérés* (*Geduldete*) were often the descendants of parents or grandparents who had immigrated to a commune without acquiring any rights of permanent residence, whether at cantonal or communal level. Their number varied in different areas, but they were always forbidden to move, hardly had any economic rights and in some cantons were not even allowed to marry. The final group was that of the *heimatloses* who, up to the mid nineteenth century, were not recognized as belonging to any community at all and thus had no canton or municipality of origin to which they could turn in time of need.[9] The term *heimatloses* was applied to many different groups of people and not only to those who were labelled travellers (*Fahrende*) or without fixed abode (*Nicht-Sesshafte*), who had always been excluded from cantonal and local citizenship. The group also included illegitimate children and 'tolerated' people who had lost their right of abode because of reduced job opportunities and who risked becoming vagrants. A distinctive characteristic of this group, which all cantons and municipalities tried to prevent from settling within their territories, was its increase with the passage of time. Although cantonal sources are incomplete, a rough estimate made in the mid 1850s mentioned 18,300 such people, unevenly distributed among the cantons because of diverging local practices.[10]

Acquisition or Loss of the *Droit de Bourgeoisie* and Entitlement to Poor Relief

How these different groups of inhabitants navigated the rules of their residence, understood the corresponding entitlements and changed their status are more complex questions for Switzerland than in other areas covered by this volume. With very few exceptions, the principles which governed citizenship made it very difficult to acquire a new local citizenship in a different canton that would then entitle the migrant and their family to relief. Neither length of residence nor place of birth guaranteed a settlement that coincided with entitlement to welfare, in contrast to other European states. Moreover, buying naturalization was beyond the reach of most people who wanted to settle permanently elsewhere in Switzerland. Indeed, only a handful of very wealthy people managed to acquire local citizenship in another canton up to the end of the eighteenth century. Apart from the moral requirements – among them a legitimate birth – there were also several financial requirements, including the 'entry fee' (*droit d'entrage/Einzugsgeld*), often a contribution for the poor or the school fund. But the major deterrent from the seventeenth century onwards was the proof of possession of adequate financial means to guarantee that at some point in the future the new citizen or their family would not become a financial burden on the new commune. The required sum was prohibitive in all cantons, so that inter-cantonal relations were often soured by questions of migration, especially with regard to the expulsion of those in need of help.

Up to the end of the eighteenth century, the marked preference, at least in the case of male migrants, for migration destinations outside Switzerland, partly reflects existing restrictions. Other reasons, however, also played an important part. With the exception of Geneva and Basle, employment opportunities for male immigrants were restricted, whereas the urban service sector employed a large number of female immigrant servants. Rural-urban migration for men was thus constrained, and more widely generally to migrate within rural Switzerland were few with the exception of sparsely populated regions such as the territories of the Prince-Bishop of Basle. Indeed, up to the beginning of the nineteenth century most cantons suffered from overpopulation. Even in cantons where industry was expanding there was thus no real need for unqualified immigrants, since there was already a large surplus of irregularly employed or unemployed labour in both lowland and upland regions. Where proto-industrialization expanded, it merely became a partial substitute for enrolment in foreign military services and a means for the cantonal authorities to keep their labour *in situ*. Only in times of industrial crisis did the number of men going into military service increase significantly again. It is evident that, in rural regions, as long as those possessing local citizenship could combine the income from possession of a small plot of land, access to communal resources and proto-industrial work, there was no need for any additional unqualified labour immigrating from beyond the cantonal borders. And those citizens who needed to search for work outside their own commune would hesitate to move to another place as they would no longer benefit from access to the commons, which often constituted an important contribution to a household's income. For those involved in higher status occupations the situation was potentially different. Nonetheless, the demand for craftsmen and skilled workers was limited, and most immigrants were employed on contracts that specified that they had to leave the town once their work was finished.

Whilst practically all municipalities had instituted very restrictive rules for newcomers from outside the canton, practices varied regarding intra-cantonal relations and depended on the degree of autonomy of the municipalities. There were two ends to the spectrum. The development of textile-based proto-industry increased work opportunities in the upland regions of city-states such as Zürich and Basle and also in the clock- and watchmaking industry of the Jura region, particularly Neuchâtel and Vaud. But the local authorities had only very limited powers to restrict the influx of immigrants since the level of the entry fee to be paid by newcomers was often decided by, or at least had to be approved by, the cantonal authorities. These cantonal governments were often dominated by town burghers involved in putting-out activities, the *Fabrikanten*, who insisted on only a small entry fee to be paid in the proto-industrialized upland communities, as they were interested in the presence of a numerous and cheap labour-force. This policy facilitated the settlement of in-migrants from within the canton and was one of the main reasons for the large increase in the population of these regions. Nonetheless, the immigrants who now 'belonged' to these municipalities were often in a very precarious situation as the demand for relief in times of crisis tended to quickly deplete the communal poor fund.

The other end of the spectrum is represented by the pre-alpine and alpine regions with limited resources and high levels of municipal autonomy. Here each local administration was bent on protecting its economic resources from neighbours and had its own distinctive characteristics regarding the extent of restrictions on the mobility of the poor and the level of assistance provided. Immigrants were anything but welcome, though even in pre-alpine regions there could be some exceptions to this rule. Where supplementary resources might be obtained from out-migration, migrants from the neighbouring regions were welcome since their labour was necessary in agriculture to replace the men who were absent.

These general and particular rules served to make individuals and officials keenly aware of the value of the *droit de bourgeoisie/Bürgerrecht* and the serious consequences of losing it. At least up to the nineteenth century, the risks of losing citizenship status were tangible,[11] with a range of factors – dissoluteness, moral deviance, desertion, unauthorized marriage, prolonged absence, the character of migration and marriage to women 'foreign to the community' – used as an excuse to strip people of their previous entitlements and status. Some of these are worth exploring further. Thus, until the mid nineteenth century, a long absence increased probability of migrants being stripped of their local citizenship. Emigrants could not automatically return to their commune of origin, nor were they entitled to help if one's citizenship had not been renewed. But renewal was a costly business and had to take place every five, ten or twenty years depending on local regulations. It was argued that the costs reflected the expenses incurred to the community during the absence of the migrant, such as the maintenance of the commons or even increasing their extent, investments for the management of water and of rivers, and the cost of relief for others that they had not shared during their absence. These renewal costs could also sometimes vary according to the individual's place of birth or could be higher for a citizen's children not born in his or her place of origin. But the risk of losing one's citizenship was greater in some sectors of activity, such as lengthy service in foreign armies. It was not only the length of absence that was relevant for loss of citizenship, but also the type of migration, and especially unauthorized migration when it was considered to be detrimental to the economic interests of the elite, such as enrolment in non-approved Swiss regiments, emigration on the part of qualified workers whose acquired knowledge increased the risk of technology transfer, and so on.[12]

Change of religious confession, especially for those who had spent long years in France, Spain and Italy, also represented a potential hazard. Confessional warfare between protestant and catholic Switzerland – in deed as in word – was never a distant prospect, and until 1848 religious freedom, except during the short interval of the Helvétique, was never the norm. Conversion to a religion other than the cantonal religion very often resulted in banishment as well as confiscation of all property, which can be seen from several cases up to the first half of the nineteenth century, in turn a factor contributing to the increase in the group of *heimatloses*.[13] With regard to marriage, I have dwelt elsewhere on the importance of respect for the norms established by the State, all of which aimed at preventing marriages to men or women who were 'foreign to the commune of origin'.[14] Those who married without satisfying the necessary conditions were at considerable risk of losing of their *droit de bourgeoisie/Bürgerrecht*. In some cantons, assisted persons and beggars 'who persisted in marrying' were subject to draconian measures to avoid any further relief commitments, such as dissolution of their marriage. In rare cases where the permission to marry was given to people without sufficient means, it was usually on the explicit condition that the couple promised never to request any help from the commune. A note to this effect was entered, for instance, into the marriage register of the chaplain of Fischental, in the canton of Zurich.[15] Often the consequences of the transgression of the marriage regulations were that both spouses lost their citizenship. This was the case in the 1820s and 1830s in the canton of Glarus, where migrants to Russia who had married Russian women were denied the right to return to their commune of origin because of such marriages. They were even warned that the police would expel them from the canton should they return, even without their foreign wives.[16]

Change and Continuity from 1848

The period between the Swiss constitutions of 1848 and 1874 represents a milestone as far as the question of citizenship is concerned even if the developments enshrined in such legislation had limited impact on the rights of the poor. The 1848 constitution stipulated that all Swiss *nationals* automatically possessed the three citizenships with their inherent entitlement to relief, and that it was illegal for a canton or municipality to deprive a citizen of their full citizen's rights. All Swiss *residents* with limited rights (*Hintersassen, heimatlose, Geduldete*) had to be provided with a commune of origin which henceforth had the statutory duty to assist them. The allocation of citizens with limited rights to the different cantons was decided by the Federal Government. The tensions that arose between cantons and between municipalities, especially where exclusion had been a frequent practice, were numerous. This explains why in some cantons more than 5 per cent of the population had to be given full citizenship.[17] In many municipalities – especially the poor ones that already had many out-migrants to assist – dissent was forceful and the work of the Federal Court of Justice on the attribution of responsibilities correspondingly voluminous. National level estimates that 25–30,000 persons with limited rights were granted full citizenship between the 1850s and the 1870s are probably much underestimated.[18] This is not least because in some 'progressive' cantons, such as Glarus, the *Hintersassen* who made up more than 5 per cent of the cantonal population had already attained full citizenship by the 1830s. The sheer scale of such activity, especially when allied with 'escape clauses' built into much underpinning legislation, had important consequences for the practices of municipalities and the relationship between the central authorities and localities, which I will explore further in this section.

Despite the establishment of the rule that Swiss citizens could take up residence wherever they wanted on Swiss territory, some important clauses still restricted the ability of the poor to move from less developed regions to places where they were more likely to find employment or where they stood a better chance of obtaining communal or charitable relief.[19] To avoid a massive influx of needy migrants into the industrialized cantons, which would then have been faced with social problems, the Constitution of 1848 allowed the cantons and the municipalities of residence to remove migrants to their commune of origin. It also introduced a suite of 'moral' criteria, largely derived from the practice of previous centuries, as a deterrent to the migration of paupers. Between 1848 and 1874 a migrant had to meet several requirements before being able to take up legal domicile in another canton. Among the most important were conditions related to financial resources (proof that one was able to provide for oneself and family 'with his financial means [*fortune* in French], his profession or his work'), 'moral character' (a certificate – *certificat de bonne vie et mœurs/guter Leumund* – had to attest his or her good character), and proof that the migrant had not previously received welfare benefits.

In addition, all newly naturalized citizens had to wait for an interval of five years before taking up a new domicile, increasing the chances that they would fall foul over some of the other restrictive clauses in the 1848 legislation. The requirement that migrants, in contrast to settled residents, had to be able to survive on the basis of their wage alone had a particularly restrictive effect. It meant that they were not entitled to use the communal land which in some parts of Switzerland, and especially in upland communities, accounted and still accounts for a considerable part of the territory, removing a significant plank of the economy of makeshifts that might have allowed them to meet the financial criteria. When in the 1870s federal law tried to curtail the legal rights of communities to reserve their common land for the exclusive benefit of long-established families, the reaction of the communities was to change the legal status of that land into that of a semi-public corporation. Thus, these resources did not become accessible to all citizens living there.[20] In turn, of course, this sort of restrictive approach to settlement, belonging and entitlement implies that information on the financial and moral position of actual and potential migrants was readily available. While more work is needed on this issue, correspondence between the local clergy in Alsace, or between that in the canton of Berne with the clergy in Schwanden in the canton of Glarus, demonstrates that both the commune of origin and that of domicile were kept well-informed.[21]

The points of principle embedded in the 1848 constitution continued to shape Swiss attitudes towards belonging and entitlement in the later nineteenth century. The Constitution of 1874 removed some of the restrictive moral criteria and the requirement that newly naturalized citizens must stay put for a given period. It did little, however, to remedy the fact that the destination of the migrant – to another canton, within the canton of origin, or abroad – heavily influenced the criteria by which their entitlements would be judged. Moreover, the rule persisted that in cases of destitution the canton of domicile was entitled either to be reimbursed for the expenses it had incurred or, if that was not the case, to send the pauper back to his or her commune of origin. And, in common with nineteenth-century England, some cantons created specific rules which could be used as a deterrent to actioning entitlements even where a theoretical right existed. Foremost amongst such rules were those which stripped claimants of their civic rights until the cost of assistance had been repaid. Such sanctions had far-reaching economic consequences, leaving migrants unable to obtain credit, subject to supervision by a guardian, and potentially removable to their parish of origin. These ambiguities over the entitlements of Swiss nationals extended well beyond the 1870s. The organization of relief remained a cantonal matter until the 1970s and this could lead to different treatments and practices of exclusion for the poor according to the commune to which they belonged.[22]

Two exceptions were the cantons of Bern and Neuchâtel in the second half of the nineteenth century which for exactly opposite reasons abandoned the criteria of origin for relief and adopted that of the residence. The overwhelming number of migrants within the canton of Bern made it absolutely impossible for many municipalities to maintain the principle of origin, since some of them had up to four or five times more of their citizens living outside than within the commune.[23] Neuchâtel, in contrast, gave up this criterion because it had such considerable immigration from poor regions which were not prepared to grant relief to their out-migrants. However, these two cantons still had to provide relief for their own citizens living in other cantons according to the criteria of the commune of origin.

Since the question of relief remained within the competence of the cantons and the municipalities nearly everywhere in Switzerland, the possibilities for the Federal Government to intervene were limited and the scope for central-local conflict was considerable. The government's role was to make sure that the different articles of the cantonal constitutions were not in opposition to the Federal constitution. Since the competences of the Federal Government also included questions pertaining to relations with other states, it also had to settle the problems driven by the marked increase of foreign nationals living in Switzerland and of Swiss nationals living abroad. For 'foreigners', assistance and relief remained in the competence of their municipalities of residence, allowing such municipalities to expel impoverished foreigners to their country of origin. This practice impelled the Federal Government to sign international agreements with several countries from 1874 onwards, a variant of the trends explored in Paul-André Rosental's chapter for this volume. Such agreements were particularly concerned with sick people whose poor health would not allow them to be transported home, and with foreigners who had died in Switzerland.[24] The associated costs were to be met in the country where they occurred on a reciprocal basis, and in Switzerland the cantons and the municipalities where the foreigners had lived were held responsible for payment. Unsurprisingly this was a source of tension.

Another significant subject of dispute between the Federal Government and the cantons, or rather the municipalities, was the problem presented by Swiss women who had married foreigners. As the number of these marriages increased, so did the problem of support. Having lost their Swiss nationality through marriage, in the case of their needing assistance, they would be deprived of their right of residence and expelled with their children to the country of their late husband if that country refused to assist them in Switzerland. Disputes in these matters with the Grand Duchy of Baden were numerous and ongoing but it was not until 1903 that Federal legislation was enacted to deal with the re-integration of such women, something which in turn created rancorous dispute. The main problem was that for the Swiss Government a policy of re-integration had no financial consequences at all, whereas for the small municipalities to which a widow was allocated the financial consequences could be overwhelming, especially when many citizens had migrated, paid no tax whatsoever in the commune, and a number of them needed to be assisted in their place of domicile.

An appropriate example is that of a widow who was re-integrated with her seven under-age children in the canton of Aargau. Born in 1866 in a municipality of the canton of Aargau, which was not her municipality of origin, she moved to the canton of Zurich, where she married and lived for twenty years until the death of her husband. Having married a citizen from the Grand-Duchy of Baden in Germany, she had lost her Swiss citizenship. In 1909, at the time of her re-integration into the municipality of Waldhäusern, the municipality had only 111 inhabitants, and of those only 57 possessed local citizenship. The majority of the citizens of Waldhäusern lived in other municipalities, 56 in municipalities of the canton of Aargau and 129 in other Swiss cantons, with an unknown number of citizens living outside Switzerland.[25] According to the communal statistics, as few as 26 citizens – of which 14 only lived in the municipality and the other 12 in the canton – paid the poor tax. All the other citizens paid nothing at all and 'a large number of those 129 living outside the canton also have to be assisted'.[26] The burden was an impossible one, demonstrating the limits of a relief system based on the *commune d'origine/ Bürgerrecht*, which still put the burden of relief on the municipality of origin long after the migrants had departed.

At any event, less than twenty years after the adoption of the law on re-integration the Federal Government had to arrive at a compromise in view of the financial difficulties generated such that after 1922 the government co-funded the scheme. Such co-funding was crucial to resolving tensions between government and locality. The entitlements of Swiss living abroad also depended on the principle of the place of origin, but from the end of the nineteenth century the Federal Government increased its participation in the cost of relief. There were now somewhat different arguments for or against recalling impoverished people to Switzerland. The cost for the removal of one person or a whole family to Switzerland and thus uprooting them from their accustomed social environment was given greater weight since it was often cheaper to give them relief abroad. The further development of aid from Swiss private charitable organizations, together with subsidies from the Confederation, helped to support old people in Europe and overseas who had perhaps spent all their life abroad and had no wish to be uprooted and removed to their municipality of origin.

Actioning Entitlement to Relief

Of course, communal allowances for the dependent poor were only one part of the economy of makeshifts for poor families, something that has escaped attention thus far in our discussion of the centrality of the commune of origin to the formal relief process. Many cantons endeavoured to protect their communal poor fund (*Armengut*), often of limited extent in rural areas, by shifting part of the financial burden of support to wider family networks. As early as the seventeenth century, several legal codes stated that it was first and foremost the duty of the family to give support to poor kin. The responsibility of the family for its members was very far-reaching and communal support was given only when family support could not be provided. In Zürich, in the eighteenth century, it devolved on family members up to the third degree of consanguinity.[27] In Glarus, following a decision of the *Landsgemeinde* in 1754, kin were obliged to contribute up to the fourth degree of consanguinity. The circle of kin obliged to give support often correlated with succession law: those likely to be in the line of succession effectively had to contribute to the upkeep of their kin. To make the poor look after poor kin was an important item for dispute. When the family was unwilling or unable to pay for the upkeep of kin in the latter's place of residence, removal to the commune of origin was the solution adopted – after which they often had to be taken in by family relations.[28]

At the beginning of the twentieth century this notion of family responsibility was actually reinforced, becoming a formal national policy in the first Swiss Civil Code of 1912. While the extent of kinship obligations was more limited – mutual obligation to assist those in need extended from grandparents to grandchildren and vice-versa, whilst siblings, even stepbrothers and sisters, could only be made responsible for payment if their income was considered sufficient – the obligation remained enshrined as an expectation. Naturally, the flow of resources from families to paupers was a dual function of the financial situation of the kinship group and the degree of pressure which the authorities of the commune of origin put on the family to contribute to the expenses incurred. The willingness and ability of families to act was also partly dependent upon whether the support required was of a temporary or permanent nature. In the first case, support mostly consisted of goods and foodstuffs, while cash was given only in small amounts at best, and the overall level of relief remained well below subsistence level. But when it was a question of more permanent support, dependence was often associated with removal to a commune of origin and an expectation that kin would take in individuals and families thus removed. The numbers involved in this process were considerable. In the eighteenth century beggars were put on carts by the hundreds and taken to the borders of the canton to which they were thought to belong.[29] The practice persisted on a large scale in the first half of the nineteenth century and removal linked to the question of assistance was abolished only in 1977.[30] In short, while entitlements might be established, actioning them was often difficult and uncomfortable for both paupers and their families.

This observation is given further credence if we turn to situations where the families of paupers did not help or could not provide support in a co-residence environment. In this case, paupers might be boarded out by the Assistance Board through an inverted auction (*mise au rabais*)[31] or, worse even, boarded out in turn (*placement en tour de rôle/in Kehr, in Umgang*): being sent from farm to farm for periods of time which depended on the wealth of the farmers. This labour carrousel, which existed in many cantons as early as the seventeenth century, was in some places considered more as a punishment than as a help and contributed to stigmatizing the poor.[32] Until the mid nineteenth century even a wealthy town like Geneva used to put its poor people *en pension* in its rural municipalities because this was the cheapest way of dealing with them. The procedure was applied mostly in the case of older people and children.

In the nineteenth century its continued prevalence in agricultural regions like Berne reflected the social changes experienced by agriculture, but also the power of the farmers.[33] For them the boarded out children were an extremely cheap substitute for young adult agricultural workers as they did not get even a basic wage, but were just kept in food and clothes. Formal obligations to provide education could be ignored with the acquiescence of local overseers who were accustomed to turning a blind eye. In other places, such as Fribourg, the system of boarding out persisted until the end of the 1920s, especially for children.

There are a number of reasons why old methods like removal and boarding out survived for such a long time in some parts of Switzerland. In the virulent controversy as to the entity ultimately responsible for supporting a needy emigrant, the municipalities of origin very often insisted on the fact that most emigrants had emigrated when they were young, or perhaps had even never lived in their commune,[34] that they had never worked or paid taxes there, and that it was the canton of domicile that had benefited most from the migrants. To complicate matters further, the anomaly in the Swiss system was reinforced by rulings of the Swiss Government, which decreed in several cases in the 1850s and 1860s that it was illegal for the municipalities of origin to oblige those who had emigrated to another canton to pay the poor tax. Effectively, the situation for emigrants was no better either. They had in any case to pay the poor tax where they lived and would nevertheless never be entitled to benefit from it.

Meanwhile, it is important to observe that neither industrialization nor urbanization made the acquisition of citizenship-based benefits any easier. The two movements certainly tested the limits of the system of poor relief based on the *Heimatrecht*, fostering a situation in which an ever-growing proportion of Swiss population no longer lived in its commune of origin and the number of foreign nationals increased (Table 6.1). The impossibility of organising relief transfers on a corresponding scale implied that the second half of the nineteenth century witnessed the creation of parallel institutions to improve the situation of impoverished immigrants not entitled to any public support – mostly in urban municipalities. These charitable private institutions, such as the *Allgemeine Armenpflege* in Basel or the *Bureau central de bienfaisance* in Geneva, were often well-endowed and at the end of the nineteenth century they were funded not only by donations, bequests and so on, but also by cantonal contributions. Nonetheless, and particularly at times of economic crises, demand often outstripped supply. This, allied with a tendency not to make any distinction between Swiss and foreign residents, undermined the level of benefits associated with citizenship.

Table 6.1. Population in Switzerland According to Origin and Residence, 1850 and 1900 (per 1,000)

Year	Swiss citizens living in			Foreign nationals	Total Population
	municipality of origin	In another municipality of their canton of origin	In another canton		
1850	849	35	76	40	1,000
1900	384	315	184	116	1,000

Source: Swiss Censuses

Conclusion

In Switzerland, as was the case in the neighbouring South German States and Austria, communal autonomy was decisive when it came to poor relief and citizenship. Communal poor funds existed only to help those in possession of local citizenship, which was passed on from father to sons and daughters. When in need those citizens who resided outside their commune of origin were dependent for relief on the decision taken by the Assistance Board of their *commune d'origine/Bürgerort*. This decision could be quite arbitrary and it was not possible to appeal against it. It was for the authorities to decide whether they would offer assistance to such migrants or, if not, ask for their removal. This was something which still occurred in the first half of the twentieth century, albeit less frequently than in earlier centuries when it was a fairly common occurrence. Removal was a harsh measure, but for the poor without any or only partial citizenship rights the situation was even worse, as they had no right to assistance whatsoever, depended on casual private charity when in need and always ran the risk of being put into an institution. The gap in status and rights between local citizens and those without any or only partial rights narrowed from the middle of the nineteenth century onwards. The decision to confer local citizenship to all Swiss people without exception was a political decision, taken against the will of many rural municipalities, which felt that their resources would be over-burdened as a result of their obligation to assist many of these new citizens. Some local authorities continued to consider these new citizens as a danger to society, as can be seen from the title given to them by the chief of police in Geneva in 1879 who published a report on *la population flottante et les classes dangereuses à Genève*.[35]

The obligation for the commune of origin to support its citizens continued to exist when the latter had effectively become strangers to their own commune and did not even know the language spoken there. This practice was no longer in conformity with the increased mobility of the population, but the persistence of traditional legal views was at the root of the difficulties faced by the different political entities which tried to reach agreement on relief responsibility. The impoverishment of many Swiss citizens living outside their commune of origin during World War I was the cause of the first agreement that attempted to alleviate the problems. This created a mutual responsibility of the municipalities of domicile and those of origin so as to avoid the removal of thousands of Swiss to their commune of origin. A first step to a more unified practice was taken in 1923 when ten cantons agreed to share the costs of relief according to the length of time spent in a commune other than that of origin. Yet it was nearly half a century later before all the cantons agreed to sign the *Concordat intercantonal concernant l'assistance publique au lieu de domicile* which increased their obligation to assist long-time immigrants. And not until the 1970s was it decided at long last at the federal level to set a limit to the obligation of the commune of origin to support its citizens and to allow Swiss citizens an unlimited right of settlement (*une liberté d'établissement illimitée*) on the national territory.

Notes

1. During the short interlude of the Helvétique (1798–1803), the central government did change a number of important rules with regard to settlement, but not to the system of poor relief. In 1803 the cantons reverted to their original systems of settlement and assistance.
2. The first directive that each Swiss canton was individually responsible for its poor and beggars can be found as early as 1491, but it was in very general terms and had negligible effects.
3. See, for example, K. Geiser. 1975. 'Einzug, Niederlassung und Heimatrecht im alten Bernbiet', *Jahrbuch des Oberaargaus*, 18.
4. G. Le Comte. 1989. 'Quelle politique pour les pauvres? Le cas de la communauté de Vaulion sous l'Ancien Régime', in A.-L. Head-König and B. Schnegg (eds), *La pauvreté en Suisse (XVIIe-XXe siècles)*, Zurich, 95–108.
5. In the powerful city-states of Zurich and Berne, which had secularized all ecclesiastical property, rural communities considered that it was for the central government to assist the poor. For Berne, see E. Flückiger Strebel. 2002. *Zwischen Wohlfahrt und Staatsökonomie. Armenfürsorge auf der bernischen Landschaft im 18. Jahrhundert*, Zurich, 221ff.
6. Elsewhere called also *Landsassen, Beisassen. ewige Einwohner*. It is impossible to detail here all the possible categories which existed. They could be people who were citizens of a canton, but had not managed to acquire local citizenship, thus effectively being excluded from all economic advantages (no access to commons or to wood distribution, the exercise of only a limited number of activities, limited ownership of land, etc.). In the eighteenth century, they were often the descendants of in-migrants of the sixteenth and seventeenth centuries.

7. A case in point is that of the immigrant Huguenots in the canton of Bern, who remained barred from naturalization up to the nineteenth century.
8. They would have risked falling into the category of the *heimatloses,* the most vulnerable population.
9. T. D. Meier and R. Wolfensberger. 1998. *"Eine Heimat und doch keine."* Heimatlose und *Nicht-Sesshafte in der Schweiz (16.–19. Jahrhundert),* Zürich.
10. The calculations are based on *Feuille fédérale* 7, 1855, vol. 1, 419ff. (Rapport de gestion [...] [du] Conseil fédéral suisse [...] 1854); *Feuille fédérale,* 9, 1857, vol. 1, 218–41 (Rapport de gestion [...] [du] Conseil fédéral suisse [...] 1856).
11. On a nation-wide level, the conception of citizenship and the reasons for its loss began to evolve in quite different directions between 1815 and 1848. The French-speaking cantons were influenced in part by the French conception of citizenship, whilst in some Swiss-German cantons, especially the catholic ones, the ancien régime rules persisted until 1848.
12. U. Pfister. 1992. *Die Zürcher Fabriques. Proindustrieller Wachstum vom 16. zum 18. Jahrhundert,* Zürich, 183–184.
13. Meier and Wolfensberger, *Eine Heimat,* 35ff.
14. A.-L. Head-König. 1989. 'Marginalisation ou intégration des pauvres: les deux facettes de la politique matrimoniale pratiquée par les cantons suisses (XVIe-XIXe siècles)', in Head-König and Schnegg, *La pauvreté en Suisse,* 79–93.
15. Staatsarchiv Zürich, Fischental, Eheregister, 1723.
16. For instance Gemeindearchiv Mollis (canton Glarus), Stillstands-Protokoll, 6.12.1827, fol. 102ff.
17. P. Willisch. 2004. *Die Einbürgerung der Heimatlosen im Kanton Wallis (1850–1880),* Visp, 142.
18. Meier and Wolfensberger, *Eine Heimat,* 495.
19. One must, of course, distinguish between moving temporarily to undertake seasonal work, for which at that time no special documents were needed, and other forms of mobility, which implied the right of residence (domicile) outside the commune of origin and for which it was compulsory to deposit one's *acte d'origine.*
20. A.-L. Head-König. 2003. 'Les biens communaux en Suisse aux XVIIIe et XIXe siècles: enjeux et controverses', in M.-D. Demelas and N. Vivier (eds), *Les propriétés collectives face aux attaques libérales (1750–1914). Europe occidentale et Amérique latine,* Rennes, 99–118.
21. Recorded in the Stillstandsprotokolle of the parish of Schwanden.
22. In the canton of Glarus, for instance, it was left to the commune to decide whether it wanted to practice the *Heimruf* ('recalls home') to the commune of origin, or assist its poor in their place of domicile, or even wait for a decision of expulsion from the commune of domicile. See R. Wydler. 1939. *Untersuchungen über das Armenwesen im Kanton Glarus unter besonderer Berücksichtigung des Zeitraumes von 1840 bis 1930,* Glarus, 91.
23. H. R. Schmidt. 2010. 'Handlungsstrategien und Problembereiche der Armenfürsorge im alten Bern', in A. Holenstein et al. (eds), *Richesse et pauvreté dans les républiques suisses au XVIIIe siècle,* Genève, 245–247.
24. The only one signed before 1874 was that with Belgium in 1855; all the others were signed after 1874.
25. *Feuille fédérale,* éditée par la Chancellerie fédérale (FF), Bern, 6, 1909, 759ff.
26. Ibid., 768.
27. B. Keller. 1935. *Das Armengesetz des Kantons Zürich vom Beginn des 18. Jahrhunderts bis zum Armengesetz des Jahres 1836,* Winterthur, 116.
28. Removal did not concern only people who needed to be assisted within Switzerland, but also the poor living abroad, such as in the case of the children Bagnoud who were repatriated from Paris to Bagnes, an upland community in the Valais.

29. This system of removal was a time-consuming business and very ineffective because the beggars returned as soon as they could. See A.-M. Dubler. 1970. *Armen- und Bettlerwesen in der Gemeinen Herrschaft 'Freie Ämter' (16. bis 18. Jahrhundert)*, Basel.
30. It was only from this date Swiss citizens and 'established' foreigners could settle wherever they wanted without any restriction whatsoever.
31. In an inverted auction, the bidder with the lowest price for maintenance was accepted.
32. Flückiger Strebel, *Zwischen Wohlfahrt*, 296.
33. A.-L. Head-König. 2010. 'Les formes de garde des enfants placés en Suisse: politiques ambiguës, résistances et objectifs contradictoires (1850–1950)', *Paedagogica Historica*, 46(6), 770.
34. A similar problem arose after World War I, with the repatriation of many thousand Swiss from abroad, especially with those coming from Russia, who had to reintegrate into the municipalities their forefathers had left often more than a century before.
35. J. Cuénoud. 1879. *La population flottante et les classes dangerueses à Genève: nos dangers intérieurs*, Genève.

CHAPTER SEVEN

OVERRUN BY HUNGRY HORDES?

Migration and Poor Relief in the Netherlands, Sixteenth to Twentieth Centuries

Marco H. D. van Leeuwen

Introduction

Migrants' entitlement to poor relief is a much neglected theme in Dutch history in general and in that of early modern poor relief in particular. Some of what follows will therefore be speculative. I will discuss the notion of swarms of impoverished migrants besieging the wealthy towns of the Dutch Republic, the so-called geographical free-rider thesis. The persuasive logic of that thesis predicts the collapse of urban welfare under the weight of the claims of pauper migrants. Yet that did not happen. Dutch welfare remained a marvel to the world until the end of the eighteenth century, coming perilously close to being disrupted at the turn of the nineteenth century, but recovering and continuing to function, albeit with increasing problems, until 1965. Only then did the state take over responsibility for the poor who remained a charge to the community. Why did the Dutch system of poor relief not collapse? This chapter will discuss the stabilizing factors in Dutch poor relief, as well as the remaining problems it encountered. It will focus chiefly on the early modern period, in particular the situation after the Golden Age, but will also engage with developments up to 1965.

Migrants as a Burden to the Community?
The Geographical Free-rider Thesis

Fragile, continually impaired, subject to repeated collapse before being
continually rebuilt – that is how de Swaan characterized poor relief in
early modern Europe. Disease, war, and other troubles created swarms
of impoverished migrants who moved around in search of assistance, in
a continual quest that destroyed the very relief they sought. Anticipating
these movements, towns and villages in which poor relief had until then
functioned relatively well were forced to close their gates to the poor:

> The prophecies of doom were self-fulfilling: as bands of starving and diseased
> people began to roam, they would descend on any township that had a reputa-
> tion for hospitality, and as they arrived, they crushed the very charitable system
> that had attracted them.... The very fact that the poor began to wander and
> seek a better place sufficed to abolish these better places. Events have taken this
> course time and again.[1]

Poor relief had, in other words, a serious free-rider problem. Ever since
the publication of Olson's groundbreaking study in 1965, it has been assumed to be problematic for groups to organize collective welfare provision, even if they have an interest in doing so, since such provisions suffer
from the free-rider behaviour of those who are eager to take benefits but
equally eager to avoid paying for them.[2] That same problem is evident in
the case of historic poor relief structures. During periods of crisis, it was
financially necessary or at least attractive for a local authority to offer little
in the way of poor relief and so to push the migrating poor away to nearby
towns. But what one town did, others could too, causing poor relief in a
whole region to collapse under the mobile hordes of hungry, mendicant
and thieving poor. This despite the objectively good reasons – religious
motives, the need to maintain a labour reserve, the desire to maintain
peace and good order – for communities to make provision for the poor.[3]

De Swaan argues that local authorities were quite simply not in a position to coordinate their charitable activities, and so poor relief was always
prone to regular collapse. Central government ensured a degree of regional stability by requiring each city to provide for its own poor. In England, legislation to that effect had already been enacted to stand alongside
the Elizabethan Poor Law of 1601, which introduced an element of uni-
formity into poor relief throughout the country, by the later seventeenth
century.[4] Each parish was required to provide for its own poor, and poor
applicants who were not established residents could be sent back to their
parish of origin. The situation was different in the rest of Europe, where

attempts were made to coordinate relief, 'but until the nineteenth century, none of these efforts amounted to anything like a coherent or effective national policy'.[5] In The Netherlands, de Swaan argues, the regional stability of poor relief was guaranteed by the establishment of workhouses which had a local and regional function in providing for the poor. On the face of it, the workhouse was profitable, so it appeared to be an attractive solution for each locality to avert the collapse of poor relief. In fact, the workhouse was anything but profitable, but by the time this had become clear it was an established institution. Modest grants from the government were sufficient to ensure the continuation of workhouse provision. In later years, the scope of state intervention increased in modest stages, until, through statutory provisions and if necessary by compulsion, a system of uniform social welfare was prescribed and imposed throughout the country. Thus, gradually, the state and welfare grew to become the welfare state. In turn, the genesis of the welfare state is – in de Swaan's construct – the culmination of efforts to lessen the vulnerability of local poor relief institutions.

De Swaan's view that local communities were simply incapable of coordinating their charitable activities, and that that was the reason why poor relief always broke down, is disputed by Prak. He points in contrast to the continuity of poor relief. In his work on the Dutch town of 's-Hertogenbosch, Prak observed that local poor relief since the Middle Ages was not in general subject to periodic collapse. He writes that the local institutional structures offered a sufficient guarantee for the protection of local services. The availability of large charitable funds, a buffer in bad times, prevented periodic failure and ensured continuity. Persons of authority in local communities could use that authority to introduce additional measures: they could tighten eligibility criteria or reduce the support given to each individual, thereby limiting claims on local resources, or they could generate additional income through ad hoc collections.[6]

The question of the vulnerability versus resilience of local poor relief is not one whose importance is limited to the social history of the poor or even the socio-political history of towns, villages, and central government in early modern Europe. Equally, poor relief arrangements influenced the extent and direction of migration flows and thus the more or less optimal local allocation of labour. Linked to that are matters of economic growth and social stability in early modern society. An analysis of the resilience of local poor relief in terms of the geographical free-rider problem can thus reveal something not only about both Prak's continuity thesis and de Swaan's model of periodic collapse, but also about a wide range of socio-political and economic questions.

Migration in the Dutch Republic

Before considering the effect of migration on social welfare, it will be useful to say a few words about migration in general in the Dutch Republic. To a large extent, the growth of the Dutch population was determined by the arrival of migrants.[7] In the seventeenth and eighteenth centuries hundreds of thousands of migrants settled permanently in the Netherlands, while more or less equal numbers sojourned in the Republic on their way to other destinations. Still others worked as seasonal labourers in the herring fishery, Baltic shipping, peat digging, infrastructural projects such as land reclamation, canal construction, urban expansion, haymaking, harvesting and the preparation of commercial crops. In terms of numbers, the proportion of migrants in the coastal areas of the Netherlands was around half the entire male working population.[8] Not all migrants stayed and worked throughout the year, and considered in terms of the number of years worked the proportion of migrants in the economy was just 10 per cent of the Republic's population as a whole, while in the province of Holland it was twice that.[9] Internal migration was a feature alongside immigration. The economic development of the Netherlands had created a significant urban proletariat early on, and as a consequence of developments in the agrarian sector a growing number of impoverished smallholders emerged, determined to seek their fortunes in the cities.

The presence of so many migrants created fertile ground for the Republic's economic development, but was also itself a consequence of it. The education, skills, business capital, and connections enjoyed by many migrants and gained elsewhere formed a welcome addition to those of the indigenous Dutch, many of whom, incidentally, were themselves descended from immigrants, and contributed to the Republic's exceptional prosperity. At the same time, it may also be assumed that its prosperity was one of the main reasons, apart from its religious tolerance, why the Republic continued to attract immigrants for so many years.[10]

The marked openness of Dutch society to migrants was evident in many ways. Second-generation migrants were included on lists of the wealthiest residents in Amsterdam – and by extension in the Western world. In the west of the country especially, there were few barriers to migrants joining guilds.[11] Any migrant craftsman who could afford to pay would be admitted to the guild, and any immigrant could purchase citizenship for the equivalent of between one and two months' wages, though that was slightly more difficult in some areas along the border of the Republic.[12] No migrant ghettos appeared. Where immigrants lived close to one another, it was because they wished to do so, usually because others from their region of origin, or co-religionists, were already living in that neighbourhood, or because they followed an occupation that was carried out in a specific district, such as the docks. One study of the position of migrants in Amsterdam concluded, for instance,

> that in Amsterdam there were no lines demarcating migrants from the rest of society.... There certainly were huge discrepancies in terms of circumstances, power, and status, but those cannot be attributed to a dichotomy between the established population and newcomers. In that sense the Republic of the eighteenth century was a relatively 'open' society.[13]

In sum, there were indeed high levels of migration and mobility both towards and within the Dutch Republic. In normal times, few migrants had recourse to welfare; indeed, they contributed to its upkeep in the Dutch Republic. Nonetheless, unless they returned home, some migrants had to apply for welfare during winter, when employment was scarce, during times of economic recession, or when hit by personal misfortune. How did that work? Could they have formed a sort of travelling circus of the unfortunate, crushing by their sheer numbers the welfare agencies to which they were attracted?

Poor Relief in the Dutch Republic

Organized poor relief existed as early as the Middle Ages.[14] Indeed, canon law included provisions requiring a parish to care for its destitute. If parishes were unable to meet the cost, churchwardens would apportion a levy among the parishioners. In addition to parish-based help, the nobility and monasteries had certain obligations towards those of their servants who were ill or elderly. Institutions for the poor had been founded in Western Europe ever since the growth of towns and cities in the eleventh century. The institutions were initially less specialized than they were later to become, caring at first for orphans, the sick, the elderly, transient visitors, as well as *proveniers*, that is, paying residents. Sometimes, at the request of the city council, a hospital (*gasthuis*) would dispense alms to the poor, but responsibility for the regular distribution of food and clothing lay largely with the Masters of the Holy Spirit (*Heilige Geestmeesters*), later known as the Masters of the Homesitting poor (*Huiszittenmeesters*).

In the cities of the Late Middle Ages, charitable endowments were administered separately from general parish assets by overseers of the poor. The endowments were a feature of Catholic religiosity, an aspect of the cult of memory whereby benefactors made donations with a view to ensuring their own salvation in the afterlife. The recipients were expected to pray for the souls of the dead in exchange for posthumous gifts. The names of the dead thus 'lived on' in the alms provided to the poor, though the expenses associated with masses said for the souls of the dead were an important component of the total expenditure of poor relief institutions, which left correspondingly less for the poor. The cities meanwhile had a tangled maze of charitable foundations and endowments, set up by individuals, guilds, and clergy, administered and for the most part staffed by members of religious orders. The Church had a leading role, but if necessary the municipal authorities intervened to stave off a crisis.

In the first half of the sixteenth century, a new approach to poor relief was felt to be necessary, in part due to population growth and to the rapid expansion of major cities. Traditional poor relief arrangements were unable to cope adequately with the effects of the rapidly growing number of paupers. Another influence was humanist criticism of the monasteries and mendicant orders, and what was said to be their unrestricted, indiscriminate and haphazard approach to distributing charity to beggars. The newly critical attitude to almsgiving led to a shift in emphasis towards limiting vagrancy and the number of beggars. In 1526 the Spanish humanist Juan Luis Vives, a resident of Bruges, published his *De Subventione Pauperum* [On Assistance to the Poor]. Vives argued that mendicancy should be countered by strict prohibitions and better supervision of the poor. Only the 'real poor', by which he meant those unable to provide a livelihood because of physical incapacity, illness or old age, should receive relief, and certainly not indolent beggars. He called for a more coherent system of poor relief, one that would for instance make a distinction between the able-bodied and the infirm poor. Most importantly, uncoordinated relief by the myriad of hospitals and ecclesiastical charities, friaries and individuals had to be brought to an end. He urged the state to set up an organized system of poor relief to co-exist with private initiatives. And in many German, Italian and French cities, but also in the southern Netherlands, poor relief was indeed reorganized at that time.[15]

The northern Netherlands experienced less rapid urbanization than the south of the country, so poverty was a less pressing problem. Yet the fundamental reform of poor relief in the southern Netherlands did not go unnoticed. In 1527, the States of Holland enquired about changes implemented in Bruges and Ypres. In 1531, inspired by these innovative ideas and reforms, the Holy Roman Emperor Charles V decreed that parochial charity should be centralized within a single common fund.[16] The poor had to register with the city, and to wear an identifying badge. Begging was prohibited and vagabonds were barred from entering cities. As far as we know, the edict led to poor relief being reformed only in Friesland and even there the reforms were not implemented in their entirety. Elsewhere in the northern Netherlands, it was not until later that reforms were introduced.[17]

Indeed, greater changes in poor relief took place only after the Dutch Revolt and the start of the Reformation. In the cities that had switched their allegiance after 1572 and joined the rebel cause, Catholic endowments were appropriated and handed over to civic institutions and the Reformed Church, which acquired a privileged position as a public Church – although not a state church. Municipal administrators were often also members of the Reformed Church, but in general they set political interests above those of the church. There was no longer a union of church and state. During the Reformation a multiplicity of religious movements and denominations emerged, each of which developed its own system of poor relief in the course of time. This gave rise to a confessionally segmented system of poor relief that was exceptional in Europe, where welfare was generally supervised by a single church, be it Catholic, Protestant or Jewish. Each religious denomination of any significance wanted its own patronage and protection.[18] The biblical injunction 'As we have therefore opportunity, let us do good unto all men, especially unto them who are of the household of faith' was clearly heeded here.[19]

During the Golden Age, no nation was more charitable than the Netherlands. In terms of per capita charitable giving, England began to approximate that of the Netherlands only at the end of the eighteenth century (setting aside guild welfare, not discussed here).[20] Within the Dutch Republic, poor relief agencies in every town and city, as well as in many villages, were obliged to appeal to the generosity of the public. In principle each religious community took care of its own destitute, while municipal poor relief existed as a last resort for those whom the church failed to help. In Amsterdam, for example, almost all religious denominations maintained a special agency to provide for the 'ordinary' poor, while many also had almshouses for their elderly parishioners, and orphanages for the boys and girls of their religious community. There were also two municipal poor relief agencies – an orphanage for citizens' children, and another for those of non-citizens. Finally, like many other cities, Amsterdam had a number of almshouses founded, and in many cases managed, by individuals. The poor relief system was thus fragmented along religious and secular lines, with a further distinction according to social status and religious denomination.[21]

Charitable giving was voluntary, but well organized.[22] Alms boxes were situated strategically at busy locations, such as inns, post offices, and ferries. Churches held collections during services, and frequent door-to-door collections were made. The municipal poor relief made collections too, authorized by the municipal council and subject to a roster. Municipal authorities ensured that all collections were properly organized and audited the annual accounts, but apart from that they were reluctant to become heavily involved. In the Dutch Republic, a *modus vivendi* existed with both church and town exercising overall supervision over charitable giving, but no more and no less. Part of the responsibility felt by local government for the welfare of its poor was delegated, as it were, to the churches and to the municipal boards of administrators, often formally independent bodies. That is what today we may call corporatism, with government responsibilities delegated to semi-autonomous agencies in which members can participate.[23] Co-religionists could influence ecclesiastical poor relief, citizens could administer urban poor relief, and, moreover, by petitioning the town council they could complain if they felt relief was being mismanaged. This distribution of charitable responsibilities among church, state and citizen survived essentially until the introduction of the *Algemene Bijstandswet* in 1965.

In sum, the Netherlands provided a system of decentralized and segmented poor relief in its cities and villages. The national and provincial authorities played a minimal role in it – save for letters of surety, which we shall discuss later – leaving poor relief largely to local institutions which were frequently run along religious lines and financed privately. Many individual towns had separate poor relief institutions, each with its own board of administrators. Local authorities played a part in poor relief by monitoring church charities or by running 'residual' poor relief institutions for those paupers who did not receive help from the church. The lack of a role for central government resulted in an archipelago of autonomous institutions which treasured their independence. Idiosyncratic rules were defended tooth and nail if necessary.[24] How did the myriad charities assist the poor, migrants and non-migrants? How many, and which, people were assisted, and what were they entitled to?

It is generally difficult, if not impossible, to reconstruct precisely how many people were assisted. One approach is to start on relatively firm ground, by looking at the situation in the first half of the nineteenth century, before moving back to the seventeenth and eighteenth centuries. During the first half of the nineteenth century, a quarter of the population of Amsterdam was assisted on a regular basis. In the period 1829–1854, 55,000 men, women and children were assisted, either during the winter or all year round.[25] That figure does not include individuals who received benefits only briefly, or those helped by individual citizens or small private institutions. Most relief was outdoor (90 per cent), but some was provided in orphanages (4 per cent), homes for the elderly (2 per cent), courts of almshouses (2 per cent) and the workhouse (2 per cent). Three quarters of all relief was church-based, while the municipality provided the remainder. How many people were helped in Amsterdam in the time of the Dutch Republic is more difficult to determine, but the available indicators suggest it was fewer than in the first half of the nineteenth century. Poverty had been on the rise from the end of the eighteenth century. The number of individuals assisted by the Municipal Charity alone, for instance, had risen from 3 to between 5 and 6 per cent of the total population. Hence, possibly an eighth of the total Amsterdam population was helped on a regular basis by a charity in normal years in the Dutch Republic.[26]

The majority of paupers consisted of the sick and infirm, the elderly, widows with children, workers with large families, and sometimes poor women alone.[27] This finding serves to highlight the multifunctionality of pre-industrial poor relief. It performed tasks that today are performed by a multitude of independent bodies. Poor relief was important not only for a large group of poor men and women but also for many different categories of the poor. Roughly a fifth of the total male labour force received charity in the first half of the nineteenth century, and a large proportion of them worked in the harbour or in related trades. For the period of the Republic scattered evidence makes it clear that the sick, infirm, widows and the elderly also figured prominently on the lists of those helped by relief agencies.[28] Workers with large families were assisted too. As will become apparent later, in the seventeenth century at any rate they included a sizeable number of sailors.

What were they entitled to? In the first half of the nineteenth century, the monetary value of assistance (received by those regularly assisted) ranged from 10 to 25 guilders a year per family.[29] A man in the lowest wage category, working regularly (275 days), earned approximately 230 guilders per year. Lutheran poor relief per family amounted to just 11 per cent of that, municipal to 9 per cent, and Jewish assistance to just 4 per cent. No one could survive on charity alone, and of course nobody was expected to do so. Claiming relief was only one of the survival strategies open to the poor. Assistance needed to be combined with other sources of income. Serial data on per capita support during the Republic are available only for one of the two municipal poor relief charities, from 1687 onwards. The data include cash distributions and the value of relief in kind. Single people with no dependents but in good health, families with no children, and one-parent families received least, and most poor people fell into one of those categories.[30] The level of distributions gradually fell during the Batavian and French period (1795–1815) and then stabilized at the much lower level of the first half of the nineteenth century. Deep cuts were made as a consequence of the large number of recipients and the financial difficulties facing the poor relief agencies.

In sum, a sizeable proportion of the urban population was assisted with income supplements. About the Dutch countryside we know less, though underemployed labourers with insufficient income to support their families were sometimes supported alongside other groups such as the elderly or the sick.[31]

Did Dutch Welfare Collapse under the Weight of Migrants' Entitlements?

The annual accounts of poor relief organizations can help us to establish whether poor relief was subject to periodic collapse. If no funds were distributed to the poor at certain times, that might imply a periodic collapse of relief, while continuity of distribution suggests continuity of support. We can begin by examining total expenditure on the poor in Amsterdam, a city of high immigration and a flourishing welfare system. If migrants, attracted like bees to subsidized honey, caused the welfare system to collapse, we should certainly expect to see that happening in Amsterdam.

Figure 7.1 gives information for the Reformed Charity during the Golden Age and Figure 7.2 provides information for that body and for

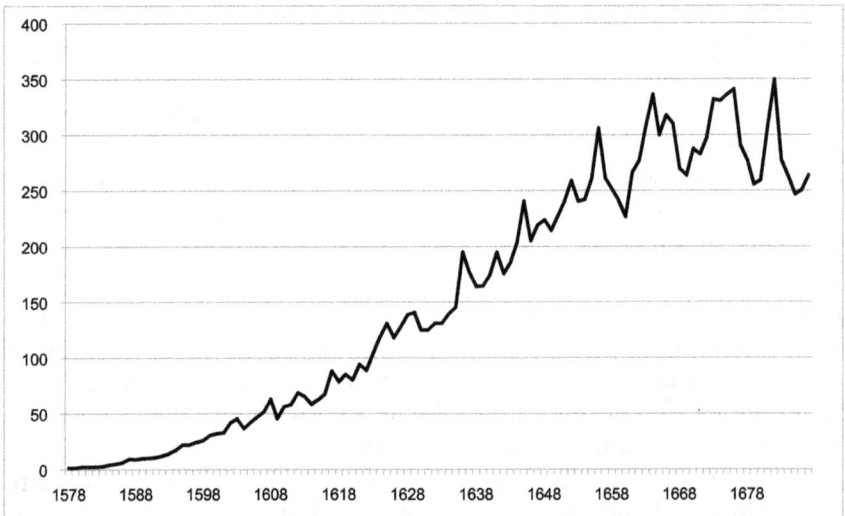

Figure 7.1. Annual Expenditure of the Reformed Charity in Amsterdam 1578–1687, in DFL

Source: J. Wagenaar. 1760–1767. *Amsterdam in zyne opkomst, aanwas, geschiedenissen etc.,* Amsterdam, vol. 2, 149–51.

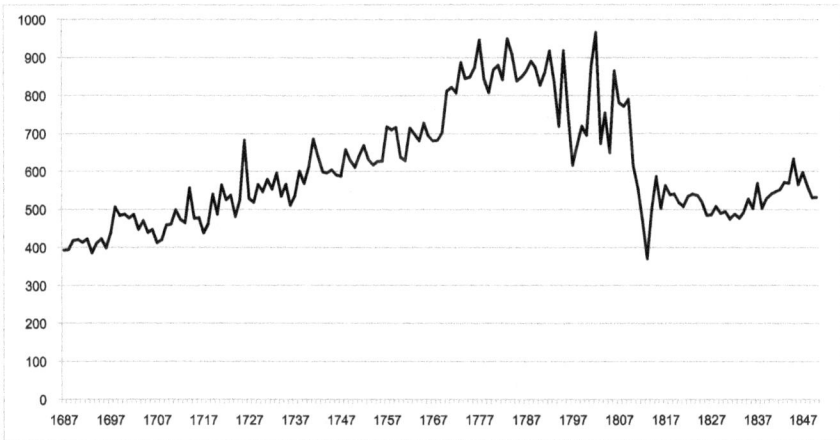

Figure 7.2. Annual Income of the Four Biggest Charities in Amsterdam 1687–1850, in DFL

Source: Leeuwen, *Bijstand,* appendix, for the period 1800–1850; M. H. D. van Leeuwen. 2012. 'Giving in Early Modern History: Philanthropy in Amsterdam's Golden Age', *Continuity and Change,* 27(1).

Note: The biggest charities are the Reformed, the two municipal charities each covering half of the city, the Lutheran and the Catholic charities. Linear interpolations for some years.

Amsterdam's three other major charitable institutions for a subsequent period. During the Golden Age the poor relief organization run by the Reformed Church grew from nothing to become an organization capable of dispensing 250–300,000 guilders a year by the mid seventeenth century. From 1687 data are available for the three other major poor relief organizations as well. The provision of relief grew until the last quarter of the eighteenth century. That was followed by a period of stabilization, a dramatic drop during the period of Batavian and French rule, and then renewed stabilization. The total level of support provided by all four relief organizations grew from around 400,000 guilders at the end of the seventeenth century to just short of a million guilders at the end of the eighteenth century. Expenditure then fell briefly to the levels seen at the end of the seventeenth century, before rising again to 600,000 guilders by about 1850. The exact level of relief expenses varied from year to year, but there is no question of any periodic collapse. There was only one clear period of crisis: the period of Batavian and French rule, but even then poor relief continued. That is not insignificant. It was one of the worst periods in Amsterdam's history but even under such extreme pressure the system of poor relief continued to function.

How this continuous provision worked in per capita real terms is not
an easy question. An index of prices of consumables rose from 40 to 70
from the end of the sixteenth to the end of the seventeenth centuries,
while nominal wages doubled.[32] Allowing for inflation, the expenditure
of the Reformed charity in this period still shows an enormous rise. The
growth of Amsterdam's population can only be approximated for this
period. The estimated population in 1681–1685 amounted to 220,000
inhabitants. The 1622 census gives about half of this number while the
population around 1580 may have been 25–30,000.[33] Which proportion
of the population was Reformed, and whether this changed over time, is
unknown. In all, inflation and population growth together may account
for a growth factor of say 20, which is huge but still not enough to explain the growth in Reformed charitable expenditure.

After 1687 we have better data. The population had ceased to increase,
and even declined a little to around 214,000 in 1791–1795. The consumables' price index rose from 70 to 95 in 1795, while the index of nominal
wages increased from about 100 to 110. Taken together, population size
and inflation therefore explain a rise of around 25 per cent of charitable
expenditure, whereas the expenses of the four charities in reality more
than doubled from around 400,000 guilders per year to 1,000,000 in
1783. After 1687 there was thus a clear real rise in charitable expenditure
until after 1783, when a period of increasing poverty, rising prices and
declining relief expenses set in.[34]

Was the continuity of poor relief observed in the case of Amsterdam, as
well as that observed in 's-Hertogenbosch by Prak, an exception? Studies
of a limited number of other towns and villages in the Republic provide
an answer. In Graft, a prosperous village in North Holland, continuity
was the rule in the seventeenth century, as it was in the villages of a poor
province such as Drenthe. The same was true of the city of Middelburg,
in Zeeland, between 1600 and 1811. Evidence from Leiden suggests
there was no periodic nor even incidental collapse of relief there from the
second half of the eighteenth to the first half of the nineteenth century;
the same conclusion can be reached for Rotterdam for the seventeenth,
eighteenth, and the first half of the nineteenth centuries. Nor is any evidence to be found of collapse of poor relief in some other cities.[35] These
findings are sufficient to reject the thesis of periodic collapses in Dutch
poor relief in the seventeenth and eighteenth centuries. The key issue remains, therefore, how the Dutch relief agencies achieved such continuity.
I will argue that three strategies mattered here: Two – raising income or
cutting costs, and capital buffers – were internal to the organization of
relief, while a third – the system of surety letters – dealt directly with the
influx of newcomers.

Raising Income and Cutting Costs

Evidence on sources of income shows that Dutch relief agencies were on a permanent life line from Dutch citizens. Over half the income of the three church-run institutions in Amsterdam came from 'living' sources: collections, legacies or gifts.[36] The value of charitable bequests varied not only with individual wills, but also from year to year. One year a charity found itself endowed with a small fortune; the next year it received no bequests at all. Members of Amsterdam's elites sometimes gave enormous sums, but small bequests were also possible. It is remarkable that many benefactors came from the middle classes, and a few even from the lower classes. Collections formed an important component.[37] Most donations were probably made during church services, as the Protestant vicar or Catholic priest, or for that matter the Jewish rabbi, urged his congregation to give for the poor.[38] All of Amsterdam's churches held collections. There were also door-to-door collections, as well as collection boxes placed throughout the city, tapping the purses of men and women of modest means too. In times of crisis, Amsterdam charities tried to increase income by collecting more frequently and by making more forceful appeals. The effect of that was limited, however, since many of the factors that caused charitable expenditure to rise (dearth, winters or wars) also limited the benevolence of charitable donors.

Cutting expenditure and stockpiling were two other options pursued to make ends meet in difficult times. One instance of the former was the fall in the level of distributions during the financial difficulties of the Batavian and French period (1795–1815).[39] Yet such a sudden and steep decline was exceptional: in general, Amsterdam's charities did not tend to adjust the level of distributions to negative circumstances in any immediate manner.[40] Stockpiling was a further option to save costs: by storing grain when prices were low, agencies could limit the expenses caused by price fluctuations of in-kind relief. Selective data on grain purchases by the Reformed Charity in the eighteenth century suggests that it repeatedly resorted to this avenue.[41] Strategies of raising income and cutting costs, then, were obviously used, but could only get charities so far.

Capital Buffers

Prak attributes the continuity of poor relief in 's-Hertogenbosch primarily to the ready availability of capital assets held by the poor relief organizations. Interest on capital was almost sufficient to fund all the assistance given to the poor. As a result, poor relief organizations in 's-Hertogenbosch were not excessively dependent on gifts from individuals, a source of income that might dry up in times of crisis. The supply of charitable capital in 's-Hertogenbosch might have been exceptionally favourable. In Leiden, for example, in the second half of the eighteenth century only a tenth of charitable income derived from returns on capital, and in Rotterdam in subsequent decades the figure was never above a half.[42] The situation in Amsterdam was somewhere between that in Leiden and Rotterdam, while in all cases remaining less favourable than in 's-Hertogenbosch.

Over the period 1687 to 1799, Amsterdam's relief agencies obtained about a third of their income from interest on capital. This figure was in decline, since at the end of the seventeenth century return on capital had accounted for just over half their income. The figure fell in absolute terms too, from around 60,000 to around 50,000 guilders a year. This might have been due to lower returns on higher capital, but a different scenario is more likely. In the eighteenth century the municipal charity acquired very little new capital by means of legacies, rarely bought assets and only occasionally sold them. It is likely then that its capital base hardly increased at all over the course of the eighteenth century. An exception is to be made for the position of the Catholic charity, where gifts and legacies remained a significant source of income, and whose capital base continued to expand markedly in the course of the eighteenth century.[43]

The well-informed eighteenth-century historian Wagenaar claimed that the capital of the Reformed Charity acted as a buffer in times of need.[44] In normal years it received more money than it needed for day-to-day poor relief. The surplus on the current account was transferred to the capital account to be appropriated in times of need. When things were especially difficult, the process was reversed.[45] In extreme conditions Amsterdam's charities drew on their capital or took out loans. This enabled them to survive what was probably the most serious crisis which they ever faced, that of the period of Batavian and French rule. But there was a third reason why they did not go bankrupt, and that was one that dealt directly with the influx of newcomers.

Letters of Surety

From the end of the seventeenth century onwards Dutch towns employed a simple remedy to stem the influx of the poor: they just sent them back unless they were covered by the relief agreements concluded with other municipalities, so-called letters of surety. A letter of surety (*acte van indemniteit, acte van cautie*) was a promise by a person or an organization to pay for the relief of named individuals if they required assistance within a specified number of years. Normally the letter took the form of a certificate, or surety, delivered by a town council or a poor relief organization to a resident upon leaving that town. From 1682 to 1785, for example, Leiden issued letters of surety to outmigrants which were valid for periods of two to three years, while requiring immigrants to present their own letters of surety if they wanted to settle in the city or purchase citizenship.[46] Similar documents have been preserved for a large area of the Republic's territory, including the towns and rural areas of South and North Holland, and parts of Gelderland, North Brabant and Overijssel. An analogous system was in operation in other parts of the Netherlands, including the city of Rotterdam and the province of Drenthe.[47] The specifics of the relationship between poor relief and migration in the Netherlands in the early modern era may, in certain respects, have been unique, but letters of surety were used elsewhere, e.g., in England.[48]

Why did the Dutch system of letters of surety emerge when it did, at the close of the country's Golden Age? In the preceding century, cities had grown considerably.[49] This growth had been spurred by immigration: migrants were needed to meet the high labour demand of the flourishing urban economies, the more so since urban death rates were high and large numbers of young men were necessary to man the fleets that left for the Dutch East Indies. Under such conditions, town councils scarcely had any reasons to limit the flow of migrants, for in places where work was scarce, newcomers left of their own accord. Poor relief for the sick, infirm, elderly, widows and large families with inadequate resources – for native-born citizens and newcomers alike – was an acceptable price to pay. Hence, for most of the seventeenth century there was little reason to introduce entry conditions.

However, things changed when economic growth gave way to stagnation. After the mid-seventeenth century, the demand for migrant labour fell, and what demand there was could increasingly be met by seasonal migrants, who came every year and returned home once the work had been done. Work was scarce outside the busy season, and, more than before, tended to be monopolized by insiders who knew their way around the increasingly fragmented labour market better than migrants did. When there was insufficient work to go round, newcomers started to rely on survival strategies that were less popular with the locals, such as begging. They became increasingly dependent on charity and came to be seen as both rivals on the labour market and financial burdens for relief agencies. The free-rider problem described by de Swaan raised its ugly head: if every town closed its doors to poor people from outside, a roving army of rootless people would develop.

Under those circumstances the 'central' authority intervened by issuing regional residence rules. In 1682 the States of Holland declared that 'all such persons who have moved from any place to the towns or to the countryside shall, after a period of one year, be deemed no longer to belong to the place from which they have moved.'[50] Other provinces followed that example and introduced similar rules in order to stop towns from passing indigent groups back and forth.[51] The central authorities intervened, in other words, not by building workhouses as de Swaan would have it, but by passing rudimentary local poor laws. Yet while the new measures limited opportunities for impoverished people to be sent away, towns were confronted with an influx of poor immigrants whom they now had to support after a year's residence. Towns appear to have started demanding letters of surety to put a stop to that. Leiden, for instance, introduced the surety letter system in order to keep away 'poor people from outside the town, beggars, wheedlers, vagrants, vagabonds, idlers, and other undesirables' whom the town would otherwise have to support.[52] In 1697 Rotterdam defended its surety letters policy by referring to the

> many poor and undesirable people [coming] from all sides to this town and jurisdiction with the intention of being supported by its Protestant charities and almshouses [which] is greatly to the detriment not only of the poor people of this town ... but also leads to the total ruin of the aforementioned Protestant charities and almshouses.[53]

In many instances we do not know whether or when individual towns started requesting letters of surety (and we know much less about villages), and so we cannot describe exactly how the system developed. It is clear, however, that it was well-established during the eighteenth century.

How were these local entry conditions enforced in practice? To safeguard relief organizations from immigrants' future relief costs, financially liable immigrants had to be singled out and sent back, either upon arrival or at least before a year had passed. This sometimes happened at the city gates, when beggars and other 'hopeless cases' were sent away, while bargemasters involved in human trafficking were punished, and where some paupers were given a modest amount of travel money to move on.[54] The latter was a common response to migrants, as Jeremy Boulton shows for eighteenth-century London, elsewhere in this volume. Selection also happened in town, in the districts or wards. From the end of the seventeenth century wardens, for example in the city of Rotterdam, closely monitored who lived in their district. They checked whether non-Rotterdammers had a certificate of admission (*akte van admissie*) and referred them to the Commissarissen van Admissie (Admissions Commissioners) or denounced them to the constabulary. Admission was granted only if applicants could provide for themselves and held the necessary papers, which included a letter of surety to the value of 300 guilders – around a year's minimum wages – issued by their place of origin or by family members, friends, fellow countrymen or employers. Illegal migrants without the necessary papers were to be evicted by the constabulary. Only immigrants who had been awarded a right of admission and had lived in Rotterdam for more than two years without recourse to assistance were eligible for relief.[55]

From the middle of the seventeenth century onwards Haarlem's magistrate also used wardens of the various neighbourhoods to monitor local population movements. Haarlem residents were required to report to the warden when they rented out accommodation to strangers. The warden kept a list of everyone living in his neighbourhood, registering co-residents and their occupation or trade. The magistrate was particularly concerned to keep out poor immigrants, in order to protect the city's relief funds. In 1678 the wardens were ordered explicitly to keep a close watch on poor immigrants. They were to advise the burgomasters on certificates of admission, which were given only to those newcomers who could support themselves or held a letter of surety. Only those having resided in town for four consecutive years with a certificate of admission were eligible for municipal poor relief. Despite these strict rules, the wardens sometimes failed to observe them, and permitted strangers without certificates of admission to stay.[56]

Other Dutch cities also used wardens to distinguish 'valuable' migrants from 'liabilities'. Leiden was divided into 130 districts, and district wardens were to ensure that no one offered accommodation to migrants without a letter of citizenship or surety.[57] Groningen, Delft and Leeuwarden used similar practices.[58] In Leeuwarden the district wardens were selected from the lower ranks of society in the hope that they had intimate knowledge of the poor. From the middle of the seventeenth century onwards, Leeuwarden magistrates also periodically checked whether relief recipients had all the necessary papers and removed those who did not. As Leeuwarden was a garrison city, this included impoverished families of soldiers or former soldiers, who were not considered as residents and could therefore not claim relief.[59] In the province of Drenthe, secular and ecclesiastical authorities together regulated the coordination of poor relief between various localities, and also endorsed the use of surety letters.[60]

Letters of surety and associated residence rules, then, were used from the late seventeenth century onwards to limit urban immigration. The system did not, however, enjoy universal support. In 1785, for instance, textile manufacturers in Leiden complained that the requirement to present a letter of surety hindered the immigration of skilled workers to the town. In Rijnland, the authorities even stopped demanding letters of surety because 'it led to a shortage of building workers'.[61]

Amsterdam as a Safety Valve

Amsterdam found itself in a very particular situation with regard to immigration policies. It was, and always had been, a city of immigrants. The city attracted large numbers of newcomers looking for work on its ships and quaysides, and in its warehouses and industries.[62] Some of those migrants, or their wives and children, applied for poor relief.[63] According to the Municipal Charity, sailors and textile workers received most support, and the availability of poor relief was one factor attracting them to the city. In 1681, when the guardians of the Municipal Charity in the west of the city were asked for advice on how to stop the growth of the indigent population, they warned against any measures that could hinder the immigration of sailors: it was exactly because they knew that their wives and children would be taken care of that sailors came to Amsterdam. Sailors' families accounted for more than half the support given to the poor in their part of town, and the councillors considered it essential to 'support their wives and children so as to ensure that the men were available in times of need', such as war efforts.[64] The Municipal Charity guardians in the east of the city argued that measures to restrict migration ran the risk of deterring valuable labour from coming to the city. It was vital to ensure that entry restrictions 'do not keep away all types of worker and travelling folk'. Because 'the wheat is mixed with the chaff', they advised 'leav[ing] the separation to the Lord's harvest'.[65]

Amsterdam could not participate in the system of letters of surety and associated entry rules, in other words, because this would have restricted the influx of labour needed for the fleet. Other towns were probably not particularly troubled by Amsterdam's failure to take part in the scheme, as it meant migrants could always turn to Amsterdam. On balance, the number of people moving to Amsterdam exceeded the number leaving the city, and so the number of potential poor people in Amsterdam increased. That brings us to an important explanation as to why there was no periodic breakdown in poor relief as a result of the geographical free-rider problem. During the Golden Age, a dynamic labour market absorbed large numbers of migrants. When the economic downturn of the late seventeenth century caused an increasing number of cities to tighten their entry rules, migrants expelled elsewhere were always able to move to Amsterdam in the hope of finding work there. Migration to the Dutch Indies, via the port of Amsterdam, was also an option, albeit as a last resort. In that way, Amsterdam acted as a kind of safety valve, relieving excess pressure on local poor relief. Amsterdam absorbed excess poor migrants like a sponge, shipping large numbers of them to the Orient. Those who remained could rely on a well-developed charitable structure in the city and a culture of charitable giving. Generous donations to the poor came from the world of international trade and high finance, as well as from the middle class in the broad sense of the word.

Any sponge needs to be wrung out now and then if it is to work properly, but how was that to be done in the case of Amsterdam? Having rejected the use of letters of surety, what did Amsterdam do to prevent excessive demands on its poor relief funds without deterring the influx of labour? In 1682 the Municipal Charity guardians in the west of the city suggested paying closer attention to the kind of people coming into the city, although their colleagues from the east thought that was unfeasible; they also wanted to punish 'such shipowners and captains (especially from the East and Norway) who transport poor people here, where they fall to the charge of the church'. Restricting the numbers of unwanted new-comers would also make the work of district wardens easier. A monitoring body of district wardens had been set up in 1652, but it had not been particularly effective. We know little about the responsibilities of district wardens in Amsterdam, but we do know that they had to approve applicants for poor relief and keep records of how long they had lived in the city. A second way of preventing charitable over-stretch was to provide support for migrants only after they had lived in Amsterdam for a specific time, and Figure 7.3 shows that the length of residence required for relief eligibility rose gradually over time, especially in the seventeenth century.

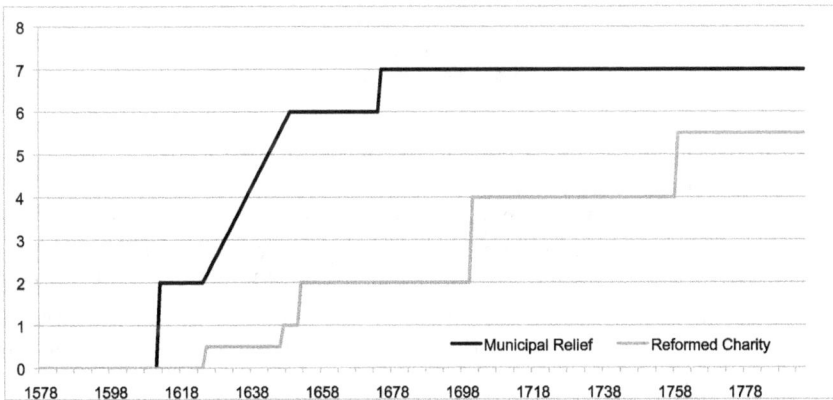

Figure 7.3. Number of Years of Residence Required for Relief Eligibility in Amsterdam, 1578–1795

Source: ACA PA 377, no. 221, fos 157, 163; no 25bb, 25, 42; Wagenaar, *Opkomst* 2(156); Heerma van Voss, 'De armenzorg in Amsterdam', 37, 54.

Note: From 1759 the line for the Reformed Charity is the average number of years for those born in the Netherlands (five years) and those born outside the Nether-lands (six years). The municipal relief organization raised the number of residence years required from two in 1612 via four 'some years later' to six in 1650, which has been represented in the graph via linear interpolation.

A third strategy was to tighten conditions for support, and that was done between 1675 and 1682: the unemployed no longer received support from the Municipal Charity in the summer and could no longer receive support from more than one source. A fourth method was to cut the value of winter relief.[66]

All those measures were used by the urban authorities to enable local poor relief to operate effectively until the end of the eighteenth century. At that point, things became more difficult. The proportion of indigents in the city's population grew rapidly, as did the cost of in-kind relief. During the period of Batavian and French rule, deep cuts were made in the value of poor relief and the charitable institutions had to sell some of their assets. Poor relief in Amsterdam almost collapsed, but that was not an example of the collapse of local poor relief described by de Swaan. The situation he describes arose from an influx of the poor from outside the city, whereas migration to Amsterdam dried up at the end of the eighteenth century and became an exodus in the period of Batavian and French rule. In other words, the poor relief crisis experienced in Amsterdam at the end of the eighteenth century was not the consequence of other towns expelling their poor, but an internal affair caused by the lack of employment opportunities – including the decline of the Dutch East India Company (VOC) – and a rise in food prices. Furthermore, as noted earlier, it was a temporary breakdown and not a periodic meltdown.

The Workhouse

Another of de Swaan's arguments, on the importance of the workhouse, also requires qualification. Established in Amsterdam in 1596, workhouses spread across Western Europe in the following centuries. The fact that they form part of a European-wide process of cultural diffusion, combined with the Dickensian horror stories of workhouse life and the fact that many workhouse buildings still exist may explain part of the scholarly and public fascination with workhouses.[67] Yet their actual importance in the context of local relief policies was limited.

We know most about the Amsterdam workhouse for the first half of the nineteenth century. It catered to all and sundry: convicted beggars, intransigent children placed by their parents as a lesson in obedience, debtors taken hostage by their creditors in the hope of persuading them into payment, and, on a modest scale, individuals who voluntarily went along with their families. This varied group picked oakum, knitted socks and gloves, and made rugs from cattle hair. The workhouse cared for between several hundred and one thousand poor men and women every year, a figure which, although not unsubstantial, pales in comparison with the average of 55,000 who were in regular receipt of outdoor relief each year.[68]

In practice, it was impossible to direct all migrant paupers to the workhouse for a variety of reasons. First, it would have caused problems for the underemployed, such as transport workers. They roamed the streets of Amsterdam, combing the city for odd jobs. They worked wherever they saw work. It would not have made sense to lock them up, as that would have ended their on-and-off participation in the labour force.[69] Secondly, incarcerating the poor in the workhouse was expensive. Supplying clothing, shelter, fuel for heating, and food entailed costs much higher than those of a modest poor relief allowance supplementing other sources of income. For the workhouse, the annual average cost per inmate was ninety-six guilders, as opposed to between four and nine guilders for institutions providing outdoor relief. Thirdly, some Amsterdam workers, artisans, and journeymen refused to go to the workhouse willingly, since it made them feel like prisoners.

The workhouse did serve a purpose for a particular group of unemployed men and their families during wintertime. A small number of people were desperate enough to seek and be granted admittance. That was the case with destitute migrants who had recently arrived in the city and were faced with the bleak prospect of a winter without food, friends or family, and without the means to return to where they came from. Despite the high costs, those individuals were admitted into the workhouse, not so much out of a desire to maintain them as part of a labour reserve but out of fear. Municipal officials believed that such an underclass might resort to stealing and plundering if left to itself. Furthermore, municipal authorities argued that they needed a 'less eligible' place to use as a deterrent against begging, the more so as desperately hungry beggars could not be prevented from begging without giving them an alternative.

The workhouse capacity was so limited that it could function only as a threat to the masses of the poor. A few troublesome paupers could be held in check, but it was not a feasible way to deal with hungry masses of hundreds or thousands of poor. Even arresting a modest number of beggars often proved difficult, as bystanders would often intervene on their behalf. It was economically inefficient to incarcerate the mass of the poor: it was much more costly than outdoor relief, it acted as a disincentive to underemployed workers to find work, and it was resisted by many and therefore even more costly to realize. The workhouse was of importance, however, both in keeping a small underclass of desperate newcomers from stealing or plundering, and because it could serve as a threat to the masses of the poor.

Migrants' Relief Entitlements in
the Nineteenth and Early Twentieth Centuries

In 1811, the system of letters of surety was abolished, or, more accurately put, it was replaced by another scheme, covering the entire country, established by the *Wet op het Domicilie van Onderstand* (Domiciliary Relief Act). That scheme became the first in a series of national laws designed to prevent municipalities from engaging in a policy of 'pass the parcel' with the poor.[70] There are several reasons why it is useful briefly to consider those laws here. First, it will dispell the myth that the free-rider problem haunted only the early modern period, and that there therefore was a sharp discontinuity in the ability of Dutch society to solve it. Second, it helps clarify the scope for, and limitations on, resolving the geographical free-rider problem. Third, it casts further light on the consequences of potential solutions.

The 1811 *Wet op het Domicilie van Onderstand* stipulated that a poor person could apply for relief only in his or her place of birth, unless that individual had moved to a different municipality, in which case that new municipality would be responsible for poor relief after a period of one year. The subsequent 1818 *Wet op het Domicilie van Onderstand* extended that period to four years. Some poor relief authorities circumvented the new law.[71] The fragmentation of poor relief, the absence of population records, the lack of clarity as to whether these residential requirements also applied to ecclesiastical poor relief, and the initial unwillingness of the Gedeputeerde Staten (Provincial Estates) to adjudicate in disputes, resulted in the law triggering drawn-out disputes and correspondence.[72]

Nonetheless, the new system did represent an improvement over the letters of surety. For the first time, there was a national scheme, in principle compulsory, designed to address the geographical free-rider problem. In the course of time, case law and royal decrees improved the law by implementing rules designed to clarify those doubtful cases which had initially given rise to disputes. Thus, in 1833, it was finally resolved that the law also applied to ecclesiastical poor relief. The 1854 *Armenwet* (Poor Law) made place of birth the place of legitimate support, though only for public relief. Where a person received poor relief in a municipality other than that in which he or she was born, the municipality bearing the costs could reclaim them from the municipality of birth – in which case the municipality of birth had the right to demand that the recipient return to his or her place of origin.[73]

The right of restitution caused problems for villages and small municipalities. Migration from rural areas to the city meant that, on balance, small rural municipalities had to pay more for their poor living elsewhere than they could reclaim for relief paid to the poor from outside their own municipality, so in 1870 the law was amended. From then on, the municipality of residence became the place of legitimate support, and that applied to both ecclesiastical as well as civic poor relief, which further encouraged migration from rural areas to cities.[74] During the agricultural depression of the 1880s many unemployed agricultural labourers moved to towns and cities in the hope of either finding work or receiving poor relief, the provision of which was generally better developed in cities than in rural areas.[75] Sometimes, that migration was instigated by rural poor relief bodies themselves, keen to shift the burden of assistance on to the cities and prompting complaints that the urban 'Alsmhouses and orphanages were an enticement to the rural indigent'.[76] A new poor law was drafted, the explanatory memorandum to which asserted that 'apart from owing to the drift from the countryside, large municipalities repeatedly experienced injurious consequences because small municipalities endeavoured to pass on their sick or needy'.[77]

The 1912 Poor Law included a provision whereby the local authorities where a migrant applied for relief could, within one year, petition the Gedeputeerde Staten to charge the cost of that relief to the recipient's municipality of birth. The court would then consider the case, with the final decision lying with the Gedeputeerde Staten, although an appeal to the Crown was possible.[78] The provision quickly proved to be a dead letter. The major cities, which had to bear the costs, were thus confronted with a new problem. The high level of taxes necessary to finance poor relief drove the better off to the more affluent villages nearby. The towns and cities responded by endeavouring to drive away poor newcomers, often using improper means, for example by preventing them from registering in the population register and thus effectively denying them a right of admission, by reducing the level of relief, by making it impossible for them to engage in a profession – by refusing to issue hawkers with a license for instance – or by setting up agreements with other cities akin to the erstwhile letters of surety.

In the first half of the twentieth century, the Netherlands experienced a similar classic geographical free-rider problem. One can therefore hardly maintain that the free-rider problem was intrinsic to poor relief in the early modern period, causing its collapse, after which the national government assumed control and resolved the problem. During World War II the geographical free-rider problem was alleviated to some extent because municipalities (beginning with the seven largest in 1942 but expanding very soon to include ninety-one by 1943 and 194 by 1952) undertook to collaborate, under certain conditions of a medical and social nature, in relocating their respective indigents.[79] Moreover, social security legislation gradually took over the work of providing for the poor. It was not until the *Algemene Bijstandswet* (Social Assistance Act) of 1965 that the geographical free-rider problem was finally resolved, because from then onwards it was the state, and no longer the municipalities, which paid and administered assistance.

Any arrangement designed to relieve poverty had consequences for migration flows and thus also for economic life and social order. The simplest option was for relief to be provided by the municipality of birth. In almost all cases, it was clear which that was. However, such an arrangement hindered migration because any potential migrant would take account of the loss of entitlement when deciding whether or not to move. Furthermore, it might lead to problems maintaining order among those who nonetheless left. Impoverished migrants, denied relief in the municipality to which they moved, might be more inclined to resort to undesirable survival strategies, or form gangs and cause disorder in the countryside. An alternative was to have the place of residence pay the costs of relief, which would not have impeded migration but could have imposed a heavy burden on poor relief funds in those municipalities to which many went in search of work or who were perhaps attracted by the relief provided. Hybrid solutions along the lines of 'the place of birth, unless the applicant had not lived there for a time' or 'the place of residence, but only after the applicant had lived there a number of years' were compromises involving those two extremes. The system of letters of surety was such a hybrid solution. It acted as a brake on migration, to a lesser extent than if relief were to be paid automatically by the place of birth but to a greater extent than if the costs always lay with the place of residence. It is no coincidence that the letters of surety system was introduced at the end of the seventeenth century at a time of economic stagnation, labour market segmentation, and a desire to reduce migration, just as it is no coincidence that the first poor law requiring the place of residence to pay the costs of support – that of 1870 – was introduced at a time of economic growth, labour market desegmentation, and increasing migration.

Conclusion

During the Republic, urban poor relief in the Netherlands did not periodically collapse. On the contrary, it operated continuously and as a rule relatively satisfactorily, although in Amsterdam it did come close to collapse during the Batavian and French period. Even through that disastrous period, poor relief survived. Moreover, the near collapse of poor relief in Amsterdam was not the consequence of an influx of paupers rejected by other municipalities, as the thesis of periodic collapse would have it. In fact, at that time there was actually an exodus of poor from the city. During the Republic the lack of periodic crises meant that pressure on poor relief was muted. The first national scheme to regulate the relationship between domicile and relief at the start of the nineteenth century was therefore not an act of 'crisis management'. The national state had been created for completely different reasons and expanded upon the existing system of interlocal and interregional support arrangements – that of the letters of surety in the broadest sense.

The geographical free-rider problem was certainly an issue and would continue to exist until well into the twentieth century. However, during the Golden Age it was probably not a matter of great concern: the expanding local Dutch labour markets absorbed large numbers, and migrants could always move to Amsterdam in the hope of finding work there, or, as a last resort, sail with the fleet to the East. When after the Golden Age, economic growth stagnated and labour market rigidity set in, urban labour markets no longer benefitted from migrants as much as before and cities were tempted to repatriate non-local poor. It was then that the regional authorities intervened, as de Swaan claims, though it was to prevent local poor relief from collapsing rather than in response to its collapse, and more by way of issuing rudimentary regional poor laws than by setting up workhouses with a supralocal function. Many municipalities responded by participating in the letters of surety system. That system had a regulatory effect on migration, so improving the stability of local poor relief. At least as important for the continuity of poor relief as other stabilizing factors – the role of capital assets as a buffer, toughening the criteria for relief eligibility, cutting levels of relief, and stockpiling – was the letters of surety system and Amsterdam's special position within it.

Even after the Golden Age, Amsterdam remained the prototypical migration city. The demand for migrant labour, to man the fleet for example, deterred the city from participating in the letters of surety system. Migrants continued to arrive and continued to go to the Dutch Indies. Some newcomers, or their wives, applied for poor relief. By using the stabilizing methods outlined above, the city attempted to limit the costs of relief, and the many poor relief bodies continued to help large numbers of non-Amsterdammers. That Amsterdam's poor relief agencies were able to do so can be attributed partly to the availability of large charitable endowments and the existence of a charitable culture, characterized by many voluntary contributions from broad groups within the population. During the Republic, Amsterdam acted as a 'safety valve', preventing the pressure on local poor relief in the Netherlands from becoming excessive.

Notes

I would like to thank Chris Gordon, Tirtsah Levie Bernfeld, Henk Looijesteijn, Elise van Nederveen Meerkerk and Danielle Teeuwen for their valuable comments. I have reworked material from M. H. D. van Leeuwen. 1996. 'Amsterdam en de armenzorg tijdens de Republiek', *NEHA-Jaarboek* 59, 132–161, for this chapter.

1. A. de Swaan. 1988. *In Care of the State: Health Care, Education and Welfare in Europe and the USA in the Modern Era*, New York, 31–32, and also 6–7, 30–32, 37–41, 50.
2. M. Olson. 1965. *The Logic of Collective Action: Public Goods and the Theory of Groups*, Cambridge, MA.
3. M. H. D. van Leeuwen. 1994. 'Logic of Charity: Poor Relief in Preindustrial Europe', *Journal of Interdisciplinary History* 24, 589–613.
4. See e.g., S. King. 2000. *Poverty and Welfare in England, 1700–1850. A Regional Perspective*, Manchester, 18–24; S. Hindle. 2004. *On the Parish. The Micro-Politics of Poor Relief in Rural England, c. 1550–1750*, Oxford, chapters 5 and 6.
5. Swaan, *In Care of the State*, 36.
6. M. Prak. 1994. 'Goede buren en verre vrienden. De ontwikkeling van onderstand bij armoede in Den Bosch sedert de Middeleeuwen', in H. Flap and M. H. D. van Leeuwen (eds), *Op lange termijn. Verklaringen van trends in de geschiedenis van samenlevingen*, Hilversum, 165.
7. That was not the case in all cities. Moreover, we do not know whether it was true also for those rapidly expanding towns during the Golden Age to which many young people migrated. Young migrants had relatively more children and perhaps a relatively lower mortality rate. On this problem, see A. Sharlin. 1978. 'Natural Decrease in Early Modern Cities: A Reconsideration', *Past and Present* 79, 126–138; A. M. van der Woude. 1982. 'Population Developments in the Northern Netherlands* (1500–1800) and the Validity of the Urban Graveyard Effect', *Annales de démografie historique*, 55–75; P. R. D. Stokvis. 1993. 'Het sterftepatroon in preïndustrieel Den Haag (ca. 1700–1855). De mythe van de stedelijke oversterfte en de sterfte naar jaargetijde en doodsoorzaken', *De Negentiende Eeuw* 17, 201–216.
8. J. Lucassen. 1995. 'Labour and Early Modern Economic Development', in K. Davids and J. Lucassen (eds), *A Miracle Mirrored. The Dutch Republic in European perspective*, Cambridge, 401 n. 9.
9. J. de Vries and A. van der Woude. 1995. *The First Modern Economy: Success, Failure, and Perseverance of the Dutch Economy, 1500–1815*, Cambridge, 72–73.
10. See e.g., T. Levie Bernfeld. 2012. *Poverty and Welfare among the Portuguese Jews in Early Modern Amsterdam*, Oxford, chapter 2, dealing with the extent of migration of Jews to Amsterdam in the early modern period.
11. The position of Jews represented an exception to this: they were seldom, if ever, permitted to join. There were no major barriers to immigrants in the labour market.
12. Again, Jews, and certainly gypsies too, were an exception to the rule. C. M. Lesger and M. H. D. van Leeuwen. 2012. 'Residential Segregation from the Sixteenth to Nineteenth Century: Evidence from the Netherlands', *Journal of Interdisciplinary History* 42(3), 333–369.
13. C. M. Lesger. 1997. 'Migranten in Amsterdam tijdens de achttiende eeuw: residentiële spreiding en positie in de samenleving', *Jaarboek Amstelodamum* 89, 67.
14. See, among others, J. Israel. 1995. *The Dutch Republic: Its Rise, Greatness, and Fall 1477–1806*, Oxford, 26–29, 367ff; M. Prak. 1998. 'Armenzorg 1500–1800', in J. van Gerwen and M. H. D. van Leeuwen (eds), *Studies over zekerheidsarrangementen: risico's, risicobestrijding en verzekeringen in Nederland vanaf de middeleeuwen*, Amsterdam, 54; M. van der Heijden. 2007. 'Juan Luis Vives: icoon van de vroegmoderne armenzorg', in J. van

Eijnatten, Fred van Lieburg, and Hans de Waardt (eds), *Heiligen of helden. Opstellen voor Willem Frijhof,* Amsterdam, 61–71.

15. *L. de Rivière.* 1908. '*De armenzorg in Nederland*', *Tijdschrift voor Armenzorg en Kinderbescherming,* 58–65; A. J. Adriani. 1926. "Johannes Ludovicus Vives en zijn geschrift 'De Subventione Pauperum' na vier eeuwen herdacht", *Tijdschrift voor Armwezen, Maatschappelijke Hulp en Kinderbescherming,* 23 October 1926, 1067–69, and 28 November 1926, 1109–1110.

16. This and what follows is based on Vries and Woude, *The First Modern Economy,* 655ff.

17. Israel, *The Dutch Republic,* 353–60; Vries and Woude, *The First Modern Economy,* 655ff; Prak, 'Armenzorg', 57ff.; J. Spaans. 1997. *Armenzorg in Friesland 1500–1800. Publieke zorg en particuliere liefdadigheid in zes Friese steden: Leeuwarden, Bolsward, Franeker, Sneek, Dokkum en Harlingen,* Hilversum, 17, 367–368; E. van Nederveen Meerkerk and G. Vermeesch. 2009. 'Reforming Outdoor Relief. Changes in Urban Provisions for the Poor in the Northern and Southern Low Countries (c. 1500–1800)', in Van der Heijden et al. (eds), *Serving the Urban Community: the Rise of Public Facilities in the Low Countries,* Amsterdam, 135–154.

18. See H. Nusteling. 1985. *Welvaart en werkgelegenheid in Amsterdam, 1540–1860,* Amsterdam, 161.

19. Galatians 6: 10. This biblical passage was displayed for example in the offices of the Reformed Charity in Amsterdam. See M. H. D. van Leeuwen. 2000. *The Logic of Charity: Amsterdam 1800–1850,* Aldershot and New York, 88.

20. P. Lindert. 2004. *Growing Public: Social Spending and Economic Growth since the Eighteenth Century,* Cambridge. For guild help, see M. H. D. van Leeuwen. 2012. 'Guilds and Middle-Class Welfare 1550–1800: Provisions for Burial, Sickness, Old Age, and Widowhood', *Economic History Review* 65(1), 61–90. For mutual aid in the nineteenth century, see M. H. D. van Leeuwen. 2007. 'Historical Welfare Economics from the Old Regime to the Welfare State. Mutual Aid and Private Insurance for Burial, Sickness, Old Age, Widowhood, and Unemployment in the Netherlands during the Nineteenth Century', in B. Harris and P. Bridgen (eds), *Charity and Mutual Aid in European and North America since 1800,* London, 89–130. Dutch guilds generally did not provide travel money for unemployed artisans, journeymen or apprentices to try their luck in another city, unlike their counterparts in England and Germany. Perhaps there was less need to do so, as the country was smaller and travelling, with barges, easier. Dutch guilds, like charities, were urban phenomena, and so where their welfare arrangements.

21. Prak, 'Armenzorg'; Leeuwen, *The Logic.* Jews were supposed to take care of themselves and stay away from poor relief provided by the city or any other denomination. It was expressly stated thus by the city and repeated in many ordinances or petitions drawn up by the Portuguese community. See T. Levie Bernfeld. 2002. 'Financing Poor Relief in the Spanish-Portuguese Jewish Community in Amsterdam in the Seventeenth and Eighteenth Centuries', in J. I. Israel and R. Salverda (eds), *Dutch Jewry: Its History and Secular Culture,* Leiden, 63–102.

22. See also the recent collection of articles by L. Heerma van Voss, M. H. D. van Leeuwen, H. Looijestein, D. Teeuwen, and E. Van Nederveen Meerkerk on the *Giving in the Golden Age* (GIGA) project, in the theme issue of *Continuity and Change,* 27(1) in 2012. Within the Amsterdam Portuguese Jewish community, however, there was an element of compulsion through the payment of internal taxes, next to voluntary contributions. See Levie Bernfeld, 'Financing', 71–75; Levie Bernfeld, *Poverty,* chapter 5. Taxes included those imposed on general wealth, one on the consumption of kosher meat and one on the imports and exports as well on a number of commercial transactions. See also D. M. Swetschinki. 2000. *Reluctant Cosmopolitans: The Portuguese Jews of Seventeenth-Century Amsterdam,* London, 197–199.

23. M. Prak. 1999. *Republikeinse veelheid, democratisch enkelvoud. Sociale verandering in het Revolutietijdvak, 's-Hertogenbosch 1770–1820*, Nijmegen.

24. Prak, 'Armenzorg' provides an overview. See also the scattered references in Israel, *The Dutch Republic*.

25. M. H. D. van Leeuwen. 1993. 'Surviving With a Little Help: The Importance of Charity to the Poor of Amsterdam 1800–1850, in a Comparative Perspective', *Social History* 18, 320; Leeuwen, *Logic*.

26. For numbers of assisted poor, see van M. H. D. van Leeuwen, J. Schoenmakers and F. Smits. 1981. 'Armoede en bedeling in Amsterdam ten tijde van de Republiek' (Unpublished Paper, University of Amsterdam). For an estimate of population totals in Amsterdam, see M. H. D. van Leeuwen and J. E. Oeppen. 1993. 'Reconstructing the Demographic Regime of Amsterdam 1681–1920', *Economic and Social History in the Netherlands* 5, 61–102.

27. Leeuwen, 'Surviving', 321–327; Prak, 'Armenzorg'; Leeuwen, *Logic*.

28. Prak, 'Armenzorg', 76–81; H. van Wijngaarden. 2000. *Zorg voor de kost. Armenzorg, arbeid en onderlinge hulp in Zwolle, 1650–1700*, Amsterdam, 87–94 and passim; I. van der Vlis. 2001. *Leven in Armoede. Delftse bedeelden in de zeventiende eeuw*, chapter 3.

29. Leeuwen, 'Surviving', 327–331.

30. From 1808 to 1854, 60 per cent of newly registered families received the minimum level of support during the winter; only 2 per cent were given the maximum. M. H. D. van Leeuwen. 1992. *Bijstand in Amsterdam, ca. 1800–1850. Armenzorg als beheersings- en overlevingsstrategie*, Zwolle, 202 n. 77. Single men or women who were severely handicapped, physically or mentally, might receive more.

31. See, for the scattered evidence in other cities, Prak, 'Armenzorg', 76–81; Wijngaarden, *Zorg*, 87–94 and passim; Vlis, *Leven*, chapter 3.

32. Calculated as a 13-yearly moving average from the data (indexed 1650–54=100) collected by H. Nusteling. 1985. *Welvaart en werkgelegenheid in Amsterdam 1540–1860*, Amsterdam, 260–261. In the same period nominal wages in the building industry rose from 41 to 96. Ibid., 235–236.

33. Nusteling, *Welvaart*, 234; Leeuwen and Oeppen, 'Reconstructing', 87.

34. Graphs with information on yearly income of Amsterdam charities can be found in M. H. D. van Leeuwen. 2012. 'Giving in Early Modern History: Philanthropy in Amsterdam's Golden Age', *Continuity and Change*, 27(1), 301–343. In the Amsterdam Portuguese Jewish community the growth of expenditure on welfare was similar. The cost of welfare approximately increased by a factor 4.7 between 1650/1 and 1740/1, both in nominal and in real terms. See Levie Bernfeld, *Poverty*, chapter 5.

35. The study by A. T. van Deursen. 1994. *Een dorp in de polder. Graft in de zeventiende eeuw*, Amsterdam, is exceptional in covering a small village; generally we know less about charity in the countryside. Urban examples include: F.H.M.C. Adriaens. 1956. *De magistraat van Nijmegen en de armenzorg (1750–1800)*, Nijmegen; A.P.A.M. Spijker. 1979. 'Van Aalmoes tot bijstand. Een overzicht van de stedelijke armenzorg in Haarlem', *Haerlem Jaarboek*, 66–98; C. J. van Baar and L. Noordegraaf. 1982. 'Werkschuwheid en misbruik van sociale voorzieningen? Het beleid in de Alkmaarse armenzorg 1750–1815', *Alkmaarse Historische Reeks* 5, 55–67; P. D. 't Hart. 1983. *De stad Utrecht en haar inwoners. Een onderzoek naar samenhangen tussen sociaal-economische ontwikkelingen en de demografische geschiedenis van de stad Utrecht 1771–1825*, Utrecht, 74–99; J. L. Kool-Blokland. 1990. *De zorg gewogen: zeven eeuwen godshuizen in Middelburg*, Middelburg; Spaans, *Armenzorg*. The same applies to specialist institutions such as orphanages. See S. Groenveld, J. J. H. Dekker and T. R. M. Willemse. 1997. *Wezen en boefjes. Zes eeuwen zorg in wees- en kinderhuizen*, Hilversum; A. McCants. 1997. *Civic Charity in a Golden Age: Orphan Care in Early Modern Amsterdam*, Urbana. See also Nederveen Meerkerk and Vermeesch, 'Reforming'.

36. Leeuwen, 'Giving'. For sources of income of the Portuguese Jewish community, see Levie Bernfeld, 'Financing', 100 fig. 4.

37. Leeuwen, 'Giving'.

38. For sermons of rabbis within the Portuguese Jewish community urging the congregation to give to charity, see Levie Bernfeld, *Poverty*, chapter 6; for collections and door-to-door collections, see chapter 5 and Levie Bernfeld, 'Financing', 74. The Portuguese community also contributed to the poor of the city with a yearly contribution on condition the city authorities would stay away from the doors of the Portuguese Jews to collect money. ACA, PA 334, no. 992, 4 (14 April 1644), 1 (5 May 1676).

39. See Figure 7.1. See also the Jewish cost-cutting measures discussed in Levie Bernfeld, 'Financing', 83–85; Levie Bernfeld, *Poverty*, chapter 5. See also Leeuwen, *The Logic*, 120.

40. Even the price rise of relief in kind in the last quarter of the eighteenth century, a problem made worse by an increase in the number of recipients, did not immediately lead to cuts in the level of relief. On the increase in poverty, see P. C. Jansen. 1975. 'Armoede in Amsterdam aan het eind van de achttiende eeuw', *Tijdschrift voor Geschiedenis*, 88, 613–625.

41. M. H. D. van Leeuwen and N. Lucas. 1981. 'De diakonie van de hervormde kerk' (Unpublished paper, University of Amsterdam) 17.

42. P. A. C. Douwes. 1977. *Armenkerk. De hervormde diaconie te Rotterdam in de negentiende eeuw*, Schiedam, 125; G. P. M. Pot. 1994. *Arm Leiden. Levensstandaard, bedeling en bedeelden, 1750–1854*, Hilversum, 170.

43. H. C. de Wolf. 1964. *Geschiedenis van het R.C. Oude-Armenkantoor te Amsterdam*, Hilversum, 201–6. Another Catholic body, the Catholic Girls Orphanage, also multiplied its capital during the seventeenth and eighteenth centuries. R. Meischke. 1980. *Amsterdam. Het R. C. Maagdenhuis, het huizenbezit van deze instelling en het St. Elizabeth-gesticht*, The Hague, 69–73. This was also the case for the Sephardic charity as well as for the burgher orphanage. Levie Bernfeld, *Poverty*, chapter 5, and McCants, *Civic Charity*, chapter 7.

44. J. Wagenaar. 1760–1767. *Amsterdam in zyne opkomst, aanwas, geschiedenissen etc.*, Amsterdam, vol. 2, 149. For a similar mechanism of the use of capital as a buffer and surplus income to be transferred to a special fund in order to protect erosion of the capital, see Levie Bernfeld, 'Financing', 82–83; Levie Bernfeld, *Poverty*, chapter 5.

45. H. W. van der Hoeven. 1985. *Uit de geheime notulen van de "Eerwaarde Groote Vergadering" 1785–1815. Het beleid van de diakonie van de Hervormde kerk te Amsterdam*, The Hague, 178, 184. It should be added that we do not know which valuation principles were applied in estimating the value of the capital held by the Reformed Charity and the Catholic relief agencies.

46. C. A. Davids. 1978. 'Migratie te Leiden in de achttiende eeuw. Een onderzoek op grond van de acten van cautie', in H. A. Diederiks et al. (eds), *Een stad in achteruitgang. Sociaalhistorische studies over Leiden in de achttiende eeuw*, 146–192, esp. 174.

47. C. W. van Voorst van Beest. 1955. *De katholieke armenzorg te Rotterdam in de zeventiende en achttiende eeuw*, The Hague; H. Gras. 1989. *Op de grens van het bestaan. Armen en armenzorg in Drenthe 1700–1800*, Zuidwolde. For a recent overview of types of indentity registration, see H. Looijesteijn and M. H. D. van Leeuwen. 2012. 'Establishing and Registering Identity in the Dutch Republic', in K. Breckenridge and S. Szreter (eds), *Registration and Recognition. Documenting the Person in World History*, Oxford, 211–251.

48. See P. Styles. 1963. 'The Evolution of the Law of Settlement', *Birmingham Historical Journal* 9, 33–63; S. King. 2000. *Poverty and Welfare in England 1700–1850. A Regional Perspective*, Manchester, 23; Hindle, *On the Parish*, chapters 5 and 6. See also A. Winter. 2008. 'Caught between Law and Practice: Migrants and Settlement Legislation in the Southern Netherlands in a Comparative Perspective (c. 1700–1900)', *Rural History* 19, 137–162.

49. Vries and Woude, *The First Modern Economy*, 72–78, 632–664, esp. 659–660. See also Prak, 'Armenzorg'.

50. Quoted in Davids, 'Migratie', 187 n. 16.

51. The states of Utrecht in 1687, Zeeland in 1705, Overijssel in 1767, and the Estates General acting for Limburg and Brabant in 1792. See G. Luttenberg. 1837. *Vervolg op het Groot Plakkaatboek of verzameling van wetten betrekkelijk het openbaar bestuur in de Nederlanden. Armwezen,* Zwolle, 13–15, 41–42, 49–53.
52. Quoted in Davids, 'Migratie', 147.
53. Quoted in Voorst van Beest, *Katholieke armenzorg,* 11–12.
54. See e.g., E. Kuijpers. 2005. *Migrantenstad. Immigratie en sociale verhoudingen in zeventiende-eeuws Amsterdam,* Hilversum, 297–98; A. Buursma. 2009. *'Dese bekommerlijke tijden'. Armenzorg, armen en armoede in de stad Groningen 1594–1795,* Assen, 91.
55. Voorst van Beest, *Katholieke armenzorg,* 10–22.
56. G. Dorren. 1998. *Het Soet Vergaren. Haarlems buurtleven in de zeventiende eeuw,* Haarlem, 65–78.
57. Davids, 'Migratie', 138.
58. Buursma, *Dese bekommerlijke tijden,* 90–95, 137 (Lutheran relief), 142 (Jewish relief) on Groningen; Vlis, *Leven,* 53 on Delft.
59. Spaans, *Armenzorg,* 258–263.
60. Gras, *Op de grens,* 63–84.
61. P. B. A. Melief. 1955. *De strijd om de armenzorg in Nederland, 1795–1854,* Groningen, 74; Davids, 'Migratie', 149.
62. Among European Jews, Amsterdam was reputed for its tolerance: Jews could come in and settle down without a numerus fixus or without the obligation to pay a common tax to the authorities, while Amsterdam offered economic chances in the city or overseas. Moreover, the Portuguese Jewish community had a reputation of being extremely benevolent to Jews from other centres in Europe. Therefore poor Jews, rejected elsewhere, streamed into the city and expected help from the Portuguese community which in principle was set up and intended for refugees from the Iberian peninsula only. For restrictions on unwanted immigrants, see Levie Bernfeld, *Poverty,* chapter 2. The Amsterdam Portuguese community tried to relocate 'non-local' or undesirable poor ever since the community established itself in Amsterdam at the turn of the seventeenth century.
63. L. Heerma van Voss. 1958. 'De armenzorg te Amsterdam in de 17e eeuw' (unpublished dissertation, University of Amsterdam), esp. 58 and 69 on applications for relief in 1682, 45 on poor relief as a pull factor, and 46–47 on the distribution of peat to the Huguenots.
64. Ibid., 107.
65. Ibid., 58.
66. Ibid., 41–42, 54–57, and 82 on the value of winter relief; 46 and 59 on restrictions on summer relief; 44 on ships' captains; and 47 on multiple relief.
67. C. Lis and H. Soly. 1979. *Poverty and Capitalism in Pre-industrial Europe,* Brighton, chapter 4; Swaan, *In Care of the State,* 47; P. Spierenburg. 1991. *The Prison Experience: Disciplinary Institutions and Their Inmates in Early Modern Europe,* New Brunswick, 55–59. For the Portuguese Jewish workhouse, intended for Ashkenazi Jews and copied from the Amsterdam city institution, established 1642 and functioning until 1670, see Levie Bernfeld, *Poverty,* chapter 4.
68. Leeuwen, *The Logic.*
69. In that respect the workhouse was nevertheless more advantageous than the labour colonies in the north of the country. Placement there ended labour force participation totally, whereas volunteers in the workhouse could, on request, be granted a short leave of absence to solicit work. Such leave of absence, although useful, still could not wholly solve the problem of labour force participation.
70. This is not entirely true. The national Poor Law of 1800 (section 15) had already abolished the letters of surety system. It also stipulated that relief would be the responsibility of the municipality of residence, on the understanding that church poor relief bodies were not required to support the poor from elsewhere who had received relief during the past three

years or who had applied for such relief within a year of arriving. Those poor would be able to apply to a general poor relief fund. However, it quickly became apparent that this fund was not going to be set up, and in 1802 section 15 was abrogated. Luttenberg, *Vervolg,* 59–60, 63–64.

71. Melief, *De strijd,* 146–147; Leeuwen, *The Logic,* 49–50.
72. Luttenberg, *Vervolg,* 83–84. For the 1818 law, see ibid., 127–139. See also the additional details set out by royal decree over the years, including that of 1833 concerning ecclesiastical poor relief. Ibid., 242–243. See also G. Ramaker. 1936. 'Afwenteling van kosten van armenzorg op andere gemeenten', in J. G. Ramaker, F. M. J. Jansen and J. de Bruin, *Prae-adviezen over het onderwerp: afwenteling van kosten van armenzorg op andere gemeenten,* Haarlem, 19. The 1818 law stipulated that existing letters of surety would retain their validity (section 9), but that new letters would have no legal force (section 14).
73. Ramaker, 'Afwenteling', 11, and also 15 on the cost of restitution.
74. Ibid., 11–12; Leeuwen, 'Amsterdam', 158.
75. Ramaker, 'Afwenteling'; P. T. Kok. 2000. *Burgers in de bijstand. Werklozen en de ontwikkeling van de sociale zekerheid in Leeuwarden van 1880 tot 1930,* Franeker, 229; A. L. Kort. 2001. *Geen cent te veel. Armoede en armenzorg op Zuid-Beveland, 1850–1940,* Hilversum, 119.
76. A. L. Kort. 1985. 'Armoede en armenzorg in Goes 1860–1914', *Historisch Jaarboek voor Zuid- en Noord-Beveland* 11, 74.
77. F. M. J. Jansen. 1936. 'Afwenteling van kosten van armenzorg op andere gemeenten. De huidige stand van het vraagstuk, bezien uit het gezichtspunt van de centrum-gemeente', in Ramaker, Jansen and de Bruin, *Prae-adviezen over het onderwerp,* 44.
78. Section 40 of the Poor Law. Ramaker, 'Afwenteling', 25–26. See also ibid., 25–26 on the 'tax refugees'; ibid., 75–81 for the response of the cities; and for the case law, see ibid., 28–42, as well as Jansen, 'Afwenteling', 57–59.
79. See J. C. van Dam. 1952. 'De intercommunale verhuisregeling in een nieuwe versie', *Tijdschrift voor Maatschappelijk Werk* 6, 239–420.

CHAPTER EIGHT

AGRARIAN CHANGE, LABOUR ORGANIZATION AND WELFARE ENTITLEMENTS IN THE NORTH-SEA AREA, C. 1650–1800

Thijs Lambrecht

Introduction

In May 1772 the sexton of the village of Reningelst recorded in his diary that parishes throughout the coastal area of the Austrian Netherlands were ordering immigrants to return to their parishes of birth. In some cases pauper families were loaded on a cart and transported back collectively. The author noted that these pauper evictions were illegal because they also targeted migrants who had not applied for poor relief. In other words, able-bodied labourers and their households were also compelled to leave.[1] The expulsion of agricultural labourers and their families characterizes an interesting episode in the history of poor relief organization and settlement regulation in the region. The scale and intensity of pauper removals was probably unprecedented in the Southern Low Countries. Parishes proved eager not only to chase away paupers, but also to remove all excess labour power from their communities.

The timing and place of these pauper expulsions were no coincidence. In this chapter I will argue that the restrictive policies adopted by rural parishes in the North Sea area in this period were the result of a range of socio-economic changes taking place in these communities. From the middle of the seventeenth century onwards, the Flemish coastal region was characterized by the gradual disappearance of medium-sized farms, resulting in a dual social structure: a small group of wealthy farmers who retained the majority of the land on the one hand, and a large group of day labourers with restricted access to land on the other hand. The growing dominance of large farms created a need for a flexible and mobile labour force, which in turn entailed a potential threat to local relief resources. This chapter focuses on identifying and explaining the various strategies adopted by these communities to restrict migrants' entitlements to local resources. Surveying these strategies reveals that the bundle of welfare rights that migrants could obtain constituted an important element in local migration policies. They were, however, complemented by other formal and informal strategies to discourage migration and safeguard relief provisions.

My focus of study is on the region commonly referred to as Flanders. In current language, Flanders is often taken to refer to the northern Dutch-speaking part of Belgium. Historically and geographically, however, 'Flanders' refers to a cross-border coastal area that includes adjacent areas of present-day France, Belgium and the Netherlands. Although this region was divided between three different states also during most of the period under consideration here (France, Southern Netherlands and the Dutch Republic), there are good reasons to treat it as one economic zone. The chapter will thus employ the terms *Flanders* to refer to the 'Belgian' part of the area (the present-day provinces of Western and Eastern Flanders), *Zealand Flanders* to refer to the Dutch part (the western part of the present-day province of Zealand), and *Flandre Maritime* to identify the northern French region bordering the North Sea and the present-day Belgian province of Western Flanders. Although this chapter is mainly concerned with Flanders, the comparable socio-economic developments taking place across the region necessitates frequent reference to these neighbouring regions.

Agrarian Change

From the late Middle Ages to the nineteenth century two main sub-regions existed in Flanders, differentiated by soil conditions, property relations, labour relations and farm size.[2] In the coastal areas, characterized by heavy clay soil or polder land, farms were in general larger than in the inland region. Because of their larger size, these farms also required more hired labour than the family-operated farms and cottages characteristic of the inland regions. Around 1800 a government report stated that the largest farms were encountered along the coasts of the North Sea: in this area 'large' farms frequently constituted more than 40 hectares of land, well above the 20-hectare threshold operable by family hands alone. In the inland regions most holdings were smaller than 20 hectares.[3] Similar structures existed in the neighbouring coastal regions. In the western part of Zealand Flanders more than 52 per cent of the farms were larger than 20 hectares in the mid eighteenth century, together occupying more than 90 per cent of the soil.[4] In northern France, especially around Dunkirk and north of Lille, large farms likewise dominated the rural landscape.[5]

The marked differences between coastal and inland Flemish regions also emerge when we look at sub-regions in closer detail. Data available for the *Franc de Bruges*, the rural district surrounding the city of Bruges, demonstrates that to the north and south of the city a different agrarian structure was in place in the mid eighteenth century (Table 8.1).

Table 8.1. Farm Size North and South of Bruges, 1748 (% of holdings)

Farm Size	North (Polder Area)	South (Inland Area)
0 – 0.5 ha	*51.7*	*41.5*
0.5 – 5 ha	*19.0*	*39.4*
5 – 15 ha	*6.7*	*15.5*
15 – 50 ha	*16.2*	*3.6*
> 50 ha	*6.5*	*0.0*
Total	*100*	*100*

Source: Database Population Census Rural District of Bruges, 1748.

The 1748 census data demonstrate that both in the polder and inland regions of the *Franc de Bruges* small farms (less than 5 hectares) were dominant. Belonging to day labourers, there existed however important differences in the way they were operated. In inland Flanders most cottagers were also active in proto-industrial production: small-scale farming was then combined with textile industries to ensure the survival of the household. In the coastal area, however, no proto-industrial activities existed, making smallholders solely dependent on agricultural wage labour as the main source of their income.[6] Furthermore, purely wage-dependent households were much more prevalent in the coastal area: most of the smallholders there had less than 0.5 hectare of land and were thus forced to sell their labour on the market to ensure their survival. A second striking difference is that the typical 'family farm' (5 to 15 hectares) that could operate independently from labour markets was nearly absent in the coastal area, whereas it was more frequent in inland Flanders. The third major difference is that large farms, which required hired labour, were much more dominant in the coastal area. There were few farms larger than 15 hectares in the inland area of the *Franc de Bruges* and compared to the northern area, they were quite limited in size. In adjacent coastal regions similar agrarian structures existed. In the *chatellenie de Furnes*, situated west of the Bruges district, for instance, large holdings dominated the rural landscape: in 1765 holdings with more than 25 hectares of land made up 58 per cent of all farms.[7]

In sum, the coastal area of Flanders was less diversified in terms of the size of agricultural holdings. It was characterized by profound social polarization: in the polder villages a large number of small cottages co-existed with a few large farms. In inland Flanders rural society was more diversified. Here, farms were on average smaller but also more evenly spread between different size categories. Small and medium-sized farmers were also active in proto-industrial textile production whereas by-employments in the polder area were largely absent. Moreover, while such differences are identifiable from an early date, there is also considerable evidence that the social structure of the coastal areas was undergoing further and profound social transformations in the course of the eighteenth century. Driving these transformations was the success of large farmers in enlarging their holdings even further. Data available for the villages of Ramskapelle and Sint-Joris from the mid seventeenth to the late eighteenth centuries provide a clear illustration of this trend towards even larger farms (Table 8.2).

Table 8.2. Distribution of Land in the Villages of Ramskapelle and Sint-Joris, 1659–1780 (% of holdings)

Farm Size	1659	1765	1780
0.5 – 3 ha	*1.4*	*0.3*	*0.4*
3 – 10 ha	*5.3*	*2.1*	*2.2*
10 – 25 ha	*31.7*	*7.8*	*13.2*
> 25 ha	*61.6*	*89.7*	*84.1*
Total	*100*	*100*	*100*

Source: Vandewalle, *De geschiedenis*, 107.

While in 1659 large farms of more than 25 hectares occupied around 60 per cent of the land, their share had risen to over 80 per cent little than a century later. Similar trends of farm engrossment are observable for other villages too. In Steenkerke, for example, the land held by farms larger than 25 hectares increased from 39 per cent in 1684 to 67 per cent in 1785.[8] As Table 8.2 illustrates, this came at the expense of all other groups in these villages. Although middling farmers were especially vulnerable to losing land to the large farms, smallholders were equally struck by these developments.

Because the data used here only indicate how much land farmers held within a single village, it is possible that they actually underestimate the size of large farms, which could combine multiple holdings over different villages. When in the 1750s and 1760s the magistrates of the coastal regions launched an enquiry into the true extent of large farms, they found that a vast number of large farmers indeed combined multiple holdings. In most cases, they leased two farms in adjacent villages, but sometimes they even leased three or four farms.[9] Especially after the middle of the eighteenth century this seems to have become fairly common practice, notwithstanding the fact that such practices were legally forbidden.[10] The emergence of a class of large farmers was thus probably more elaborate than the data in Table 8.2 indicate. Although less research has been done for the 'Flemish' part of northern France, the frequent complaints voiced by village communities about the destruction of small farms and engrossment of large holdings bear witness to similar trends in this region.[11] In Zealand Flanders, too, similar trends towards a further concentration of land in the hands of a small class of wealthy farmers have been recorded. Especially between 1650 and 1750, large holdings were able to extend their share of the land in rural communities in this region.[12]

The gradual transformation of the Flemish economic landscape did not go unnoticed by eighteenth-century economists and welfare reformers. After 1750 many commentators took a hostile stance towards large farms and condemned the negative effects they produced in terms of agricultural efficiency, population growth and wealth distribution.[13] Because landed interests were for obvious reasons divided on this matter, few projects aimed at curtailing the size of large farms were eventually translated into policy.[14] Yet it is worth noting that several economists and reformers explicitly saw farm engrossment as a cause of rising poor relief expenses. Some of them therefore openly advocated the redistribution of land into smaller holdings. The reformer François-Joseph Taintenier argued in 1775 that dismantling large farms would create more employment in the countryside and decrease the pressure on rural poor relief institutions.[15] Theodore-Agustin Mann, in an influential analysis of the negative effects of large farms on the economy and society, explicitly referred to England to make his point. Here, he argued, rising poor relief expenditure was the direct result of farm engrossment.[16] Among many late-eighteenth-century intellectuals in the Austrian Netherlands there was a strong sense that the economic gains from farm engrossment were not evenly distributed. The attempts at reforming welfare provisioning, and more specically to introduce poor taxes for large farmers, discussed below probably owe some of their trajectory to this intellectual climate.

Labour Organization

The trend towards a greater concentration of land in the hands of large farmers had profound effects on labour demand and organization. As farms grew in size, employment per unit of land dropped and employment rates on large farms declined, especially when they specialized in pastoral husbandry.[17] Data on employment on farms in the North Sea area testify to this economic logic. In Zealand Flanders, for example, farms between 10 and 30 hectares employed on average 7.4 living-in servants in 1748, while on farms of over 70 hectares this was only 4.6 servants.[18] Moreover, large farms also preferred to hire day labourers instead of living-in servants, especially after 1750 when food prices were rising.[19] This was also because on large farms year-round employment was more difficult to achieve: as large farms tended to specialize in either pastoral or arable agriculture, there were marked seasonal peaks in labour demand. Trends towards farm engrossment, combined with rising food prices after 1750, then, resulted in a preference for day labourers over living-in servants.

The details of labour organization and demand on large farms in these regions can be reconstructed from the data collected by an Irish traveller in the early nineteenth century. The report of Thomas Radcliff on the agriculture and the rural economy in the former county of Flanders contains a detailed description of a farm of 66 hectares in the region of Cadzand in Zealand Flanders, which can be considered characteristic of large farms in the coastal areas of Flanders (Figure 8.1).[20]

The information collected by Radcliff indicates that the labour force employed on this farm can be divided into three different categories. First, the farm employed a number of servants. This category of workers lived with their employer and received a cash wage in addition to food and board. They were generally unmarried young adults who had left the parental household to acquire some savings and skills with an eye to establishing a household later in their lifecycle. The vast majority of the servants in the region were aged between 15 and 30.[21] This particular farmer employed six servants from March to October. From November to February only four servants were hired. Next to these servants the farm also provided year-round employment for four day labourers and their households. Unlike servants, this type of worker did not live with the employer. In most cases day labourers lived in the same village as their employer and in some cases also operated a small agricultural holding.

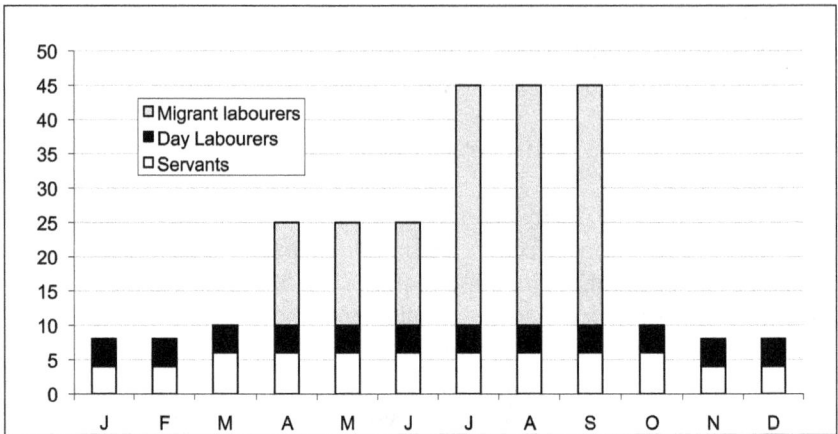

Figure 8.1. Labour Demand on a Farm in Cadzand (Zealand Flanders), c. 1815–1820 (Average Daily Number of Workers per Month)
Source: Calculations from Radcliff, *A Report*, 191–92.

Finally, this farm also employed 15 male migrant labourers from April to June for the weeding season. From July to September, when labour demand peaked, their numbers rose to 35. During these harvest months, migrant labourers were employed in cutting wheat, barley and beans and mowing hay, and housed by their employer in primitive dwellings called 'Vlaamse keten' (Flemish sheds).[22] Radcliff noted that the harvest work was carried out by migrant labourers 'who come in from the neighbouring part of Flanders'.[23]

It is beyond the scope of this chapter to discuss all categories of farm workers in detail, but it is important to highlight that data such as those collected by Radcliff demonstrate that few categories of labourers could expect year-round employment on large farms. One of the main characteristics of the large farms that came to dominate the landscape after 1650 was the controversial seasonal demand for labour. This had important implications for the labourers working on these farms. Data for individual farms in the coastal area show that the terms offered to servants were very different in coastal Flanders compared to the inland region. In inland Flanders, all servants were offered one-year contracts, and May hiring for the year was the dominant labour agreement between farmers and their servants. In the polder regions two dates appear on which servants were hired and dismissed: Mayday and the first of October. A distinction was made between a summer term (5 months) and a winter term (7 months). Whereas nearly all servants were offered yearly contracts in inland Flanders, slightly over half were offered the same terms in the coastal areas. In the coastal areas most servants were hired for the summer term and part of them dismissed in autumn.[24]

The emergence of large and specialized farms thus reduced year-round employment opportunities both for servants and for day labourers. The counterpart was an increase in the employment of migrant labourers. The aldermen of Westkapelle, for instance, described in 1775 how dozens of migrant labourers invaded their parish during the weeding and harvest season. It was estimated that 225 migrant labourers worked and lived there during that part of the year. Their impact on the local labour supply becomes apparent when we take into account that there were only 156 households living in the village on a permanent basis.[25] Zealand Flanders also attracted vast numbers of migrant labourers in the eighteenth century. Here too, it was stated that the additional labour had to be attracted from other regions to take in the harvest.[26] It is estimated that the western part of Zealand Flanders attracted around 1,300 migrant labourers each year by the middle of the eighteenth century, accounting for approximately one-third of all labourers in the region.[27] Farmers around Dunkirk also relied heavily on migrant labourers. In 1789, 377 individuals entered the arrondissement with the intention to return after a few months. The majority of these migrants labourers were employed on large farms for the harvest season.[28]

The wider effects of this evolution towards shorter-term labour contracts were considered by a member of the magistracy of the rural district of Bruges in 1786. He observed that the trend towards a highly seasonal labour demand produced a number of negative effects. Because labour demand was increasingly concentrated in the weeding and harvest season, many workers experienced unemployment during autumn and winter. Both day labourers and farm servants dismissed in autumn had to appeal to the local welfare institutions to tide them over the winter months. Conversely, the summer months witnessed actual labour shortages, especially when the harvest needed to be taken in: even the numerous migrant labourers did not suffice to harvest all the crops in time. The relative labour shortage during the summer months caused particular problems for medium-sized holdings.[29]

From 1650 onwards, then, patterns of labour demand and organization in coastal Flanders underwent fundamental changes, resulting in a highly seasonal demand for labour. The problems of seasonal unemployment and temporary labour shortages confronted local communities with new challenges with regard to poor relief and migration. In order to adequately interpret the strategies they devised to deal with these challenges, it is necessary first to take a closer look at the evolution of the local labour supply and wage levels in this period.

Population and Wages

The coastal regions were characterized not only by a specific constellation of farm size and labour demand, but also by a specific pattern of demographic growth. Throughout the eighteenth century it was frequently noted that the local labour supply in the area fell short of demand, especially during the harvest period, explaining the need to attract migrant labourers from elsewhere. One factor appears to have been that population grew at a much slower pace in the coastal areas than in inland regions: whereas in inland Flanders the population more than doubled over this period, population growth in the coastal areas was considerably less impressive.[30] More detailed data on the rural district of Bruges help to illustrate the marked difference between polder regions to the north and inland regions to the south (Figure 8.2). In the second quarter of the eighteenth century population levels remained more or less stationary in the inland regions, while the coastal areas even witnessed a slight population decline. After 1750 population levels rose steadily in both regions. Yet whereas the coastal areas recorded a population increase of around 20 per cent between 1725 and 1800, in the southern part the increase was more than double that rate over the same period.[31] Explaining these marked differences is difficult in the absence of family reconstitutions. Some contemporary commentators argued that the proportion of the population not marrying was higher and that the average age at marriage was substantially higher in the coastal areas. They blamed large farms and

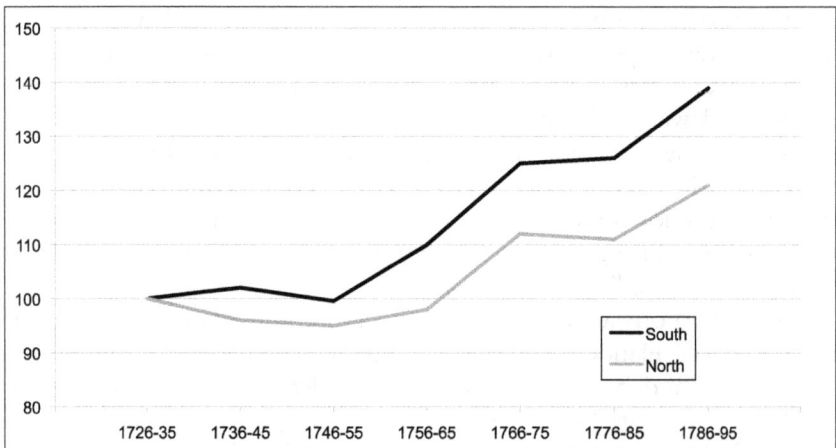

Figure 8.2. Population Levels in the Rural District of Bruges (1726–1735 = 100)

Source: Calculations from Spanhove, 'De bevolkingsevolutie'.

their monopolization of land and resources: household formation was delayed or rendered impossible because there was insufficient land for the smallholder to lease or purchase.[32]

Although this hypothesis has not been tested, it is clear that fertility was not the only factor explaining these different population dynamics. Mortality also intervened and determined the natural growth rate of the population in this area (Figure 8.3). Lack of detailed population data precludes the calculation of death rates. A rather crude measure of the intensity of mortality, the ratio of baptisms to burials, does however suggest that mortality patterns were different in both regions. The data collected for the rural district of Bruges indicates that mortality was higher in the coastal areas than in the inland areas – although the situation improved in both regions throughout the eighteenth century. Different levels of mortality therefore probably partly explain why population growth was slower in polder villages compared to inland communities. The more reliable data we have for the early nineteenth century confirm that mortality rates in the coastal areas were high, oscillating between 30 and 50 per thousand, compared to the inland regions where rates ranged between 20 and 30 per thousand.[33]

Recent research has indicated that the higher levels of mortality in the coastal areas can be attributed to malaria.[34] The ecological conditions of the polder regions constituted a fertile habitat for the Anopheles mosquito. Parishes with extensive marshlands were particularly receptive to malaria in this period. Especially during warm and dry years the disease

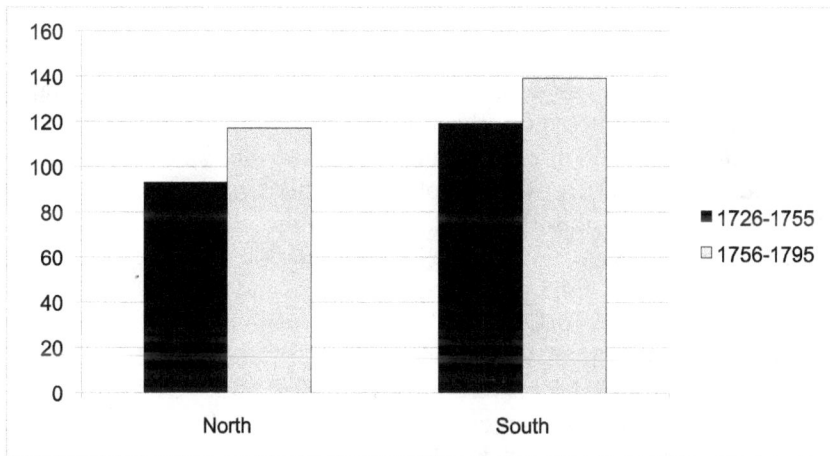

Figure 8.3. Baptisms per 100 Burials in the Rural District of Bruges, 1726–1795

Source: Calculations from Spanhove, 'De bevolkingsevolutie'.

hit the coastal area hard. As a result, the polders enjoyed a bad reputation with regard to health and mortality. Eighteenth-century commentators frequently referred to the effects of malaria on the local population. Although at that time the origins and treatment of the fevers resulting from malaria were poorly understood, it was common knowledge that living and working in the polders posed a health risk. Most contemporary writers conceded that the coastal regions were affluent societies – highlighted by the cleanliness of the peasant dwellings and their rich material possessions – but that the risk of disease and mortality was pressing. In the descriptive accounts accompanying the military map of the Austrian Netherlands compiled by the Count de Ferraris all polder regions were characterized as unhealthy and infected by disease and therefore unsuited for military encampments.[35] The frequent complaints of priests assigned to a polder parish also testify to the unhealthy environment.[36] Whenever they had the chance, they migrated to more inland parishes.[37]

The fevers associated with malaria resulted in mortality, but also in more frequent and recurrent periods of sickness. In 1761 the aldermen of the parish of Verreboek (in the polder region of the *Waasland*) painted a grim picture of the living condition of their parishioners. Although the inhabitants of this region enjoyed some fiscal privileges the village was only thinly populated. Unhealthy 'vapours' rising from the numerous ponds and creeks were seen as the main cause of limited population growth. The effects of malaria on the local population were not restricted to high mortality and low fertility. It was claimed that most inhabitants suffered from recurrent fevers that prevented them from carrying out work on a regular basis.[38] Others observers of the rural coastal economy likewise stated that sickness reduced the work capacity of the local population.[39] As a result, these malaria-infested regions frequently encountered labour shortages during the late summer and early autumn.

One solution was to attract labourers from the more 'healthy' parishes in inland Flanders. Most of the employers in the coastal areas resorted to this tactic, but the unhealthy environment of the polder villages proved to be a serious hindrance. While the local population had developed some degree of immunity, immigrants from inland Flanders were particularly vulnerable to malaria. In 1772, for example, it was claimed that migrants workers in the parish of Westkapelle (near Bruges) suffered massively from fevers when doing harvest work. The unhealthy environment of the coastal area was a challenge that employers in this region needed to overcome. Additional labour could be hired only if the wages that large farmers were willing to pay reflected the health risk run by these immigrants.[40] Malaria in this region thus had a multiple impact on the labour supply. First, its endemic nature resulted in higher mortality rates that checked population growth. Second, many inhabitants suffered from this disease physically, reducing their work capacity and their availability on the labour market. Lastly, the bad reputation of the coastal regions with reference to health resulted in higher wages that necessarily included a health risk premium.

Wage rates between the thinly populated coastal regions and the more densely populated inland regions differed considerably. In the early nineteenth century, the practice of offering relatively high wages was identified as a conscious strategy to attract labour from elsewhere.[41] Employment opportunities and attractive salaries served as a stimulating force for labourers from inland Flanders and more distant areas such as Hainaut to move north for a couple of weeks or months. The first detailed data on regional wage differences date from the early eighteenth century. Whilst under French occupation all servants working in husbandry in the rural district of Furnes were enumerated and their annual wages recorded. In total we have data for more than 1,000 individual servants (Table 8.3). These lists display a wide range of annual wages, a pattern well-known among servants. Yet next to various differences between servants, striking geographical differences emerge. Servants working in the coastal area dominated by large farms received wages that were on average 20 per cent higher compared to their colleagues in the inland areas. Not only servants benefitted from high wages. An analysis of the wages paid during harvest equally reveals substantial differences between the coastal and inland regions. Between 1760 and 1766 harvest labourers on the farm 'Ter Hoyen' (in the inland village of Markegem) were paid 7.05 *schellingen* per hectare for reaping grain. On the farm 'Ter Doest' in the polder village of Lissewege wages were substantially higher: here labourers could earn 11.3 *schellingen* per hectare or some 60 per cent more.[42] Although the distance between these two farms was relatively short (some 40 km), substantial wage differences existed. High wages thus probably stimulated inter-parish mobility and served to attract labourers from regions with a labour surplus.

Table 8.3. Annual Wages of Servants in Husbandry in the District of Furnes, 1701 (£ parisis per year)

	Male Servants		Female Servants	
	N	Average Wage	N	Average Wage
Coastal Area	351	99.45	228	50.24
Inland Area	311	81.54	224	41.63
Total	662	91.01	452	45.98
Wage Difference (%)		+ 22 %		+ 21 %

Source: City Archives Furnes, Old Archives, 752.

Poor Relief, Mobility and Welfare Entitlements

Changes in farm size were accompanied not only by changes in labour organization. As one contemporary observer remarked in the 1780s, the nature of labour demand and organization on large farms – highly seasonal and a marked preference for short contracts – also posed potential threats to poor relief resources.[43] The parishes in the coastal region were thus faced with a double challenge. On the one hand they had to create the conditions to stimulate labour mobility since local labour reserves were insufficient during the peak months of agricultural activity. On the other hand, these communities did not want to run the risk of supporting and maintaining these labourers when dismissed by their employers. In other words, they would need to dissuade immigrants from settling in these parishes on a permanent basis. As local relief resources were financed primarily by charitable donations, the supply of poor relief was, unlike welfare systems based on taxation, highly inelastic. Labour mobility thus had to be reconciled with restricted access to local relief resources.[44] In the course of the eighteenth century, and in particular after 1750, the villages in the region took various measures aimed at both controlling the influx of labour and restricting the access to local relief resources. The available evidence suggests that they changed their policies towards immigration and settlement during this period as a result of the structural changes in the agrarian production system.

In order to adequately analyze these policies, it is important to realize that different types of migrant labour posed very different risk to local relief resources. Seasonal labourers were among those least likely to apply for relief. As the research of Jan Lucassen has demonstrated, many of them were only temporary wage labourers: seasonal labour served as an income supplement to a yearly work cycle that also included agricultural work on their own smallholdings. Once the harvest was taken in most returned home with their wages.[45] The coastal regions however also attracted individuals and households intending to settle there permanently or semi-permanently. Interrogations of individuals arrested for vagrancy frequently refer to agricultural work undertaken in the coastal area and to semi-permanent residence that lasted many years.[46] The high labour demand during the summer months and the possibility of relief during the slack season could in other words attract workers without access to land or relief in their home parish. Data for northern France confirm that population movements with a permanent character existed alongside patterns of seasonal migration. Some 40 per cent of the immigrants to the arrondissement of Dunkirk recorded in 1789 intended to settle there permanently.[47] Servants too posed a threat to local relief resources. As many of them would have been employed for only five months per year, they could become a welfare charge after their dismissal. We may assume, however, that authorities in the coastal regions were most anxious about the permanent settlement of households intending to work as day labourers. Unlike seasonal migrants and servants, such migrants would also bring their children and thus posed the greatest financial threat. That is why settlement laws in the coastal provinces were first and foremost aimed at preventing the permanent settlement of the latter type of migrants.

The first recorded attempts aimed at discouraging labourers from settling permanently in coastal Flanders date from the first decades of the eighteenth century. In 1718 and 1732 the aldermen of the town and rural district of Furnes explicitly forbade the construction of cottages and primitive dwellings on public land in order to limit the influx of poor and 'unproductive' elements – measures that were subsequently extended to private land.[48] From the mid eighteenth century onwards households intending to settle in the area had to apply for a special license to build a new dwelling. These applications could be refused on economic grounds, as for instance when the aldermen turned down an application by an agricultural labourer because the parish was already sufficiently stocked with labourers.[49] In the context of the Southern Netherlands these measures were relatively strict and exceptional. In inland Flanders no such restrictions on immigration and the erection of new dwellings existed. The motives of the magistrate of Furnes were clear: they were granting building permissions only to households and individuals who were unlikely to become chargeable.

These initial attempts to curtail permanent settlement were soon accompanied by measures related to poor relief. In 1750 an agreement was forged between the coastal regions of the Austrian Netherlands and northern France on the issue of settlement and poor relief.[50] This 'Concordat of Ypres' stated that individuals could settle freely wherever they wanted without having to produce a certificate from their parish of origin, thus removing some of the administrative barriers to mobility. More importantly, however, the convention required migrants in need of relief to apply to their parish of birth: irrespective of the duration of their residence elsewhere, their relief needs would always remain a responsibility of their parish of birth.[51] As Franklin Mendels has already observed, the concordat thus facilitated temporary migration into the area, but hindered permanent settlement and access to poor relief in the parish of residence.[52] This Concordat thus suited the interests of the rural village elites in the coastal areas: it stimulated temporary migration to the coastal areas, but also denied those immigrants access to local welfare resources. Yet the Concordat proved a short-lived experiment. Although it catered to the needs of large farmers, many Flemish villages pulled out of the convention by the 1770s. One of the many complaints voiced against the convention referred to spiralling welfare costs, but at this point it is not clear whether they were the result of the convention or a more structural feature of this period. Other complaints focused on the impracticalities of providing relief to individuals residing outside their parish of birth, a consequence of the observed increase of out-resident relief practices. Although the convention was short-lived, it demonstrates that regional authorities did invest time and energy in alternative arrangements that catered to their specific economic needs.[53] In northern France the basic principles of the Concordat remained in place until the Revolution.

The Concordat left another important imprint on the coastal parishes, as it was accompanied by measures to ensure that parishes held sufficient charitable resources to meet their relief responsibilities. In northern France and Flanders, in 1750 and 1751 respectively, local relief institutions were granted the right to tax parishioners if the revenues from charitable donations proved insufficient. These measures should be viewed against the background of relatively meagre welfare resources at parish level, especially in northern France. Some parishes refused to take care of their poor claiming that their parish had insufficient charitable funds. Poor taxes were thus introduced to ensure that these parishes could raise the financial means to take care of their poor.[54] Although the convention was abandoned by the 1770s, it proved a landmark in the sense that it fostered the successful introduction of poor taxes in the region.

Nowhere in the coastal regions was the question of labour migration and relief entitlements debated more vividly than in Zealand Flanders. Especially in the villages bordering the Southern Netherlands, local authorities were engaged in various attempts to restrict and regulate migrants' entitlement to poor relief.[55] In this predominantly Protestant region, questions of settlement and relief entitlement were tied in with religious issues. In the seventeenth century, when the number of Catholics in Zealand Flanders was still relatively small, Protestants and Catholics still enjoyed equal rights to poor relief. In the later decades of the seventeenth century, however, recurrent warfare, military destructions and food shortages fostered an important migration stream from the Spanish Netherlands to Zealand Flanders. Although most of these refugees probably did not intend to settle down permanently, the Spanish War of Succession eventually resulted in the permanent settlement of Catholic families in the region, reflected in the fact that they were granted the right to organize their own religious services in the early eighteenth century.[56] Next to these permanent settlers, many hundreds of labourers also frequently crossed the border in search of work on the large holdings in this area.

From the early eighteenth century onwards, local authorities were increasingly worried about the impact of these Catholic migrants and their families on local relief provisions, and undertook efforts to separate relief responsibilities along religious lines. In 1700 migrants from the Southern Netherlands were ordered to produce a settlement certificate from their parish of birth or else to leave the territory. In the course of the eighteenth century, Catholics became excluded from access to Protestant welfare resources during periods of sickness, old age and unemployment. As the Catholic communities in Zealand Flanders did not possess immovable assets, they were forced to resort to taxation to maintain their poor, in addition to sporadic transfers from co-religionists in the Southern Low Countries.[57] It is no coincidence that efforts to create a parallel circuit of Catholic poor relief originated in a period when the agricultural sector passed through a severe crisis in the first half of the eighteenth century. In other words, the farmers of Zealand Flanders did not want to both pay high wages to migrant workers and support them during sickness and unemployment.[58]

The heavy reliance on taxation to cover relief expenses created considerable tensions within the Catholic communities. In principle, all Catholics had to contribute to the poor fund, from seasonal labourers over servants to settled farmers. Large Protestant farmers however actively supported their labourers in evading taxation, fearing that these welfare taxes would ultimately raise wages. The small Catholic farmers therefore complained that they were forced to pay for the relief expenses of labourers who were primarily employed on the farms of large Protestant farmers – that the latter, in other words, shifted the welfare costs of their labourers to the small Catholic peasants. The settled Catholic community therefore decided to restrict assistance to seasonal labourers to the harvest months only, and insisted that farmers could not retain their migrant labourers longer than was necessary for the harvest season. In the last decades of the eighteenth century a range of financial mechanisms was introduced to further limit the large farmers' opportunities for exploiting Catholic poor relief. They could be held financially accountable for the poor taxes payable by their labourers, and could be forced to refund certain welfare costs incurred by them in the case of sickness or unemployment.[59]

The example of these tensions over relief taxation in Zealand illustrates the risk that large farmers could in certain conditions exploit welfare resources for their own purposes. For example, if large farmers did not have to pay for the welfare costs involved they might prefer to retain their workers after the harvest season, which would place a heavy burden on local relief resources. In this respect, the introduction of poor taxes in the Flemish coastal regions from the mid eighteenth century onwards is likely to have stimulated them to employ local labour reservoirs first before attracting non-residents. Threatening farmers with taxation for welfare purpose, in other words, can be seen as a successful attempt to spread risks more evenly within rural communities. At the same time, it forced them to take an active interest in the material well-being of their settled and less wealthy co-parishioners.

In both Zealand and Flanders, in other words, the second half of the eighteenth century witnessed the introduction of a range of mechanisms to avoid exploitation of the welfare system. This also indicates that the interests of employers and public authorities did not necessarily coincide. Responsibility mechanisms installed by local and especially regional public bodies clearly tried to prevent farmers from using the welfare system to their advantage within their own community.

Control over Land and Labour

The previous section highlights some of the policies to discourage permanent settlement in regions characterized by large farms. Although access to welfare probably played a role when individuals and households contemplated staying or leaving, other factors influenced this decision too. There are some indications that village elites adopted other strategies to avoid permanent settlement, even from those who did not present an immediate threat to welfare resources, for instance to avoid competition for land – which could result in rising rents. To maintain their farms and avoid competition with smallholders, large farmers employed strategies that extended their control over both land and labour. In this section I will analyze these strategies and mechanisms with particular reference to northern France, on which we are best informed. It is likely, however, that similar techniques were adopted in Flanders and Zealand.

The high-wage economy of the polder region was at first sight a stimulus for the under- and unemployed inhabitants of the densely populated inland regions to migrate north. In reality, however, we find that these regions attracted few permanent settlers above the social rank of day labourer and farm servant. The lists compiled by the parishes in the rural district of Furnes in 1771 of heads of households who lived outside their parish of birth show that those active in the primary sector overwhelmingly consisted of day labourers. There are almost no references to smallholders who migrated to this region.[60] This suggests that there were also other factors at play preventing permanent settlement from social groups for whom access to welfare resources was less important.

At first sight wages were high in the coastal area, both in nominal and real terms, but wages should be placed in their social and economic context. Throughout Flanders, wages were part of a wider farmer-peasant ecosystem, engaging large farmers and smallholders in specific forms of exchange of capital and labour.[61] Peasants with small plots of land basically faced two options when it came to preparing the soil. The first was to till their fields using the spade, which was a relatively cheap implement, easily accessible to nearly all households, and operable by human energy. The second was to use animal traction to plough and harrow the fields. But since their plots were too small to raise horses, this was generally not an option unless they could use horse and plough on a temporary basis. That is exactly what happened in eighteenth-century Flanders: smallholders frequently hired large farmers' horse teams for a short period of time. By doing so they actually bought time: while two horses could plough one hectare in approximately 2 days, it would take an adult male some 55 to 65 days to dig over the same surface. Although spade cultivation was more highly regarded – because it increased soil productivity – this nevertheless represented a very labour-intensive activity. The smallholders therefore preferred to use horses and repay the costs with their own labour.

Data available for the inland farm of Ter Hoyen testify to this practice. The farmer charged smallholders in his parish 113 *stuiver* for the use of a plough-team for one hectare. As a male day labourer earned 6 *stuiver* per day, he had to work for 19 days to repay the costs involved. Compared to digging, this represented a net gain of 35 to 45 days.[62] Day labouring was thus part of a time saving strategy by small peasants: because they were willing to sell their labour on the market, they could acquire temporary access to the capital goods of their employers. It allowed them to cultivate their land faster than with a spade and the time won could be devoted to other activities such as proto-industry. In doing so they were able to increase the overall productivity of their household, allocate labour more productively and rationalize their work efforts.

In northern France, and in Artois in particular, a similar exchange system existed between large and small farms. But whereas this exchange system in inland Flanders stimulated social stability, in Artois it became a source of class conflict in village communities. While it had been customary for the richest farmers to lend their plough and wagon teams to smallholders, this usage was disrupted when large farmers started to refuse to lend their capital goods or to charge exuberant rates from the 1760s onwards. Without access to a plough team it was virtually impossible to exploit a small farm of three to four hectares efficiently, so that smallholders

were forced to downsize their holdings. In other words, large farmers in
Artois manipulated the capital/labour ratio in order to force smallholders
to give up some of their land. This land was in turn rented by the large
farmers who could thus expand their holdings. And because smallholders
were forced to downsize, more labour became available. It was an efficient strategy on the part of large capitalist farmers to gain control over
the local land and labour market. Ultimately, the regional authorities of
Artois had to set official rates for plough and wagon services in order to
prevent further social upheaval.[63] These tensions no doubt contributed
to the hostile attitudes towards large farms and farmers at the end of the
eighteenth century.[64]

The events in Artois illustrate how large farmers could gain control over
local means of production. An unfavourable capital/labour ratio for smallholders seriously constrained their options for survival. Eighteenth-century
data for the polder region of Furnes indicate that the capital/labour ratio
there differed considerably from that in inland Flanders. Whereas in Flanders one day of plough work cost the equivalent of approximately 20 days
of manual labour, this was more than 50 in the polder area.[65] Although
wages were high in the polder regions, then, their exchange value relative
to the price of capital goods was low. The unfavourable capital/labour
ratio is likely to have discouraged potential migrants from settling there
permanently. It was only when they exchanged the wages they received in
coastal Flanders with plough and wagon services in inland Flanders that
they actually profited from the higher wages. As they held a monopoly
on capital goods in their parishes, large farmers could thus create conditions that made it very difficult for farmers to exploit small holdings. As
such they were able to neutralize competition for land with smallholders
and to control the local labour supply. As a result, migrants were not only
excluded from local welfare, but also from the land market.

This example indicates that formal rules on immigration and settlement could be accompanied by more informal and at first sight less visible strategies by the local socio-economic elites. Access to welfare and
land markets are probably only two of the many strategies that were used
to shield local resources from outsiders. Interventions in the marriage
market could for instance also be used to deter permanent settlement. In
Zealand Flanders, for instance, regulations on mixed marriages between
Catholics and Protestants were tightened in the course of the eighteenth
century: it was stated that many Catholic youth from poor backgrounds
used mixed marriages in order to gain access to the rights that were tradi-
tionally reserved for locals. Notes in the parish registers kept by the priest
of Krombeke suggest a hostile environment towards immigrants.[66] The
conditions for entry into the parish community were thus defined and

manipulated at different levels that extended beyond welfare and poor relief.

Conclusion

Between 1650 and 1800 there were significant changes in the social and agrarian structures of parishes in the Continental regions bordering the North Sea, producing a very dualistic society formed of a small group of wealthy farmers on the one hand and a large group of agricultural day labourers on the other. These changes in agrarian organization and labour demand created a set of challenges that resulted in a process of institutional innovation in terms of welfare entitlements. As a result of land concentration processes in the course of the seventeenth and eighteenth centuries, rural communities in coastal Flanders, northern France and Zealand Flanders came to display some of the characteristics of 'closed' parishes. As large farmers successfully controlled the rental market, there was a concentration of productive resources into the hands of the wealthy few.[67] However, the wealth that large farmers could accumulate during this period came at a cost, and, especially after 1750, large farmers were forced by regional authorities to share the welfare burdens of their less fortunate co-parishioners.[68] Financial solidarity with the settled poor in their parishes probably was the price they had to pay for their larger holdings. Large farmers could no longer opt out of the relief bill. This shared solidarity and responsibility probably strengthened the sense of community within these parishes and may have attributed to a more hostile environment, both legally and informally, towards outsiders trying to get a foot into the parish door. Large farmers, backed by regional authorities, aimed to stimulate labour mobility but restrict the permanent settlement of outsiders to avoid additional pressures on local poor relief resources.

Reconciling labour mobility, agrarian capitalism and welfare proved a difficult challenge. This chapter illustrates that within a relatively restricted geographical area, different strategies and trajectories could be observed particularly with respect of welfare entitlements. In some way these policies served as an experiment and were later abandoned. Many of the measures adopted relating to welfare and settlement also produced unintended consequences that were later corrected.[69] Although the welfare policies of this period might seem unjust and discriminatory viewed from a contemporary perspective, these experiments probably contributed to the emergence of the comprehensive welfare system that characterizes the North Sea countries today. For it was during this period of experiment and trial and error that one of the basic characteristics of our present-day welfare system was born: risks are shared between all members of society.

Notes

1. J. De Smet (ed). 1970. *Zuid-Westvlaamse tijdskroniek uit de Oostenrijkse en Franse Tijd. Het memoriael van Reninghelst door koster P. L. Cuvelier*, Bruges, 33.
2. See E. Thoen. 2004. 'Social Agrosystems as an Economic Concept to Explain Regional Differences. An Essay Taking the Former County of Flanders as an Example (Middle Ages–19th Century),' in B. J. van Bavel and P. Hoppenbrouwers (eds), *Landholding and Land Transfer in the North Sea Area (Late Middle Ages–19th century)*, Turnhout, 47–66.
3. J. Mertens and W. Vanderpijpen. 1970. 'Schets van de Westvlaamse Landbouw eind achttiende-begin negentiende eeuw. Het rapport van B.J. Holvoet en zijn belang voor de Mémoire Statistique du Département de la Lys', *Handelingen van het Genootschap voor Geschiedenis* 107, 290.
4. P. J. van Cruyningen. 2000. *Behoudend maar buigzaam. Boeren in West-Zeeuws-Vlaanderen, 1650–1850*, Wageningen, 99.
5. G. Lefebvre. 1959. *Les paysans du nord pendant la Révolution Française*, Bari, 41–52; P. Vandewalle. 1994. *Quatre siècles d'agriculture dans le région de Dunkerque 1590–1990: Une étude statistique*, Ghent, 112–113.
6. F. F. Mendels. 1975. 'Agriculture and Peasant Industry in Eighteenth-Century Flanders,' in W. Parker and E.L. Jones (eds), *European Peasants and their Markets*, Princeton, 179–204; C. Gyssels and L. van der Straeten. 1986. *Bevolking, arbeid en tewerkstelling in West-Vlaanderen (1796–1815)*, Ghent, 134–143; C. Vandenbroeke. 1996. 'Proto-industry in Flanders: a Critical Review', in S. C. Ogilvie and M. Cerman (eds), *European Proto-industrialization*, Cambridge, 102–103; W. Vanderpijpen. 1988. 'De proto-industrialisatie in Vlaanderen: een grote regionale diversiteit', in G. Peeters and M. De Moor (eds), *Arbeid in veelvoud. Een huldeboek voor Jan Craeybeckx en Etienne Scholliers*, Brussels, 123–130.
7. P. Vandewalle. 1986. *De geschiedenis van de landbouw in de kasselrij Veurne (1550–1645)*, Brussels, 104.
8. P. Lambrecht. 1986. *De Westhoek: Demografisch profiel en materiële leefwereld (17de–18de eeuw)* (Unpublished MA dissertation, Ghent University), vol. 1, 143.
9. State Archives Bruges, *Brugse Vrije Bundels*, nr. 1782; D. Dalle. 1963. *De bevolking van Veurne-Ambacht in de 17de en de 18de eeuw*, Brussels, 77–82.
10. In 1628 the rural district of Bruges stipulated that no farmer was allowed to rent more than one holding: *Wetten ende Costumen der Stede van Brugghe*, Ghent, 1767, 151. Probably to ensure their fiscal revenues, the aldermen of the rural district of Bruges did not intervene to actively try and halt this trend.
11. See A. de Saint-Léger and P. Sagnac (eds). 1906. *Les cahiers de la Flandre maritime en 1789*, Dunkirk-Paris, vol. 1, 22, 29, 35, 110, 144, 184; vol. 2, 117, 123, 130, 145; Lefebvre, *Les paysans*, 60–63. Other regions in northern France displays similar trends of farm engrossment in the seventeenth and eighteenth centuries. See D. Rosselle. 1983. 'La mise en valeur de la terre dans la France du nord (XVIe-XVIIIe siècles). Réflexions à partir d'un modèle artésien,' in *La terre à l'époque moderne*, Paris, 68–70.
12. P. Priester. 1998. *De geschiedenis van de Zeeuwse landbouw circa 1600–1900*, Wageningen, 184–88 (A. A. G. Bijdragen: 37); Cruyningen, *Behoudend*, 98–103. J. de Vries and A. van der Woude. 1997. *The First Modern Economy. Success, Failure, and Perseverance of the Dutch Economy, 1500–1815*, Cambridge, 550–553, have argued that land concentration was characteristic of the coastal areas in the Dutch Republic during the early modern period.

13. See H. Hasquin. 1981. 'Moyenne culture et populationnisme dans les Pays-Bas autrichiens ou les ambiguïtés du despotisme éclairé', *Revue Belge d'Histoire Contemporaine* 12, 691–712; C. Bruneel. 1990. *l'Hostilité à l'égard des grandes fermes, un aspect du populationnisme dans les Pays-Bas autrichiens. Théorie et réalités brabançonnes,* Louvain-la-Neuve, 7–44.
14. See, for example, F. Zelck. 1988. 'De Staten van Brabant op het einde van het Ancien Régime: hun invloed op de besluitvorming op sociaal-economisch gebied (1770–1794)', in J. Craeybeckx and F. Daelemans (eds), *Bijdragen tot de geschiedenis van Vlaanderen en Brabant: Sociaal en economisch, vol. 3,* Brussels, 190–194.
15. F.-J. Taintenier. 1775. *Supplément au traité sur la mendicité,* Brussels, 37–38.
16. T.-A. Mann. 1783. 'Mémoire sur la question: Dans un pays fertile et bien peuplé, les grandes fermes sont-elles utiles ou nuisibles à l'Etat en général?', *Mémoires de l'Académie Impériale et Royale des Sciences et Belles-Lettres de Bruxelles* 4, 218–219.
17. See R. Allen. 1992. *Enclosure and the Yeoman: The Agricultural Development of the South Midlands 1450–1850,* Oxford, 215–217.
18. Cruyningen, *Behoudend,* 174–175.
19. As has been noted for England by A. Kussmaul. 1981. *Servants in Husbandry in Early Modern England,* Cambridge, 120–134; R. M. Smith. 1999. 'Relative Prices, Forms of Agrarian Labour and Female Marriage Patterns in England, 1350–1800,' in I. Devos and L. Kennedy (eds), *Marriage and Rural Economy. Western Europe since 1400,* Turnhout, 32–37.
20. T. Radcliff. 1819. *A Report on the Agriculture of Eastern and Western Flanders Drawn up at the Desire of the Farming Society of Ireland,* London, 191–193; J. de Hullu. 1943. *Thomas Radcliff's beschrijving van de landbouw in het Land van Cadzand omstreeks 1819,* Oostburg.
21. On the institution of service in Flanders, see Gyssels and Straeten, *Bevolking,* 144–155; T. Lambrecht. 2009. 'Peasant Labour Strategies and the Logic of Family Labour in the Southern Low Countries during the 18th Century,' in S. Cavaciocchi (ed.), *The Economic Role of the Family in the European Economy from the 13th to the 18th Centuries,* Florence, 638–643.
22. See Cruyningen, *Behoudend,* 173.
23. Radcliff, *A Report,* 192.
24. For inland Flanders, see T. Lambrecht. 2002. *Een grote hoeve in een klein dorp. Relaties van arbeid en pacht op het Vlaamse platteland tijdens de 18de eeuw,* Gent, 145–163. For coastal Flanders, see the detailed accounts of large farms of the Abbey of the Dunes in Seminar Bruges, Accounts of the Abbey of the Dunes, nrs. 134–136, 261–266.
25. State Archives Bruges, *Aanwinsten:* 3279. See also J. Lucassen. 1984. *Naar de kusten van de Noordzee. Trekarbeid in Europees perspectief, 1600–1900,* Gouda, 307–310.
26. G. A. C. van Vooren. 1973. 'De armenzorg voor de Katholieken in het Middelburgse missiegebied gedurende de 18de eeuw I,' *Appeltjes van het Meetjesland* 24, 51.
27. Cruyningen, *Behoudend,* 171–173.
28. M. Dieudonné. 1804. *Statistique du Département du Nord,* Douai: Marlier, vol. 1, 525; F. F. Mendels. 1981. *Industrialization and Population Pressure in Eighteenth-Century Flanders,* New York, 113–114.
29. State Archives Bruges, Collection Sanders, 181.
30. C. Vandenbroeke. 1984. 'Le cas flamand: Evolution sociale et comportements démographiques aux XVIIe-XIXe siècles', *Annales E.S.C.* 39, 917–920.
31. L. Spanhove. 1972. 'De bevolkingsevolutie van het platteland omheen Brugge in de achttiende eeuw (1725–1795)', *Standen en Landen* 58, 75–108.
32. With particular reference to the region of Bruges, see the comments in B. Détert. 1786. *De Rapsodisten.* Bruges, vol. 12, 187–188.
33. I. Devos. 2006. *Allemaal beestjes. Mortaliteit en morbiditeit in Vlaanderen, 18de–20ste eeuw,* Ghent, 169.

34. I. Devos. 2001. 'Malaria in Vlaanderen tijdens de 18de en 19de eeuw', in J. Parmentier en S. Spanoghe (eds), *Orbis in orbem. Liber amicorum John Everaert*, Ghent, 197–234.

35. J. De Ferraris. 1966 (1777). *Mémoires historiques, chronologiques et oeconomiques*, Brussels, vol. 3, 16, 51, 129, 143, 175, 194.

36. N. Leplae. 1972. Betwistingen rond de benoeming van parochieherders in de Oostenrijkse Nederlanden, bijzonder in het bisdom Brugge in de eerste helft der XVIIIe eeuw', *Standen en Landen* 50, 29.

37. See for example Grand Seminar Bruges, Manuscript Collection, S. 154.

38. State Archives Ghent, Staten van Vlaanderen, 6726.

39. J. F. De Lichervelde. 1815. *Mémoire sur les fonds ruraux du département de l'Escaut*, Ghent, 57.

40. See for example the statement by the aldermen of Verreboek: 'In the polder villages, labourers are always short. Farmers cannot hire servants unless they are willing to pay double of what they could earn elsewhere.' See State Archives Ghent, Staten van Vlaanderen, 6726.

41. Lichtervelde, *Mémoire*, 57.

42. Lambrecht, *Een grote hoeve*, 139 for inland Flanders. For the coastal regions, see Seminar Bruges, Accounts of the Abbey of the Dunes, 135–136.

43. State Archives Bruges, Collection Sanders, 181.

44. On these issues, see also P. M. Solar and R. M. Smith. 2005. 'An Old Poor Law for the New Europe? Reconciling Local Solidarity with Labour Mobility in Early Modern England,' in P. A. David and M. Thomas (eds), *The Economic Future in Historical Perspective*, Oxford, 463–477.

45. J. Lucassen. 1987. *Migrant Labour in Europe 1600–1900. The Drift to the North Sea*, London, 95–99.

46. See for example State Archives of Courtray, Old City Records of Courtray, nr. 11442, 11506, 11606, 14084 and 14290. The interrogations indicate that some migrants arrested under the vagrancy laws sometimes stayed in the coastal provinces for many consecutive years. Some of them also reported that they had no property and fixed residence or had deserted from the army. On vagrants and their motives, see also A. Winter. 2004. 'Vagrancy as an Adaptive Strategy: The Duchy of Brabant, 1767–1776', *International Review of Social History* 49, 249–277.

47. Calculated from data in Dieudonné, *Statistique*, 252. Data for the province of Western Flanders from 1796 indicate that the share of 'foreign' inhabitants (defined as those who had not been born in their parish of residence) was highest in the regions characterized by large farms. See Gyssels and Straeten, *Bevolking*, 95–96.

48. Dalle, *De bevolking*, 84–85.

49. Ibid., 85–87.

50. The Concordat of Ypres was probably one of the first international agreements concerning poor relief and welfare.

51. On this Concordat of Ypres, see P. Bonenfant. 1934. *Le problème du paupérisme en Belgique à la fin de l'ancien régime*, Brussels, 408–414; A. Winter. 2008. 'Caught Between Law and Practice : Migrants and Settlement Legislation in the Southern Low Countries in a Comparative Perspective, c. 1700–1900', *Rural History* 19, 144–148; A. Winter and T. Lambrecht. 2013. 'Migration, Poor Relief and Local Autonomy: Settlement Policies in England and the Southern Low Countries in the Eighteenth Century', *Past and Present*, 218.

52. Mendels, *Industrialization*, 115.

53. Winter and Lambrecht, 'Migration'.

54. For coastal Flanders, see *Placcaert-Boeck van Vlaenderen V*, Ghent, 1763, vol. 2, 1066–1070. For northern France, see J. Moreau de Séchelles, 'Mémoire concernant les précautions qui ont été prises pour bannir la mendicité dans le Département de Flandre (1750)',

in G. Thuillier (ed.). 2003. *Aux origines de l'administration sociale: le rapport de Loménie de Brienne en 1775*, Paris, 454–470.

55. Vooren, 'De armenzorg I', 5–32.

56. J. de Hullu. 1915. 'De stichting der Rooms-Katholieke parochiën te Sluis en IJzendijke in de achttiende eeuw', *Nederlands Archief voor Kerkgeschiedenis* 12, 35–62.

57. The accounts of these Catholic relief institutions indicate that the majority of their income was indeed derived from taxes. On the structure of the income of these Catholic poor relief institutions, see G. A. C. van Vooren. 1974. 'De armenzorg voor de katholieken in het Middelburgse missiegebied gedurende de 18de eeuw. II. De uitvoering,' *Appeltjes van het Meetjesland* 25, 13–28. In addition, during the second half of the eighteenth century it was not uncommon in the parishes of the diocese of Bruges to collect alms that were distributed among Catholic relief funds in Zealand Flanders: G. A. C. van Vooren. 1969. 'De toestand der Staatse Katholieken en de Middelburgse Missie van 1737 tot 1804', *Appeltjes van het Meetjesland* 20, 48.

58. Cruyningen, *Behoudend*, 56–60 on the crisis of the rural economy of Zealand Flanders during this period.

59. Vooren, 'De armenzorg I', 5–31.

60. W. Beele. 2010. 'Vremde cortgestenen in de kasselrij Veurne anno 1771', *Westhoek* 26, 159–235.

61. For northern France, see D. Rosselle. 1989. 'La vente des biens nationaux et le changement des structures de l'exploitation agricole: l'exemple artésien', in G. Gayot and J.-P. Hirsch (eds), *La Révolution Française et le développement du capitalisme*, Lille, 314–316. For Zealand Flanders, see T. Radcliff, *A Report*, 192; Cruyningen, *Behoudend*, 180–181. For 'Belgian' Flanders, see T. Lambrecht. 2003. 'Reciprocal Exchange, Credit and Cash: Agricultural Labour Markets and Local Economies in the Southern Low Countries during the Eighteenth Century', *Continuity and Change* 18, 251ff.

62. Lambrecht, 'Reciprocal Exchange', 251–252.

63. F. Loriquet. 1891. *Cahiers de doléances de 1789 dans le département du Pas-de-Calais*, Arras, vol. 1, 407; F. Laude. 1914. *Les classes rurales en Artois à la fin de l'Ancien Régime (1760–1789)*, Lille, 252–57; A. de Calonne. 1920. *La vie agricole dans la Nord de la France*, Paris; M. Bloch. 1966. *French Rural History. An Essay on its Basic Characteristics*, Berkeley, 195–196.

64. See the numerous complaints in the cahiers of 1789.

65. Calculated from Ghent University Library, Ms. 1759: A. J. Boedt, *Diversche remarquen op verdeelynghe ende prysen*, 1733. Unfortunately I could not find similar data for the polder regions for the second half of the eighteenth century.

66. J. Toussaert. 1956. *La population de Krombeke au XVIIIe siècle d'après les registres paroissiaux*, Lille, 92–93.

67. The extent to which this development was paralleled by a concentration of property rights, however, remains unclear.

68. Regional political authorities also represented and safeguarded urban interests. The aldermen of Furnes for example governed both the city and rural district of Furnes. As was already noted by Moreau de Séchelles, cities (like Lille) suffered especially from vagrancy and begging if rural parishes failed or refused to assume financial responsibility for their poor. This could explain why at this level of decision-making, mechanisms were constructed to ensure that the welfare costs were evenly distributed between town and countryside and within rural parishes. See Moreau de Séchelles, *Mémoire*, 455–466.

69. See for example the anonymous and trenchant commentary on the effects of Concordat of Ypres in *Mémoire représentant les suites préjudiceuses et imprévues du Concordat*, 1–8 [c. 1770, Bruges?].

Chapter Nine

Settlement Law and Rural-Urban Relief Transfers in Nineteenth-Century Belgium

A Case Study on Migrants' Access to Relief in Antwerp

Anne Winter

In most European regions, poor relief remained a largely local affair throughout the transition from preindustrial to industrial society: organized and financed by local bodies, poor relief was in principle intended only for the local poor. The question of how to deal with migrants and their relief needs, already a matter of considerable concern under the ancien régime, became a particularly pressing issue for urban authorities in the nineteenth century, when an unprecedented concentration of population and employment in towns took shape. As urban immigration levels proliferated, so did the challenges of urban relief organization, which were exacerbated by the precariousness of early industrial labour markets. How to deal with the relief claims of the many newcomers, many of whom stayed in town only temporarily, and regularly fell on hard times? Giving all newcomers access to local relief would jeopardize the already hard-pressed urban relief funds, but a complete denial of access to relief could create socially explosive situations and might seriously hinder the influx of workers needed to man the expanding urban labour markets.

In this chapter I will demonstrate how settlement legislation in nineteenth-century Belgium helped urban authorities to deal with this challenge in ways that enabled them to mobilize substantial relief subsidies from the countryside. The evolution of Belgian settlement legislation and practice is a complex issue, which has so far received almost no scholarly attention.[1] What I intend to do here is to provide a first estimate of the scale and direction of rural-urban relief transfers that took place as a result of nineteenth-century settlement legislation, and to explore their impact on urban relief practices. Drawing upon data from poor relief accounts in the booming international port city of Antwerp, I will argue that these relief transfers were considerable and amounted to de facto wage subsidies from the countryside to cities, facilitating rural-urban migration on a macro level, and influencing actual relief distribution practices on a micro-level.

These findings have important implications for our understanding of urbanization processes and relief policies in the long nineteenth century. Although completely neglected in standard accounts on urbanization and industrialization in nineteenth-century Belgium, settlement-based relief transfers – so I shall argue – were an important factor in allowing the young state to become the 'First Industrial Nation' on the Continent, which makes it an interesting case for comparison with England and other early industrializers. In order to structure my argument, I shall first discuss the possible relation between migration, relief and the industrial transition, then sketch the evolution of settlement legislation in nineteenth-century Belgium, before exploring its implications for rural-urban relief transfers and migrants' access to relief in the city of Antwerp. What remains beyond the scope of this chapter are the causes of legislative change over this period, as well as the experiences and perspectives of the poor migrants themselves – but its findings provide important leads for further research on these questions too.

Migrants, Out-Resident Relief and Urbanization in the Industrial Transition

While early legislation had simply aimed to keep the poor put, by the eighteenth century many European regions provided possibilities for migrants to 'gain a settlement', i.e. to transfer eligibility for relief from one's home parish to a new place of residence. Migrants who did not meet the conditions, however, remained 'sojourners': residing in a place where they did not have a settlement, they were therefore not eligible for relief and were at times in danger of expulsion. Between gaining a settlement or not, however, an important but little-studied intermediate option to deal with migrants' relief entitlements existed: the practice of out-resident relief. Migrants who had not (yet) acquired a new settlement, could receive relief from their home community while residing elsewhere. Whether or not to give relief to out-residents was a decision at the discretion of migrants' home communities, and often implied intricate negotiations on the part of the poor themselves, sometimes also involving the relief authorities in their place of residence.[2]

Out-resident relief practices developed most precociously in England and Wales, where relief obligations were laid down in the Poor Laws of 1598–1601 and the Settlement Law of 1662, and where profound economic transformations rendered the relief of the mobile poor a more pressing issue from a comparatively early date.[3] Several authors have argued how Britain's settlement-based relief system contributed to the country's precocious path of economic growth and industrialization in the long nineteenth century, by stimulating an efficient allocation of labour.[4] By allowing centres of economic expansion the best pick of workers while shifting their relief costs to their parishes of origin, prevalent criteria of settlement and systems of out-resident relief would have amounted to a de facto wage subsidy from the countryside to the booming towns when urbanization levels proliferated in the wake of the Industrial Revolution.[5] Although the tone of contemporary debate and the available empirical data suggest that out-resident relief transfers represented a sizeable or even major contribution to urban relief expenses at least up to mid-century, the actual scale of rural-urban relief transfers during England's industrial transition remains difficult to establish in any comprehensive or systematic manner, due to the essentially informal nature of out-resident relief practices, which left few systematic traces in the sources.[6]

However, our understanding of the role of out-resident relief as a system of migration subsidization in an era of urbanization and industrialization can be greatly improved by looking at other European regions. While many studies on the subject assume or imply a sense of English particularity in this respect, England was not the only country to develop elaborate settlement legislation, nor was it the only country where increasing levels of mobility and urbanization fostered the expansion of out-resident relief practices in the long nineteenth century. Expanding the debate to include the experience of other European countries provides better insight into both the particularities of the English case and the relationship between out-resident relief, migration and urbanization in the long nineteenth century more generally.

There are two main reasons why Belgium provides a particularly relevant case study in this respect. One is that Belgium embarked upon a trajectory of extensive industrialization and urbanization from a relatively early date, mirroring many of the societal transformations of nineteenth-century Britain. While it was one of the first areas on the Continent to follow England's path of mechanization and industrialization, the proportion of Belgium's population living in cities of more than 5,000 inhabitants grew from around 30 per cent in 1800 to 52 per cent by 1900. By that time, one in four Belgians lived in one of the five major cities or their mushrooming suburbs, and the 'new industries' had come to employ a large part of the country's workforce. While net migration was not the sole nor necessarily the major contributor to urban growth, gross levels of urban migration were markedly on the rise throughout the long nineteenth-century, coming to engage the equivalent of more than 10 per cent of the urban population on a yearly basis by mid century, and exacerbating problems of urban congestion and the provision of relief.[7] The second reason is that the peculiarities of Belgium's settlement legislation over this period have provided us with a wealth of serial sources on out-resident relief that simply did not exist elsewhere. Unlike England, for which only fragmentary evidence exists, the Belgian sources allow us to study the magnitude, limits and possibilities of out-resident relief practices in the long nineteenth century with a degree of comprehensiveness unparalleled in any other country, which in turn allows us to address questions of rural-urban labour subsidization from a varied set of angles.

Settlement Legislation in Nineteenth-Century Belgium

Although already a pressing issue under the ancien régime, no uniform settlement legislation existed on a central or national level in the Habsburg Netherlands – the region that more or less made up present-day Belgium.[8] Notwithstanding earlier attempts, the move towards a general harmonization of legislation had to await the discontinuities wrought by French rule, when in 1797 a one-year residence was declared sufficient for access to relief provisions in a migrant's place of residence – as in the Rhinelands discussed in Andreas Gestrich's chapter in this volume.[9] After the downfall of Napoleon, a more encompassing law on *onderstandswoonst* (settlement) was proclaimed by King William I in 1818, which aimed to determine each person's lawful settlement – i.e., the local community responsible for his or her relief – in the newly established United Kingdom of the Netherlands. The length of residence required in order to transfer one's settlement was raised considerably to four consecutive years (six for non-nationals). At the same time, temporary support to sojourners could now be reclaimed from their rightful settlement, *'lorsque l'exception trouve son motif dans la justice et l'humanité'*.[10]

These principles were strengthened and refined by the next major revision of settlement legislation by the then Belgian government in 1845. On the one hand, the conditions for acquiring a new settlement were tightened further, to no less than eight consecutive years of residence, not counting the periods during which public assistance of some kind had been received, and excluding non-nationals from the possibility of gaining a settlement via residence. On the other hand, the law further clarified and facilitated the procedures for reclaiming disbursements for sojourners' relief from their rightful settlement.[11] These instructions governed settlement policy for another thirty years, until the law of 1876 brought down the required length of residence from eight to five years, still excluding periods during which relief had been received, and restored the possibility for non-nationals of gaining a settlement. The new regulations also established that local authorities were no longer charged in full for the relief of out-resident poor when the latter had been away for more than five years: only one quarter of the costs was to be reimbursed by their place of settlement, while the remaining sum was to be paid out by a newly created provincial *fonds commun*. This provincial fund was to be sustained by contributions by all towns and villages in proportion to their numbers of inhabitants.[12] A new major revision of poor relief administration in 1891, finally, maintained the principle of settlement only for disbursements of indoor relief in beggars' colonies, almshouses, lengthy hospital admissions and other forms of residential care, which in practice greatly reduced the importance of settlement legislation in relation to questions of urban migration.[13]

The overall trend of Belgian legislation in the nineteenth century, then, was to make it more difficult to acquire a new settlement via residence – which was, in fact, the opposite of what was taking place in England and Wales at the time.[14] The Belgian trend towards a gradual lengthening of the required period of residence was only partly reversed in 1876, when residential requirements were brought down from eight to five years. Even then, however, the additional clauses made sure that only a small proportion of sojourners could qualify for a transfer of settlement on these grounds. Yet each move towards a toughening of residential criteria was accompanied by a facilitation of out-resident relief procedures: the possibility of granting out-resident relief was legally endorsed in King William's 1818 law, and significantly elaborated in the laws of 1845 and 1876. These specifications placed the decision to grant relief to sojourners entirely in the hands of their place of residence, while obliging their place of settlement to reimburse any relief costs made. The latter's only say in the whole operation was that they could have their sojourners sent back if they wished.[15] Relief costs incurred for non-settled non-national paupers were to be reimbursed in a similar manner by the state finances. National legislation even specified standard accounting procedures to be followed for out-resident relief and provided standard forms by which to settle out-resident relief balances between different local (and central) authorities.[16] The actual import of nineteenth-century settlement legislation, both de jure and de facto, was a growing dissociation between one's place of settlement and that of residence. While impeding the spatial transfer of settlement, it greatly facilitated the possibilities of relief transfers between the places of settlement and residence.

The combination of a general toughening of settlement criteria on the one hand, and the facilitation of out-resident relief on the other hand, provided new devices by which the contentious issue of migrants' access to relief could be handled by local authorities. As cities were the main net beneficiaries of migration streams throughout the nineteenth century, a growing number of urban dwellers retained their settlement in their – mostly rural – places of origin. With the authorities in the place of residence the sole judge of sojourners' needs, these could in theory choose who they helped and how they helped them, and they could have other authorities pay the bills. To what extent did this result in urban relief expenses being paid by rural communities? The increasing inequality in the distribution of sojourners' relief costs between town and countryside was in any case a source of mounting political debate in contemporary opinion. In the 1860s and 1870s especially, rural representatives lobbying for legislative reform repeatedly accused urban authorities of draining rural relief provisions by their disproportionate generosity to immigrants.[17] Did cities benefit as much from out-resident relief flows as contemporary critics would have us believe?

Rural-Urban Relief Transfers in Nineteenth-Century Belgium and Antwerp

Systematic data on the scale and direction of out-resident relief flows for the first half of the nineteenth century are on the whole difficult to find. While King William's law of 1818 provided the first legal basis for out-resident relief practices, and the scale of out-resident relief appears to have increased significantly as a result, the true take-off of out-resident relief flows had to await the combined impact of the crisis of the 1840s and the legislative reform of 1845. While the harvest failures and the collapse of rural industry in the 1840s ushered in a new phase of spiralling relief costs and increasing geographical mobility, the new *Loi sur le domicile de secours* further facilitated the possibilities of out-resident relief and ensured a more systematic recording of these flows in various sources.[18]

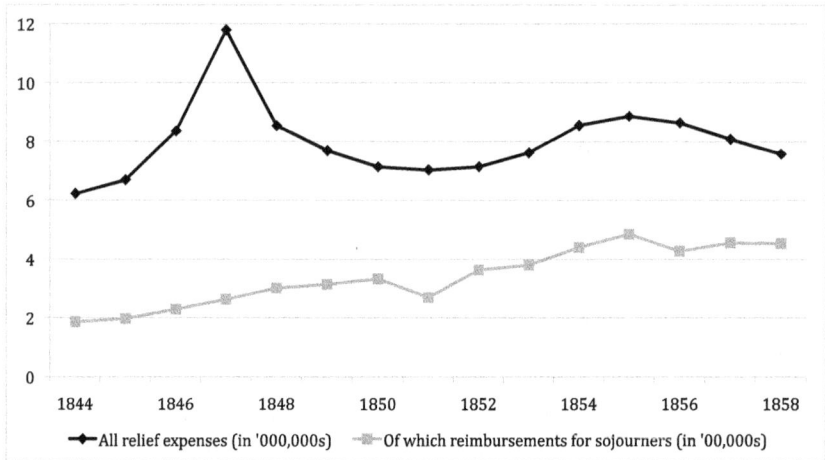

Figure 9.1. Relief Expenses and Sojourners' Reimbursements in Belgium, 1844–1858 (in BFR)

Source: Exposé de la situation du Royaume ... 1851–1860, vol. III, 100Q ff.

Figure 9.1 gives a first indication of the evolution of out-resident relief practices in the aftermath of the crisis and the new law. It provides an overview of all local relief expenses in Belgium as well as the sum of all re-imbursements for sojourners as derived from aggregate national statistics between 1844 and 1858. The first series of figures illustrates the long-run tendency for relief expenses to increase strongly in Belgium over the nineteenth century, driven by growing proletarianization and boosted by periodic crises such as the dramatic events of the 1845–1847 famine. As the traditional and largely self-reliant sources of income of relief institutions increasingly fell short of meeting the rising costs, subsidies by local authorities took up an ever more important and regular part in relief ex-penses.[19] At the same time, the proportion of out-resident recipients was clearly on the rise. The second series of figures expressed in Figure 9.1 indicates how the law of 1845 substantially facilitated the transfer of relief made for sojourners, which more than doubled from less than 200,000 Belgian francs in 1844 to more than 450,000 francs by 1855. Over this period, recorded reimbursements for sojourners increased from 3 to 6 per cent of all relief expenses made. Given the many problems in collecting trustworthy accounting details, there is no doubt that this percentage represents an absolute minimum. Moreover, it is not so much the ag-gregate relief sums paid out to sojourners that interest us here, but rather the possible *imbalances* in the spatial distribution of out-resident relief transfers. Hence, a more appropriate perspective is provided by the relief accounts of individual cities.

The case studied in greater detail here is the city of Antwerp, which was transformed from a middle-sized regional textile centre in the second half of the eighteenth century to a booming international port town by the middle of the nineteenth century.[20] This economic transformation went hand in hand with a strong demographic expansion, from 50,000 in 1800 to 100,000 by 1850 and 270,000 in 1900, and with a growing proportion of immigrants in the town's population, from 22 over 32 to 43 per cent respectively. Immigrants became dominant on the urban labour market not only in numerical terms – already in the 1830s they provided more than half of the city's active population – but also in a more qualitative way, as they took up almost all of the new, port-related employment. For the expansion of its nineteenth-century port activities, in other words, Antwerp relied heavily on immigrant labour.[21] In addition, fluctuations in maritime activity and the inherent irregularity of most port-related employment increased the importance of poor relief as a means of overcoming temporary unemployment.[22] In other words, the characteristics of Antwerp's urban economy fostered both a strong reliance on immigrants on the one hand, and growing relief burdens on the other hand.

Public relief provisions in Antwerp, as in other Belgian cities, were divided between the Charity Office and the Commission of Hospices. The first was responsible for the provision of *outdoor* relief, i.e., the disbursement of in-kind and cash benefits to poor households. Two main types of recipients existed: 'permanent' poor who received weekly support – often a combination of in-kind benefits and cash doles, either in wintertime or throughout the year – and 'casual' poor who were helped on an irregular basis. The criteria for permanent support were very stringent, so that only very old, invalid and single-parent households figured among the 'permanent' poor. Casual relief, including in-kind (bread, coal, clothing) and cash support as well as medical assistance (doctors' visits and pharmacy coupons), was typically granted to a wider range of households suffering a temporary setback or expense, such as childbirth, sickness or temporary unemployment. In addition, the Charity Office also financed the meals and doles of paupers in the *atelier de charité*, a non-residential workhouse where by mid century several hundreds of paupers spun, knitted, sewed and wove in return for a meal and a subsidized wage.[23] The Commission of Hospices in turn organized all forms of *indoor* relief for specific pauper groups in residential institutes: the two city hospitals, the boys' and girls' orphanage, the asylum, a number of almshouses, and boarding costs for elderly and children placed with private charities and foster families. By far the most important institutes exploited by the Commission of Hospices were the city hospitals – the Saint-Elisabeth hospital and from 1885 onwards the Stuivenberg hospital – which admitted up to 10,000 patients per year in the later nineteenth century and consumed more than half of the Commission's budget.[24]

We know from existing research that the Antwerp relief authorities were haunted by permanent shortages of funds throughout the nineteenth century, which led them to continuously tighten the criteria for eligibility for support.[25] At the same time, research into the survival strategies of the urban poor has time and again demonstrated the importance of outdoor and indoor relief as part of a complex income pooling strategy, especially for newcomers with smaller support networks, even when the monetary equivalent of the relief provided was relatively small.[26] To what extent could the Charity Office and Commission of Hospices make use of settlement provisions to mitigate the relief responsibilities towards the city's immigrant labour force? And how did this affect newcomers' chances of gaining access to local relief provisions?

Both the Charity Office and the Commission of Hospices produced yearly accounts by which it is possible to chart the volume of outresident relief in relation to total expenses. Let us start the analysis with the figures on outdoor relief distilled from the Charity Office accounts (Figure 9.2). These show that total disbursements involved a yearly expense from around 250,000 francs in mid century to 500,000 francs at the end of the period, representing a declining per capita average of 2.5 to 2 francs per inhabitant.[27] When these total expenses are compared with incoming and outgoing relief transfers, three main observations can be made. First, these figures confirm that expenses as regards in-resident sojourners (whose settlement was based in a place other than Antwerp) were substantially greater than those towards out-resident poor (whose settlement was based in Antwerp, but who lived elsewhere). In other words, Antwerp's disbursements to other municipalities remained much smaller than the volume of relief transfers in the opposite direction, i.e., the reimbursements which the Antwerp Charity Office claimed from other municpalities as a compensation for relief expenses paid out to sojourners residing in Antwerp: 'outgoing' relief transfers were only between 3,000 and 15,000 francs, while 'incoming' transfers ranged from 20,000 to 60,000 francs. This tilted balance between outgoing and incoming relief transfers – also demonstrated for the city of Ghent in the same period – confirms that the direction of nineteenth-century rural-urban migration flows made Belgium's growing cities into large net receivers of relief transfers in the context of settlement legislation.[28]

A second major observation from Figure 9.2 is that the overall benefits accruing to the Antwerp Charity Office increased significantly over time, both in absolute and relative terms, until the legislative reforms of

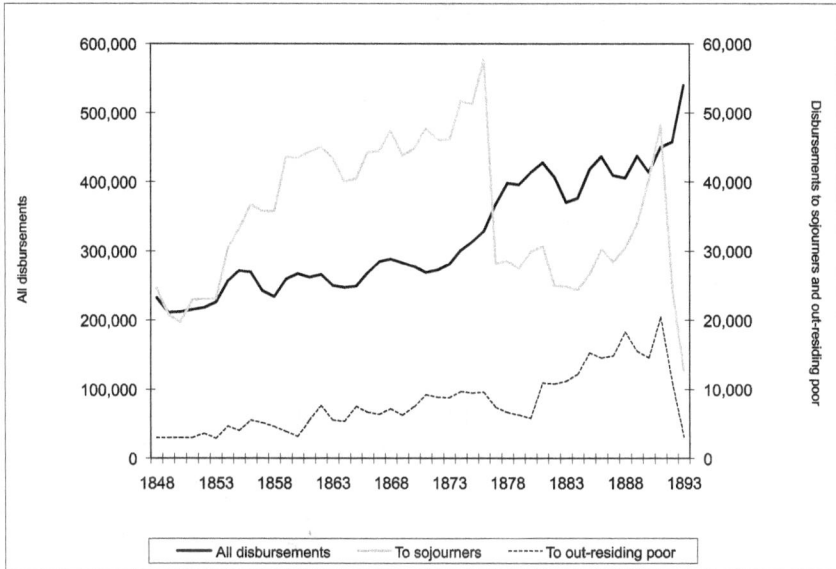

Figure 9.2. Relief Disbursements by the Antwerp Charity Office, 1848–1893 (in BFR)

Source: OCMWA, BW Registers, 148–193: *Jaarrekeningen,* 1848–1893.

1876 and 1891 intervened to redraw the picture. By mid century, relief expenses to sojourners still stood at a relatively modest level of 20,000 francs, or the equivalent of 10 per cent of total outdoor distributions by the Antwerp Charity Office. Given that outgoing relief transfers at that time amounted to only 3,000 francs (i.e., 2 per cent of total expenses), this meant that out-resident relief transfers provided the Antwerp Charity Office with a net subsidy equivalent to 8 per cent of its distributions. By the 1870s, expenses as regards resident sojourners had increased steadily up to 58,000 francs, representing 18 per cent of outdoor distributions, while the equivalent sum that Antwerp paid out to other municipalities was still less than 3 per cent, adding up to a net subsidy of 15 per cent of overall relief expenses.

Thirdly, the 1876 act radically reshaped the balance of payment of the Antwerp Charity Office. The shortening of residential criteria from eight to five years and the inclusion of non-nationals implied that the settlement of many erstwhile sojourners was suddenly transferred to Antwerp, together with their relief responsibilities. Relief costs paid back by other authorities fell from 58,000 to 28,000 francs in one year's time, from 18 to only 8 per cent of all relief expenses. Conversely, the expenses paid to settled poor out of the Charity Office's own pocket shot up accordingly. Although costs for out-resident Antwerp poor declined somewhat too, they stabilized at around the equivalent of 3 per cent of all outdoor relief in the following years. Antwerp's balance of payment to the newly installed provincial fund was initially slightly positive – never more than the equivalent of 1 per cent of overall relief costs – but deteriorated over time: by the late 1880s the city paid more to the provincial fund than it received. The net result of all these changes after the 1876 reform was to reduce drastically the net benefits which the Antwerp (and probably other urban) relief administrations derived from the Belgian settlement system. From a net gain of up to 15 per cent of local relief disbursements in the 1870s, out-resident relief transfers declined to a net gain of only 3 per cent at the end of the 1880s, and approximated a zero-sum when payments to the provincial fund are taken into account. When the 1891 reform abolished settlement as far as outdoor relief expenses were concerned, the scale of out-resident relief transfers, both incoming and outgoing flows, fell to negligible levels.

Let us now turn to the expenses for residential care, which reveal a similar trend. By far the largest expense category within the Commission of Hospices pertains to the financial administration of the two city hospitals: the centuries-old Saint-Elisabeth hospital and, from 1885 onwards, the newly built Stuivenberg hospital.[29] Admission was free upon referral by the Charity Office's doctors. The number of patients was continuously on the rise in the course of the nineteenth century, leading to increasing problems of overcrowding – prior to the opening of the Stuivenberg hospital the Saint-Elisabeth hospital recorded up to 7,000 admissions per year, against around 1,000 at the beginning of the century. With the exception of a small number of paying – and therefore privileged – admissions, most patients belonged to the poorer sections of the Antwerp population, among whom the risk and frequency of illness was high for all: young adults supplied the majority of the hospital's population in the nineteenth century, and only ten per cent was over 65. While part of the non-local patients had been sent there on purpose and with the consent of their place of settlement for specific medical treatment, the majority were immigrants who had fallen ill during their stay and who stayed in hospital for a few days or weeks to recover.[30]

Data pertaining to the financial administration of the city hospitals are represented in Figure 9.3. Overall expenses towards patient care in the city's two main hospitals combined expanded from around 200,000 francs at mid century to more than 600,000 at the close of the century. Although fluctuating heavily – partly attributable to fluctuations in shipping and diseases on board – the contribution of sojourners' reimbursements to these expenses was clearly on the rise between 1850 and 1875,

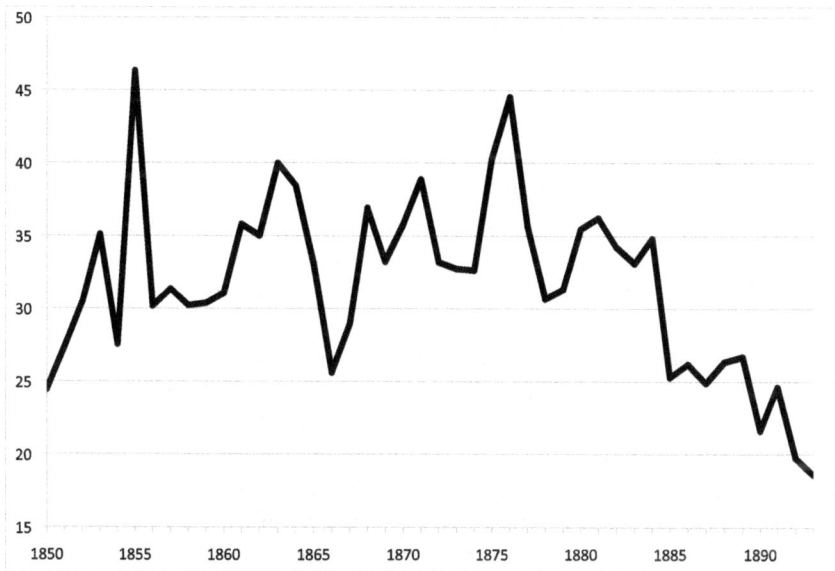

Figure 9.3. Reimbursements for Sojourners' Hospital Stays as Percentage of Hospital Care Expenses by the Antwerp Commission of Hospices, 1850–1893

Source: Compte moral, 1870–1895; Vermeiren, L. 'Het Sint-Elisabethgasthuis te Antwerpen in de 19de eeuw. Een analyse van de financiële structuur (1820–1913)' (unpublished dissertation, University of Louvain, 1984), vol. II, 68–76; Vermeiren, 'Van gasthuis'.

supplying up to 45 per cent of all hospital care expenses on the eve of the 1876 reform. After the new law the sojourners' share in overall expenses declined to less than 20 per cent in the 1890s.

Taken together, the figures for the Charity Office and city hospitals in Antwerp indicate that the net benefits which urban relief authorities derived from out-resident relief transfers could at times be very substantial, financing up to one-third of the combined costs for outdoor relief and hospital care. Extensive accounting documentation moreover attests to the fact that this source of finance was mobilized very smoothly: the overall pace of reimbursement was generally high and constant.[31] While the number of conflicts between different municipalities over out-resident relief also increased in the course of the second half of the nineteenth century, litigation was mainly over determining a pauper's actual settlement rather than about reimbursements. There were in fact no legal grounds whatsoever for a recognized settlement to refuse to reimburse relief costs made on behalf of its paupers residing elsewhere, even if the relief given was deemed too generous.[32]

Migrants' Access to Relief

The above figures indicate that urban authorities like in Antwerp were to a certain extent able to distribute 'free lunches' paid for by newcomers' places of origin. Did this make urban relief authorities more generous towards immigrant poor than to local paupers, as was claimed by their adversaries in political debate? And did this imply that it was actually easier for sojourners to gain access to poor relief than their settled counterparts? Exploring these questions requires consideration of many aspects, and the following is only a first and tentative exploration.

The observation that sojourners' share in relief distributions increased markedly between 1850 and 1875 is based on aggregate figures only. To assess its implications for migrants' access to relief on a household basis, we should be able to relate it to the number of poor relieved. A source that provides important indications in this respect is provided by the nominal accounts kept by the Antwerp Charity Office to monitor the re-imbursement process. These record all the sojourner household heads relieved, whether on a casual or permanent basis, together with the amount and type of relief received in a certain time interval: every six months for Belgian sojourners, every three months for non-Belgian sojourners.[33] By dividing the total sum of relief by the number of names mentioned per time interval, it is possible to gain an idea of the evolution of per capita (or in fact, per household) relief distributions to sojourners.

Figure 9.4 represents the number of names appearing on these lists together with average per capita expenditure for Belgian (per semester) and non-Belgian (per trimester) sojourners respectively. These indicate that both the numbers of sojourners' households receiving relief *and* the average amount of relief given were on an upward trend between 1850 and 1875: among non-Belgian sojourners, the average numbers of households relieved each trimester increased from 230 at mid century to more than 300 twenty-five years later, while the average relief received varied between 12 and 14 francs per trimester. Among Belgian sojourners, the numbers of households increased from around 300 to over 800 while their average support increased from around 15 to 20 francs per semester over the same period. After 1876, the numbers of sojourner households fell back substantially due to the shortening of residential criteria,[34] but the average relief distributions per household continued to reveal an upward trend, albeit with considerable fluctuations.

Between 1845 and 1875, then, both the numbers of sojourners relieved by the Antwerp Charity Office and the average amount of relief received by them increased. Yet both trends are difficult to interpret. First of all, no figures exist on the evolution of the *total* number of sojourners

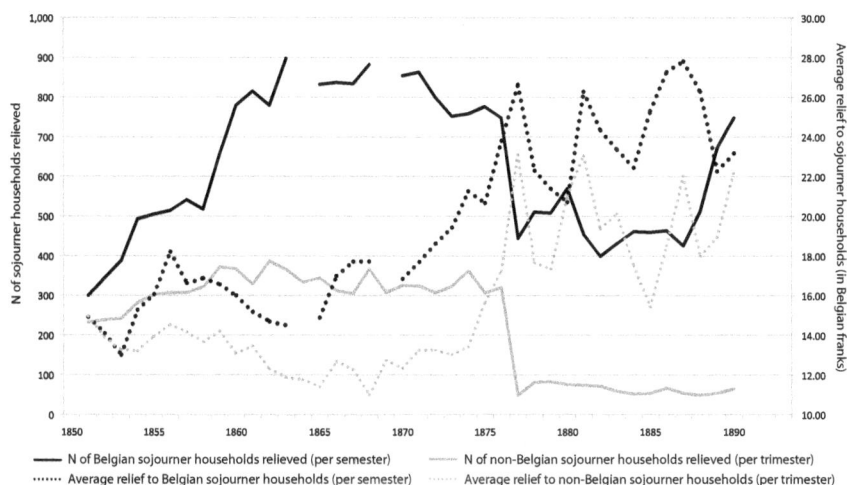

Figure 9.4. Sojourner Households Relieved by the Antwerp Charity Office, 1850–1895

Source: OCMWA, BW, Registers, 151–160: *Jaarrekeningen*, 1851–1860; 813–830: *Jaarregisters Belgen*, 1862–1880; 918–927: *Jaarregisters Belgen*, 1881–1890; 913–916: *Jaarregisters buitenlanders*, 1855/9–1890.

residing in Antwerp: one's settlement status was generally examined only if and when one turned to public relief assistance. Tentative extrapolations on the basis of immigration data from censuses and population records suggest that the sojourners helped by the Antwerp Charity Office represented between 4 and 6 per cent of *all* resident sojourners between 1850 and 1875, and stabilized at a level of around 3 per cent after 1876 – not revealing any trend towards greater accessibility.[35] Secondly, average per capita relief is a very blunt measure, as the types and amounts of relief distributed varied considerably. While administrative reports concerning the local poor always distinguished clearly between permanent and casual relief, this was not the case with sojourners, for whom relief expenses were lumped together in one sum irrespective of the regularity, level or type of relief provided. The only way to gain insight in the variety of relief provided to sojourners, therefore, is a detailed household-centred analysis on the basis of the nominal distribution lists – which I have undertaken for the year 1855. This analysis shows that relief to sojourners in 1855 varied from 0.15 franc in medical assistance to the Somers family from the small town of Lier, to 325.04 francs to the widow and children Langewouters from the village of Retie, in the form of cash (312 fr.), shirts (1.46 fr.) and medical assistance (11.58 fr.). While the average relief given to a sojourner household amounted to 29 francs, the standard deviation was no less than 38 francs. The median lay at only 13 francs, while three quarters of sojourner households received less than 39 francs, and 80 per cent less than 52 francs, i.e., less than one franc per week. Given that one franc could buy around four kilograms of rye bread, it is clear that the support given to the majority of sojourners was very modest.[36] Yet even modest help could be vital in tiding over difficult times in a varied economy of makeshifts.

Table 9.1. Types of Relief to Sojourner Households by the Antwerp Charity Office, 1855

	Households (%)	Average relief per household (in BFR)
Medical or in-kind relief only	39	6.32
Monetary support	55	44.56
Once	*26*	*18.08*
Repeated	*29*	*68.58*
Admission to workhouse	7	36.76
Once	*4*	*19.34*
Repeated	*2*	*70.28*
Total	100	29.26
Total (N)	1,128	

Source: OCMWA, BW 155–163: *Jaarrekeningen,* 1855–1863.

When we differentiate sojourners recorded in the 1855 lists according to the type of help received and their numbers of occurrences, two main groups emerge (Table 9.1). Those who received *regular* – i.e., repeated – support in the form of doles or workhouse wages made up 31 per cent of all sojourner households but received 73 per cent of all support – with an average of 69 francs per household per year. Sojourners who appeared on the lists only once or received nothing but in-kind relief made up the large majority (69 per cent) but received only 27 per cent of all support paid out to sojourners – the equivalent of 12 francs per household per year. This demonstrates that the lion's share of sojourners was given only modest help on a casual basis, while a minority nevertheless received regular monetary support of a more substantial nature – up to the equivalent even of permanent doles paid out to settled poor.[37] The latter is an interesting anomaly, since settlement legislation in principle envisaged only casual or unforeseen needs to be covered by out-resident relief – which hints at the complexity of considerations and negotiations that underlay out-resident relief *in practice*.

All said and done, however, the majority of sojourners was relieved on a casual basis only, and this contrasts with relief policies towards the local poor. Although a lack of data hampers systematic comparisons of relief distributions to settled and non-settled poor per capita,[38] it is nevertheless clear that the proportion of local poor receiving permanent doles was several times larger than the proportion of sojourners receiving regular support.[39] In addition, available aggregate figures confirm that *types* of relief provided to sojourners were very different from those distributed to settled poor.[40] Figure 9.5 expresses the proportions paid out to sojourners in the different types of relief provided by the Charity Office and the Commission of Hospices between 1850 and 1890. These demonstrate that sojourners were represented strongest in medical support: their share in hospital care and medical support – the latter consisting of doctor's visits and medicines distributed by the Charity Office's pharmacy – oscillated between 35 to over 50 per cent between 1850 and 1876. Their respective share in workhouse support and doles was comparatively much smaller, while their share in in-kind support – such as clothing and extra rations for women with newborn children – was somewhere in between. In all kinds of relief, sojourners' shares displayed a marked decline after 1876, but the proportion remained highest for medical support.

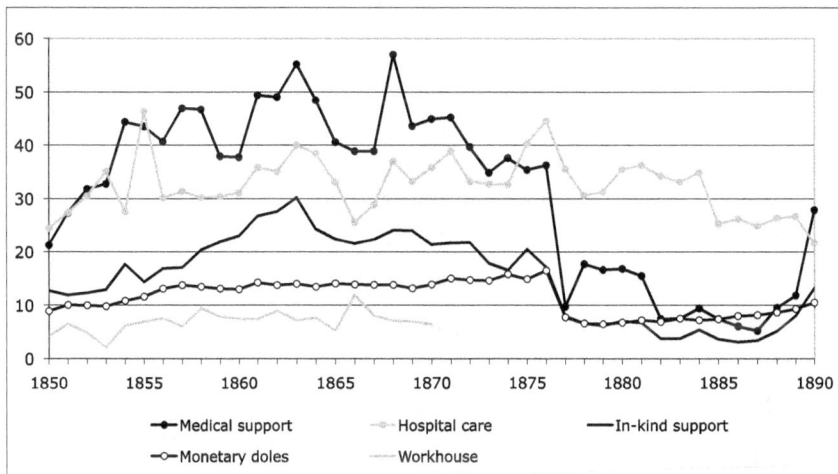

Figure 9.5. Sojourners' Shares in Different Types of Relief, 1850–1890 (%)

Sources: OCMWA, BW Registers, 148–193: *Jaarrekeningen*, 1848–1893; 813–830: *Jaarregisters Belgen*, 1862–1880; 918–927: *Jaarregisters Belgen*, 1881–1890; 913–916: *Jaarregisters buitenlanders*, 1855/9–1890; *Rapport sur l'administration*, 1850–1890; *Compte moral*, 1870–1895; Vermeiren, 'Het Sint-Elisabethgasthuis', vol. II, 68–76.

These figures indicate that sojourners' access to relief was highest for those types of relief aimed at covering temporary periods of need, and lowest for more structural and permanent forms of support directed mainly at widows, the elderly, and single parents or couples with many children. This need not surprise us, given the intention of the law and the demographic characteristics of contemporary migration flows: as the majority of Antwerp immigrants consisted of young, single adults, the life-cycle profile of sojourners was on average less structurally relief-dependent than that of the Antwerp-born population, who included comparatively more vulnerable groups such as the elderly and children.[41] Our available data suggest that sojourners appear to have enjoyed comparatively easy access to relief provisions to cover temporary forms of relief dependence, due to for instance illness or temporary unemployment, but were much less successful in gaining access to more permanent or structural forms of relief. Whether this was due to selectivity on the part of the Antwerp relief authorities and/or of the relief authorities in their place of settlement – who could have them sent back in case of more structural relief dependence – has to be ascertained by further research. Yet so far, the tentative conclusion seems warranted that the main result of relief transfers in the case of out-resident relief was to enable otherwise relatively employable sojourners to cover temporary periods of work disability, and that their main beneficiaries were relatively 'productive' migrants with relatively low *structural* relief needs. That Antwerp authorities were disproportionately generous to sojourner households as compared to settled poor cannot be substantiated on the basis of the data explored here, although the upward trend of both the numbers of sojourners relieved and the amount of relief given after the mid century suggests that they might have become more sensitive to the benefits which temporary out-resident relief could provide in a highly unstable labour market.

Conclusion

For the larger part of the nineteenth century, Belgian settlement legislation combined with growing levels of rural-urban migration to create a situation in which a substantial and growing part of urban relief provisions was paid out of the pockets of migrants' mainly rural places of origin. As the Antwerp example has shown, the relief transfers involved could amount to one third of all urban relief expenses, and this was possibly even higher for other cities such as Brussels. At the same time, relief policies towards sojourners appear to have been selective, in the sense that they were disproportionately oriented towards forms of irregular relief aimed at overcoming temporary setbacks, such as medical assistance and casual in-kind relief. This suggests that the main beneficiaries of out-resident relief were relatively 'productive' migrants with low structural relief needs in times of temporary work disability.

While more general claims need to be corroborated by further research for other cities, the evidence explored so far suggests that the net effect of Belgian settlement legislation and relief transfers, up to the last quarter of the nineteenth century at least, was a selective stimulus to 'productive' migration in much the same way as has been argued for England. The possibilities of maintaining and mobilizing relief entitlements from a distance mitigated the risks associated with migration and therefore probably encouraged decisions to move by those who stood to gain most. At the same time, access to temporary relief probably played an important role in allowing otherwise employable migrants to stay in the case of temporary unemployment or work disability, and therefore helped to overcome the marked fluctuations of irregular labour markets by smoothing the supply of labour. Because these costs were reimbursed by migrants' mainly rural places of origin, this would have resulted in a de facto wage subsidy from the countryside to cities, which eased Belgium's precocious urban and industrial transitions. Although more cross-local and cross-national research is needed, these observations suggest that out-resident relief transfers were an important, if largely neglected, dimension of the urbanization processes in those countries that took the lead in Europe's industrial transition.

Apart from these main trends that need to be corroborated by further research, the anomalies that emerge from the case study are likewise interesting. While the majority received relief only on a casual basis, a minority of sojourners in mid-nineteenth-century Antwerp received support on a par with the levels paid out to settled poor on the permanent dole lists. As such a scenario obviously runs counter to the intention of the law, and to a certain extent also to the logic of out-parish relief, it highlights the need for further in-depth research into the process of negotiation and bargaining that underlay distribution practices to sojourners in practice, with an eye to the complexity and subtlety that has been demonstrated for the English case by Steven King and Jeremy Boulton in this volume. One promising way forward here are the many letters between paupers, municipality of origin, municipality of residence, and other parties involved that have been kept in local archives but have so far received very little attention from Belgian historians. Research on the actual negotiation processes over out-resident relief will help to provide insight in the positions and motives of the different parties involved, to establish the extent to which some sojourners could be refused relief and asked to return home, and to draw in the perspectives and experiences of migrants themselves. Research on the relief accounts of rural municipalities, in turn, can help us to gain insight into the scale of the financial drain which rural-urban relief transfers implied.

Another set of questions in need of further research revolves around the direction and timing of legislative reform over settlement in nineteenth-century Belgium. The data gathered on the scale and direction of out-resident relief seem to confirm that the laws of 1818 and 1845 played into the hands of urban interests, while the legislative reforms of 1876 and 1891 favoured rural interests. Why did the balance of interests shift? I have hypothesized elsewhere that the laws of 1818 and 1845 represented a compromise between rural and urban interests as a means to slow down the volume of rural-urban migration in times of severe rural crisis, which by 1876 had been superseded by rural opposition against the large financial drain it implied.[42] The figures collected for Antwerp add credibility to this interpretation, in the sense that the net-benefits of out-resident relief flows were still modest when the 1818 and 1845 laws were adopted, but grew to be very substantial in the run-up to the 1876 reform. Yet only a detailed analysis of parliamentary discussions with reference to the changing economic outlook and balances of power in town and country alike can help to establish further insight into the motives and power relations underlying the legislative changes of the long nineteenth century.

Notes

Preliminary results of the research on which this chapter is based were published in Dutch in A. Winter, 'Migratiebeleid en economische verandering: Nieuwkomers en armenzorg in Antwerpen, 1750–1900', *Noordbrabants Historisch Jaarboek* 26 (2009), 99–128, and A. Winter, 'Eigen armen eerst? Migranten en de toegang tot armenzorg in Antwerpen, ca. 1840–1900', in M. De Koster et al. (eds), *Werken aan de Stad. Stedelijke actoren en structuren in de Zuidelijke Nederlanden, 1500–1900*, Brussels, 2011, 135–56. The author wishes to thank the Francqui Foundation for the research leave as a Francqui Research Professor, which enabled her to finalize this chapter.

1.   The only historian to have documented the question of settlement in the Southern Low Countries under the ancien régime at some length is P. Bonenfant. 1934. *Le problème du paupérisme en Belgique à la fin de l'ancien régime*, Brussels, 112–132, 408–421. D. Van Damme. 1990. 'Onderstandswoonst, sedentarisering en stad-platteland-tegenstellingen: Evolutie en betekenis van de wetgeving op de onderstandswoonst in België (einde achttiende tot einde negentiende eeuw)', *Belgisch Tijdschrift voor Nieuwste Geschiedenis* 21, 484–489 provides a preliminary exploration of the situation in nineteenth-century Ghent. A. Winter. 2008. 'Caught between Law and Practice: Migrants and Settlement Legislation in the Southern Low Countries in a Comparative Perspective, c. 1700–1900', *Rural History* 19, 144–148 provides a first discussion of some of the issues that are pursued further in the present chapter.

2. See the other chapters in this volume.
3. K. D. M. Snell. 2006. *Parish and Belonging. Community, Identity and Welfare in England and Wales, 1700–1950*, Cambridge, 103–113.
4. J. S. Taylor. 1976. 'The Impact of Pauper Settlement 1691–1834', *Past and Present* 73, 67–68; J. S. Taylor. 1991. 'A Different Kind of Speenhamland: Nonresident Relief in the Industrial Revolution', *Journal of British Studies* 30(2), 183–208; K. D. M. Snell. 1991. 'Pauper Settlement and the Right to Poor Relief in England and Wales', *Continuity and Change* 6(3), 400–401; P. Solar. 1995. 'Poor Relief and English Economic Development Before the Industrial Revolution', *Economic History Review* 48(1), 1–22; P. M. Solar and R. M. Smith. 2003. 'An Old Poor Law for the New Europe? Reconciling Local Solidarity with Labour Mobility in Early Modern England', in P. A. David and M. Thomas (eds), *The Economic Future in Historical Perspective*, Oxford, 463–477.
5. Taylor, 'The Impact', 67–68; Taylor, 'A Different Kind', 183–208.
6. On contemporary debates, see M. Caplan. 1978. 'The New Poor Law and the Struggle for Union Chargeability', *International Review of Social History* 23, 267–300. For important case studies, see D. Ashforth. 1976. 'The Urban Poor Law', in D. Fraser (ed.), *The New Poor Law in the Nineteenth Century*, London and Basingstoke, 128–148; D. Ashforth, 'Settlement and Relief in Urban Areas', in M. E. Rose (ed.). 1985. *The Poor and the City: The English Poor Law in Its Urban Context, 1834–1914*, Leicester, 58–91; Taylor, 'A Different Kind'; T. Sokoll. 2001. *Essex Pauper Letters, 1731–1837*, Oxford; S. King. 2005. "It Is Impossible for Our Vestry to Judge His Case into Perfection from Here': Managing the Distance Dimension of Poor Relief, 1800–1840', *Rural History* 16(2), 161–189.
7. Pierre Lebrun et al. 1979. *Essai sur la révolution industrielle en Belgique, 1770–1847;* K. Veraghtert. 1981. 'De economie in de Zuidelijke Nederlanden 1790–1970', in D. P. Blok (ed.), *Algemene Geschiedenis der Nederlanden*, vol. 10, Haarlem, 128–129; P. Deprez and C. Vandenbroeke. 1989. 'Population Growth and Distribution and Urbanisation in Belgium During the Demographic Transition', in R. Lawton and R. Lee (eds), *Urban Population Development in Western Europe from the Late Eighteenth to the Early Twentieth Century*, Liverpool, 233–235.
8. For a detailed discussion of settlement legislation in the late Habsburg period compared to the situation in England and Wales, see Winter, 'Caught'; A. Winter and T. Lambrecht. 2013. 'Migration, Poor Relief and Local Autonomy: Settlement Policies in England and the Southern Low Countries in the Eighteenth Century', *Past and Present*, 218.
9. *Décret concernant des mesures pour l'extinction de la mendicité*, 15/10/1793 (Promulgated in Belgium in 1797: *Pasinomie*, série 1, vol. V, 501–5).
10. *Loi tendant à determiner les lieux où les indigents peuvent participer au secours publics*, 28/11/1818 (*Pasinomie*, série 2, vol. IV, 481–485).
11. *Loi relative au domicile de secours*, 18/02/1845 (*Pasinomie*, série 3, vol. XV, 13–24). The only category of non-nationals who could still acquire a settlement on the same footing as Belgians were those who had acquired the status of *domicilié* – a very small and exceptional group. See F. Caestecker, *Alien Policy in Belgium, 1840–1940: The Creation of Guest Workers, Refugees and Illegal Aliens*, Oxford, 2000, 11.
12. *Loi sur le domicile de secours*, 14/03/1876 (*Pasinomie*, série 4, vol. XI, 34–94).
13. *Loi sur l'assistance publique*, 27/11/1891 (*Pasinomie*, série 4, vol. XXVI, 459–509). See also *Pandectes Belges*, vol. 96, Brussels, 1909, s.v. 'Secours (domicile de)', art. 8–10. Henceforth, hospital stays could be charged to the municipality of settlement only from the eleventh day onwards, and the latter was discharged from reimbursement if admission had been the result of a work-related accident.
14. Caplan, 'The New Poor Law'.
15. Even the ministry of internal affairs interpreted the clauses facilitating out-resident relief as installing a 'duty' to relieve non-settled paupers, while retaining a 'right' to disbursement: 'la loi du 18 février 1845 a reproduit le système de la loi de 1818 en formulant plus

explicite, l'obligation de l'assistance aux indigents étrangers à la commune, et le droit au remboursement', in *Exposé de la situation du Royaume. Statistique générale de la Belgique (Période décennale de 1851–1860)*, III (Bruxelles, 1864), 100 Q. Compare with the qualifications in *Pandectes Belges*, vol. 96, Brussels, 1909, s.v. 'Secours (domicile de)', art. 11: 'Cette administration [de bienfaisance du lieu où se produit la nécessité des secours] est seule juge du point de savoir si les dits indigents réunissent les conditions requises pour être assistés ... ni l'autorité supérieure ni la commune du domicile de secours n'ont action sur l'administration charitable de la commune où l'indigent se trouve: celle-ci est souveraine, elle ne peut subir ni injonction d'avoir à accorder des secours à tel ou tel individu, ni défense d'en accorder. La commune du domicile de secours ne pourrait donc se soustraire au remboursement des secours fournis ... sous prétexte que l'individu secouru n'était pas indigent.'

16. See for instance the *Circulaire du ministre de la justice, relative au domicile de secours,* 23/04/1851 (*Pasinomie*, série 3, vol. XXI, 161–163).

17. *Annales Parlementaires de Belgique. Chambre des Répresentants,* Session 1861–1862, 437; Session 1874–1875, nr. 175, 2–4. See *Circulaire de M. le ministre de la justice Alph. Nothomb,* 15 April 1857, nr. 19470, cited in E. Hellebaut and C. de Gronckel. 1879. *Commentaire de la loi du 14 mars 1876 sur le domicile de secours,* Brussels, 69.

18. Openbaar Centrum voor Maatschappelijk Welzijn Antwerpen (henceforth OCMWA), Bureel van Weldadigheid (henceforth BW), Doos 169: *Rapport décennal 1846 à 1855,* f. 32: 'Antérieurement à 1849 les pauvres n'ayant pas leur domicile de secours reconnu à Anvers étaient en général compris dans le nombre secouru pour compte de la ville. Une recherche minutieuse et l'application rigoureuse des lois ont établi le domicile de secours ailleurs qu'à Anvers d'un grand nombre des pauvres qui étaient antérieurement considérés à charge de la ville.'

19. Although there existed – at least in the first half of the nineteenth century – no *direct* link between the level of local taxes and the volume of local relief subsidies, other expenses and sources of income played a role, too. E. Vanhaute. 1988 . 'De armenzorg op het Antwerpse platteland, 1750–1850: Onderzoek naar een instelling tijdens de scharniereeuw', in *Machtsstructuren in de plattelandsgemeenschappen in België en aangrenzende gebieden (12de–19de eeuw),* Brussels, 641–665; E. Vanhaute and T. Lambrecht. 2011. 'Famine, Exchange Networks and the Village Community. A Comparative Analysis of the Subsistence Crises of the 1740s and the 1840s in Flanders', *Continuity and Change* 26(2), 155–186.

20. On this transformation, see C. Lis. 1986. *Social Change and the Labouring Poor: Antwerp, 1770–1860,* New Haven.

21. A. Winter. 2009. *Migrants and Urban Change: Newcomers to Antwerp, 1760–1860,* London, 101–146.

22. See for instance Lis, *Social Change;* R. Lee. 1998. 'The Socio-economic and Demographic Characteristics of Port Cities: A Typology for Comparative Analysis', *Urban History* 25(2), 147–172; A. Knotter. 2004. 'Poverty and the Family-Income Cycle: Casual Laborers in Amsterdam in the First Half of the 20th Century', *History of the Family* 9(2), 221–237.

23. On the different types of relief provided by the Charity Office, see the 'Statistique de l'indigence' in the yearly *Rapport sur l'administration et la situation des affaires de la ville d'Anvers,* published from 1836 onwards. On the Antwerp workhouse, see M. Abelshausen. 1982. 'De Antwerpse werkhuizen van liefdadigheid (1802–1870)', *Annalen van de Belgische vereniging voor de geschiedenis van de hospitalen en de volksgezondheid* 20, 61–108.

24. On the institutes and budget of the Commission of Hospices, see the yearly *Compte moral administratif de l'administration des hospices civils d'Anvers,* published from 1870 onwards.

25. See Lis, *Social Change,* chapters 9 and 10.

26. M. H. D. van Leeuwen. 1993. 'Surviving with a Little Help: The Importance of Charity to the Poor of Amsterdam, 1800–1850, in a Comparative Perspective', *Social History* 18, 319–338.

27. OCMWA, BW Registers, 148–193: Jaarrekeningen, 1848–1893. All calculations pertain to permanent and casual relief disbursements only, and disregard administrative expenses and 'private' charity legacies administered via the Charity Office.
28. Damme, 'Onderstandswoonst', 524–527.
29. The other, smaller, expense categories of the Commission of Hospices, such as residential care for elderly and children, were often explicitly reserved for local poor. Apart from the hospitals, the only other residential institution with substantial numbers of sojourners was the asylum, but most of them had been sent there by their municipality of settlement rather than interned during their stay in Antwerp.
30. L. Vermeiren. 1988. 'Van gasthuis tot ziekenhuis. De negentiende eeuw (tot 1925)' in *750 Jaar St.-Elisabethgasthuis te Antwerpen, 1238–1988,* Brussels, 145–226.
31. The cumulated deficit of costs never reimbursed at the Antwerp Charity Office over the period 1850 and 1891 amounted to less than 4 per cent of all the costs made on behalf of other localities. At the Commission of Hospices the equivalent figure over the period 1870–1891 was less than 3 per cent. In Ghent too reimbursements appear to have taken place smoothly: Damme, 'Onderstandswoonst', 526–527.
32. While relief to non-settled paupers was conceived by law as exceptional and temporary, both the laws of 1845 and 1876 explicitly stated, 'Reimbursement could not be refused on the grounds that relief had not been necessary.' An attempt to include a clause in the 1876 law that allowed local authorities to deny reimbursement if the relief had not been absolutely necessary was rejected. See also note 16.
33. OCMWA, BW, Registers, 151–160: Jaarrekeningen, 1851–1860; 813–830: Jaarregisters Belgen, 1862–1880; 918–927: Jaarregisters Belgen, 1881–1890; 913–916: Jaarregisters buitenlanders, 1855/9–1890.
34. The comparatively strong drop in non-national sojourners is explained by the fact that they had been excluded from the possibility of gaining settlement by residence before 1876, so that they included a comparatively large number of long-resident poor.
35. On the calculations involved, see Winter, 'Eigen armen eerst', 152.
36. E. Scholliers. 1965. 'Prijzen en lonen te Antwerpen en in het Antwerpse (16e–19e eeuw)', in C. Verlinden, ed., *Dokumenten voor de geschiedenis van prijzen en lonen in Vlaanderen en Brabant,* vol. II, Bruges, 946. Compare with Lis, *Social Change,* 107–112.
37. In 1855 the average expenses towards settled poor receiving permanent support was 68 francs per household: 'Statistique de l'indigence', in *Rapport sur l'administration* (1855).
38. Accounts and statistics on settled poor inform us only on the number of households receiving permanent doles; for casual, medical and in-kind relief we have information only on the total sums disbursed, but not on the number of persons helped. This contrasts with the detailed billing of all types of expenses made towards non-settled poor.
39. According to Lis, *Social Change,* 111–114, the number of settled poor figuring on the permanent support lists in the mid 1850s amounted to around 10 per cent of Antwerp's *total* population.
40. Reconstituted from OCMWA, BW Registers, 148–193: Jaarrekeningen, 1848–1893.
41. See Winter, *Migrants,* 101–146
42. See Winter, 'Caught', 152.

CHAPTER TEN

TRAJECTORIES OF
GERMAN SETTLEMENT REGULATIONS
The Prussian Rhine Province, 1815–1914

Andreas Gestrich

Introduction

The German territories on the West Bank of the Rhine provide an interesting example for the study of the history of poor relief, and particularly the problem of settlement, in Germany. For centuries most of these areas had belonged to the Catholic prince-bishoprics of Trier and Cologne. In 1801, however, they were annexed by revolutionary France and divided up between four newly created French departments. As part of the French Republic they not only introduced the Napoleonic Code Civil as their common law code, but also France's reforms of its system of poor relief which broke radically with traditions of Catholic charity and monastic and other forms of religious poor relief.[1] Having been made part of Prussia at the Vienna Congress of 1815, the Rhinelands were able to maintain some of the French regulations but soon came under the influence of a new Prussian trajectory of modernization of poor relief, which profoundly changed regulations governing settlement and parish responsibility for the poor. In turn, the new Prussian settlement laws formed the blueprint of what became later general law in the German Kaiserreich of 1871.

The first section of this chapter will provide a brief overview of the origins of settlement regulations in Germany which formed the background of the respective laws of the German federal states well into the nineteenth century. It will then analyse the effects of the Napoleonic regulations on the organization of poor relief in the Rhineland, and finally it will look at Prussian policies in the field of poor relief, its controversies with the liberal Rhenish bourgeoisie as well as the Catholic church over principles of poor relief, the growing role of the state in this field and its attempts to establish a framework for relief under increasing demands for better labour mobility.

Medieval and Early Modern Legacies of German Settlement Regulations

To render the relief of the poor the primary responsibility of their home parish rather than leave it to the charity of ecclesiastical institutions or pious individuals in the host or home parishes was one of the major shifts from medieval to early modern systems of poor relief. This trend commenced in the late fourteenth and fifteenth centuries and was accompanied by the institutional enforcement of a differentiation between deserving and non-deserving poor as well as between migrants and those 'belonging' to the parish. This was a European phenomenon, as other contributors to this volume show, and was due to new levels of mobility after the Black Death, to rapid urban growth, as well as to a new work ethic and a growing hostility towards 'strong beggars' who would have been physically able to work but preferred to beg.[2]

To exclude the able-bodied and those not belonging to the parish from support were not entirely new ideas, but the attempt of secular powers to institute clear rules for the exclusion from parish relief added a new dimension to traditional religious charity. Whereas it has always been part of Christian teaching that those who are able to work should do so rather than ask for support, Canon Law had no regulation that deservingness had to be checked.[3] As far as the donors and their individual 'economy of salvation' was concerned, the right intention to help was the relevant yardstick for the religious validity of their gift, not the differentiation between deserving and undeserving poor.[4] Similarly, Canon Law and its medieval interpreters offered various possibilities to exclude strangers, but never suggested it as a general rule. The main argument in favour was that a Christian was always obliged to support close relatives and neighbours, but others only if there were sufficient means to extend one's charity beyond these close circles. This argument supported not only the strong emphasis which was put in Germany (and other places like Switzerland, as Anne-Lise Head-König shows in her chapter for this volume) on the obligation of families to support their siblings,[5] but also the attempt of parishes to restrict their charitable efforts to their own members in need.

From the late fourteenth century charitable institutions in Germany became more discriminating, particularly in their dispensation of regular support or institutional care. Urban hospices and monasteries concentrated their means on caring for their local clientele.[6] In addition, the Imperial City of Nuremberg restricted as early as 1370 the licence to beg within the city boundaries to the local poor who had registered with the authorities and were given a badge which they were obliged to wear:[7]

> In Nuremberg the poor wear this badge on their arms or their hats. It is made from yellow brass. A similar badge is carried by many paupers who live outside the city but belong to it. They also receive alms. Their badge, however, is made from white material.[8]

These Nuremberg regulations were followed by similar measures in other cities and also on the level of the entire Holy Roman Empire. In 1530 a so-called 'Reichspoliceyordnung' (Reich Police Ordinance), issued by Emperor Charles V at the Imperial Diet held at Augsburg, stipulated that every parish had the duty to provide for its own deserving poor and allow only its own feeble or disabled members to beg within its territory. Beggars should be prevented from moving freely and begging outside their home territory. Mobile poverty became stigmatized and even criminalized.[9]

The ordinance of the Imperial Diet served as a framework for subsequent legislation of the many territories of the Holy Roman Empire. The Augsburg regulations concerning the primary responsibility of the home parishes remained in force right to the end of the Holy Roman Empire. They were supported by the legislation of the territorial states.[10] As a consequence, it was not only Imperial Cities like Nuremberg that introduced restrictions concerning foreign beggars. Rural parishes were also supposed to adopt similar regimes of discriminating relief as the other side of the coin that the parishes became legally obliged to care for their poor. In this context local citizenship and its various differentiations became important as they comprised some sort of entitlement to support in times of hardship, reflecting a similar position in Switzerland and other central European states. The regulation of the multilayered forms of belonging to a parish from full citizenship to the right of stay without any access to community rights and relief funds went along with these politics of inclusion and exclusion from relief in a way explored also by others in this volume.[11]

As transfer payments between parishes, particularly those belonging to a different territory of the Empire, were difficult, the way of dealing with foreign beggars was normally their expulsion by way of a 'Bettelschub', a forced mass transportation of beggars and vagrants beyond the boundaries of a town or a state.[12] Originally part of a medieval system of sharing the burdens of charity by feeding particularly old and weak beggars and then taking them on a cart to the next village for support, the "Bettelschub" became a rigid and increasingly state-organized system of exclusion. In 1753 the Habsburg territories, for example, introduced an ordinance that all foreign beggars had to removed across the borders back into their homelands. The Habsburg military organized removals to Bavaria and other neighbouring territories twice per year which often comprised groups of around one hundred beggars.[13] Prussia regularly ordered the expulsion of foreign beggars from its territories by general ordinances, e.g., in the years 1680, 1684, 1696, 1698, 1704, 1710, etc.[14] This was, of course, ineffective, as beggars regularly returned. The alternative was incarceration into prisons and workhouses, the development of which were contemporaneous with attempts to suppress vagrancy and begging.[15]

Despite the importance of acts of charity in Catholic theology, legislation against beggars in Catholic territories was often just as rigid as in Protestant ones. Even prince-bishoprics such as Trier and Cologne made no exception. Particularly since the eighteenth century they, too, tried to introduce harsh regulations to suppress begging and the mobility of the poor.[16] However, as always the reality differed from the rules. The practice of providing relief was much more complex, particularly in Catholic areas. Here, the persistence of monasteries and religious and charitable foundations preserved a more varied and flexible system of relief institutions than was to be found in Protestant territories. Particularly monasteries provided food and other support for local paupers as well as for foreigners. In many cases their help was vital also for the local poor as parish funds tended to be insufficient to provide the necessary support for all paupers. Even in the eighteenth century Catholic monasteries and religious foundations often distributed more help and money than the parish itself and defied all attempts by secular authorities to control their charity. Moreover, closer examination also shows that contrary to the legal regulations, foundations and other institutions under parish control supported not only locals but also 'foreign beggars' throughout the early modern period.[17]

Other complexities in the everyday organization of poor relief could derive from multi-confessionalism within parishes. Despite the tendency towards increasing control of secular institutions over the administration of poor relief, this was often difficult to achieve, particularly in parishes where the population adhered to several different Christian confessions. The small town of Duisburg, which was to become a major industrial centre of the Rheinprovinz, for example, had a majority of Calvinist citizens, but also housed Lutherans, Catholics and Jews. Right through the early modern period, poor relief in Duisburg was in the hands of the different churches which supported their own members only. As the Calvinists also formed the economically strongest part of the population, their relief funds were much greater than those of the other denominations and they could afford much more generous relief than their Lutheran or Catholic neighbours.[18] Settlement was, therefore, not necessarily the only parameter which determined the access to relief, and often religious funds were more likely to support foreign members of their confession or denomination than fellow parishioners adhering to a competing belief.

The legacy of the early modern period concerning settlement regulations for the poor was, therefore, particularly for Catholic territories like the prince-bishoprics in the Rhine area, an ambivalent one. On the one hand they formed no exception to the long tradition of legally restricting relief to deserving parishioners and making the home parishes responsible for the support of their own poor. On the other hand, they preserved the multiplicity of religious institutions and practices which were not only vital for the survival of the poor in times of distress, but formed also a core element of Catholic piety and religious commitment. Both these tendencies continued to influence and shape poor relief and the notion of settlement during the nineteenth century, albeit under radically changed political and economic circumstances.

French Legislation on Poor Relief in the Rhinelands and Its Effects

The German territories on the West Bank of the Rhine were annexed by France in 1801 and divided up between the newly created French departments Sarre, Rhin-Moselle, Mont-Tonerre (Donnersberg) and Roer, with Trier, Koblenz, Mainz and Aachen as their respective administrative centres. Fully belonging to France, these regions not only introduced the Napoleonic Civil Code as their common law code, but also France's revolutionary reforms of its system of poor relief.[19] The 1793 Declaration of the Rights of Man had declared the relief of the poor a 'social debt' of society towards its poorer members.[20] The right to relief or work was, therefore, granted to every citizen, and begging was to be eradicated. New communal institutions for dispensing relief were to be founded, and the property and funds of religious orders and foundations for the poor to be used towards their endowment. [21]

This did not work under the circumstances of the time, and Napoleon reversed most of the revolutionary regulations, particularly by returning to orphanages and hospices their former property and funds. In 1796 the directory created a new uniform system of poor relief by regulating that every parish should establish at least one *bureau de bienfaisance* to administer outdoor relief and – in a later regulation of 1806 – ordered the foundation of *dépôts de mendicité* as workhouses for beggars. Vagrants, whose disciplining remained the main impetus of reform under Napoleon, were to be detained in prisons (*maisons de détention*).[22] To receive outdoor relief paupers had to register with the *bureau de bienfaisance,* and only people who had lived in the parish for more than twelve months were eligible. They also needed trustworthy witnesses for their neediness. Vagrant beggars were to be barred from any outdoor relief.[23]

The Napoleonic system remained as fragmentary an attempt to reform the French system of poor relief (particularly in many rural areas) as the previous revolutionary reforms, yet both formed part of the administrative innovations which were superimposed on many of the occupied territories in Europe. Moreover, and in the context of this chapter, they were of considerable importance in the sense that in several of the occupied territories they supported reforms which were already underway before the Revolution. In others they started such reforms. Thus, while mostly the new structures collapsed with the French rule, a complete return to the old regime of poor relief was also rare. The former Imperial City of Cologne, for example, was occupied by France as early as 1794 and made part of the Roer Departement in 1798. The majority of Cologne's inhabitants were Catholic, and the relief of the poor had rested on a complex mix of hospices controlled by the city magistrates on the one hand, and on charity of the numerous pious foundations of the city's ecclesiastical parishes on the other. In 1794 these funds were put under the control of a commission for the hospices (*Hospizienkommission*) and later the *bureau de bienfaisance.* In a similar process in Trier, the seat of a prince-bishop, the many foundations and hospices were united under Napoleon to form a single administration – an administrative structure which, in principle, persists until today. In other places, like Duisburg, the Calvinist community resisted the handing over of their relief funds to the new central general fund and succeeded in keeping it as a separate endowment for their members, albeit officially now under the control of the secular institutions.[24]

With the introduction of the French system the poor of places like Trier or Cologne gained, for the first time, something like a right to relief. This was not an indiscriminate right, as French legislation also differentiated strictly between deserving and undeserving poor, good and bad paupers. There were also no legal procedures established through which paupers could enforce these rights. The only suggested way of redress was a complaint to the mayor. This has led some legal historians to interpret the stipulations of the French constitutions of 1793 in a way that the right to relief meant the obligation of the parish to provide poor relief, but could not be understood as a pauper's subjective right to relief.[25] Even though the idea of subjective rights to relief were certainly present in the discussions of the *Comité pour l'extinction de la mendicité de l'Assemblée constitutante* which prepared the respective legislation for the *Constituante*,[26] no framework for implementing it was designed or put into practice in France or the occupied territories. As the financing of the new system soon proved difficult, the situation of the paupers in the Rhenish territories had by no means improved; it was merely that controls of deservingness and settlement had become stricter.

Deservingness had to be testified to by witnesses. Applicants needed a certificate of poverty, which had to be signed by four citizens and a police officer. Until recently the now destroyed city archive of Cologne held a collection of about 2,000 applications for such pauper certificates from the years 1799 to 1801.[27] As far as the regulation of a pauper's right of settlement was concerned, France had introduced into the newly acquired departements a requirement that poor relief settlement should no longer be bound to local citizenship, but could be acquired by registering with the local police after having taken up residence in a parish. After one year of permanent stay a person would automatically be entitled to ask for relief without having to fear removal or lengthy negotiations with his or her place of origin.[28] Whereas an application for citizenship continued to be a lengthy and difficult as well as costly process, the establishment of settlement rights for poor relief was reduced to registering with the police immediately after having taken up residence in a parish. Similar rules were introduced in England (albeit registering with welfare rather than legal officials) as others in this volume show. The strict control of mobility through the police was, therefore, at the centre of these new regulations. Even though it might seem that these reforms were primarily driven by the desire to enforce the right to individual mobility and the freedom to choose one's place of residence, one of their core aims was in fact to fight begging and render vagabonds illegal. All beggars and paupers who could not prove their settlement were to be interned into *dépôts de mendicité*.

As in France it is also unclear for the new Rhenish departments to what extent the new settlement regulations were put into practice, a common theme for this volume. Studies on poor relief practices in this area show that some of the old regulations continued to be applied on a local level. This was particularly noticeable in the case of settlement. Often relief continued to be restricted to established local citizens. This was, for example, the case in Cologne, where no major changes in the local patterns of relief seem to have occurred after the introduction of the new regulations. In her analysis of a list of paupers supported by the town in 1810, Ursula Dorn could show that all of them were Cologne citizens and nearly all of them were even born there.[29] The city archive seems to contain only very few records from these early years of the nineteenth century in which questions of settlement (or the lack of it) were debated. None of these cases, however, give a clear indication of whether the local poor relief commissioners followed the new rules or whether there were any conflicts about them.

It is unsurprising, therefore, that little change seems to have occurred in the sense of belonging and identity on the side of the poor. If one looks at their written applications for support, it seems that the majority of paupers continued to use the old rhetoric of citizenship and belonging in order to establish their entitlement to relief. With few exceptions – those who used the new language of equality and addressed the mayor as 'Bürger (citizen) Maire' for instance – most applicants wrote in a style indicating that they respected the social hierarchy. It is also interesting in this context, that about a third of the applicants still turned to the Catholic priest for the necessary support of their application.[30] Only a few miles away from Cologne, in the town of Essen, similar letters survive in the town archives. They are all from the years 1803 or 1804, which is only a few months before the town was handed over to Napoleon. In the Essen letters it is particularly noticeable how the applicants still stressed the fact that they were citizens or had obtained the right of settlement in the town decades ago and, as one applicant wrote, had always fulfilled their duties as taxpayers and citizens. An old tailor of 83 also stressed that he had lived and worked as a citizen in the town for 56 years without ever asking the authorities for relief. He based his application on the argument that he was too ill and weak to go back to his native town of Erfurt and ask for relief there. This old man obviously still thought that his place of origin was the right place to turn to for relief despite the fact that he had had citizenship in Essen for decades.

Mobility of the workforce did not constitute the main target of these new regulations. Despite all revolutionary rhetoric, by the time they were introduced in the Rheinprovinz, they were rather designed to fight begging and vagrancy. This was one of the main problems in the area. Some contemporary reports maintained that there were literally thousands of beggars in Cologne at the end of the ancien régime.[31] At the beginning of the French period, this situation hardly improved due to the poor economic circumstances. The fact that the new French system of financing poor relief was not functioning properly also increased the number of beggars and vagrants in the town. In 1810 the French legislation for not only punishing beggars and vagrants but also detaining them for a (not clearly defined) period of time in a workhouse for their 'moral improvement' was introduced to the Rhenish departments.[32] In 1811 the dissolved monastery of Brauweiler – situated about 15 kilometres west of Cologne – was turned into a workhouse for beggars and vagrants. Soon after its opening it already housed about five hundred people. It was to become the main institution of this kind for the area. Thus, the authoritarian turn of the French regulations on poor relief reshaped the former laissez faire system of Catholic cities like Cologne, where beggars and vagrants, even though they had never been welcome, had mostly succeeded in finding some kind of charitable support. The reform and liberalization of settlement rights under French rule has to be viewed together with the increasing intolerance towards those without clear settlement.

Prussian Legislation and Practices of Poor Relief

After Napoleon's defeat and the collapse of the French Empire, the European powers assembled at the Congress of Vienna and reshaped Germany's political landscape for a second time. The congress delegates did not reverse the results of former secularization and mediatization in 1815, but redistributed large parts of former ecclesiastical territories, imperial cities and minor independent territories of the Holy Roman Empire on to the remaining larger states. Prussia did particularly well out of this. The German (and partly Dutch) speaking regions along the Middle and Lower Rhine were made part of the Prussian monarchy. To cope with its vast territorial gains in the west, Prussia was reorganized in 1815 and divided into ten administrative provinces, one of them the 'Rhine Province' of the Middle-Rhine with its administrative centre at Koblenz. In 1822 the Prussian Lower-Rhine duchy of Jülich-Cleve-Berg with its administrative centre at Cologne was incorporated into the Rhine Province. It remained the administrative framework for these most western territories of the Prussian state until its entire dissolution in 1945.

People in the Rhineland were not particularly pleased about being turned into Prussian subjects. One of the French innovations they had become particularly fond of was the Civil Code with its guarantees of personal freedom, legal equality and economic liberalism. Due to substantial opposition, particularly from local entrepreneurs, the new Prussian government had to keep the liberal French legal system in its new western provinces and was unable to introduce its General Law Code of 1794 which was valid in its eastern territories.[33] Even though this General Law Code was an impressive product of Prussian enlightenment it still preserved and protected many aspects of the feudal society of the ancien régime which the economically enterprising bourgeoisie of the Rhineland were glad to have got rid of.

In the case of institutions of poor relief the locals were less enthusiastic about the French legacy. The Catholic Church in particular was eager to regain control over its former pious funds and foundations and the dispensing of charity in general. Moreover, citizens preferred the voluntary character of ancien régime relief to any compulsory tax-based system of regular contributions. This is understandable if one looks at the level of poverty which cities like Cologne had to cope with in the early nineteenth century. In 1812 the local *bureau de bienfaissance* counted about 10,000 registered paupers. This was nearly 25 per cent of Cologne's total population of 45,000. In years of economic crisis such as 1816–1817 this figure could rise to over 40 per cent.[34] The result of the reform was generally a compromise. The new 'Armenordnung' (Poor Relief Ordinance) of Cologne divided the town into poor relief districts which more or less coincided with the Catholic parishes. Even though the secularized church funds were not returned to their former religious institutions, Catholic priests played an important role in the running of the district relief associations.[35] The fact that a rational system of relief was introduced and the influence of the Catholic Church curbed was in the interest of the Prussian state which did not want to reverse French reforms in this field completely.

It is interesting to see in this context that the Prussian General Law Code of 1794 had also introduced reforms of poor relief which were not dissimilar from those of the French Constitution of 1793. The Prussian Law regulated that the state had to care for its poor citizens if there was no other person or institution obliged to do so. In general the poor had to be cared for by the parishes, but for the poor with unclear settlements the state itself had to take on responsibility.[36] Like the French constitution of 1793 the Prussian General Law Code contained a strong legal commitment of the parishes and the state to care for its deserving poor (and definitely no subjective rights of the poor to relief), and strong aversion against begging and vagrancy.[37] According to the Law Code the state was entitled to dissolve all foundations which were thought to support begging and vagrancy and incorporate their funds into the general relief funds.

In order to suppress vagrancy and begging, the Prussian government also kept the new French regulations for acquiring settlement. Thus, unlike in the rest of Prussia, the *Rheinprovinz* continued to differentiate between citizenship and the right to relief on the basis of having taken up residence in a parish for at least one year.[38] However, running two different systems of settlement within the Prussian monarchy soon proved difficult and resulted in many legal conflicts over responsibilities for relief in an increasingly mobile society with growing pauperism.[39] In December 1842 the Prussian monarchy revised and unified its legislation for poor relief along the lines of the French system still valid in the *Rheinprovinz,* and it introduced the French system of the *domicile de secours* (*Unterstüt- zungswohnsitz*). This allowed men and single women to acquire the right of settlement in a parish after having registered there or (for children) after having lived there for a minimum of three years upon reaching the age of majority. At the same time the Prussian government introduced a law which guaranteed complete freedom of movement for all Prussian subjects in all parts of the monarchy. As long as a person was economically independent and able to provide for himself a house or a flat or rent a room, a parish was no longer entitled to deny this person the right to move into the parish. Nor was it legal to subject strangers to particularly strict and difficult preconditions in order to prevent them from moving in.[40] Parishes were only entitled to deny people the right to settle within their boundaries if they had been convicted of a crime or were already dependent on poor relief and unable to provide for themselves or their families. Suspected future poverty was not considered a sufficient reason to exclude anyone from moving into a parish – a situation similar to that in England and Wales from the much earlier date of 1795. However, a parish was entitled to remove newcomers to their former place of residence if they asked for relief within the first year of residence and if it could be proven afterwards that the person had been impoverished before. The time was to be calculated from the day when a person registered with the local police, which was compulsory. House owners renting out rooms or flats were held responsible for ensuring that their tenants registered with the police, and the owners could be fined for not doing so. The police had to issue certificates of residence. These could be produced at the poor relief offices in order to prove one's settlement.

This new law created, for the first time, a uniform framework for the entire Prussian monarchy for free labour movement and parochial poor relief. It is not surprising that support for this law came particularly from the agrarian eastern provinces of the monarchy and less from the more industrialized west. The industrialized areas did not yet see the eastern provinces as a reservoir of cheap labour supply, but rather dwelt on fears that their parishes would be inundated with migrant paupers to whom they could no longer refuse participation in their poor relief.[41] The fact that the new law met with such opposition in Prussia's western territories might be surprising as at first glance it seemed to present no real innovation for the *Rheinprovinz* which had preserved its regulation of the

Unterstützungswohnsitz responsible for relief from the French legislation. However, the period of residence which was needed to establish a right of settlement was reduced by the Prussian law of 1842 to the act of registering or to three years of residence after reaching the age of majority. Only if a parish could prove within the first year that the cause for the application for poor relief had existed before the applicant had moved to the new place of residence, was it entitled to refuse to help and have the applicant removed to his or her former place of residence. The new Prussian law also introduced a differentiation which was not spelled out properly in the French regulations and which soon became the source of much confusion and conflict. The Law of 1842 had regulated that no independent Prussian subject (*selbständiger Preußischer Untertan*) was to be prevented from moving into a parish and acquiring the right of settlement. However, in the subsequent law regulating poor relief it was stipulated that the mere fact that a person was employed by someone in the parish as a house servant, apprentice, journeyman or a factory worker did not automatically imply residence in the legal sense, as long as he or she lived in or were part of the household of the employer.[42] Thus, the most mobile groups of the labour force, servants and journeymen, were mostly excluded from the reform of the poor relief system and had to continue to turn to their place of origin for relief except in limited cases like illness, where the employer or the parish of residence was made responsible without being able to claim back the costs for medical treatment from their employees' home parishes.

These regulations resulted in much uncertainty for many of the most vulnerable professions. At the same time they quickly led to a run on the relief funds of the larger towns and cities, where many people tried to search for work and to establish a settlement. Another problem was created by the fact that a person lost his or her settlement after having been away from his or her place of settlement for three years. Mobile workers on their search for work could lose their original settlement without acquiring new settlement rights or were at least prone to get into that grey area where a parish could maintain during the first year that the causes for their having to apply for relief predated their arrival, and that the parish was therefore not liable to grant support. Analogous regulations were to be found in Switzerland, as we have already seen in this volume.

These uncertainties created a considerable space for the parishes to debate the right to relief of large groups of their mobile workforce or at least to question whose responsibility they were. Often parishes debated for years whose obligation it was to pay. However, for cases where no clear answer could be reached, the Prussian state had introduced the institution of the *Landarmenverbände*. These were regional unions which were partly financed by the parishes, partly by the state, and were responsible for all unclear cases as well as for the support of those local parishes who were unable to fulfil their legal obligations towards the poor. It also controlled the care for the mentally ill as well as the deaf and the blind poor. The *Rheinprovinz* was subdivided into five *Landarmenverbände,* which financed their specific Landarmenhäuser – a mixture of workhouses and hospices. However, in order to prevent such lengthy disputes over financial responsibilities parishes often resorted to the most powerful tool they had, i.e., to decide whether a pauper was deserving of a subsidy or not. Whereas in cases of serious illness or with orphans a parish had little space for withholding immediate support, times of unemployment and general economic crises gave them ample opportunity to mark particularly young men as workshy or immoral and deny them any relief. In ordinary cases relief was outdoor relief, and Prussian citizens had no legal entitlement to relief in the sense that there was any way to take legal action against the decision of the local poor relief commission. This observation speaks to the discussion of rights by the editors in the Introduction to this volume.

The 1842 Law was also accompanied by new regulations against vagrancy and begging. The Prussian government had kept the workhouse established under the French government in Brauweiler and extended it over the years. The support through the *Landarmenverbände* for people without clear settlement was, therefore, accompanied by strict laws against all those who took to the street and to begging. In the second half of the nineteenth century Brauweiler housed up to 1,600 inmates at a time and often catered to over 3,000 people per year in total. The new Prussian law of 1842 partly created this situaton. It also resulted in a particularly difficult situation for the early industrial centres which were the target for many people searching for work. Protests from these towns and cities led to a revision of the legislation in 1855, extending the time before one could apply for relief to a fixed minimum of one year. This frequently resulted in silent agreements between migrants and their villages of origin that they would be subsidized from home until they had acquired legal settlement after having lived in the new place for a year without having had to apply for relief.

In 1867 the Prussian settlement regulations of 1855 were extended to the North German Confederation founded in 1866 and then to the German Reich of 1871. It was an attempt to extend the right to free movement beyond Prussian territory and also to form something like a common German citizenship before the actual political unification of the German Empire in 1871. The Freizügigkeitsgesetz of 1867 (Ordinance of Free Movement) stipulated that all citizens of the Confederation had the right to stay or settle at any place within its territory where they could provide themselves with a place of residence. Local authorities were no longer allowed to introduce tedious special regulations to make settlement difficult and they could only prevent someone from taking up residence in a parish if they could prove that the applicant was not able to provide a living for himself or his dependent relatives. Fear of future impoverishment was not sufficient to refuse residence. If a new resident applied for poor relief within a year of taking up residence within the parish, the person could be removed. However, removal was not allowed to take place before the parish legally responsible for the person's support had accepted this responsibility. This sort of legal requirement stands in contradistinction to England and Wales, where removal before liability had been accepted was both legal and common.

This law, which was extended to the Empire after 1871, restricted the autonomy of local authorities to exclude foreigners from any entitlement to relief. However, this did not prevent frequent and lengthy negotiations and legal disputes between parishes trying to pass on responsibility. In the 1870s the town of Düsseldorf, for instance, had about one hundred foreign paupers on its distribution lists. Within this group about five or six cases were disputed because the reality of mobility patterns tended to be more complex than the legal regulations of the settlement laws.[43] The widow of a Düsseldorf postmaster with seven children, for instance, was stuck in lengthy disputes with and between two parishes, because her husband had been transferred to the town of Elberfeld where he registered as a resident but died before his family moved.[44] The weaver Carl Wüst moved from Crefeld to Düsseldorf in 1866 and also left his wife behind in Crefeld. When they followed the main breadwinner after three months, they forgot to register immediately with the authorities and did so only two months later. Another two months later the husband left his wife and family and disappeared. The women and her children were removed from Düsseldorf to Crefeld, because their time of residence in Düsseldorf was officially less than a year due to the late registration, and back again from Crefeld to Düsseldorf, because she maintained that she still had her flat and furniture in Düsseldorf. After several months it was decided by the Prussian *Kreisregierung* (district government) that Crefeld had no right to send the woman back to Düsseldorf and had to carry the costs made, but that Düsseldorf had to keep the family as they wanted to stay in Düsseldorf rather than in Crefeld.[45]

Such cases were complicated enough when they involved only one territory. They became even more complex when they involved migration across borders. In order to stop the brutal and irrational removal practices of the early modern 'Bettelschübe', several states within the German

Confederation, the loose political compound of German states which succeeded the Holy Roman Empire in 1815, concluded treaties on the exchange of beggars and vagrants, based on the principle that every state had to take on board the vagrants born in its territory. These bilateral agreements, subject as a genre to more sustained treatment by Paul-André Rosental later in this volume, were superseded in 1851 by a convention by most member states of the German Confederation agreeing on multilateral principles of removal or compensation. One of the main principles of this Convention of Gotha was that a state had to take its citizens back if they had not acquired citizenship elsewhere, even if they had lost their original citizenship through absence. Support for sick paupers who could not be sent home had to be given by their parish of residence for up to three months. Only if paupers had to be supported for longer than three months could the supporting parishes claim their expenses back from the parish of settlement.[46] The Gotha convention was subsequently incorporated into the Free Movement Ordinances of the German Empire.

However, the Gotha Convention and the subsequent settlement laws of the German Empire did by no means put an end to removals, which remained frequent and were often used as tools of social disciplining of either expensive paupers or those unwanted for social or political reasons. This has been shown in the case of removals between the newly conquered territory of Alsace-Loraine and its neighbouring Saar region which was part of the Prussian Rheinprovinz. In the first half of the 1880s the town of Saarbrücken and its suburbs registered about fifty removed paupers from Alsace yearly. The parishes in the Saar area acted similarly and tried to remove people whom they feared particularly expensive or whom they classified as undeserving of relief if unclear settlement provided them with a legal loophole to do so.[47]

The nineteenth century was, on the one hand, a period of tremendous political, economic and constitutional change for Germany which also affected the ways settlement was defined and how problems of entitlement and responsibility were dealt with. The major trend was towards unrestricted mobility within the Empire and the erosion of the older form of settlement through local citizenship which became increasingly dysfunctional. The social consequences of enhanced mobility had to be mitigated by facilitating access to support at new places of residence. Even though progress had been made, local authorities still used the instrument of removal to save money or to rid themselves of paupers whom they classified as undeserving. This mechanism of local self-interest, which resulted in many paupers being caught up in endless disputes between local administrations and transferred backwards and forwards between places of unclear settlement, opened up a wide field of action for private and particularly religious charities which thrived again in the later nineteenth century and became an important feature of Germany's new 'mixed economy of welfare'.

Conclusion

The trajectory of German settlement regulations from the late Middle Ages to the end of the nineteenth century went through several stages following a winding path of modernization in the sense that voluntary and religiously motivated charity was replaced by increasingly secular, rational and bureaucratically administered welfare regimes. The main determining factors of its development were the many profound political changes which particularly affected the notion of citizenship and settlement as well as its use as a tool for inclusion in and exclusion from poor relief. French occupation and Napoleonic reforms as well as gradual moves towards national unity, free movement within the new German Empire and a more integrated federalism all helped to gradually replace the old notion of belonging and entitlement through citizenship by birth or an extended period of residence with a more flexible system of relief for mobile citizens of the state. This situation stands in contradistinction to the United Kingdom, where differences in law and practice between its constituent countries persisted throughout the nineteenth century. However, it should also have become clear that legal developments set normative standards which might be ignored at the level of everyday decision-making. This was certainly the case with the early modern ordinances against support for beggars and vagrants who remained a feature of society right through into and beyond the nineteenth century. However, it was also the case with modern settlement laws which left parishes enough leeway to rid themselves of many unwanted paupers.

This said, one can still perceive the increasing obligation of the state and the local parishes to care for their poor as one of the most persistent and clearest legal developments across the centuries. Unlike in France this obligation entered German poor relief ordinances and other legal texts as early as the sixteenth century. It never developed into a legal entitlement in the sense that paupers could take parishes to court for it. Particularly Prussian regulations made it clear that there was no right to support and that the amount of support granted was entirely left to the discretion of the authorities. Paupers could launch complaints within the administration but not fight through the courts for a right to support. The idea of a subjective right and entitlement entered the German system of poor relief only with the introduction of insurance-based relief.

However, there was some progress all the same. The decision of whether a person who moved to a new parish should be granted settlement was initially also open to complex processes of applying for citizenship and having to prove one's ability to feed oneself and one's dependants. Here the discretionary elements were certainly reduced during the nineteenth century, particularly through French but also Prussian reforms. Despite the leeway and many loopholes which could be used by the authorities, the bureaucratic act of having to register as a resident took the decision of whether a person had lived in a place for long enough without having asked for support out of the hands of poor relief administrators and rendered attempts of exclusion more difficult.

Notes

1. For a survey of European welfare structures, see S. King. 2011. 'Welfare Regimes and Welfare Regions in Britain and Europe, c. 1750–1860', *Journal of Modern European History* 9, 42–66.

2. B. Geremek. 1988. *Geschichte der Armut. Elend und Barmherzigkeit in Europa*, München, 78ff.; M. Rheinheimer. 2000. *Arme, Bettler und Vaganten. Überleben in der Not 1450–1850*, Frankfurt a. M., 16. For the wide discussion of the causes of this shift, see also L. Frohman. 2008. *Poor Relief and Welfare in Germany from the Reformation to World War I*, Cambridge, 18–21. For similar trends in England, see B. Tierney. 1959. *Medieval Poor Law. A Sketch of Canonical Theory and its Application in England*, Berkeley and Los Angeles, 111–113.

3. Tierney, *Medieval Poor Law*, 55–61; H. Scherpner, *Theorie der Fürsorge*, Göttingen, 1962, 36; S. Schmidt and A. Wagner. 2004. 'Gebt den Hußarmen umb Gottes willen. Religiös motivierte Armenfürsorge und Exklusionspolitik gegenüber starken und fremden Bettlern', in A. Gestrich and L. Raphael (eds), *Inklusion / Exklusion. Studien zu Fremdheit und Armut von der Antike bis zur Gegenwart*, Frankfurt, 481ff.

4. Tierney, *Medieval Poor Law*, 52ff.

5. Albeit not always part of codified poor relief regulations, the rule was that parents had to care for their children and vice versa. The Prussian General Law Code, the 'Allgemeine Landrecht' of 1794, stipulated this obligation clearly.

6. Geremek, *Geschichte*, 61–63.

7. W. Rüdiger. 1932. *Mittelalterliches Almosenwesen. Die Almosenordnungen der Reichsstadt Nürnberg*, Nürnberg. See also Schmidt and Wagner, 'Gebt den Hußarmen', 482ff.; H. Bräuer. 2007. 'Bettler in frühneuzeitlichen Städten Europas', in B. Althammer (ed.), *Bettler in der europäischen Stadt der Moderne. Zwischen Barmherzigkeit, Repression und Sozialreform*, Frankfurt, 33; Frohmann, *Poor Relief*.

8. A. Berner. 1981. 'Erkundungen über das Armenwesen in Süddeutschland und der Schweiz, 1531', in C. Sachße and F. Tennstedt (eds), *Jahrbuch der Sozialarbeit*, vol. 4, Reinbek, 70.

9. M. Weber (ed.). 2002. *Die Reichspolizeiordnungen von 1530, 1548 und 1577. Historische Einführung und Edition*, Frankfurt a. M., 161. For an excellent general overview of early modern legal developments in Germany, see K. Härter. 2005. 'Recht und Armut', in C. Kühberger and C. Sedmak (eds), *Aktuelle Tendenzen der historischen Armutsforschung*, Münster, 91–128.

10. Bräuer, 'Bettler', 33–39. For additional regional examples, see also Rheinheimer, *Arme*, 104.

11. H.-P. Zimmermann. 1991. 'Das Heimatrecht im System der Gemeindeangehörigkeit am Beispiel Schleswig-Holsteins 1542 bis 1864. Ein Beitrag zur rechtlichen Volkskunde', in S. Götsch and K.D. Sievers (eds), *Kieler Blätter zur Volkskunde* 23, 86ff.

12. On the Bettelschub, see, e.g., Härter, 'Recht', 107. For an interesting regional example for the regulation of Bettelschübe, see S. Gernhäuser. 1995. 'Bettler und Vagantenwesen in Schlesien in der Frühen Neuzeit (16.–18. Jahrhundert)', in K. Droege (ed.), *Alltagskulturen zwischen Erinnerung und Geschichte. Beiträge zur Volkskunde der Deutschen im und aus dem östlichen Europa*, München, 240ff.

13. E. Schubert. 1983. *Arme Leute. Bettler und Gauner im Franken des 18. Jahrhunderts*, Neustadt a.d. Aisch, 219ff.

14. E. Nathans. 2004. *The Politics of Citizenship in Germany. Ethnicity, Utility and Nationalism*, Oxford and New York, 19.

15. Frohmann, *Poor Relief*, 32–52.

16. Schmidt and Wagner, 'Gebt den Hußarmen', 489–94; A. Wagner. 2011. *"Gleicherweiß als wasser das feuer, also verlösche almuse die sünd." Frühneuzeitliche Fürsorge- und Bettelgesetzgebung der geistlichen Kurfürstentümer Köln und Trier*, Berlin.

17. For examples from the Rhineland, see Schmidt and Wagner, 'Gebt den Hußarmen', 500–507. Particularly interesting examples also come from Catholic Bavaria where rigid attempts to control begging were introduced in the seventeenth century with very limited effect. See, e.g., F. Präger. 1997. *Das Spital und die Armen. Almosenvergabe in der Stadt Langenzenn im 18. Jahrhundert*, Regensburg; E. Schepers. 2000. *Als der Bettel in Bayern abgeschafft werden sollte. Staatliche Armenfürsorge in Bayern im 16. und 17. Jahrhundert*, Regensburg.

18. R. Jägers. 2001. *Duisburg im 18. Jahrhundert: Sozialstruktur und Bevolkerungsbewegung. Eine niederrheinische Kleinstadt im Ancien Régime*, Köln, 116–119.

19. See C. Hudemann-Simon. 1996. 'La politique sociale de l'État français sur la rive gauche du Rhin occupée puis annexée, 1794–1814', *Histoire, économie et société* 15(4), 601–613.

20. 'Les secours publics sont une dette sacrée. La Société doit la subsistence aux citoyens malheureux, soit en Assurant les moyens d'exister à ceux qui sont hors d'état de travailler.' Quoted by E. G. Balch. 1893. *Public Assistance of the Poor in France* (Publications of the American Economic Association) 8(4/5), 68.

21. A. de Watteville. 1843. *La législation charitable ou receuil des lois* [etc.], Paris, vol. 1, 20–24; Balch, *Public Assistance*, 36–70; A. Forrest. 1981. *The French Revolution and the Poor*, Oxford; I. Woloch. 1986. 'Charity to Welfare in Revolutionary Paris', *Journal of Modern History* 58, 794ff; R. Castel. 2000. *Die Metamorphosen der sozialen Frage. Eine Chronik der Lohnarbeit*, Konstanz, 162–170. See also N. Finzsch. 1990. *Obrigkeit und Unterschichten. Zur Geschichte rheinischer Unterschichten gegen Ende des 18. und zu Beginn des 19. Jahrhunderts*, Stuttgart, 48ff.

22. Balch, *Public Assistance*, 73f.

23. A. Birnie. 1930. *An Economic History of Europe, 1760–1930*, Abingdon, 260–320.

24. Jägers, *Duisburg*, 119ff.

25. U. Dorn. 1990. *Öffentliche Armenpflege in Köln von 1794 – 1871*, Köln, 96–98.

26. See, e.g., Castel, *Die Metamorphosen*, 162ff.

27. Finzsch, *Obrigkeit*, 55.

28. 'Pour acquérir le domicile de secours il faut un séjour d'un an dans une commune.' See for this regulation in other territories, e.g., T. Küster. 1995. *Alte Armut un neues Bürgertum. Öffentliche und private Fürsorge in Münster von der Ära Fürstenberg bis zum Ersten Weltkrieg (1756–1914)*, Münster.

29. Dorn, *Öffentliche Armenpflege*, 27.

30. Dorn, *Öffentliche Armenpflege*, 83; Finzsch, *Obrigkeit*, 112.

31. Finzsch, *Obrigkeit*, 46–47.
32. B. Althammer. 2006. 'Functions and developments of the Arbeitshaus in Germany: Brauweiler in the nineteenth and early twentieth centuries', in A. Gestrich, S. King, L. Raphael (eds), *Being Poor in Modern Europe. Historical Perspectives, 1800–1940*, Frankfurt a. M., 273–297.
33. K. G. Faber. 1966. *Die Rheinlande zwischen Restauration und Revolution. Probleme der Rheinischen Geschichte von 1814 bis 1848 im Spiegel der zeitgenössischen Publizistik*, Wiesbaden, 118–85; R. Schütz. 1979. *Preußen und die Rheinlande. Studien zur preußischen Integrationspolitik im Vormärz*, Wiesbaden, 87–113; G. Mettele. 1998. *Bürgertum in Köln, 1775–1870. Gemeinsinn und freie Association*, München, 110–120.
34. Mettele, *Bürgertum*, 133.
35. Mettele, *Bürgertum*, 137–142.
36. 'Dem Staat kommt es zu, für die Ernährung und Verpflegung derjenigen Bürger zu sorgen, die sich ihren Unterhalt nicht selbst schaffen und denselben auch von anderen Personen, welche durch besondere Gesetze dazu verpflichtet sind, nicht erhalten können.' H. Hattenhauer (ed.). 1970. *Allgemeines Landrecht für die preußischen Staaten von 1794*, Frankfurt a. M., 669.
37. This legal commitment of the parishes and the state can also be found in earlier Prussian poor relief legislation of the eighteenth century. See F. Bitzer. 1863. *Das Recht auf Armenunterstützung und Freizügigkeit. Ein Beitrag zur Frage des allgemeinen deutschen Heimathrechts*, Stuttgart and Oehringen, 182–184.
38. A. Emminghaus (ed.). 1870. *Das Armenwesen und die Armengesetzgebung in den Europäischen Staaten*, Berlin, 45. In contrast to this, the southern parts of the former French *départements* Sarre and Mont-Tonnerre, the former Palatinate, which came to Bavaria in 1815, returned to a strict system of making the place of origin or the parish where a person had acquired citizenship responsible for the relief of its poor, irrespective of their place of residence (*Heimatrecht*).
39. For figures see Emminghaus, *Das Armenwesen*, 33–41.
40. '§ 1. Keinem selbständigen Preußischen Untertan das an dem Orte, wo er eine eigene Wohnung oder ein Unterkommen sich selbst zu verschaffen im Stande ist, der Aufenthalt verweigert oder durch lästige Bedingungen erschwert werden.' Gesetz über die Aufnahme neu anziehender Personen, v. 31.12.1842, quoted by C. Sachße and F. Tennstedt. 1988. *Geschichte der Armenfürsorge in Deutschland*, vol. 2, Stuttgart, 276.
41. H.U. Wehler. 1987. *Deutsche Gesellschaftsgeschichte, vol. 2: Von der Reformära bis zur industriellen und politischen 'Deutschen Doppelrevolution', 1815–1845/49*, München, 294–296.
42. '§2. Ein Wohnsitz im Sinne des §1 Nr. 2 wird für Personen, welche als Dienstboten, Haus- oder Wirtschaftsbeamte, Handwerksgesellen, Fabrikarbeiter u.s.w. im Dienste eines Anderen stehen, an dem Orte, wo sie im Dienst sich befinden, durch dieses Dienstverhältnis allein niemals begründet.' Gesetz über die Verpflichtung zur Armenpflege v. 31.12.1842, quoted by C. Sachße and F. Tennstedt, *Geschichte*, 278.
43. Stadtarchiv Düsseldorf, II 1634, BI 23–48.
44. Stadtarchiv Düsseldorf, II 1645.
45. Stadtarchiv Düsseldorf, II 1634.
46. Bitzer, *Recht*, 265ff.; D. Gosewinkel. 2001. *Einbürgern und Ausschließen. Die Nationalisierung der Staatsangehörigkeit vom Deutschen Bund bis zur Bundesrepublik Deutschland*, Göttingen, 155–157.
47. M. Boldorf. 2003. 'Armenfürsorge im Spannungsfeld der Konflikte eines Grenzlandes: Die Saarregion im Kaiserreich (1870–1914)', in Jürgen Schneider (ed.), *Natürliche und politische Grenzen als soziale und wirtschaftliche Herausforderung*, Stuttgart, 114.

NATIONAL CITIZENSHIP AND MIGRANTS' SOCIAL RIGHTS IN TWENTIETH-CENTURY EUROPE

Paul-André Rosental

Introduction

In their contributions to this volume, Andreas Gestrich and Anne-Lise Head-König have pointed to nineteenth- and twentieth-century settlement systems and citizenship criteria which made an explicit distinction between the status of those from individual Swiss cantons or Prussian states and 'foreigners' from the same country. Yet, and as is clear from the other contributions to the volume, for many settlement systems the most acute problem was what to do with 'foreigners' from outside the state borders. In England this 'foreign' status extended to the Scots and the Irish, but across Europe the problem was chronic and, when war, disease, famine or religious or political persecution occasioned forced migration, periodically acute. For the eighteenth and nineteenth centuries, as we have seen from other contributions, solutions ranged from the ad hoc (payment of small allowances to move people on) to the repressive (removing foreigners who were not economically useful) or cautionary (allowing migration of foreigners if they established their own welfare structures) and to the severe (blanket restrictions on the in-migration of certain groups, allied with practical enforcements such as pulling down cottages and restricting access to the waste lands and communal lands). Such measures did not stop migration across national boundaries but they did colour attitudes towards foreigners at the level of politics and public debate, if not always in terms of attitudes towards individual travellers which could, as Jane Humphries shows, sometimes be remarkably humane.

Yet, as Gestrich and Head-König also hint, the late nineteenth century was a period when national policy makers began to seek bigger and more co-ordinated approaches to the problem of outsiders in general and foreigners in particular. These might include inter-cantonal or inter-state agreements and involve compensating financial flows. Local and regional officials were also, by the later nineteenth century and across Europe, forced to seek pragmatic solutions to the problem of 'foreignness' as residence-based criteria rather than birth or contribution came to dominate the answer to the question 'who belongs?'. Unsurprisingly, the watering down of exclusionary mechanisms created intense pan-European debate, which took a particular aspect in France. Here, traditions of locally tailored and financed welfare systems gave way only partially and incrementally by the late nineteenth and early twentieth centuries to the extension of central control,[1] and the different potential models of belonging were keenly played out.[2] These models are the subject of this chapter.

Thinking Internationally

In 1893 Baron de Reitzenstein, then vice president of the German Society for Assistance and Charity, suggested that:

> Assistance will most probably grow and be submitted to fixed rules, not any longer for [native] citizens exclusively but also for foreign citizens. The very understanding that assistance must from now on concern foreign indigents too, is one of the major contemporary conquests of humanitarian idea. Assistance therefore is both human, which means *international,* for what concerns its normal basis, and *national* for what concerns its implementation and collaboration of all citizens.[3]

His position was not an isolated one. Rather, the author was typical of a transnational network of social reformers who, in the last decades of the nineteenth century, militated in favour of an accommodation of economic liberalism. To various degrees depending on the individual, they advocated state intervention on matters of social welfare – from social insurance to labour law – aiming more broadly at legally and sociologically instituting solidarity between citizens and, more broadly speaking, within 'society'.

Migration, of course, was one of the key issues for this project. Should foreigners be entitled to the same rights as nationals? Answers to this question diverged, but a significant kernel of social reformers advocated greater equality of treatment between natives and immigrants. Created in 1873 in Ghent, the Institute for International Law exemplified the limits of this prospect. Its numerous motions related to migration (1877-1, 1880-1, 1888-1, 1892-1, 1897-1, 1897-2) demonstrate that the aim was not so much to treat migrants as citizens, not even for instance to avoid expulsions, but rather to include them into a system of fixed and transparent social regulations protecting the most vulnerable populations. This particularly meant more rights for children and women, two categories which included people who, being legally considered as minors, escaped the principle of individual responsibility which was at the basis of a liberal society. From this standpoint, Reitzenstein's conceptions may be considered as radical, not only because they tended more clearly towards an equal treatment of all claims as a social right, but also because they strongly addressed migrants' rights as a way to foster legal, compulsory assistance to national citizens as well.

Reitzenstein is probably one of the first authors to have imagined a virtuous circle between the circulation of people and the development of the welfare state, a process which actually *did* happen in the twentieth century. His 1893 book can therefore be considered as the foundation for a development which started in the mid nineteenth century and blossomed in the age of the International Labour Organization (ILO) in the 1920s. During this period, the influence of nationality on social citizenship was progressively reduced, a process which developed further after World War II. Migrants and citizens are still treated unequally today, but in terms of welfare the gap between the two has dramatically been reduced, and most inequalities have taken refuge in the grey zones of subtle technical legal arrangements or of discriminating grass roots procedures by the administrators who implement welfare bureaucracy. This process, though, has not been one of unilateral progress. It has brought about a widening of the gap between 'legal' and 'illegal' migrants and, when mixed with periodic soul searching about the future of the welfare state and the relative powers and responsibilities of national versus local bodies, fostered a fluid and inconclusive debate about belonging and national identity.

Modelling this process is important but not easy. In the first instance, we might turn to the French historian Gérard Noiriel and his 1991 book *La Tyrannie du National*.[4] This volume has intrinsic importance in France. It continues to inform debates about the dominant problematics in migration history, a field which has boomed since the 1980s and taken the place once devoted to concepts such as class and social structures in social history. Although Noiriel's influence has remained largely 'Franco-French', his 'Tyranny of the National' Model (TNM) has led to an understanding of contemporary migration as a struggle between the repressive control of the states, and the libertarian aspiration to transnational citizenship and absolute liberty of mobility. Indeed, the TNM maintains that modern, bureaucratic states have intentionally created barriers to free circulation, particularly through identification procedures, which have become tighter and tighter since the 1880s, as the current introduction of biometrics demonstrates. An extension of this model would suggest that more recently (say since the 1980s) this repressive trend has been counterbalanced by legal measures which strive to limit the over-weaning power of the state, and by civil society movements (via non-governmental organizations, or NGOs) which press for migrants' universal rights.

The TNM claims a growing severity of the state against migrants and, implicitly, a growing resistance from civil society. The alternative model that I wish to propose here – one could use the expression 'Social Citizenship Model' (SCM) – suggests that, for at least one important segment of migrant rights, i.e., social rights, migrants and native citizens have moved ever closer to an equal treatment, though this does not mean that they are or were equally treated. This process was initiated in the second half of the nineteenth century by individuals, organized labour and policymakers such as Reitzenstein in order to counter the xenophobic effects of the 'tyrannie du national'. At the core of the SCM is the observation that while in political terms citizenship becomes an increasingly important variable from the later nineteenth century, the concept becomes ever less central to the practical operation of society and especially the nature of social rights. While outcomes for individuals, regions and states depend on context and the balance of socio-political power, SCM at least offers a less linear vision of history.[5] It also emphasizes the importance of understanding multi-layered concepts of belonging as opposed to simply focussing on the legislative process, particularly settlement laws which have figured so centrally in this volume, in respect of entitlement.

Migration, Welfare and Civility

To understand the interplay of TNM and SCM, and particularly to locate the importance of the historical dimension to modern debates about migration, we might start with contemporary definitions of 'transnational citizenship'. This modern ideal combines three dimensions. Firstly, the transnational citizen's link to his or her country of origin does not define personal identity. Contemporary human beings are potential citizens of the world, rather than members of archaic and chauvinistic national entities. The individual right to mobility is considered a component of human rights. Secondly, then, the status of the transnational citizen is partially guaranteed by and inscribed into universal rights, deriving initially from the 1948 declaration on human rights. For the moment these entitlements are mainly concerned with family rights to regrouping, but they also extend to attempts to guarantee refugees' rights. Finally, the transnational citizen has agency. Politically, the contemporary era witnesses the growing activity and influence of associations and NGOs, which disrupt the traditional and conservative games of international diplomacy.[6] By fighting against the state, they both symbolize and express the resistance of civil society against institutions, or more precisely against public institutions. A combination of identity, status and agency – I will call it a 'civility model'[7] – in relation to migration as a process problematizes the role of the states which, through their current forms of action, constitute a major obstacle to the fulfilment of a modernity represented by the transnational citizen.

It would be incorrect, however, to see debate about the meaning and desirability of transnational citizenship as somehow 'new'. Indeed, a detailed analysis of the work of Reitzenstein and others from the 1890s will show that it clearly shapes and underpins contemporary discussions. Standing behind his work is an explicit ethos based on public morality and the acknowledgement of human personality. This acknowledgement is based on Reitzenstein's conception of a Christian humanity, but naturally finds equivalents among secular reformers at the same period. Also implicit in Reitzenstein's work is the concept of subsidiarity. He did not argue for a right to mobility, but to assistance. What he aimed at was both a decent treatment of migrants (here in the name of mercy) and the fulfilment of a principle of equality with national citizens which means of course, implicitly, that he accepted the legitimacy of immigration. In matters of detail, Reitzenstein and others showed striking similarity to the rationale for transnational citizenship currently in vogue. Thus, he strongly emphasized humanitarian ideas in the two meanings of humanity and mankind.[8] As well as observing that '[t]he very understanding that assistance must from now on concern foreign indigents too, is one of the major contemporary conquests of humanitarian idea', he went on to assert that '[a]ccomplishment and improvement of charity are a branch of social life which is not exclusively national[;] it can only reach its fullness if it also includes the entire mankind'.[9]

The melding together of the national and international/universal here is repeated often in Reitzenstein's work and resonates clearly with the language in which current discussion of immigrant rights are inscribed.[10] Yet, and again in common with modern debate, there was also an element of utilitarianism; Reitzenstein suggested that the principle of immigrant rights combined both ethics and humanitarianism with self-interest: 'It is

a moral law to which *everybody* has to obey in the interest of *everybody*'.[11]
Providing assistance, and treating equally native citizens and foreigners,
was a matter of morality *and* calculus and would lead cumulatively to a
virtuous circle: 'The more numerous the peoples who reach civilized life,
the larger the accomplishment of those theoretical considerations – both
for assisting and assisted people – and the solution of poverty issues'.[12]
One of Reitzenstein's contemporaries, the French Dr Drouineau, was
even more insistent on this crucial point: assistance to foreign migrants
involved 'humanitarian obligations as well as private and public interests'
and a nations' charity should be pragmatic ('pratiquement charitable').[13]

Implicit in such observations, and in modern debates about migrant
rights, is a sense that states should engage in 'social benchmarking' in
which granting social rights becomes a flag for the political and civic supe-
riority of one state over another. This aspect of the competition between
states, a peaceful but tight 'emulation', is ignored by exclusively negative
visions of 'the state' as represented by TNM.[14] In turn, the principle goes
much further than a simple question of 'levelling' (even though Reitzenstein explicitly mentioned this notion in his book): the idea is that
through a feedback effect, migratory processes will transform the *national*
structure of assistance. This constitutes the conclusion of Reitzenstein's
treaty: countries with no compulsory system of assistance such as France
or Italy would be obliged to implement it because of the interactions
between nations and the generation of a 'race to the top' in welfare standards. Reitzenstein considered the relatively recent laws adopted by Italy
in 1888 on public hygiene and 1889 on public safety, as well as the then-
current French project on compulsory medical assistance, as expressions
of this process.

Here, then, we see the importance of history writ large. An SCM
rooted in the socio-political thought and evolving practice of the nineteenth century – particularly the Gotha Treaty in 1851 between German
states as we shall see below – has as its driving force the broad intent of
society building as a means of ensuring civility.[15] While such an SCM does
not exclude the possibility of conflicts between human and social rights,
as starts to be the case in contemporary European social regulations,[16] it
has three integral and long established principles: in terms of ethos, the
explicit desirability of granting equal social rights to natives and 'foreigners' in a process of equalization that contributes to the building of the
very notion of society and brings about feedback effects for the whole
social body; in terms of agency, the interplay and articulation between
national and international dynamics, as well as between public institutions
and civil society; and in terms of status, the inscribing of social citizenship

within a framework of human rights.[17] All of these principles were clearly elaborated by the time of the late nineteenth century.

Meanwhile, an SCM, in contrast to alternatives such as the TNM which focus on unilear relationships between individuals and the state, brings the market into the picture. This is important for a counry like France, where private companies played a crucial role in the history of twentieth-century immigration. They defined demand for migrant labour at a time when mobility was first and foremost based on work. Indeed in the interwar period some private societies literally produced migration flows, recruiting manpower, transporting it and providing it directly to the firms which hired them, coming to dominate the 'migration business'. They often entered into tight partnership with the state which was willing to delegate to them elements of sovereign power such as identification procedures. On the other hand, the state also increasingly regulated labour conditions, itself part of the process of establishing and enforcing the social rights of all workers irrespective of origin.[18] Indeed, from the end of the nineteenth century to the 1970s the extension of social protection and the extension of migration went hand in hand through various phases. In the first half of the twentieth century, international associations, and then the ILO, successfully advocated workers' rights in the name both of a humanitarian ideal and of fair economic competition based on utilitarian principles.[19] Crudely, if two countries exchanged people and commodities and wanted their citizens to be treated as natives, they needed to raise and equate their level of social protection, which was a way to create the conditions of fair competition between their companies.[20]

After World War I, the argument was reformulated as social provisions became a way to attract labour from elsewhere. At the same time, international conventions promoted by the ILO allowed for bilateral provisions and eventually for a more universal extension of social right for foreign immigrants. In this process, which blossomed after 1945, human rights (in the name of mankind and universality) and social rights (in the name of justice and efficiency) were simultaneously mobilized by reformist movements, echoing the principles, structures and language elaborated by Reitzenstein. In turn, however, the virtuous circle which had been triggered in the later nineteenth century by transnational social reformers in the name of fair economic competition and free market has tended to fade away since the 1980s. Instead of remaining the deepest basis for the extension of social provisions, human rights have started to become a concern in their own right. Most of all, the combination of rights and interest, or more precisely of social, humanitarian and utilitarian principles, was jeopardized when at the end of the twentieth century US and British neo-liberals managed to monopolize the reference to economic free markets and used it to legitimize a rise in social inequalities and jeopardize the principles of social citizenship so painstakingly laid down more than a century earlier.

Yet, a historically grounded social citizenship model allows a more sophisticated understanding of the role of the state in the generalization of rights. The TNM relies on a unilateral conception of the state which leaves in the background its internal divisions, its accountability (in the case of democracies at least), and the way that each state was constrained by its diplomatic relationships and socio-economic exchanges with the other. SCM is founded on a dual vision of sovereignty, in which bureaucratization, international relations *and* self-limitation of power through bilateral and international conventions, have gone hand-in-hand in the twentieth century and provided migrants with a growing agency. This conception has a much clearer basis in reality than TNM.

International conventions through which the nation state has had to accept limitation of sovereignty are a key component of transnational citizenship and, when enforced through the courts, often the last judicial shield for immigrants. Yet paradoxically the origin of such conventions lies not in a positive desire to equilibrate social rights between natives and migrants but in the burden represented and the international tensions occasioned by repatriation of expelled citizens from one country to another. Starting in 1851 with the Gotha Treaty within the German *Bund*, states reciprocally committed themselves to welcome back their paupers or sick citizens. This 1851 international convention, which is still the basis of modern international refugee laws, expresses the dialectical limit of state sovereignty. By providing each state with an absolute power over its national territory, the convention in effect obliges it to require the agreement of other states before displacing people outside of its national borders. In other words, repatriation problems have obliged the sophisticated diplomatic construction of legal obligations between the states, not without similarity to what happened *internally* in England with the development of the out-parish system and reported by Steven King elsewhere in this volume.[21] Nor does the analogy with the English and Welsh poor law stop here; the same interrelationship between national and local dynamics in this system underpins the SCM from the later nineteenth century. Thus, while TNM focuses on national regulations, the nineteenth-century reformers advocated the building of social protection on a *double* principle, *Stadt-* (local) and *Staatsbürgerlichkeit* (national), the respective proportions of which have varied from one country and period to the other. The reason why Baron von Reitzenstein thought that foreign immigration would lead to national compulsory assistance was precisely the expectation that international pressure would be strong enough to oblige the states to promote social *Staatsbürgerlichkeit* and equalize statuses and conditions among residents, including the immigrants.[22]

Are Migrants' Social Rights Just 'Formal Rights'?

In order to explore the dynamics of an SCM and to test the effectiveness of the international conventions that increasingly came to underpin transnational citizenship, I have implemented research on the Czechoslovakian administration and the protection it tried to provide to its citizens who had emigrated into France between the wars. Inter-ministerial dynamics were at the core of the study: Czechoslovakian outmigration issues involved the respective ministries of Foreign Affairs of course, but also Agriculture and Labour. There is not the space here to rehearse the detail of the research itself, but the conclusions of the project are compelling.[23] First, even though a member of the consulate in Lyons suggested in 1920 that Czechoslovakia 'cannot declare war if its workers suffer under bad housing conditions, are treated as gypsies and valued less than Niggers or Chinese',[24] bilateral agreements and international conventions were a major concern not only for the various Czechoslovakian ministries (Labour, Agriculture, Foreign Affairs) but also for Czechoslovakian migrants' associations in France. The archives show that they followed literally day-by-day the negotiations that other countries, particularly Poland (Czechoslovakia's main migratory rival), held with France, and pressured their government to obtain the same extension of their rights as the Poles managed to. In addition to international conventions, bilateral treaties made a difference to not only the social but also the economic treatment of migrants in France. Being well protected, as was the case for the Poles, meant that the French state would provide financial assistance in case of disease for instance. By contrast, after eight days of unemployment Czechoslovakians who suffered from diseases were obliged to rely on benefits from their employers, who were in turn obliged to provide such benefits. This made such workers less attractive for employers, both at the moment when the firms needed to hire new workers, but also when considering who to fire in cases of economic depression. Comparative advantages or handicaps varied according to social rights. They were stronger for health insurance, which was national, than for unemployment provisions, which were provided by municipalities.

At base, however, migration policy was a compromise between theoretically incompatible interests. Financial logic impelled Czechoslovakia to claim rights for its emigrants in order to prevent them from applying for French citizenship, something that would make them less prone to send remittances. At the same time the social rights needed to be comprehensive; otherwise Czechoslovakian migrants might return home, a prospect which, according to a well-known 'poor-law logic', was hardly desirable for their country of origin. On the other hand, too-generous bilateral treaties would have dragged too many Czechoslovakians toward France, and particularly too many skilled glassworkers, a classical fear since the early modern period. Another consideration was tied up with ethnic identities. As with many Europeans countries, Czechoslovakia was ready to use out-migration to dispense with its less attractive citizens (delinquents, political militants) but also of its undesired minorities. Slovak citizens, in particular, were less protected by their consulate in France than Czechs. Contrarily to what TNM postulates, emigrants' protection through their state of origin (which is supposed to be a paradoxical expression of the *tyrannie du national*) is therefore neither automatic nor systematic.[25] Nonetheless, and in line with thinking from the later nineteenth century onwards, we do see an extension of migrants' social rights and the development of a transnational citizenship compatible with an SCM.

Conclusion

In the model underpinning the *tyrannie du national,* migration policy is often elided easily with the unilateral will of an over-weaning state. In practice, however, the freedom of action of individual states in dealing with the perennial problem of the nature and level of social rights that one should attach to native citizens versus immigrants was bounded. Economic logic, Christian and republican values, international conventions and diplomacy, and administrative weaknesses in social welfare systems themselves, meant that the simple methods of expulsion or discrimination were not the easiest responses. Nor were they uncontested. In such matters one cannot expect nor observe a steady, consistent line of action by the states, but rather a subtle and ever changing balance of power. Since the 1990s Western immigration policies have experienced an ever more repressive turn, a blending of rhetoric on social control and national strength that has resulted in ingrained structures of exclusion.[26] Yet we should not allow this modern perspective to turn our attention from the agenda of the later nineteenth century social reformers, and their checklist of measures required to 'make' transnational citizenship. The SCM which in effect they proposed – one that encapsulated the notion of *dosage,* in other words of balance in public action – was implemented, as the case of Poland and Czechoslovakia in their relations with France begins to show. This shift in perspective allows and obliges us to take into account the role of NGOs, private companies, trade unions, charities and churches in the intertwining processes of migration and the guaranteeing of equality in migrant rights. Ultimately, though, we must return to the question of the power of the state. In this sense what is striking is the way in which applying an SCM to welfare development reveals an increasingly dualistic vision of sovereignty, in which bureaucratization and self-limitation of power went hand in hand in the twentieth century, supporting both migrants' agency and a race to the top in social rights for the transnational citizen.

Notes

This chapter complements P.-A. Rosental. 2011. 'Migrations, souveraineté, droits sociaux. Protéger et expulser les étrangers en Europe du 19e siècle à nos jours', *Annales HSS* 66, 335–73, which provides further empirical and bibliographic elements to the general argument.

1. T. Smith. 2003. *Creating the Welfare State in France, 1880–1940,* Montreal.
2. On the passing of Dutch leadership on modelling social welfare during the nineteenth century, see C. Nottingham and P. de Rooy, 'The Peculiarities of the Dutch: Social Security in the Netherlands', in S. King and J. Stewart (eds), *Welfare Peripheries: The Development of Welfare States in Nineteenth and Twentieth Century Europe,* Bern, 39–66.
3. Translated from the French in F. von Reitzenstein. 1893. *L'assistance des étrangers en Allemagne,* Paris (offprint from *Bulletin de la Société internationale pour l'étude des questions d'assistance*). Italics are from the present author.
4. G. Noiriel. 1991. *La tyrannie du national. Le droit d'asile en Europe 1793–1993,* Paris.
5. On the contextualization and non-linearity of migration policies, see M. Lewis. 2007. *The Boundaries of the Republic: Migrant Rights and the Limits of Universalism in France, 1918–1940,* Stanford.
6. Cf. B. Badie. 2007. *Le diplomate et l'intrus. L'entrée des sociétés dans l'arène internationale,* Paris.
7. B. Baumgarten, D. Gosewinkel and D. Rucht. 2011. 'Civility: Introductory Notes on the History and Systematic Analysis of a Concept', *European Review of History* 18, 289–312.
8. At the same period, Dr Drouineau, general inspector for charitable institutions (*Inspecteur général des établissements de bienfaisance*), in his *Rapport sur l'assistance aux étrangers* to the 1896 International Congress for Assistance in Geneva, also referred to a 'humanitarian ideal', but he only expected its accomplishment in a distant future.
9. Reitzenstein, *L'assistance des étrangers.*
10. 'Assistance therefore is both human, which means *international,* for what concerns its normal basis (base normale), and *national* for what concerns its implementation and collaboration of all citizens', in Reitzenstein, *L'assistance des étrangers,* 5.
11. Ibid.
12. Ibid.
13. Drouineau, *Rapport sur l'assistance,* 1–2.
14. On the impact of this process on the development of social insurances in Europe, see A. Hu and P. Manning. 2010. 'The Global Social Insurance Movement since the 1880s', *Journal of Global History* 5, 125–148.
15. Rosental, 'Migrations'.
16. As it was the case in 2011 France with the legal and social contradictions between mothers' and fathers' entitlement to retirement schemes.

17. M. A. Mazower. 2004. 'The Strange Triumph of Human Rights, 1933–1950', *Historical Journal* 47(2), 379–398, has described how human rights in the 1948 sense were a reaction against the minority rights which dominated the interwar period. This is one possible reading of the survival of the ILO in contrast with the League of Nations.
18. C. Douki. 2011. 'Protection sociale et mobilité transatlantique: les migrants italiens au début du 20ᵉ siècle', *Annales HSS* 66, 375–410.
19. This process which is hardly conceivable today has been a standard in long-term history: for a recent discussion by an early modern historian, see L. Fontaine. 2008. *L'Economie morale*, Paris.
20. On this principle see P.-A. Rosental. 2006. 'Géopolitique et État-Providence : le Bureau International du Travail et la politique mondiale des migrations dans l'entre-deux-guerres', *Annales HSS* 61, 99–134.
21. In a vast literature, see J. S. Taylor. 1976. 'The Impact of Pauper Settlement 1691–1834', *Past and Present* 73, 42–74; K. Snell. 1991. 'Pauper Settlement and the Right to Poor Relief in England and Wales', *Continuity and Change* 6, 375–415.
22. Drouineau's *Rapport sur l'assistance* shows how foreign immigrants who live close to their country of origin are worse off than the ones who live at the other extremity of their new country of residence. In case of repatriation, their parishes or *communes* are less prone to pay the costs of transfer to their country of birth.
23. For a further development see Rosental, 'Migrations, souveraineté'.
24. Archives of the Czechoslovakian Foreign Office, Prague, Consulate of Lyons, correspondence of 19 Dec. 1920.
25. N. L. Green and F. Weil (eds). 2007. *Citizenship and Those Who Leave: The Politics of Emigration and Expatriation*, Urbana.
26. C. Dauvergne. 2008. *Making People Illegal: What Globalization Means for Migration and Law*, Cambridge.

CONTRIBUTORS

Jeremy Boulton is professor of urban history at Newcastle University. He has published widely on many aspects of the capital's economy, society and demography. Since 2004 he has, together with Romola Davenport (Cambridge) and Leonard Schwarz (Birmingham), been leading the Pauper Lives Project (http://research.ncl.ac.uk/pauperlives), which is based on a detailed reconstruction of the lives of those who inhabited the large parish workhouse of St Martin-in-the-Fields (1725–1824). This research has been twice funded by the ESRC and also by the Wellcome Trust. Publications from the Project have been published recently in *History of Psychiatry*, *Economic History Review* and *Local Population Studies*.

Andreas Gestrich studied history and Latin in Berlin (FU) and Tübingen, received his PhD from Tübingen University (1983) and completed his post-doctoral degree (habilitation) at Stuttgart University where he was a lecturer from 1983 to 1997. He was appointed professor of modern history at Trier University in 1997 and became director of the German Historical Institute London (GHIL) in 2006. He. His main research interests are the history of family, childhood and youth, the history of poverty and poor relief, media history and the social history of religious groups.

David Feldman is professor of history and director of the Pears Institute for the study of Antisemitism at Birkbeck, University of London. He has published on the history of Jews in Britain and on Jewish/non-Jewish relations since the eighteenth century, including *Englishmen and Jews: Social Relations and Political Culture* (1994). He has also written on the history of migrants and immigrants in Britain since the seventeenth century. He is co-editor of *Metropolis London: Histories and Representations since 1800* (1989), *Postwar Reconstruction in Europe: International Perspectives, 1945–49* (2011) and *Structures and Transformations in Modern British History* (2011).

Anne-Lise Head-König is professor emeritus of economic and social history at the University of Geneva. She is a former president of the *Société suisse d'histoire économique et sociale* (SSHES-SGWSG). At present she is co-editor of the periodical *Histoire des Alpes/Storia delle Alpi/Geschichte der Alpen*. Her main fields of research are comparative studies of the history of population and of family history, of migration problems, poverty and labour markets, from the seventeenth to mid twentieth centuries.

Jane Humphries is professor of economic history at the University of Oxford and a fellow of All Souls College. Her interests include labour markets, particularly women's and children's work, and the links between the family and the economy. She has edited the *Economic History Review* and is currently president of the Economic History Society. She has written a large number of articles and papers and edited several collections and journal special issues. Her paper 'Enclosures, Common Rights and Women: The Proletarianization of Families in Late Eighteenth and Early Nineteenth Century Britain' won the Arthur H. Cole Prize for the outstanding article published in the *Journal of Economic History* in 1990. Her book, *Childhood and Child Labour in the British Industrial Revolution* was awarded the Gyorgi Ranki Biennial Prize for an outstanding book in European economic history by the Economic History Association in 2011. A documentary for BBC4, *The Children Who Built Victorian Britain*, based on this research and which Professor Humphries presented, won the award for the Best History Program at the International History Makers festival in New York in February 2012.

Elizabeth Hurren, reader in the medical humanities, is based at the School of Historical Studies at Leicester University. In *Protesting about Pauperism: Poverty, Politics and Poor Relief in Late-Victorian England* (Royal Historical Society Series: Boydell, 2007) she presented new research on how the poor law system, through its complex rules and regulations, excluded the most needy. There was a concerted campaign to save money co-ordinated by central government with the co-operation of local guardians of the poor. The chapter in this volume goes further by exploring convoluted settlement law, controversial welfare customs and practical legal redress.

Joanna Innes was educated in England and the United States. She has taught at Somerville College Oxford since 1982. Her research has focussed mainly on social policy and political culture in Britain in the eighteenth and early nineteenth centuries. Her publications include *Inferior Politics: Social Problems and Social Policies in Eighteenth-Century Britain* (2009); *Charity, Philanthropy and Reform in Europe and North America 1690–1850* (1998) (edited with Hugh Cunningham); *Rethinking the Age of Reform: Britain 1780–1850* (2003) (edited with Arthur Burns); and *Re-imagining Democracy in the Age of Revolutions: America, France, Britain, Ireland 1750–1850* (2013) (edited with Mark Philp).

Steven King is professor of medical humanities and economic history at the University of Leicester. He has published widely on the history of demography, poverty and welfare at both an empirical and theoretical level. Some of his most recent publications include (with M. Shephard) 'Courtship and the Remarrying Man in Late-Victorian England', *Journal of Family History*, 37 (2012), 1–22, and 'Forme et fonction de la parenté chez les populations pauvres d'Angleterre, 1880-1840', *Annales HSS* 65 (2010), 1147–1174.

Thijs Lambrecht obtained his PhD from Ghent University and is a researcher at the Belgian State Archives. He has published on rural credit and labour markets in eighteenth-century Flanders. At present, his research focuses on welfare regimes and poor relief in eighteenth-century European rural societies.

Marco H. D. van Leeuwen is professor in historical sociology at the University of Utrecht, where he studies social inequality from the middle ages to the present. He is currently involved in the following projects: *GIGA: Giving in the Golden Age in the Netherlands, 1550–1820* (http://socialhistory.org/en/projects/giving-golden-age); *National Campaigns for Good Causes Worldwide 1950–Present* (http://philanthropiccampaigns.org); and the ERC Advanced Investigators Grant *Towards Open Societies? Trends, Variations and Driving Forces of Intergenerational Social Mobility in Europe over the Past Three Centuries* (http://www.towardsopensocieties.org).

Paul-André Rosental is professor at Sciences Po in Paris and affiliated researcher at the *Institut national d'études démographiques* (Ined). He has founded and co-directs the team Esopp (*Études sociales et politiques des populations, de la protection sociale et de la santé*) of the *Centre de Recherches Historiques*. Recent publications include *L'intelligence démographique. Sciences et politiques des populations en France (1930–1960)* (Paris: Odile Jacob, 2003), and *La santé au travail (1880–2006)* (La Découverte, coll. Repères, 2006). He has recently edited themed issues on 'Eugenics after 1945' of the *Journal of Modern European History* 10 (2012) (with Regula Argast) and on 'Health and Safety at Work. A Transnational History' of the *Journal of Modern European History* 7 (2009).

Anne Winter is lecturer and Francqui Research Professor in the history department of the Vrije Universiteit Brussel. Her research focuses on social-economic problems of the early modern period and the long nineteenth century in an internationally comparative perspective, with a particular interest in migration, social policies, urbanization and labour relations in the Southern Low Countries. Important publications include *Migrants and Urban Change: Newcomers to Antwerp, 1760–1860* (Pickering & Chatto, 2009) and *Gated Communities? Regulating Migration in Early Modern Cities* (Ashgate, 2012, with Bert De Munck).

BIBLIOGRAPHY

Abelshausen, M. 1982. 'De Antwerpse werkhuizen van liefdadigheid (1802–1870)', *Annalen van de Belgische vereniging voor de geschiedenis van de hospitalen en de volksgezondheid* 20, 61–108.

Adriaens, F.H.M.C. 1956. *De magistraat van Nijmegen en de armenzorg (1750–1800)*, Nijmegen: Centrale Drukkerij.

Adriani, A. J. 1926. 'Johannes Ludovicus Vives en zijn geschrift 'De Subventione Pauperum' na vier eeuwen herdacht', *Tijdschrift voor Armwezen, Maatschappelijke Hulp en Kinderbescherming*, 23 Oct. 1926, 1067–1069, and 28 Nov. 1926, 1109–1110.

Allen, R. 1992. *Enclosure and the Yeoman: The Agricultural Development of the South Midlands 1450–1850*, Oxford: Clarendon Press.

Althammer, B. 2006. 'Functions and developments of the Arbeitshaus in Germany: Brauweiler in the nineteenth and early twentieth centuries', in A. Gestrich, S. King and L. Raphael (eds), *Being Poor in Modern Europe. Historical Perspectives, 1800–1940*, Bern: Peter Lang, 273–297.

Althammer, B. (ed.). 2007. *Bettler in der europäischen Stadt der Moderne: Zwischen Barmherzigkeit, Repression und Sozialreform*, Frankfurt: Peter Lang.

Althammer, B. 2012. 'Poverty and Epidemics: Perceptions of the Poor at Times of Cholera in Germany and Spain, 1830s–1860s', in A. Gestrich, E. Hurren and S. King (eds), *Poverty and Sickness in Modern Europe: Narratives of the Sick Poor, 1780–1938*, London: Bloomsbury, 93–116.

Annales Parlementaires de Belgique. Chambre des Réprésentants. 1844–. Brussels: Imprimerie du Moniteur Belge.

Asche, M., M. Herrmann, U. Ludwig and A. Schindling (eds). 2008. *Krieg, Militär und Migration in der Frühen Neuzeit*, Münster: LIT Verlag Münster.

Ashforth, D. 1976. 'The Urban Poor Law', in D. Fraser (ed.), *The New Poor Law in the Nineteenth Century*, London and Basingstoke: Macmillan, 128–148.

———. 1985. 'Settlement and Relief in Urban Areas', in M. E. Rose (ed.), *The Poor and the City: The English Poor Law in Its Urban Context, 1834–1814*, Leicester: Leicester University Press, 57–91.

'Autobiography of a Navvy', *Macmillan's Magazine* 5 (1861–1862), 146–151.

Baar, C. J. van, and L. Noordegraaf. 1982. 'Werkschuwheid en misbruik van sociale voorzieningen? Het beleid in de Alkmaarse armenzorg 1750–1815', *Alkmaarse Historische Reeks* 5, 55–67.

Badie, B. 2007. *Le diplomate et l'intrus. L'entrée des sociétés dans l'arène internationale*, Paris: Fayard.

Balch, E. G. 1893. *Public Assistance of the Poor in France* (Publications of the American Economic Association), 8(4/5), 9–179.

Baldwin, P. 1990. *The Politics of Social Solidarity and the Bourgeois Basis of the European Welfare State, 1875–1975,* Cambridge: Cambridge University Press.

Barnes, T. G. 1961. *Somerset 1625–40. A County's Government during the Personal Rule,* Cambridge MA: Harvard University Press, 1961.

Barnes, T. G. (ed.). 1959. *Somerset Assize Orders, 1629–40,* vol. lxv, Frome: Somerset Record Society.

Bates, E. H. (ed.). 1907. *Quarter Sessions Records for the County of Somerset,* vol. xxiii, London: Somerset Record Society.

Baumgarten, B., D. Gosewinkel and D. Rucht. 2011. 'Civility: Introductory Notes on the History and Systematic Analysis of a Concept', *European Review of History* 18, 289–312.

Beattie, J. M. 2001. *Policing and Punishment in London. 1660–1750,* Oxford: Oxford University Press.

Beele, W. 2010. 'Vremde cortgestenen in de kasselrij Veurne anno 1771', *Westhoek* 26, 159–235.

Beier, A. L. 1981. 'Social Problems of an Elizabethan Country Town: Warwick 1580–1590', in P. Clark (ed.), *Country Towns in Pre-Industrial England,* Leicester: Leicester University Press, 45–86.

Bellamy, C. 1988. *Administering Central–Local Relations: The Local Government Board in its Fiscal and Cultural Context,* Manchester: Manchester University Press.

Bennett, J. H. E. and J. C. Dewhurst (eds). 1940. *Quarter Sessions Records with Other Records of the Justices of the Peace for the County Palatine of Chester, 1559–1760,* vol. 94 [s.l.]: Lancashire and Cheshire Record Society.

Berner, A. 1981. 'Erkundungen über das Armenwesen in Süddeutschland und der Schweiz, 1531', in C. Sachße and F. Tennstedt (eds), *Jahrbuch der Sozialarbeit,* Reinbek: Rowohlt, vol. 4, 69–88.

Berridge, V. 1990. 'Health and medicine', in F. M. L. Thompson (ed.), *Cambridge Social History of Britain, 1750–1950,* Cambridge: Cambridge University Press, vol. 6, 171–242.

Birnie, A. 1930. *An Economic History of Europe, 1760–1930,* Abingdon: Methuen.

Birtles, S. 1999. 'Common Land, Poor Relief and Enclosure. The Use of Manorial Resources in Fulfilling Parish Obligations 1601–1834', *Past and Present* 165, 74–106.

Bitzer, F. 1863. *Das Recht auf Armenunterstützung und Freizügigkeit. Ein Beitrag zur Frage des allgemeinen deutschen Heimathrechts,* Stuttgart and Oehringen: Verlag von Aug. Schaber.

Blaug, M. 1963. 'The Myth of the Old Poor Law and the Making of the New', *Journal of Economic History,* 23(1), 151–184.

Bloch, M. 1966. *French Rural History. An Essay on Its Basic Characteristics,* Berkeley: University of California Press, 1966.

Boldorf, M. 2003. 'Armenfürsorge im Spannungsfeld der Konflikte eines Grenzlandes: Die Saarregion im Kaiserreich (1870–1914)', in J. Schneider (ed.), *Natürliche und politische Grenzen als soziale und wirtschaftliche Herausforderung,* Stuttgart: Franz Steiner Verlag (VSWG Beihefte 166), 109–128.

Bonenfant, P. 1934. *Le problème du paupérisme en Belgique à la fin de l'ancien régime*, Brussels: Royal Academy.

Boulton, J. 2000. '"It is extreme necessity that makes me do this": Some Survival Strategies of Pauper Households in London's West End during the Early Eighteenth Century', *International Review of Social History*, Supplement 8, 47–70.

Boulton, J. and L. Schwarz, 'Domestic Service and the Law of Settlement in the West End, 1725–1824', paper presented to LPSS Conference on Domestic Service in England, 1600–2000, 16 April 2011, available at http://research.ncl.ac.uk/pauperlives/esrcpresentations.htm.

Boyer, G. R. 1989. 'Malthus was Right After All: Poor Relief and the Birth Rate in South –Eastern England', *Journal of Political Economy* 97(1), 93–114.

———. 1990. *An Economic History of the English Poor Law 1750–1850*, Cambridge: Cambridge University Press.

Braddick, M. 2000. *State Formation in Early Modern England c. 1500–1700*, Cambridge: Cambridge University Press.

Bräuer, H. 2007. 'Bettler in frühneuzeitlichen Städten Europas', in B. Althammer (ed.), *Bettler in der europäischen Stadt der Moderne. Zwischen Barmherzigkeit, Repression und Sozialreform*, Frankfurt: Peter Lang, 23–58.

Bruneel, C. 1990. *L'Hostilité à l'égard des grandes fermes, un aspect du populationnisme dans les Pays-Bas autrichiens. Théorie et réalités brabançonnes*, Louvain-la-Neuve: Centre Belge d'Histoire Rurale.

Brunet, G. 2011. 'So Many Orphans ... How Could One Give Them All a Helping Hand? Family Solidarity in a Context of High Mortality in the First Half of the Nineteenth Century. A Case Study: The Dombes Province (France)', *History of the Family* 16, 1–12.

Buckatzsch, E. 1961. 'The Constancy of Local Populations and Migration in England before 1800', *Population Studies* 5, 23–42.

Burn, R. 1780. *The Justice of the Peace and the Parish Officer*, 14th ed., 4 vols, London: T. Cadell.

———. 1805. *The Justice of the Peace and Parish Officer*, 20th ed., 4 vols, London: T. Cadell.

Burne, S. A. H. (ed.). 1936. *The Staffordshire Quarter Sessions Rolls, vol. 4 (1598–1602)*, Stafford: T. Wilson & Son.

Buursma, A. 2009. *"Dese bekommerlijke tijden". Armenzorg, armen en armoede in de stad Groningen, 1594–1795*, Assen: Van Gorcum.

Bynum, W. F., R. Porter and M. Shepherd (eds). 1985–88. *The Anatomy of Madness, Essays in the History of Psychiatry*, 3 vols, London: Routledge.

Caestecker, F. 2000. *Alien Policy in Belgium, 1840–1940: The Creation of Guest Workers, Refugees and Illegal Aliens*, Oxford: Berghahn.

Calonne, A. de. 1920. *La vie agricole dans la Nord de la France*, Paris : Guillaumin.

Caplan, M. 1978. 'The New Poor Law and the Struggle for Union Chargeability', *International Review of Social History* 23, 267–300.

Carthew, T. 1728. *Reports of Cases Adjudged in the Court of the King's Bench from the Third Year of King James the Second to the Twelfth Year of King William the Third*, London: R. Gosling, J. Hooke and T. Ward.

Castel, R. 2000. *Die Metamorphosen der sozialen Frage. Eine Chronik der Lohnarbeit*, Konstanz: UVK Verlagsgesellschaft.

Chapman, S. (ed.). 2001. *The Autobiography of David Whitehead of Rawtenstall (1790–1865): Cotton Spinner and Merchant,* Helmshore: Helmshore Local History Society.

Charlesworth, L. 2010. *Welfare's Forgotten Past: A Socio-Legal History of the Poor Law,* Abingdon: Routledge.

Checkland, S. G. and E. O. Checkland (eds). 1974. *The Poor Law Report of 1834,* London: Penguin.

Clark, P. 1977. *English Provincial Society from the Reformation to the Revolution,* Hassocks: Harvester Press.

———. 1979. 'Migration in England during the Late Seventeenth and Early Eighteenth Centuries', *Past and Present* 83, 57–90.

———. 1983. *The English Alehouse: A Social History 1200–1830,* London: Longman.

Clark, P. and D. Souden (eds). 1987. *Migration and Society in Early Modern England,* London: Hutchinson.

Cockburn, J. S. (ed.) 1976. *Western Circuit Assize Orders 1629–1648: A Calendar,* London: Royal Historical Society.

Coke, E. 1642. *The Second Part of the Institutes of the Laws of England,* London: M. Flesher & R. Young.

Colwell, S. 1980. 'The Incidence of Bigamy in Eighteenth and Nineteenth-Century England', *Family History* 11, 91–102.

Compte moral administratif de l'administration des hospices civils d'Anvers. 1870–1895. Antwerp: Commission des Hospices.

Coode, B. G. 1845. *On Legislative Expression: Or, the Language of the Written Law,* London: Benning, Ridgway and Co.

———. 1848. 'Law of Settlement', *Justice of the Peace,* 6 May 1848.

Crook, T. 2008. 'Accommodating the Outcast: common lodging houses and the limits of urban governance in Victorian and Edwardian London', *Urban History* 35, 414–436.

Crowther, M. A. 1981. 'Care of the Elderly in England: Family or State Responsibility', *Historical Journal* 25(1), 131–145.

———. 1981. *The Workhouse System: The History of an English Social Institution,* London: Routledge.

Cruyningen, P. J. van. 2000. *Behoudend maar buigzaam. Boeren in West-Zeeuws-Vlaanderen, 1650–1850,* Wageningen: Afdeling Agrarische Geschiedenis (A. A. G. Bijdragen 40).

Cuénoud, J. 1879. *La population flottante et les classes dangerueses à Genève: nos dangers intérieurs,* Genève: J.-G. Fick.

Dalle, D. 1963. *De bevolking van Veurne-Ambacht in de zeventiende en de achttiende eeuw,* Brussels: Paleis der Academiën.

Dalton, M. 1666. *The Countrey Justice: Containing the Practise of the Iustices of the Peace Out of Their Sessions,* London: J. Streater, J. Flesher and H. Twyford.

Dauvergne, C. 2008. *Making People Illegal: What Globalization Means for Migration and Law,* Cambridge: Cambridge University Press.

Davids, C. A. 1978. 'Migratie te Leiden in de achttiende eeuw. Een onderzoek op grond van de acten van cautie', in H. A. Diederiks (ed.), *Een stad in achteruitgang. Sociaal-historische studies over Leiden in de achttiende eeuw,* Leiden: Rijksuniversiteit Leiden, 146–192.

De Ferraris, J. 1966. *Mémoires Historiques, Chronologiques et Oeconomiques (1777)*, Brussels: Crédit Communal.

de Hullu, J. 1915. 'De stichting der Rooms-Katholieke parochiën te Sluis en IJzendijke in de achttiende eeuw', *Nederlands Archief voor Kerkgeschiedenis* 12, 35–62.

———. 1934. *Thomas Radcliff's beschrijving van den landbouw in het Land van Cadzand omstreeks 1819*, Oostburg: [s.n.].

De Lichervelde, J. F. 1815. *Mémoire sur les fonds ruraux du département de l'Escaut*, Ghent : De Goesin.

Dench, G., K. Gavron and M. Young. 2006. *The New East End. Kinship, Race and Conflict*, London: Profile Books.

Deprez P. and C. Vandenbroeke. 1989. 'Population Growth and Distribution and Urbanisation in Belgium During the Demographic Transition', in R. Lawton and R. Lee (eds), *Urban Population Development in Western Europe from the Late Eighteenth to the Early Twentieth Century*, Liverpool: Liverpool University Press, 220–257.

de Rivière, L. 1908. '*De armenzorg in Nederland*', *Tijdschrift voor Armenzorg en Kinderbescherming*, 58–65.

de Saint-Léger, A. and P. Sagnac (eds). 1906. *Les cahiers de la Flandre maritime en 1789*, Dunkirk and Paris: Société Dunkerquoise-Picard.

de Séchelles, J. Moreau. 2003 (1750). 'Mémoire concernant les précautions qui ont été prises pour bannir la mendicité dans le Département de Flandre (1750)', in G. Thuillier (ed.), *Aux origines de l'administration sociale: le rapport de Loménie de Brienne en 1775*, Paris: Comité d'Histoire de la Sécurité Sociale, 454–470.

De Smet, J. (ed.). 1970. *Zuid-Westvlaamse tijdskroniek uit de Oostenrijkse en Franse Tijd. Het memoriael van Reninghelst door koster P.L. Cuvelier*, Bruges: Westvlaams Verbond van Kringen voor Heemkunde.

de Swaan, A. 1988. *In Care of the State: Health Care, Education and Welfare in Europe and the USA in the Modern Era*, Oxford: Oxford University Press.

Détert, B. 1786. *De Rapsodisten*, Bruges: J. Bogaert.

Devos, I. 'Malaria in Vlaanderen tijdens de 18de en 19de eeuw', in J. Parmentier and S. Spanoghe (eds), *Orbis in orbem. Liber amicorum John Everaert*, Ghent: Academia Press, 2001, 197–234.

———. 2006. *Allemaal beestjes. Mortaliteit en morbiditeit in Vlaanderen, 18de-20ste eeuw*, Ghent: Academia Press.

de Vries, J. and A. van der Woude. 1995. *The First Modern Economy: Success, Failure, and Perseverance of the Dutch Economy, 1500–1815*, Cambridge: Cambridge University Press.

de Watteville, A. 1843. *La législation charitable ou receuil des lois [etc.]*, Paris: Heois.

de Wolf, H. C. 1964. *Geschiedenis van het R.C. Oude-Armenkantoor te Amsterdam, 1600–1866*, Hilversum: P. Brand.

Dieudonné, M. 1804. *Statistique du Département du Nord*, Douai: Marlier.

Digby, A. 1976. 'The Rural Poor Law,' in D. Fraser (ed.), *The New Poor Law in the Nineteenth Century*, Basingstoke: Macmillan, 149–170.

Dorn, U. 1990. *Öffentliche Armenpflege in Köln von 1794–1871*, Köln: Böhlau.

Dorren, G. 1998. *Het Soet Vergaren. Haarlems buurtleven in de zeventiende eeuw*, Haarlem: Stadsbibliotheek Haarlem.

Dorwart, R. 1971. *The Prussian Welfare State before 1740*, Cambridge, MA: Harvard University Press.

Douki, C. 2011. 'Protection sociale et mobilité transatlantique: les migrants italiens au début du 20ᵉ siècle', *Annales HSS* 66, 375–410.

Douwes, P. A. C. 1977. *Armenkerk. De hervormde diaconie te Rotterdam in de negentiende eeuw*, Schiedam: Interbook International.

Dribe, M. 2000. *Leaving Home in a Peasant Society: Economic Fluctuations, Household Dynamics and Youth Migration in Southern Sweden, 1829–1866*, Stockholm: Almqvist & Wiksell.

Drouineau. 1896. *Rapport sur l'assistance aux étrangers*, Geneva: International Congress for Assistance.

Dubler, A.-M. 1970. *Armen- und Bettlerwesen in der Gemeinen Herrschaft 'Freie Ämter' (16. bis 18. Jahrhundert)*, Basel: Schweizerische Gesellschaft für Volkskunde.

Dunhill, S. 1831. *The Life of Snowden Dunhill, written while a convict at Hobart Town*, Beverley: W. B. Johnson.

Dupont-Bouchat, M. S. 1996. 'Enfants corrigés, enfants protégés: Gènese de la protection de l'enfance en Belgique, en France et aux Pays-Bas 1820–1914', *Droit et Sociètè* 32, 89–104.

Ellis, R. 2006. 'The Asylum, the Poor Law and a Reassessment of the Four-Shilling Grant: Admissions to the County Asylums of Yorkshire in the Nineteenth Century', *Social History of Medicine* 19(1), 55–71.

———. 2008. 'The Asylum, the Poor Law and the Growth of County Asylums in Nineteenth-Century Yorkshire', *Northern History* 45(2), 279–329.

Emminghaus, A. (ed.). 1870. *Das Armenwesen und die Armengesetzgebung in den Europäischen Staaten*, Berlin: Herbig.

Emmison, F. G. (ed.). 1970. *Early Essex Town Meetings: Braintree, 1619–1636: Finchingfield, 1626–1634*, Chichester: Phillimore.

Englander, D. 1998. *Poverty and Poor Law Reform in Nineteenth Century Britain, 1834–1914: From Chadwick to Booth*, London: Longman.

Faber, K. G. 1966. *Die Rheinlande zwischen Restauration und Revolution. Probleme der Rheinischen Geschichte von 1814 bis 1848 im Spiegel der zeitgenössischen Publizistik*, Wiesbaden: Karl Steiner Verlag.

Fahrmeir, A. 2000. *Citizens and Aliens: Foreigners and the Law in Britain and the German States, 1789–1870*, Oxford: Berghahn.

———. 2007. *Citizenship: The Rise and Fall of a Modern Concept*, New Haven: Yale University Press.

Fauve-Chamoux, A. 2006. 'Family Reproduction and Stem-Family System: From Pyrenean Valleys to Norwegian Farms', *History of the Family* 11, 171–184.

Feldman, D. 2003. 'Migrants, Immigrants and Welfare from the Old Poor Law to the Welfare State', *Transactions of the Royal Historical Society, Sixth Series* 13, 79–104.

Finzsch, N. 1990. *Obrigkeit und Unterschichten. Zur Geschichte rheinischer Unterschichten gegen Ende des 18. und zu Beginn des 19. Jahrhunderts*, Stuttgart: Franz Steiner Verlag.

Fletcher, A. 1986. *Reform in the Provinces. The Government of Stuart England*, New Haven: Yale University Press.

Flinn, M. 1976. 'Medical Services under the New Poor Law', in D. Fraser (ed.), *The New Poor Law in the Nineteenth-Century*, London: Macmillan, 45–66.

Flückiger Strebel, E. *Zwischen Wohlfahrt und Staatsökonomie. Armenfürsorge auf der bernischen Landschaft im 18. Jahrhundert*, Zürich: Chronos, 2002.

Fontaine, L. 2008. *L'Economie morale*, Paris: Gallimard.

Forrest, A. 1981. *The French Revolution and the Poor*, Oxford: Blackwell.

Forster, G. C. F. 1983. 'Government in Provincial England under the Later Stuarts', *Transactions of the Royal Historical Society, Fifth Series* 33(1), 29–48.

Fox, L. (ed.) 1986. *Coventry Constables Presentments, 1629–1742*, vol. 34, Oxford: The Dugdale Society.

Freshfield, E. (ed.) 1890. *The Vestry Minute Book of St Bartholomew Exchange, 1567–1764*, London: Rixon and Arnold.

Frohman, L. 2008. *Poor Relief and Welfare in Germany from the Reformation to World War I*, Cambridge: Cambridge University Press.

Geiser, K. 1975. 'Einzug, Niederlassung und Heimatrecht im alten Bernbiet', *Jahrbuch des Oberaargaus*, 18–25.

George, M. D. 1976. *London Life in the Eighteenth Century*, Harmondsworth: Penguin.

Geremek, B. 1988. *Geschichte der Armut. Elend und Barmherzigkeit in Europa*, München: Artemis Verlag.

Gernhäuser, S. 1995. 'Bettler und Vagantenwesen in Schlesien in der Frühen Neuzeit (16.–18. Jahrhundert)', in K. Droege (ed.), *Alltagskulturen zwischen Erinnerung und Geschichte. Beiträge zur Volkskunde der Deutschen im und aus dem östlichen Europa*, München: R. Oldenbourg, 229–246.

Gestrich, A., E. Hurren and S. King. 2012. 'Narratives of Poverty and Sickness in Europe 1780–1938: Sources, Methods and Experiences', in A. Gestrich, E. Hurren and S. King (eds), *Poverty and Sickness in Modern Europe: Narratives of the Sick Poor, 1780–1938*, London: Bloomsbury, 1–34.

Gestrich, A. L. Raphael and H. Uerlings (eds). 2009. *Strangers and Poor People: Changing Patterns of Inclusion and Exclusion in Europe and the Mediterranean World from Classical Antiquity to the Present Day*, Frankfurt: Peter Lang.

Gestrich, A. and J. Stewart. 2007. 'Unemployment and Poor Relief in the West of Scotland, 1870–1900', in S. King and J. Stewart (eds), *Welfare Peripheries: The Development of Welfare States in Nineteenth and Twentieth Century Europe*, Bern: Peter Lang, 125–148.

Gosewinkel, D. 2001. *Einbürgern und Ausschließen. Die Nationalisierung der Staatsangehörigkeit vom Deutschen Bund bis zur Bundesrepublik Deutschland*, Göttingen: Vandenhoeck & Ruprecht.

Gras, H. 1989. *Op de grens van het bestaan. Armen en armenzorg in Drenthe 1700–1800*, Zuidwolde: Stichting Het Drentse Boek.

Gray, L. 2002. 'The Experience of Old Age in the Narratives of the Rural Poor in Early Modern Germany', in S. Ottaway, L. Botelho and K. Kittredge (eds), *Power and Poverty: Old Age in the Pre-Industrial Past*, Westport: Greenwood Press, 107–123.

Green, D. R. 2010. *Pauper Capital: London and the Poor Law, 1790–1870*, Aldershot: Ashgate.

———. 2009. 'Icons of the New System: Workhouse Construction and Relief Practices in London under the Old and New Poor Law', *London Journal* 34(3), 264–284.

Green, N. L. and F. Weil (eds). 2007. *Citizenship and Those Who Leave: The Politics of Emigration and Expatriation*, Urbana: University of Illinois Press.

Griffiths, P. 2008. *Lost Londons. Change, Crime and Control in the Capital City, 1550–1660*, Cambridge: Cambridge University Press.

Groenveld, S., J. J. H. Dekker and T. R. M. Willemse. 1997. *Wezen en boefjes. Zes eeuwen zorg in wees- en kinderhuizen*, Hilversum: Verloren.

Groombridge, M. J. 1956. *Calendar of Chester City Council Minutes 1603–42*, vol. cvi, Blackpool: Lancashire and Cheshire Record Society.

Gurney, D. 2007. *Brave Community. The Digger Movement in the English Revolution*, Manchester: Manchester University Press.

Gutton, J.-P. 1971. *La société et les pauvres. L'exemple de la généralité de Lyon, 1534–1789*, Paris: Les Belles Lettres.

Guzzi-Heeb, S. 2009. 'Kinship, Ritual Kinship and Political Milieus in an Alpine valley in 19th Century', *History of the Family* 14, 107–123.

Gyssels, C. and L. van der Straeten. 1986. *Bevolking, arbeid en tewerkstelling in West-Vlaanderen (1796–1815)*, Ghent: Centre Belge d'Histoire Rurale.

Hale, M. 1683. *A Discourse Touching Provision for the Poor*, London: W. Shrowsbery.

Hamlin, C. 1988. *Public Health and Social Justice in the Age of Chadwick, Britain 1800–1854*, Cambridge: Cambridge University Press.

Hart, P. D. 't. 1983. *De stad Utrecht en haar inwoners. Een onderzoek naar samenhangen tussen sociaal-economische ontwikkelingen en de demografische geschiedenis van de stad Utrecht 1771–1825*, Utrecht: Rijksuniversiteit Utrecht.

Härter, K. 2005. 'Recht und Armut', in C. Kühberger and C. Sedmak (eds), *Aktuelle Tendenzen der historischen Armutsforschung*, Münster: LIT Verlag, 91–128.

Harvey, C. E., E. M. Green and P. J. Corfield. 1999. 'Continuity, Change, and Specialization Within Metropolitan London: The Economy of Westminster, 1750–1820', *Economic History Review* 52, 469–493.

Hasquin, H. 1981. 'Moyenne culture et populationnisme dans les Pays-Bas autrichiens ou les ambiguïtés du despotisme éclairé', *Revue Belge d'Histoire Contemporaine* 12, 691–712.

Hattenhauer, H. (ed.). 1970. *Allgemeines Landrecht für die preußischen Staaten von 1794*, Frankfurt a. M.: Luchterhand.

Head-König, A.-L. 1989. 'Marginalisation ou intégration des pauvres: les deux facettes de la politique matrimoniale pratiquée par les cantons suisses (XVIe-XIXe siècles)', in A.-L. Head and B. Schnegg (eds), *La Pauvreté en Suisse (XVIIe-XXe siècles)*, Zurich: Chronos, 79–93.

———. 2003. 'Les biens communaux en Suisse aux XVIIIe et XIXe siècles: enjeux et controverses', in M.-D. Demelas and N. Vivier (eds), *Les propriétés collectives face aux attaques libérales (1750–1914). Europe occidentale et Amérique latine*, Rennes: Presses Universitaires de Rennes, 99–118.

———. 2010. 'Les formes de garde des enfants placés en Suisse: politiques ambiguës, résistances et objectifs contradictoires (1850–1950)', *Paedagogica Historica* 46(6), 763–773.

Hearnshaw, F. J. C. and D. M. Hearnshaw (eds). 1905. *Court Leet Records*, vol. 1, Southampton: Southampton Record Society.

Heerma van Voss, H.O. 1958. 'De armenzorg te Amsterdam in de 17de eeuw' (Unpublished MA dissertation, University of Amsterdam).

Heijden, M. van der. 2007. 'Juan Luis Vives: icoon van de vroegmoderne armenzorg', in J. van Eijnatten, F. van Lieburg and H. de Waardt (eds), *Heiligen of helden. Opstellen voor Willem Frijhof,* Amsterdam: Bert Bakker, 61–71.

Hellebaut E. and C. de Gronckel. 1879. *Commentaire de la loi du 14 mars 1876 sur le domicile de secours,* Brussels: Mertens.

Hennock, E. P. 2007. *The Origins of the Welfare State in England and Germany: 1850–1914: Social Policies Compared,* Cambridge: Cambridge University Press.

Hindle, S. 2000. *The State and Social Change in Early Modern England, c. 1550–1640,* London: Palgrave Macmillan.

———. 2004. *On the Parish? The Micro-Politics of Poor Relief in Rural England, c. 1550–1750,* Oxford: Oxford University Press.

Hitchcock, T. 1992. 'Paupers and Preachers: The SPCK and the Parochial Workhouse Movement', in L. Davison, T. Hitchcock, T. Keirn and R.B. Shoemaker, *Stilling the Grumbling Hive. The Response to Social and Economic Problems in England, 1689–1750,* Stroud: Alan Sutton, 145–166.

———. 2004. *Down and Out in Eighteenth-Century London,* London: Hambledon Continuum.

Hitchcock, T. and John Black (eds). 1999. *Chelsea Settlement and Bastardy Examinations, 1733–1766,* London: London Record Society.

Hitchcock, T., P. King and P. Sharpe (eds). 1997. *Chronicling Poverty: The Voices and Strategies of the English Poor 1640–1840,* Basingstoke: Macmillan.

Hochstadt, S. 1999. *Mobility and Modernity: Migration in Germany 1820–1989,* Ann Arbor: University of Michigan Press.

Hodgkinson, R. 1967. *The Origins of the National Health Service: The Medical Services of the New Poor Law, 1834–1871,* London: Wellcome Trust publication.

Honeyman, K. 2007. *Child Workers in England, 1780–1820: Parish Apprentices and the Making of the Early Industrial Labour Force,* Aldershot: Ashgate.

Horrell, S., J. Humphries and H.-J. Voth. 1998. 'Stature and Relative Deprivation: Female-Headed Households in the Industrial Revolution', *Continuity and Change* 13(1), 73–115.

———. 2001. 'Destined for Deprivation; Human Capital Formation and Intergenerational Poverty in Nineteenth-Century England', *Explorations in Economic History* 38(3), 339–365.

Howkins, A. 2002. 'From Diggers to Dongas: The Land in English Radicalism 1649–2000', *History Workshop Journal* 54(1), 1–23.

Hu, A. and P. Manning. 2010. 'The Global Social Insurance Movement since the 1880s', *Journal of Global History* 5, 125–148.

Hudemann-Simon, C. 1996. 'La politique sociale de l'État français sur la rive gauche du Rhin occupée puis annexée, 1794–1814', *Histoire, économie & société* 15(4), 601–613.

Hudson, P. and S. King. Forthcoming. *Industrialisation, Material Culture and Everyday Life.*

Humphreys, R. 1985. *Sin, Organized Charity and the Poor Law in Victorian England,* Basingstoke: Macmillan.

Humphries, J. 1998. 'Female-Headed Households in Early Industrial Britain: The Vanguard of the Proletariat', *Labour History Review* 63(1), 31–65.

———. 2010. *Childhood and Child Labour in the British Industrial Revolution,* Cambridge: Cambridge University Press.

————. Forthcoming. 'Care and Cruelty in the Workhouse: Children's Experiences of Residential Poor Relief in Eighteenth and Nineteenth-Century England', in N. Goose and K. Honeyman (eds), *Children and Childhood in Industrial England, 1650–1900*, Aldershot: Ashgate.

Hurren, E. T. 2000. '"Labourers are Revolting": "Penalising the Poor and a Political Reaction in the Brixworth Union, Northamptonshire, 1875–1885', *Rural History* 11(1), 37–55.

————. 2007. *Protesting about Pauperism: Poverty, Politics and Poor Relief in late-Victorian England*, Woodbridge: Boydell and Brewer.

Inderwick, F. A. 1891. *The Interregnum. Studies of the Commonwealth Legislative, Social and Legal*, London: S. Low, Marston, Searle & Rivington.

Innes, J. 1998. 'State, Church and Voluntarism in European Welfare 1690–1850', in H. Cunningham and J. Innes (eds), *Charity, Philanthropy and Reform from the 1690s to 1850*, Basingstoke: Macmillan, 225–280.

Israel, J. 1995. *The Dutch Republic: Its Rise, Greatness, and Fall 1477–1806*, Oxford: Oxford University Press.

Jägers, R. 2001. *Duisburg im 18. Jahrhundert: Sozialstruktur und Bevolkerungsbewegung. Eine niederrheinische Kleinstadt im Ancien Régime*, Köln: Böhlau.

James, M. 1930. *Social Problems and Policy During the Puritan Revolution 1640–1660*, London: Routledge.

Jansen, F. M. J. 1936, 'Afwenteling van kosten van armenzorg op andere gemeenten. De huidige stand van het vraagstuk, bezien uit het gezichtspunt van de centrumgemeente', in J. G. Ramaker, F. M. J. Jansen and J. de Bruin, *Prae-adviezen over het onderwerp: afwenteling van kosten van armenzorg op andere gemeenten*, Haarlem: Tjeenk Willink (Geschriften van de Nederlandsche Vereeniging voor Armenzorg en Weldadigheid, LXV), 43–95.

Jansen, P. C. 1975. 'Armoede in Amsterdam aan het eind van de achttiende eeuw', *Tijdschrift voor Geschiedenis* 88, 613–625.

Jütte, R. 1994. *Poverty and Deviance in Early Modern Europe*, Cambridge: Cambridge University Press.

————. 2004. 'Tendenzen öffentlicher Armenpflege in der Frühen Neuzeit Europas und ihre weiter wirkenden Folgen', in T. Strom and M. Klein (eds), *Die Entstehung einer sozialen Ordnung Europas, vol. 1: Historische Studien und exemplarische Beiträge zur Sozialreform im 16. Jahrhundert*, Heidelberg: Universitätsverlag Winter, 78–104.

————. 2000. *Arme, Bettler, Beutelschneider: Eine Sozialgeschichte der Armut in der Frühen Neuzeit*, Weimar: Böhlau.

Keller, B. 1935. *Das Armengesetz des Kantons Zürich vom Beginn des 18. Jahrhunderts bis zum Armengesetz des Jahres 1836*, Winterthur: A. Vogel.

Kent, D. A. 1989. 'Ubiquitous but Invisible: Female Domestic Servants in Mid-Eighteenth-Century London', *History Workshop* 28, 111–128.

————. 1990. '"Gone for a Soldier": Family Breakdown and the Demography of Desertion in a London Parish, 1750–91', *Local Population Studies* 45, 27–42.

Kent, J. R. 1981. 'Population Mobility and Alms: Poor Migrants in the Midlands During the Early Seventeenth Century', *Local Population Studies* 27, 35–51.

Kent, J. and S. King. 2003. 'Changing Patterns of Poor Relief in Some English Rural Parishes circa 1650–1750', *Rural History* 14(2), 119–156.

Kidd, A. 1999. *State, Society and the Poor in Nineteenth Century England,* Basingstoke: Macmillan.

King, P. 2004. 'Social Inequality, Identity and the Labouring Poor in Eighteenth Century England', in H. French and J. Barry (eds), *Identity and Agency in England, 1500–1800,* Basingstoke: Palgrave MacMillan, 60–87.

King, S. 1997. 'Reconstructing Lives: The Poor, the Poor Law and Welfare in Rural Industrial Communities', *Social History* 22, 318–338.

———. 2000. *Poverty and Welfare in England 1700–1850: A Regional Perspective,* Manchester: Manchester University Press.

———. 2005. '"It Is Impossible for Our Vestry to Judge His Case into Perfection from Here": Managing the Distance Dimensions of Poor Relief, 1800–40', *Rural History* 16, 161–189.

———. 2005. 'The Bastardy Prone Sub-Society Again: Bastards and their Fathers and Mothers in Lancashire, Wiltshire and Somerset, 1800–1840', in A. Levene, T. Nutt and S. Williams (eds), *Illegitimacy in Britain, 1700–1820,* Basingstoke: Palgrave Macmillan, 66–85.

———. 2010. 'Forme et fonction de la parenté chez les populations pauvres d'Angleterre, 1880–1840', *Annales HSS* 65, 1147–1174.

———. 2011. 'The Residential and Familial Arrangements of English Pauper Letter Writers, 1800–1840s', in J. McEwan and P. Sharpe (eds), *Accommodating Poverty: The Housing and Living Arrangements of the English Poor, c.1600–1850,* Basingstoke: Palgrave Macmillan, 145–168.

———. 2011. '"In These You May Trust". Numerical Information, Accounting Practices and the Poor Law, c. 1790 to 1840', in T. Crook and G. O'Hara (eds), *Statistics and the Public Sphere: Numbers and the People in Modern Britain, c. 1750–2000,* London: Routledge, 51–66.

———. 2011. 'Welfare Regimes and Welfare Regions in Britain and Europe, c. 1750–1860', *Journal of Modern European History* 9, 42–66.

King, S., T. Nutt and A. Tomkins (eds). 2006. *Narratives of the Poor in Eighteenth Century Britain,* London: Pickering & Chatto.

King, S. and A. Stringer. 2012. '"I have once more taken the Leberty to say as you well know": The Development of Rhetoric in the Letters of the English, Welsh and Scottish Sick and Poor 1780s–1830s', in A. Gestrich, E. Hurren and S. King (eds), *Poverty and Sickness in Modern Europe: Narratives of the Sick Poor, 1780–1938,* London: Bloomsbury, 69–92.

Kirby, P. 2003. *Child Labour in Britain, 1750–1870,* London: Palgrave.

Kitch, M. 1992. 'Population Movement and Migration in Pre-Industrial Rural England', in B. Short (ed.), *The English Rural Community: Image and Analysis,* Cambridge: Cambridge University Press, 62–84.

Knotter, A. 2004. 'Poverty and the Family-Income Cycle: Casual Laborers in Amsterdam in the First Half of the 20th Century', *History of the Family* 9(2), 221–237.

Kok, P. T. 2000. *Burgers in de bijstand. Werklozen en de ontwikkeling van de sociale zekerheid in Leeuwarden van 1880 tot 1930,* Franeker: Van Wijnen.

Kool-Blokland, J. L. 1990, *De zorg gewogen: zeven eeuwen godshuizen in Middelburg,* Middelburg: Koninklijk Zeeuwsch Genootschap der Wetenschappen.

Kort, A. L. 1985. 'Armoede en armenzorg in Goes 1860–1914', *Historisch Jaarboek voor Zuid- en Noord-Beveland* 11, 21–49.

————. 2001. *Geen cent te veel. Armoede en armenzorg op Zuid-Beveland, 1850–1940,* Hilversum: Verloren.

Kuijpers, E. 2005. *Migrantenstad. Immigratie en sociale verhoudingen in zeventiende-eeuws Amsterdam,* Hilversum: Verloren.

Kussmaul, A. 1981. *Servants in Husbandry in Early Modern England,* Cambridge: Cambridge University Press.

Küster, T. 1995. *Alte Armut un neues Bürgertum. Öffentliche und private Fürsorge in Münster von der Ära Fürstenberg bis zum Ersten Weltkrieg (1756–1914),* Münster: Aschendorff.

Lambrecht, P. 1986. 'De Westhoek: Demografisch profiel en materiële leefwereld (17de-18de eeuw)' (Unpublished MA dissertation, Ghent University).

Lambrecht, T. 2002. *Een grote hoeve in een klein dorp. Relaties van arbeid en pacht op het Vlaamse platteland tijdens de achttiende eeuw,* Ghent: Academia Press.

————. 2003. 'Reciprocal Exchange, Credit and Cash: Agricultural Labour Markets and Local Economies in he Southern Low Countries during the Eighteenth Century', *Continuity and Change* 18, 237–261.

————. 2009. 'Peasant Labour Strategies and the Logic of Family Labour in the Southern Low Countries During the 18th Century', in S. Cavaciocchi (ed.), *The Economic Role of the Family in the European Economy from the Thirteenth to the Eighteenth Centuries,* Florence: Firenze University Press, 637–650.

The Lancet. 1887. 23 February 1887.

Landau, N. 1988. 'The Laws of Settlement and the Surveillance of Immigration in Eighteenth-Century Kent', *Continuity and Change* 3(3), 391–420.

————. 1990. 'The Regulation of Immigration, Economic Structures and Definitions of the Poor in Eighteenth-Century England', *Historical Journal* 33, 541–572.

————. 1991. 'The Eighteenth-Century Context of the Laws of Settlement', *Continuity and Change* 6(3), 417–439.

————. 1995. 'Who Was Subjected to the Laws of Settlement? Procedure Under the Settlement Laws in Eighteenth-Century England', *Agricultural History Review* 43(2), 139–159.

Lanzinger, M. 2003. *Das gesicherte Erbe. Heirat in lokalen und familialen Kontexten. Inichen 1700–1900,* Vienna: Böhlau.

Laude, F. 1914. *Les classes rurales en Artois à la fin de l'Ancien Régime (1760–1789),* Lille: Robbe.

Lebrun P., M. Bruwier, J. Dhondt and G. Hansotte. 1979. *Essai sur la révolution industrielle en Belgique, 1770–1847,* Brussels: Royal Academy (Histoire quantitative et développement de la Belgique, vol. II, 1).

Le Comte, G. 1989. 'Quelle politique pour les pauvres? Le cas de la communauté de Vaulion sous l'Ancien Régime', in A.-L. Head and B. Schnegg (eds), *La pauvreté en Suisse (XVIIe-XXe siècles),* Zurich: Chronos, 95–108.

Lee, R. 1998. 'The Socio-Economic and Demographic Characteristics of Port Cities: A Typology for Comparative Analysis?', *Urban History* 25(2), 147–172.

Lees, L. H. 1998. *The Solidarities of Strangers. The English Poor Laws and the People, 1700–1948,* Cambridge: Cambridge University Press.

Lefebvre, G. 1959. *Les paysans du Nord pendant la Révolution Française,* Bari: Editori Laterza.

Leimgruber, M. 2008. *Solidarity Without the State? Business and the Shaping of the Swiss Welfare State, 1890–2000,* Cambridge: Cambridge University Press.

Leonard, E. 1900. *The Early History of English Poor Relief,* Cambridge: Cambridge University Press.

Leplae, N. 1972. 'Betwistingen rond de benoeming van parochieherders in de Oostenrijkse Nederlanden, bijzonder in het bisdom Brugge in de eerste helft der XVIIIe eeuw', *Standen en Landen* 50, 1–84.

Lesger, C. M. 1997. 'Migranten in Amsterdam tijdens de achttiende eeuw: residentiële spreiding en positie in de samenleving', *Jaarboek Amstelodamum* 89, 43–68.

Lesger, C. M. and M. H. D. van Leeuwen. 2012. 'Residential Segregation from the Sixteenth to Nineteenth Century: Evidence from the Netherlands', *Journal of Interdisciplinary History* 42(3), 333–369.

Levene, A. 2010. 'Parish Apprenticeship and the Old Poor Law in London', *Economic History Review* 63(4), 915–941.

———. 2010. 'Poor Families, Removals and 'Nurture' in Late Old Poor Law London', *Continuity and Change* 25(2), 1–30.

Levie Bernfeld, T. 2002. 'Financing Poor Relief in the Spanish-Portuguese Jewish Community in Amsterdam in the Seventeenth and Eighteenth Centuries', in J. I. Israel and R. Salverda (eds), *Dutch Jewry: Its History and Secular Culture,* Leiden: Brill, 63–102.

———. 2012. *Poverty and Welfare among the Portuguese Jews in Early Modern Amsterdam,* Oxford: Littman.

Levine, D. 1977. *Family Formation in an Age of Nascent Capitalism,* New York: Academic Press.

Levine, D. and K. Wrightson. 1991. *The Making of an Industrial Society: Whickham 1560–1765,* Oxford: Clarendon Press.

Lewis, M. D. 2007. *The Boundaries of the Republic: Migrant Rights and the Limits of Universalism in France, 1918–1940,* Stanford: Stanford University Press.

Lindert, P. 2004. *Growing Public: Social Spending and Economic Growth since the Eighteenth Century,* Cambridge: Cambridge University Press.

Lis, C. 1986. *Social Change and the Labouring Poor: Antwerp, 1770–1860,* New Haven: Yale University Press.

Lis, C. and H. Soly. 1979. *Poverty and Capitalism in Pre-industrial Europe,* Brighton: Harvester Press.

Looijesteijn, H. and M. H. D. van Leeuwen. 2012. 'Establishing and Registering Identity in the Dutch Republic', in K. Breckenridge and S. Szreter (eds), *Registration and Recognition. Documenting the Person in World History,* Oxford: Oxford University Press, 211–251.

Loriquet, F. 1891. *Cahiers de doléances de 1789 dans le département du Pas-de-Calais,* Arras : Crepel.

Loth, W. and J. C. Kaiser (eds). 1997. *Soziale Reform im Kaiserreich: Proteestantismus, Katholizismus und Sozialpolitik,* Stuttgart: W. Kohlhamme.

Lucassen, J. 1984. *Naar de kusten van de Noordzee. Trekarbeid in Europees perspectief, 1600–1900,* Gouda: J. Lucassen.

———. 1987. *Migrant Labour in Europe 1600–1900. The Drift to the North Sea,* London: Croom Helm.

———. 1995. 'Labour and Early Modern Economic Development', in K. Davids and J. Lucassen (eds), *A Miracle Mirrored. The Dutch Republic in European Perspective,* Cambridge: Cambridge University Press, 367–409.

Lucassen, J. and L. Lucassen. 2009. 'The Mobility Transition Revisited, 1500–1900: What the Case of Europe Can Offer to Global History', *Journal of Global History* 4, 347–377.

Luttenberg, G. 1837. *Vervolg op het Groot Plakkaatboek of verzameling van wetten betrekkelijk het openbaar bestuur in de Nederlanden. Armwezen*, Zwolle: J. J. Tijl.

Mazower, M. A. 2004. 'The Strange Triumph of Human Rights, 1933–1950', *Historical Journal* 47(2), 379–398.

Maitland, W. 1739. *The History of London, from its Foundation by the Romans, to the Present Time*, London: Samuel Richardson.

Manfredini, M. 2003. 'Families in Motion: The Role and Characteristics of Household Migration in a 19th-Century Rural Italian Parish', *History of the Family* 8, 317–343.

Mann, T.-A. 1783. 'Mémoire sur la question: Dans un pays fertile et bien peuplé, les grandes fermes sont-elles utiles ou nuisibles à l'Etat en général ?', *Mémoires de l'Académie Impériale et Royale des Sciences et Belles-Lettres de Bruxelles*, vol. 4, 199–226.

Marcroft, W. 1886. *The Marcroft Family*, Manchester: John Heywood.

Marx, K. 2008. *Armut und Fürsorge auf dem Land: Vom Ende des 19. Jahrhunderts bis 1933*. Göttingen: Wallstein.

McCaffrey, W. 1958. *Exeter 1540–1640: The Growth of an English County Town*, Cambridge, MA: Harvard University Press.

McCants, A. 1997. *Civic Charity in a Golden Age: Orphan Care in Early Modern Amsterdam*, Urbana: University of Illinois Press.

McKay, L. 1995. 'A Culture of Poverty? The St Martin in the Fields Workhouse, 1817', *Journal of Interdisciplinary History* 26, 209–231.

———. 2001. 'Moral Paupers: The Poor Men of St. Martin's, 1815–1819', *Histoire sociale / Social History* 67, 115–131.

Meier, T. D. and R. Wolfensberger. 1998. *Eine Heimat und doch keine. Heimatlose und Nicht-Sesshafte in der Schweiz (16.–19. Jahrhundert)*, Zürich: Chronos.

Meischke, R. 1980. *Amsterdam. Het R.C. Maagdenhuis, het huizenbezit van deze instelling en het St. Elizabeth-gesticht*, The Hague: Staatsuitgeverij.

Melief, P. B. A. 1955. *De strijd om de armenzorg in Nederland, 1795–1854*, Groningen: Wolters.

Melling, J. and W. Forsythe (eds). 1999. *Insanity, Institutions and Society 1800–1914: A Social History of Madness in Comparative Perspective*, London: Routledge.

Mémoire représentant les suites préjudiceuses et imprévues du Concordat. [c. 1770]. [s.l.]: [s.n.].

Mendels, F. F. 1975. 'Agriculture and Peasant Industry in Eighteenth-Century Flanders', in W. Parker and E. L. Jones (eds), *European Peasants and Their Markets*, Princeton: Princeton University Press, 179–204.

———. 1981. *Industrialization and Population Pressure in Eighteenth-Century Flanders*, New York: Arno Press.

Merricks, L. 1994. '"Without Violence and by Controlling the Poorer Sort": The Enclosure of Ashdown Forest 1640–93', *Sussex Archaeological Collections* 132, 115–128.

Mertens, J. and W. Vanderpijpen. 1970. 'Schets van de Westvlaamse Landbouw eind achttiende-begin negentiende eeuw. Het rapport van B.J. Holvoet en zijn belang voor de Mémoire Statistique du Département de la Lys', *Handelingen van het Genootschap voor Geschiedenis te Brugge* 107, 277–300.

Mettele, G. 1998. *Bürgertum in Köln, 1775–1870. Gemeinsinn und freie Association,* München: Oldenbourg Verlag.

Midwinter, E. C. 1969. *Social Administration in Lancashire, 1830–1860: Poor Law, Public Health and Police,* Manchester: Manchester University Press.

Mommsen, W. and W. Mock. 1981. *The Emergence of the Welfare State in Britain and Germany 1880–1950,* Newton Abbott: Taylor & Francis.

Nathans, E. 2004. *The Politics of Citizenship in Germany. Ethnicity, Utility and Nationalism,* Oxford and New York: Berg.

Neven, M. 2003. 'Terra Incognita: Migration of the Elderly and the Nuclear Hardship Hypothesis', *History of the Family* 8, 267–295.

Noiriel, G. 1992. *Population, immigration et identitè nationale en France: XIXe-XXe siècle,* Paris: Hachette.

———. 1991. *La tyrannie du national. Le droit d'asile en Europe 1793–1993,* Paris: Calmann-Lévy.

Nolan, M. 1825. *A Treatise of the Laws for the Relief and Settlement of the Poor,* 4th ed., 3 vols, London: J. Butterworth.

Norberg, K. 1985. *Rich and Poor in Grenoble, 1600–1814,* Berkeley: University of California Press.

Nottingham, C. and P. de Rooy. 2007. 'The Peculiarities of the Dutch: Social Security in the Netherlands', in S. King and J. Stewart (eds), *Welfare Peripheries: The Development of Welfare States in Nineteenth and Twentieth Century Europe,* Bern: Peter Lang, 39–66.

Nusteling, H. 1985. *Welvaart en werkgelegenheid in Amsterdam 1540–1860s: Een relaas over demografie, economie en sociale politiek van een wereldstad,* Amsterdam: Bataafsche Leeuw.

Nutt, T. 2010. 'Illegitimacy, Paternal Financial Responsibility, and the 1834 Poor Law Commission Report: The Myth of the Old Poor Law and the Making of the New', *Economic History Review* 63, 335–361.

Olson, M. 1965. *The Logic of Collective Action: Public Goods and the Theory of Groups,* Cambridge, MA: Harvard University Press.

Oppenheim, J. 1991. '*Shattered Nerves*': *Doctors, Patients and Depression in Victorian England,* Oxford: Oxford University Press.

Oxley, G. 1974. *Poor Relief in England and Wales 1601–1834,* Newton Abbott: David & Charles.

Pandectes Belges. 1909. Vol. 96. Brussels: Ferdinand Larcier.

Parton, A. 1987. 'Poor Law Settlement Certificates and Migration to and from Birmingham 1726–57', *Local Population Studies* 38, 23–29.

Pasinomie. Collection complète des lois, décrets, arrêtés et règlements généraux qui peuvent être invoqués en Belgique. 1833–. Brussels: Bruylant.

Pearl, V. 1978. 'Puritans and Poor Relief. The London Workhouse, 1649–60', in D. Pennington and K. Thomas (eds), *Puritans and Revolutionaries. Essays in Seventeenth-Century History Presented to Christopher Hill,* Oxford: Clarendon Press, 206–232.

Pell, A. 1900. 'Outrelief: A Paper Read at a Poor Law Conference as Chairman of the Central Committee Held at the Crewe Arms Hotel on Tuesday October 14th 1890', *Tracts, 1843–1893,* London, 1–16.

Pfister, U. *Die Zürcher Fabriques. Proindustrieller Wachstum vom 16. zum 18. Jahrhundert,* Zürich: Chronos, 1992.

Placcaert-Boeck van Vlaenderen V. 1763. 2 vols, Ghent: De Goesin.

Plain Words on Outrelief. 1894. London: [s.n.].

Pooley, C. and J. Turnbull. 1998. *Migration and Mobility in Britain since the Eighteenth Century,* London: Taylor & Francis.

Pot, G. P. M. 1994. *Arm Leiden. Levensstandaard, bedeling en bedeelden, 1750–1854,* Hilversum: Verloren.

Präger, F. 1997. *Das Spital und die Armen. Almosenvergabe in der Stadt Langenzenn im 18. Jahrhundert,* Regensburg: Friedrich Pustet.

Prak, M. R. 1994. 'Goede buren en verre vrienden. De ontwikkeling van onderstand bij armoede in Den Bosch sedert de Middeleeuwen', in H. Flap and M. H. D. van Leeuwen (eds), *Op lange termijn. Verklaringen van trends in de geschiedenis van samenlevingen,* Hilversum: Verloren, 147–170.

———. 1998. 'Armenzorg 1500–1800', in J. van Gerwen and M. H. D. van Leeuwen (eds), *Studies over zekerheidsarrangementen: risico's, risicobestrijding en verzekeringen in Nederland vanaf de middeleeuwen,* Amsterdam: NEHA, 49–90.

———. 1999. *Republikeinse veelheid, democratisch enkelvoud. Sociale verandering in het Revolutietijdvak, 's-Hertogenbosch 1770–1820,* Nijmegen: SUN.

Priester, P. 1998. *De geschiedenis van de Zeeuwse landbouw circa 1600–1900,* Wageningen: Afdeling Agrarische Geschiedenis (A.A.G. Bijdragen: 37).

Radcliff, T. 1819. *A Report on the Agriculture of Eastern and Western Flanders Drawn up at the Desire of the Farming Society of Ireland,* London: John Harding.

Ramaker, G. 1936. 'Afwenteling van kosten van armenzorg op andere gemeenten', in J. G. Ramaker, F. M. J. Jansen and J. de Bruin, *Prae-adviezen over het onderwerp: afwenteling van kosten van armenzorg op andere gemeenten,* Haarlem: Tjeenk Willink (Geschriften van de Nederlandsche Vereeniging voor Armenzorg en Weldadigheid, LXV), 9–42.

Rapport sur l'administration et la situation des affaires de la ville d'Anvers. 1836–1900, Antwerp: City of Antwerp.

Redlich, F. 1964. *The German Military Enterpriser and his Work Force: A Study in European Economic and Social History,* Wiesbaden: F. Steiner.

Redwood, B. C. (ed.) 1954. *Sussex Quarter Sessions Order Book, 1642–49,* vol. 54, Lewes: Sussex Record Society.

'Report of a Committee of the Statistical Society of London, on the State of the Working Classes in the Parishes of St. Margaret and St. John Westminster'. 1840. *Journal of the Statistical Society of London* 3(1), 14–24.

'Report of George Coode, Esq to the Poor Law Board on the Law of Settlement and Removal of the Poor'. 1851. In *House of Commons Papers,* 113–125.

Rheinheimer, M. 2000. *Arme, Bettler und Vaganten. Überleben in der Not 1450–1850,* Frankfurt a. M.: Fischer Taschenbuch Verlag.

Rogers, N. 1989–90.'Carnal Knowledge: Illegitimacy in Eighteenth-Century Westminster', *Journal of Social History* 23, 355–375.

———. 1991. 'Policing the Poor in Eighteenth-Century London: The Vagrancy Laws and Their Administration', *Histoire sociale / Social History* 24, 127–147.

Rollison, D. 2010. *A Commonwealth of the People. Popular Politics and England's Long Social Revolution,* Cambridge: Cambridge University Press.

Rose, M. E. 'The Crisis of Poor Relief in England, 1860–1900', in W. Mommsen and W. Mock (eds), *The Emergence of the Welfare State in Britain, 1850–1950,* London: Croom Helm, 1981, 50–70.

Rosenheim, J. M. (ed.) 1989. *The Notebook of Robert Doughty 1662–1665,* vol. 54, Norfolk: Norfolk Record Society.

Rosental, P.-A. 1999. *Les sentiers invisibles: Espace, familles et migrations dans la France du 19e siècle,* Paris: Ecole des Hautes Etudes en Sciences Sociales.

———. 2006. 'Géopolitique et état-providence: le Bureau International du Travail et la politique mondiale des migrations dans l'entre-deux-guerres', *Annales HSS* 61, 99–134.

———. 2011. 'Migrations, souveraineté, droits sociaux. Protéger et expulser les étrangers en Europe du XIXe siècle à nous jours', *Annales HSS* 66, 335–373.

Rosselle, D. 1983. 'La mise en valeur de la terre dans la France du nord (XVIe–XVIIIe siècles). Réflexions à partir d'un modèle artésien', in *La terre à l'époque moderne,* Paris: Association des Historiens Modernistes, 53–80.

———. 1989. 'La vente des biens nationaux et le changement des structures de l'exploitation agricole: l'exemple artésien', in G. Gayot and J.-P. Hirsch (eds), *La Révolution Française et le développement du capitalisme,* Lille (Revue du Nord Hors Série, 5), 311–319.

Ruggles, S. 1992. 'Marriage, Migration and Mortality: Correcting Sources of Bias in English Family Reconstitutions', *Population Studies* 46, 507–522.

Sabine, G. H. (ed.). 1941. *The Works of Gerard Winstanley,* Ithaca, NY: Cornell University Press.

Sachße, C. and F. Tennstedt. 1980–1992. *Geschichte der Armenfürsorge in Deutschland,* 3 vols, Stuttgart: W. Kohlhammer.

Sánchez-Barricarte, J. 2002. 'Developments in Household Patterns in Three Towns in Navarre, Spain, 1786–1986', *History of the Family* 7, 479–499.

Sanderson, T. 1873. *The Life and Adventures of Thomas Sanderson,* Darlington: Brag, Machine Printer.

Saville, J. 1848. 'Autobiography' in F. A. West, *Memoirs of Jonathan Saville of Halifax; Including his Autobiography,* London: Hamilton, Adams, Mason & Co.

Saxby, M. 1806. *Memoirs of a Female Vagrant Written by Herself,* London: J. W. Morris.

Schepers, E. 2000. *Als der Bettel in Bayern abgeschafft werden sollte. Staatliche Armenfürsorge in Bayern im 16. und 17. Jahrhundert,* Regensburg: F. Pustet.

Scherpner, H. 1962. *Theorie der Fürsorge,* Göttingen: Vandenhoeck und Ruprecht.

Scheutz, M. 2003. *Ausgesperrt und gejagt, geduldet und versteckt: Bettlervisitationonen im Niederösterreich des 18. Jahrhunderts,* St Pölten: NÖ Institut für Landeskunde.

Schmidt, A. 2007. 'Survival Strategies of Widows and Their Families in Early Modern Holland, c.1580–1750', *History of the Family* 12, 268–281.

Schmidt, H. R. 2010. 'Handlungsstrategien und Problembereiche der Armenfürsorge im alten Bern', in A. Holenstein, B. Kapossy, D. Tosato-Rigo, S. Zurbuchen (eds), *Richesse et pauvreté dans les républiques suisses au XVIIIe siècle,* Genève: Slatkine, 239–251.

Schmidt, S. and A. Wagner. 2004. 'Gebt den Hußarmen umb Gottes willen. Religiös motivierte Armenfürsorge und Exklusionspolitik gegenüber starken und fremden Bettlern', in A. Gestrich and L. Raphael (eds), *Inklusion / Exklusion. Studien zu Fremdheit und Armut von der Antike bis zur Gegenwart*, Frankfurt: Peter Lang, 479–510.

Scholliers, E. 1965. 'Prijzen en lonen te Antwerpen en in het Antwerpse (16e-19e eeuw)', in C. Verlinden (ed.), *Dokumenten voor de geschiedenis van prijzen en lonen in Vlaanderen en Brabant*, Bruges: De Tempel, vol. II, 641–1056.

Schubert, E. 1983. *Arme Leute. Bettler und Gauner im Franken des 18. Jahrhunderts*, Neustadt a.d. Aisch: Kommissionsverlag Degener.

Schütz, R. 1979. *Preußen und die Rheinlande. Studien zur preußischen Integrationspolitik im Vormärz*, Wiesbaden: Steiner.

Schwarz, L. 2001. 'Hanoverian London: The Making of a Service Town', in P. Clark and R. Gillespie (eds), *Two Capitals: London and Dublin, 1500–1840*, Oxford: Oxford University Press (Proceedings of the British Academy 107), 93–110.

Scull, A. 1979. *Museums of Madness: The Social Organisation of Insanity in Nineteenth-Century England*, London and New York: Allen Lane.

Sharlin, A. 1978. 'Natural Decrease in Early Modern Cities: A Reconsideration', *Past and Present* 79, 126–138.

Sharp, B. 1980. *In Contempt of All Authority: Rural Artisans and Riot in the West of England, 1586–1660*, Berkeley: University of California Press.

Sharpe, F. R. (ed.). 1965. 'The Order Book of Ormskirk 1613–1721', in F. R. Sharpe (ed.), *A Lancashire Miscellany*, [s.l.]: Lancashire and Cheshire Record Society, vol. 109, 31–56.

Sharpe, P. 1997. '"The Bowels of Compation": A Labouring Family and the Law, c. 1790–1834', in T. Hitchcock, P. King and P. Sharpe (eds), *Chronicling Poverty. The Voices and Strategies of the English Poor, 1640–1840*, London: Palgrave Mac-Millan, 87–108.

Sheppard, W. 1652. *The Whole Office of the Country Justice of Peace*, 2nd ed. London: W. Lee, D. Pakeman, G. Bedell.

Slack, P. 1974. 'Vagrants and Vagrancy in England, 1598–1664', *Economic History Review* 27, 360–379.

———. *Poverty and Policy in Tudor and Stuart England*, London: Longman.

———. 1999. *From Reformation to Improvement: Public Welfare in Early Modern England*, Oxford: Clarendon Press.

Slack, P. (ed.). 1975. *Poverty in Early Stuart Salisbury*, Devizes: Wiltshire Record Society.

Smith, D. L. 1999. *The Stuart Parliaments 1603–1689*, London: Hodder Arnold.

Smith, R. 1996. 'Charity, Self-Interest and Welfare: Reflections from Demographic and Family History', in M. Daunton (ed.), *Charity, Self-Interest and Welfare in Britain, 1500 to the Present*, London: UCL Press, 23–50.

Smith, R. 1998. 'Ageing and Well-Being in Early Modern England: Pension Trends and Gender Preferences under the English Old Poor Law c. 1650–1800', in P. Johnson and P. Thane (eds), *Old Age from Antiquity to Post-Modernity*, London: Routledge, 64–95.

Smith, R. M. 1999. 'Relative Prices, Forms of Agrarian Labour and Female Marriage Patterns in England, 1350–1800', in I. Devos and L. Kennedy (eds), *Marriage and Rural Economy. Western Europe since 1400*, Turnhout: Brepols (CORN Publications Series, 3), 32–37.

Smith, T. B. 2003. *Creating the Welfare State in France, 1880–1940*, Montreal: Mc-Gill-Queen's Press.

Snell, K. D. M. 1984. 'Parish Registration and the Study of Labour Mobility', *Local Population Studies* 33, 29–44.

———. 1985. *Annals of the Labouring Poor: Social Change and Agrarian England, 1660–1900*, Cambridge: Cambridge University Press.

———. 1991. 'Pauper Settlement and the Right to Poor Relief in England and Wales', *Continuity and Change* 6, 375–415.

———. 1992. 'Settlement, Poor Law and the Rural Historian: New Approaches and Opportunities', *Rural History* 3(2), 145–172.

———. 2006. *Parish and Belonging. Community, Identity and Welfare in England and Wales 1700–1950*, Cambridge: Cambridge University Press.

Snell, K. D. M. and J. Millar. 1987. 'Lone Parent Families and the Welfare State: Past and Present', *Continuity and Change* 2(3), 387–422.

Sokoll, T. 2001. *Essex Pauper Letters, 1731–1837*, Oxford: Oxford University Press.

Solar, P. 1995. 'Poor Relief and English Economic Development Before the Industrial Revolution', *Economic History Review* 48(1), 1–22.

Solar, P. M. and R. M. Smith. 2003. 'An Old Poor Law for the New Europe? Reconciling Local Solidarity with Labour Mobility in Early Modern England', in P. A. David and M. Thomas (eds), *The Economic Future in Historical Perspective*, Oxford: Oxford University Press, 463–477.

Spaans, J. 1997. *Armenzorg in Friesland 1500–1800. Publieke zorg en particuliere liefdadigheid in zes Friese steden: Leeuwarden, Bolsward, Franeker, Sneek, Dokkum en Harlingen*, Hilversum: Verloren.

Spanhove, L. 1972. 'De bevolkingsevolutie van het platteland omheen Brugge in de achttiende eeuw (1725–1795)', *Standen en Landen* 58, 75–108.

Spence, C. 2000. *London in the 1690s. A Social Atlas*, London: Centre for Metropolitan History.

Spierenburg, P. 1991. *The Prison Experience: Disciplinary Institutions and their Inmates in Early Modern Europe*, New Brunswick: Rutgers University Press.

Spijker, A.P.A.M. 1979. 'Van aalmoes tot bijstand. Een overzicht van de stedelijke armenzorg in Haarlem', *Haerlem Jaarboek*, 66–98.

Stapleton, B. 1992. 'Marriage, Migration and Mendicancy', in B. Stapleton (ed.), *Conflict and Community in Southern England*, New York: St. Martin's Press, 51–91.

Statistique générale de la Belgique. Exposé de la situation du Royaume. Période décennale de 1851–1860. 1863–1865. 4 vols, Brussels: Th. Lesigne.

Stokvis, P. R. D. 1993. 'Het sterftepatroon in preïndustrieel Den Haag (ca. 1700–1855). De mythe van de stedelijke oversterfte en de sterfte naar jaargetijde en doodsoorzaken', *De Negentiende Eeuw* 17, 201–216.

Styles, P. 1963 'The Evolution of the Law of Settlement', *Birmingham Historical Journal* 9, 33–63.

Suzuki, A. 1988. 'The Household and the Care of Lunatics in Eighteenth-Century London', in P. Horden and R. M. Smith (eds), *The Locus of Care: Families, Communities, Institutions, and the Provision of Welfare since Antiquity*, London: Routledge, 153–175.

Swetschinki, D. M. 2000. *Reluctant Cosmopolitans: The Portuguese Jews of Seventeenth-Century Amsterdam*, London: Littman.

Szołtysek, M. 2007. 'Central European Household and Family Systems, and the 'Hajnal-Mitterauer' Line: The Parish of Bujakow (18ᵗʰ–19th Centuries)', *History of the Family* 12, 19–42.

———. 2008. 'Three Kinds of Preindustrial Household Formation System in Historical Eastern Europe: A Challenge to Spatial Patterns of the European Family', *History of the Family* 13, 223–257.

Tabili, L. 2011. *Global Migrants, Local Culture: Natives and Newcomers in Provincial England, 1841–1939,* Basingstoke: Palgrave Macmillan.

Taintenier, F.-J. 1775. *Supplément au traité sur la mendicité,* Brussels: [s.n.].

Taylor, J. S. 1976. 'The Impact of Pauper Settlement 1691–1834, *Past and Present* 73, 42–74.

———. 1989. *Poverty, Migration and Settlement in the Industrial Revolution: Sojourners' Narratives,* Palo Alto: Society for the Promotion of Science and Scholarship.

———. 1991. 'A Different Kind of Speenhamland: Nonresident Relief in the Industrial Revolution', *Journal of British Studies* 30, 183–208.

Teibenbacher, P. 2009. 'Natural Population Movement and Marriage Restrictions and Hindrances in Styria in the 17th to 19th Centuries', *History of the Family* 14, 292–308.

Thirsk, J. 1978. *Economic Policy and Projects. The Development of a Consumer Society in Early Modern England,* Oxford: Clarendon Press.

Thoen, E. 2004. 'Social Agrosystems as an Economic Concept to Explain Regional Differences. An Essay Taking the Former County of Flanders as an Example (Middle Ages–19th century)', in B. J. van Bavel and P. Hoppenbrouwers (eds), *Landholding and Land Transfer in the North Sea area (Late Middle Ages–19th century),* Turnhout: Brepols (CORN Publication Series, 5), 47–66.

Thomas, K. 1969. 'Another Digger Broadside', *Past and Present* 42, 57–68.

Thomson, D. 1991. 'Welfare of the Elderly in the Past, a Family or Community Responsibility?', in M. Pelling and R. Smith, *Life, Death and the Elderly: Historical Perspectives,* Oxford: Oxford University Press, 194–222.

———. 1984. '*I Am Not My Father's Keeper:* Families and the Elderly in Nineteenth-Century England', *Law and History Review* II, 265–286.

Tierney, B. 1959. *Medieval Poor Law. A Sketch of Canonical Theory and its Application in England,* Berkeley: University of California Press.

Toone, W. 1813. *The Magistrate's Manual: Or, a Summary of the Duties and Powers of a Justice of the Peace,* London: J. Butterworth.

———. 1815. *A Practical Guide to the Duty and Authority of Overseers of the Poor,* London: J. Butterworth & Son.

Toussaert, J. 1956. *La population de Krombeke au XVIIIe siècle d'après les registres paroissiaux,* Lille: Université de Lille.

Turner, D. M. 2005. 'Popular Marriage and the Law: Tales of Bigamy at the Eighteenth-Century Old Bailey', *London Journal* 30(1), 6–21.

Underdown, D. 1992. *Fire From Heaven: The Life of an English Town in the Seventeenth Century,* London: Harper Collins.

van Dam, J. C. 1952. 'De intercommunale verhuisregeling in een nieuwe versie', *Tijdschrift voor Maatschappelijk Werk* 6, 239–240.

van Damme, D. 1990. 'Onderstandswoonst, sedentarisering en stad-platteland-tegenstellingen: Evolutie en betekenis van de wetgeving op de onderstandswoonst in België (einde achttiende tot einde negentiende eeuw)', *Belgisch Tijdschrift voor Nieuwste Geschiedenis* 21(3), 483–534.

Vandenbroeke, C. 1984. 'Le cas flamand: Evolution sociale et comportements démographiques aux XVIIe-XIXe siècles', *Annales ESC* 39(5), 915–938.

———. 1996. 'Proto-industry in Flanders: a Critical Review', in S. C. Ogilvie and M. Cerman (eds), *European Proto-industrialization,* Cambridge: Cambridge University Press, 102–117.

van der Hoeven, H. W. 1985. *Uit de geheime notulen van de 'Eerwaarde Groote Vergadering' 1785–1815. Het beleid van de diakonie van de Hervormde kerk te Amsterdam,* The Hague: Uitgeverij Boekencentrum.

Vanderpijpen, W. 1988. 'De proto-industrialisatie in Vlaanderen: een grote regionale diversiteit', in G. Peeters and M. De Moor (eds), *Arbeid in veelvoud. Een huldeboek voor Jan Craeybeckx en Etienne Scholliers,* Brussels: VUB Press, 123–130.

van der Vlis, I. 2001. *Leven in Armoede. Delftse bedeelden in de zeventiende eeuw,* Delft: Prometheus/Bert Bakker.

van der Woude, A. M. 1982. '*Population Developments in the Northern Netherlands* (1500–1800) and the Validity of the Urban Graveyard Effect', *Annales de démografie historique,* 55–75.

van Deursen, A. T. 1994. *Een dorp in de polder. Graft in de zeventiende eeuw,* Amsterdam: Bert Bakker.

Vandewalle, P. 1986. *De geschiedenis van de landbouw in de kasselrij Veurne (1550–1645),* Brussels: Gemeentekrediet (Historische Uitgaven, 66).

———. 1994. *Quatre siècles d'agriculture dans le région de Dunkerque 1590–1990: Une etude statistique,* Ghent: Centre Belge d'Histoire Rurale.

van Ginderachter, M. and M. Beyen (eds). 2011. *Nationhood from Below: Europe in the Long Nineteenth Century,* Basingstoke: Palgrave Macmillan.

Vanhaute, E. 1988. 'De armenzorg op het Antwerpse platteland, 1750–1850: Onderzoek naar een instelling tijdens de scharniereeuw', in *Machtsstructuren in de plattelandsgemeenschappen in België en aangrenzende gebieden (12de-19de eeuw),* Brussels: Gemeentekrediet van België (Historische Uitgaven Reeks in-8, 77), 641–656.

Vanhaute E. and T. Lambrecht. 2011. 'Famine, Exchange Networks and the Village Community: A Comparative Analysis of the Subsistence Crises of the 1740s and the 1840s in Flanders', *Continuity and Change* 26(2), 155–186.

van Leeuwen, M. H. D. 1992. *Bijstand in Amsterdam, ca. 1800–1850. Armenzorg als beheersings- en overlevingsstrategie,* Zwolle: Waanders.

———. 1993, 'Surviving With a Little Help: The Importance of Charity to the Poor of Amsterdam 1800–50, in a Comparative Perspective', *Social History* 18, 319–338.

———. 1994. 'Logic of Charity: Poor Relief in Preindustrial Europe', *Journal of Interdisciplinary History* 24, 589–613.

———. 1996. 'Amsterdam en de armenzorg tijdens de Republiek', *NEHA Jaarboek* 59, 132–161.

———. 2000. *The Logic of Charity: Amsterdam 1800–1850,* Aldershot and New York: Macmillan.

———. 2007. 'Historical Welfare Economics from the Old Regime to the Welfare State. Mutual Aid and Private Insurance for Burial, Sickness, Old Age, Widowhood, and Unemployment in the Netherlands during the Nineteenth Century', in B. Harris and P. Bridgen (eds), *Charity and Mutual Aid in European and North America since 1800,* London: Routledge, 89–130.

———. 2012. 'Giving in Early Modern History: Philanthropy in Amsterdam's Golden Age', *Continuity and Change* 27(1), 301–343.

———. 2012. 'Guilds and Middle-Class Welfare 1550–1800: Provisions for Burial, Sickness, Old Age, and Widowhood', *Economic History Review* 65(1), 61–90.

van Leeuwen, M. H. D., and N. Lucas. 1981. 'De diakonie van de hervormde kerk' (Unpublished Paper, University of Amsterdam).

van Leeuwen, M. H. D., and J. E. Oeppen. 1993. 'Reconstructing the Demographic Regime of Amsterdam 1681–1920', *Economic and Social History in the Netherlands* 5, 61–102.

van Leeuwen, M. H. D., J. Schoenmakers and F. Smits. 1981. 'Armoede en bedeling in Amsterdam ten tijde van de Republiek' (Unpublished Paper, University of Amsterdam).

van Nederveen Meerkerk, E., and G. Vermeesch. 2009. 'Reforming Outdoor Relief: Changes in Urban Provisions for the Poor in the Northern and Southern Low Countries (c. 1500–1800)', in M. Van der Heijden, E. van Nederveen Meerkerk and G. Vermeesch (eds), *Serving the Urban Community: The Rise of Public Facilities in the Low Countries,* Amsterdam: Aksant, 135–154.

van Vooren, G. A. C. 1969. 'De toestand der Staatse Katholieken en de Middelburgse Missie van 1737 tot 1804', *Appeltjes van het Meetjesland* 20, 22–86.

———. 1973. 'De armenzorg voor de Katholieken in het Middelburgse missiegebied gedurende de 18de eeuw. I. De organisatie,' *Appeltjes van het Meetjesland* 24, 5–72.

———. 1974. 'De armenzorg voor de Katholieken in het Middelburgse missiegebied gedurende de 18de eeuw. II. De uitvoering,' *Appeltjes van het Meetjesland* 25, 5–60.

van Voorst van Beest, C. W. 1955. *De katholieke armenzorg te Rotterdam in de zeventiende en achttiende eeuw,* The Hague: Excelsior.

van Wijngaarden, H. 2000. *Zorg voor de kost. Armenzorg, arbeid en onderlinge hulp in Zwolle, 1650–1700,* Amsterdam: Prometheus.

Veits-Falk, S. 2000. *'Zeit der Noth': Armut in Salzburg 1803–70,* Salzburg: Freunde der Salzburger Geschichte.

Veraghtert, K. 1981. 'De economie in de Zuidelijke Nederlanden 1790–1970', in D. P. Blok (ed.), *Algemene Geschiedenis der Nederlanden,* Haarlem: Fibula-Van Dishoeck, vol. 10, 127–139.

Vermeiren, L. 1984. 'Het Sint-Elisabethgasthuis te Antwerpen in de 19de eeuw. Een analyse van de financiële structuur (1820–1913)' (Unpublished Licentiaat Thesis, Katholieke Universiteit Leuven).

———. 1988. 'Van gasthuis tot ziekenhuis. De negentiende eeuw (tot 1925)' in *750 Jaar St.-Elisabethgasthuis Te Antwerpen, 1238–1988,* Brussels: Gemeentekrediet, 145–226.

Viegas de Andrade, C. 2010. 'Marriage Patterns in Nineteenth-Century Vila de Conde: The Study of an Urban Centre in Northwest Portugal', *History of the Family* 15, 34–54.

von Reitzenstein, F. 1893. *L'assistance des étrangers en Allemagne*, Paris: Impr. de Troublé (offprint from *Bulletin de la Société internationale pour l'étude des questions d'assistance*).

Wagenaar, J. 1760–1767. *Amsterdam in zyne opkomst, aanwas, geschiedenissen etc.*, 3 vols, Amsterdam: Tirion.

Wagner, A. 2011. *'Gleicherweiß als wasser das feuer, also verlösche almuse die sünd': Frühneuzeitliche Fürsorge- und Bettelgesetzgebung der geistlichen Kurfürstentümer Köln und Trier*, Berlin: Duncker & Humblot, 2011 (Schriften zur Rechtsgeschichte, 153).

Walter, J. 1989. 'The Social Economy of Dearth in Early Modern England', in J. Walter and R. Schofield (eds), *Famine, Disease and the Social Order in Early Modern Society*, Cambridge: Cambridge University Press, 75–128.

Walter, J. and K. Wrightson. 1976. 'Dearth and the Social Order in Early Modern England', *Past and Present* 71, 22–42.

Webb, S. and B. Webb. 1927. *English Local Government. English Poor Law History, Part 1: The Old Poor Law*, London: Longmans, Green.

Webb, S. and B. Webb. 1929. *English Local Government. English Poor Law History, Part 2: The Last Hundred Years*, 2 vols, London: Longmans, Green.

Weber, M. (ed.). 2002. *Die Reichspolizeiordnungen von 1530, 1548 und 1577: Historische Einführung und Edition*, Frankfurt a. M.: Klostermann.

Wehler, H. U. 1987. *Deutsche Gesellschaftsgeschichte, vol. 2: Von der Reformära bis zur industriellen und politischen 'Deutschen Doppelrevolution', 1815–1845/49*, München: Büchergilde Gutenberg.

Weiss, J. 1983. 'Origins of the French Welfare State: Poor Relief in the Third Republic 1871–1914', *French Historical Studies* 13, 47–77.

Wells, R. 1993. 'Migration, the Law and Parochial Policy in Eighteenth and Early Nineteenth Century England', *Southern History* 15, 86–139.

Wetten ende Costumen der Stede van Brugghe. 1767. Ghent: De Goesin.

Willcox, W. B. 1940. *Gloucestershire. A Study in Local Government*, New Haven: Yale University Press.

Williams, J. B. 1835. *Memoirs of the Life, Character and Writings of Sir Matthew Hale*, London: Jackson and Walford.

Williams, K. 1981. *From Pauperism to Poverty*, Manchester: Manchester University Press.

Williams, S. 2004. 'Caring for the Sick Poor: Poor Law Nurses in Bedfordshire, 1770–1834', in P. Lane, N. Raven and K. D. M. Snell (eds), *Women, Work and Wages in England, 1600–1850*, Woodbridge: Boydell Press, 102–118.

———. 2005. 'Poor Relief, Labourers' Households and Living Standards in Rural England c. 1770–1834: A Bedfordshire Case Study', *Economic History Review* 58(3), 485–519.

Willisch, P. 2004. *Die Einbürgerung der Heimatlosen im Kanton Wallis (1850–1880)*, Visp: Rotten.

Winter, A. 2004. 'Vagrancy as an Adaptive Strategy: The Duchy of Brabant, 1767–1776', *International Review of Social History* 49, 249–277.

———. 2008. 'Caught between Law and Practice: Migrants and Settlement Legislation in the Southern Netherlands in a Comparative Perspective (c. 1700–1900)', *Rural History* 19, 137–162.

————. 2009. *Migrants and Urban Change: Newcomers to Antwerp, 1760–1860,* London: Pickering and Chatto (Perspectives in Economic and Social History 1).

————. 2009. 'Migratiebeleid en economische verandering: Nieuwkomers en armenzorg in Antwerpen, 1750–1900', *Noordbrabants Historisch Jaarboek* 26, 99–128.

————. 2011. 'Eigen armen eerst? Migranten en de toegang tot armenzorg in Antwerpen, ca. 1840–1900', in M. De Koster, B. De Munck, H. Greefs, B. Willems and A. Winter (eds), *Werken aan de Stad. Stedelijke actoren en structuren in de Zuidelijke Nederlanden, 1500–1900,* Brussels: VUB Press, 135–156.

————. 2012. 'Regulating Urban Migration and Relief Entitlements in Eighteenth-Century Brabant', in B. De Munck and A. Winter (eds), *Gated Communities? Regulating Migration in Early Modern Cities,* Aldershot: Ashgate, 175–196.

Winter, A. and T. Lambrecht. 2013. 'Migration, Poor Relief and Local Autonomy: Settlement Policies in England and the Southern Low Countries in the Eighteenth Century', *Past and Present* 218.

Woloch, I. 1986. 'Charity to Welfare in Revolutionary Paris', *Journal of Modern History* 58, 779–812.

Woodward, D. 1980. 'The Background to the Statute of Artificers: The Genesis of Labour Policy 1558–63', *Economic History Review* 33(1), 32–44.

Woolrych, A. 1982. *Commonwealth to Protectorate,* Oxford: Clarendon Press.

Wright, D. and P. Bartlett (eds). 1999. *Outside the Walls of the Asylum: the History of Care in the Community, 1750–2000,* London: Continuum.

Wrightson, K. and D. Levine. 1995. *Poverty and Piety in an English Village: Terling 1525–1700,* Oxford: Oxford University Press.

Wrigley, E. A. 2004. *Poverty, Progress and Population,* Cambridge: Cambridge University Press.

Wydler, R. 1939. *Untersuchungen über das Armenwesen im Kanton Glarus unter besonderer Berücksichtigung des Zeitraumes von 1840 bis 1930,* Glarus: Tschudi & Co.

Zelck, F. 1988. 'De Staten van Brabant op het einde van het Ancien Régime: hun invloed op de besluitvorming op sociaal-economisch gebied (1770–1794)', in J. Craeybeckx and F. Daelemans (eds), *Bijdragen tot de geschiedenis van Vlaanderen en Brabant: Sociaal en economisch,* Brussels: VUB Press, vol. 3, 169–210.

Zimmermann, H.-P. 1991. 'Das Heimatrecht im System der Gemeindeangehörigkeit am Beispiel Schleswig-Holsteins 1542 bis 1864. Ein Beitrag zur rechtlichen Volkskunde', in S. Götsch and K. D. Sievers (eds), *Kieler Blätter zur Volkskunde* 23, 67–101.

INDEX

www.ingramcontent.com/pod-product-compliance
Lightning Source LLC
Chambersburg PA
CBHW060026030426
42334CB00019B/2203